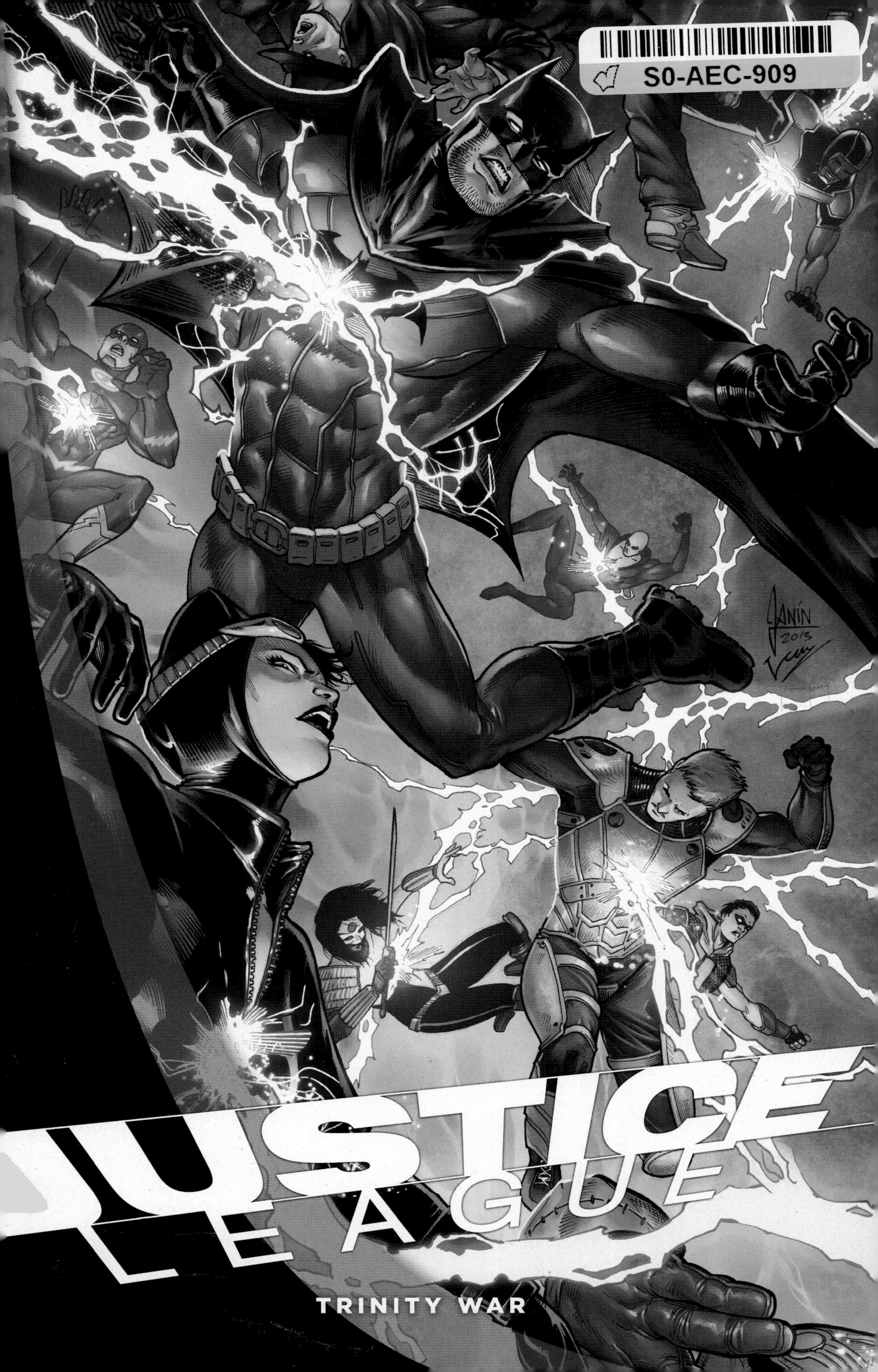
JANÍN
2013
JUSTICE
LEAGUE
TRINITY WAR

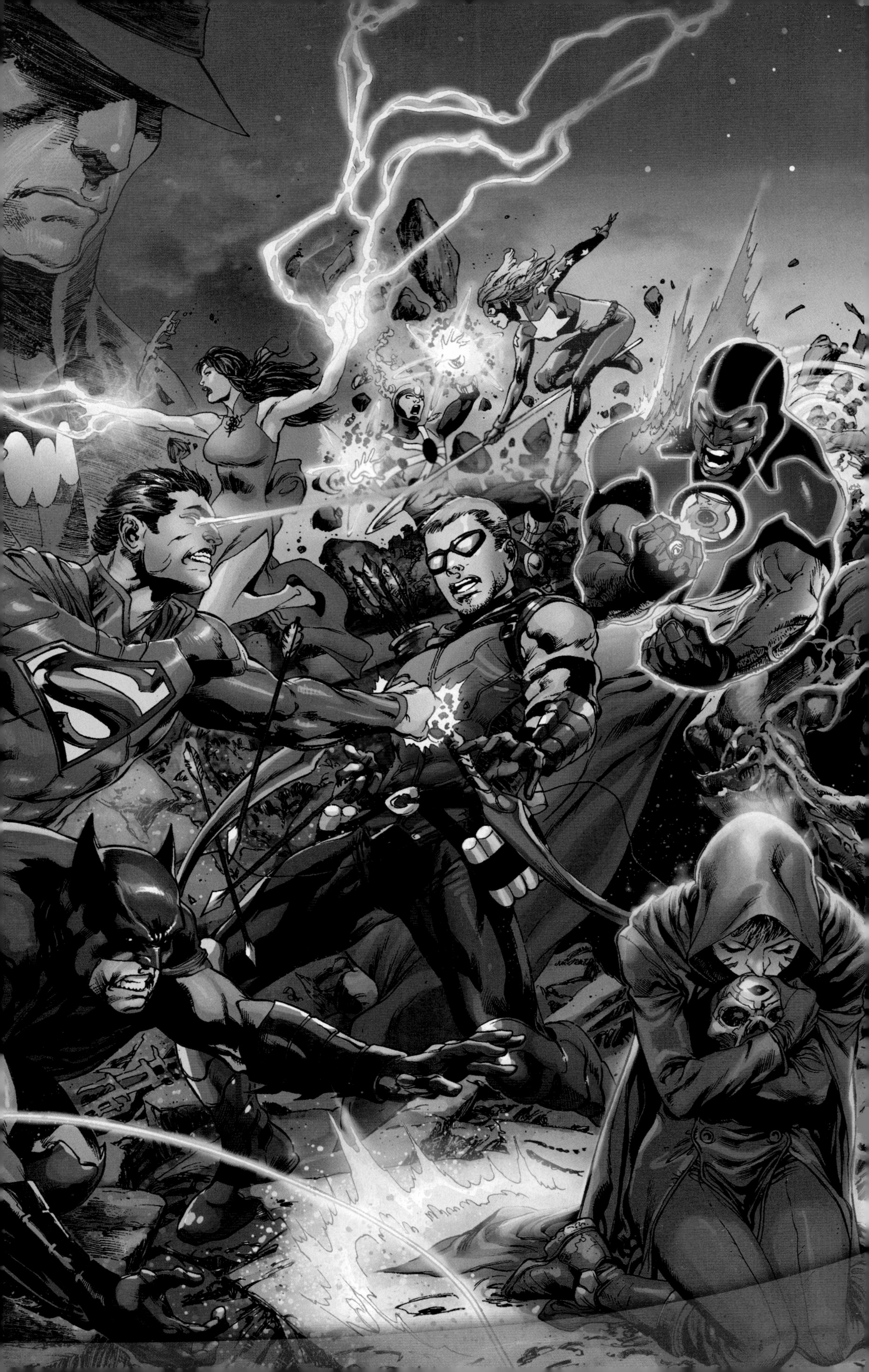

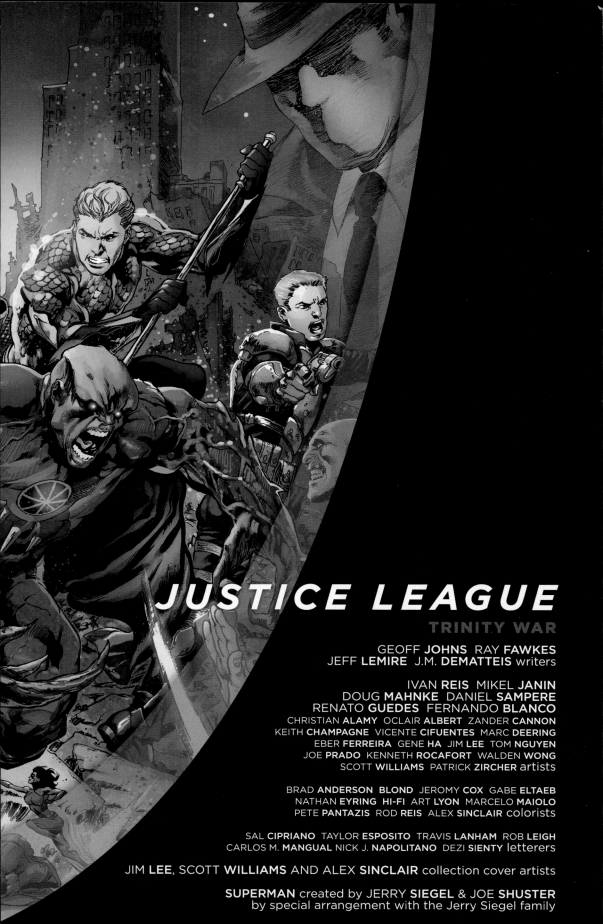

JUSTICE LEAGUE
TRINITY WAR

GEOFF **JOHNS** RAY **FAWKES**
JEFF **LEMIRE** J.M. **DEMATTEIS** writers

IVAN **REIS** MIKEL **JANIN**
DOUG **MAHNKE** DANIEL **SAMPERE**
RENATO **GUEDES** FERNANDO **BLANCO**
CHRISTIAN **ALAMY** OCLAIR **ALBERT** ZANDER **CANNON**
KEITH **CHAMPAGNE** VICENTE **CIFUENTES** MARC **DEERING**
EBER **FERREIRA** GENE **HA** JIM **LEE** TOM **NGUYEN**
JOE **PRADO** KENNETH **ROCAFORT** WALDEN **WONG**
SCOTT **WILLIAMS** PATRICK **ZIRCHER** artists

BRAD **ANDERSON** BLOND JEROMY **COX** GABE **ELTAEB**
NATHAN **EYRING** HI-FI ART **LYON** MARCELO **MAIOLO**
PETE **PANTAZIS** ROD **REIS** ALEX **SINCLAIR** colorists

SAL **CIPRIANO** TAYLOR **ESPOSITO** TRAVIS **LANHAM** ROB **LEIGH**
CARLOS M. **MANGUAL** NICK J. **NAPOLITANO** DEZI **SIENTY** letterers

JIM **LEE**, SCOTT **WILLIAMS** AND ALEX **SINCLAIR** collection cover artists

SUPERMAN created by JERRY **SIEGEL** & JOE **SHUSTER**
by special arrangement with the Jerry Siegel family

EDDIE BERGANZA DAN DIDIO WIL MOSS BRIAN CUNNINGHAM Editors – Original Series
HARVEY RICHARDS Associate Editor – Original Series KATE STEWART Assistant Editor – Original Series
JEB WOODARD Group Editor – Collected Editions PETER HAMBOUSSI Editor – Collected Edition
STEVE COOK Design Director – Books ROBBIE BIEDERMAN Publication Design

BOB HARRAS Senior VP – Editor-in-Chief, DC Comics

DIANE NELSON President DAN DIDIO and JIM LEE Co-Publishers
GEOFF JOHNS Chief Creative Officer AMIT DESAI Senior VP – Marketing & Global Franchise Management
NAIRI GARDINER Senior VP – Finance SAM ADES VP – Digital Marketing BOBBIE CHASE VP – Talent Development
MARK CHIARELLO Senior VP – Art, Design & Collected Editions JOHN CUNNINGHAM VP – Content Strategy
ANNE DEPIES VP – Strategy Planning & Reporting DON FALLETTI VP – Manufacturing Operations
LAWRENCE GANEM VP – Editorial Administration & Talent Relations ALISON GILL Senior VP – Manufacturing & Operations
HANK KANALZ Senior VP – Editorial Strategy & Administration JAY KOGAN VP – Legal Affairs
DEREK MADDALENA Senior VP – Sales & Business Development JACK MAHAN VP – Business Affairs
DAN MIRON VP – Sales Planning & Trade Development NICK NAPOLITANO VP – Manufacturing Administration
CAROL ROEDER VP – Marketing EDDIE SCANNELL VP – Mass Account & Digital Sales
COURTNEY SIMMONS Senior VP – Publicity & Communications JIM (SKI) SOKOLOWSKI VP - Comic Book Specialty & Newsstand Sales
SANDY YI Senior VP – Global Franchise Management

JUSTICE LEAGUE: TRINITY WAR

Originally published in single magazine form as JUSTICE LEAGUE 22-23, JUSTICE LEAGUE OF AMERICA 6-7, JUSTICE LEAGUE DARK 22-23,
TRINITY OF SIN: PANDORA 1-3, TRINITY OF SIN: PHANTOM STRANGER 11, CONSTANTINE 5, NEW 52 FREE COMIC BOOK DAY SPECIAL 2012
© 2012, 2013 DC Comics. All Rights Reserved. All characters, their distinctive likenesses and related elements featured in this publication are
trademarks of DC Comics. The stories, characters and incidents featured in this publication are entirely fictional.
DC Comics does not read or accept unsolicited ideas, stories or artwork.

DC Comics, 2900 W. Alameda Avenue, Burbank, CA 91505
Printed by Solisco Printers, Scott, QC, Canada. 2/12/16. Second Printing.

ISBN: 978-1-4012-4944-1

Library of Congress Cataloging-in-Publication Data

Johns, Geoff, 1973-
Justice League : Trinity War / Geoff Johns, Jeff Lemire.
pages cm. — (The New 52!)
ISBN 978-1-4012-4944-1
1. Graphic novels. I. Lemire, Jeff. II. Title. III. Title: Trinity War.
PN6728.J87J6558 2014
741.5'973—dc23
2013045590

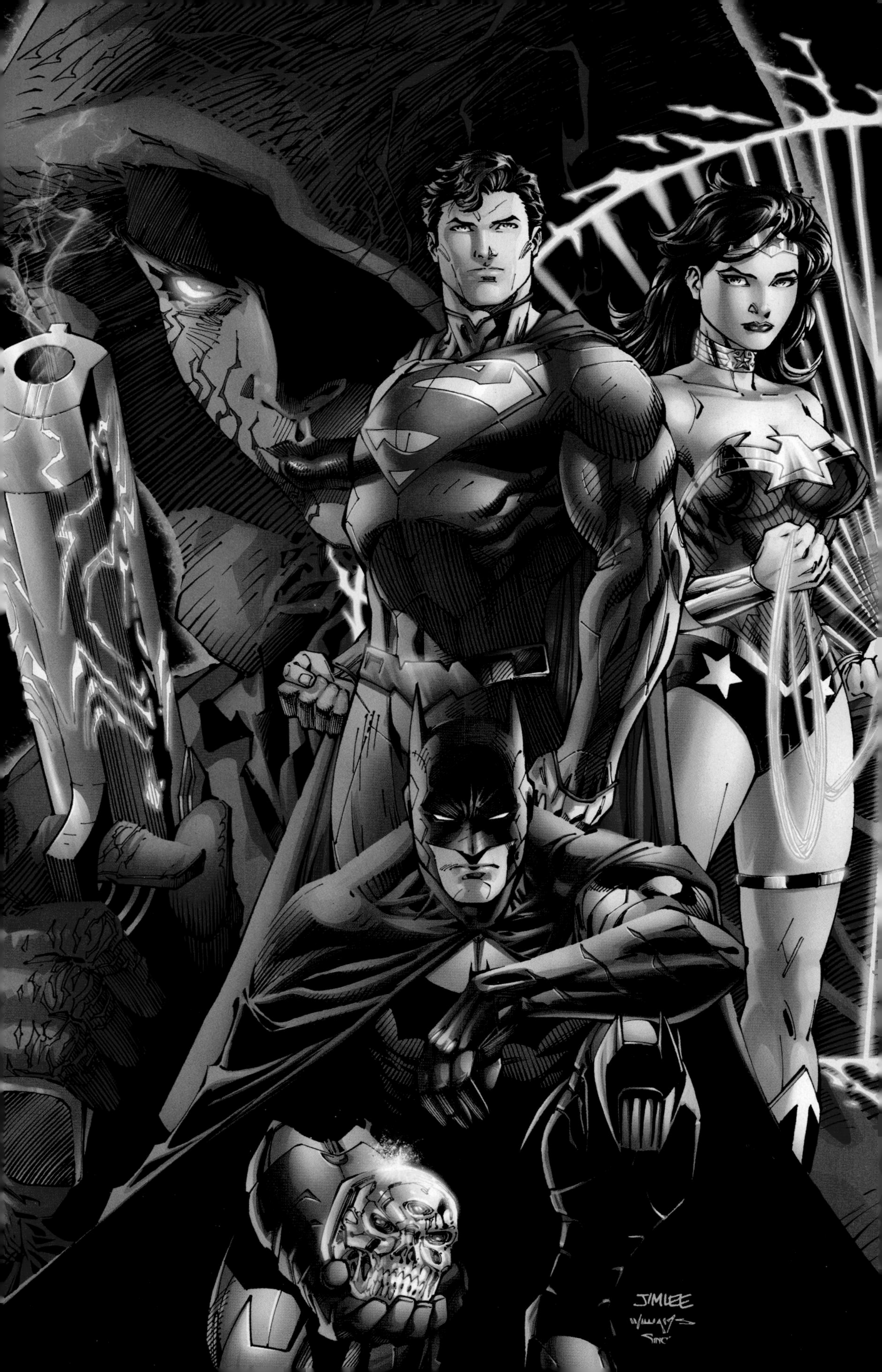
JIMLEE

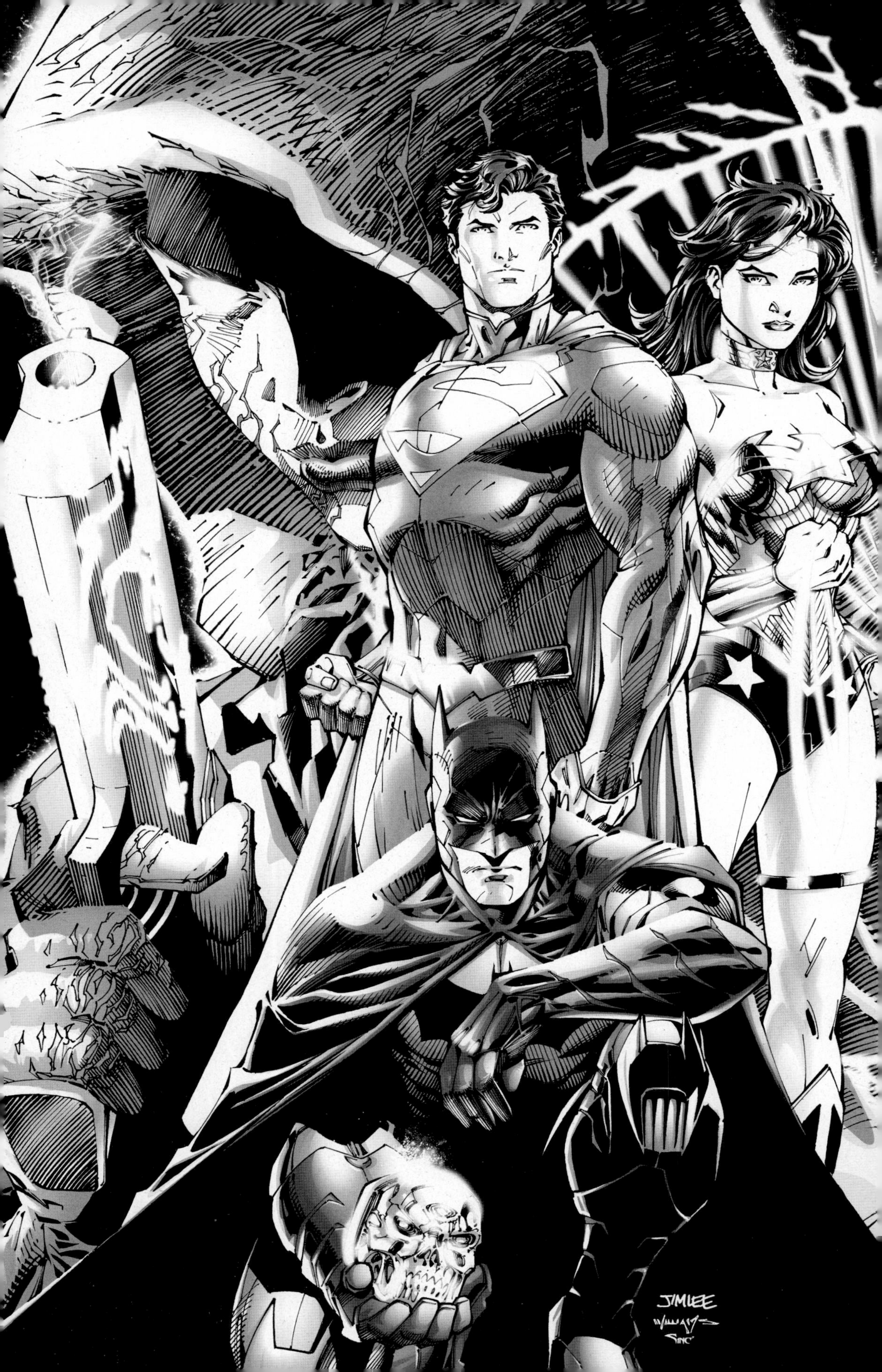
JIM LEE

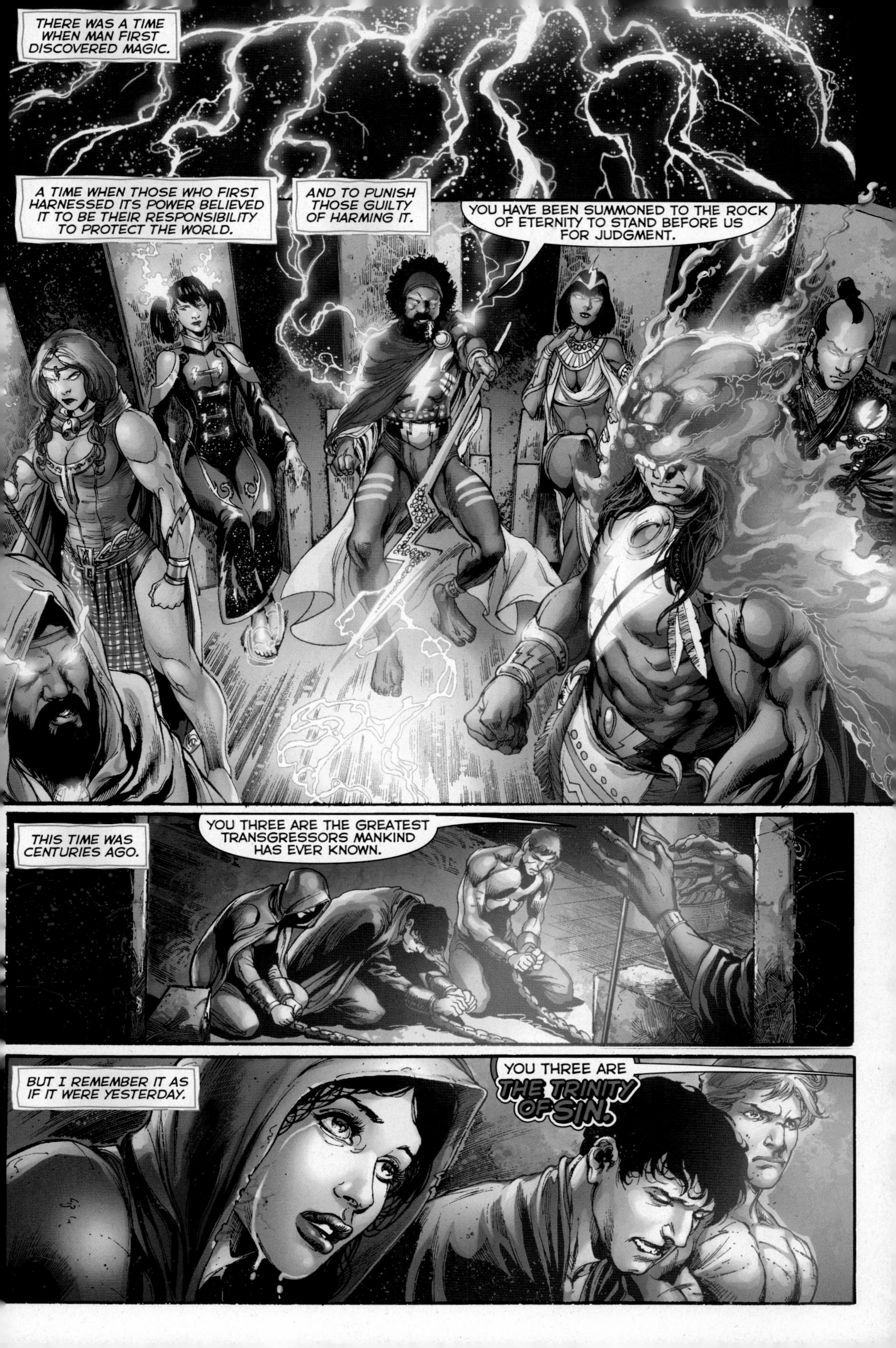
THERE WAS A TIME WHEN MAN FIRST DISCOVERED MAGIC.
A TIME WHEN THOSE WHO FIRST HARNESSED ITS POWER BELIEVED IT TO BE THEIR RESPONSIBILITY TO PROTECT THE WORLD.
AND TO PUNISH THOSE GUILTY OF HARMING IT.
YOU HAVE BEEN SUMMONED TO THE ROCK OF ETERNITY TO STAND BEFORE US FOR JUDGMENT.
THIS TIME WAS CENTURIES AGO.
YOU THREE ARE THE GREATEST TRANSGRESSORS MANKIND HAS EVER KNOWN.
BUT I REMEMBER IT AS IF IT WERE YESTERDAY.
YOU THREE ARE THE TRINITY OF SIN.

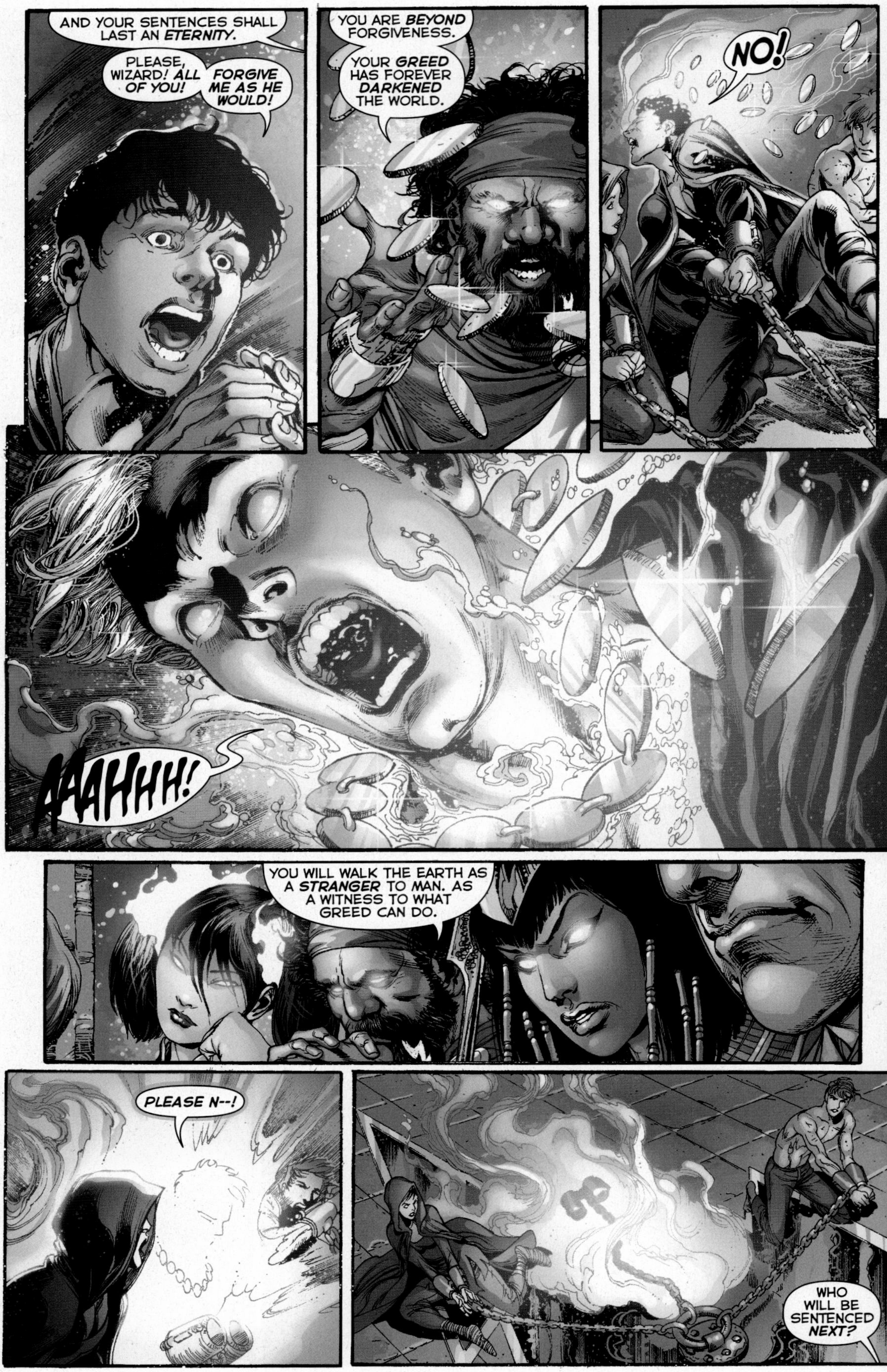
AND YOUR SENTENCES SHALL LAST AN ETERNITY.
PLEASE, WIZARD! ALL OF YOU!
FORGIVE ME AS HE WOULD!
YOU ARE BEYOND FORGIVENESS.
YOUR GREED HAS FOREVER DARKENED THE WORLD.
NO!
AAAHHH!
YOU WILL WALK THE EARTH AS A STRANGER TO MAN. AS A WITNESS TO WHAT GREED CAN DO.
PLEASE N--!
WHO WILL BE SENTENCED NEXT?

I WILL NOT BEG, WIZARDS. I *DEFY* THE *AUTHORITY* YOU CLAIM!

DO WHAT YOU WISH TO ME!

BUT IF YOU DO NOT *KILL* ME, I WILL RISE TO POWER AGAIN!

AND YOU WILL FEAR MY NAME AS DOES THE WORLD!

YOU WILL *FORGET* YOUR NAME AS WILL EVERYONE.

I... AM... *YNNN!*

MMNFNN!

LET GO OF ME! PLEASE!

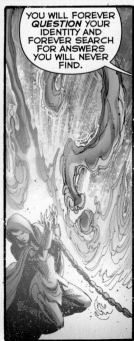

YOU WILL FOREVER *QUESTION* YOUR IDENTITY AND FOREVER SEARCH FOR ANSWERS YOU WILL NEVER FIND.

AND *YOU,* PANDORA.

HAVE YOU ANY *SPITEFUL WORDS* FOR US BEFORE *SENTENCING?*

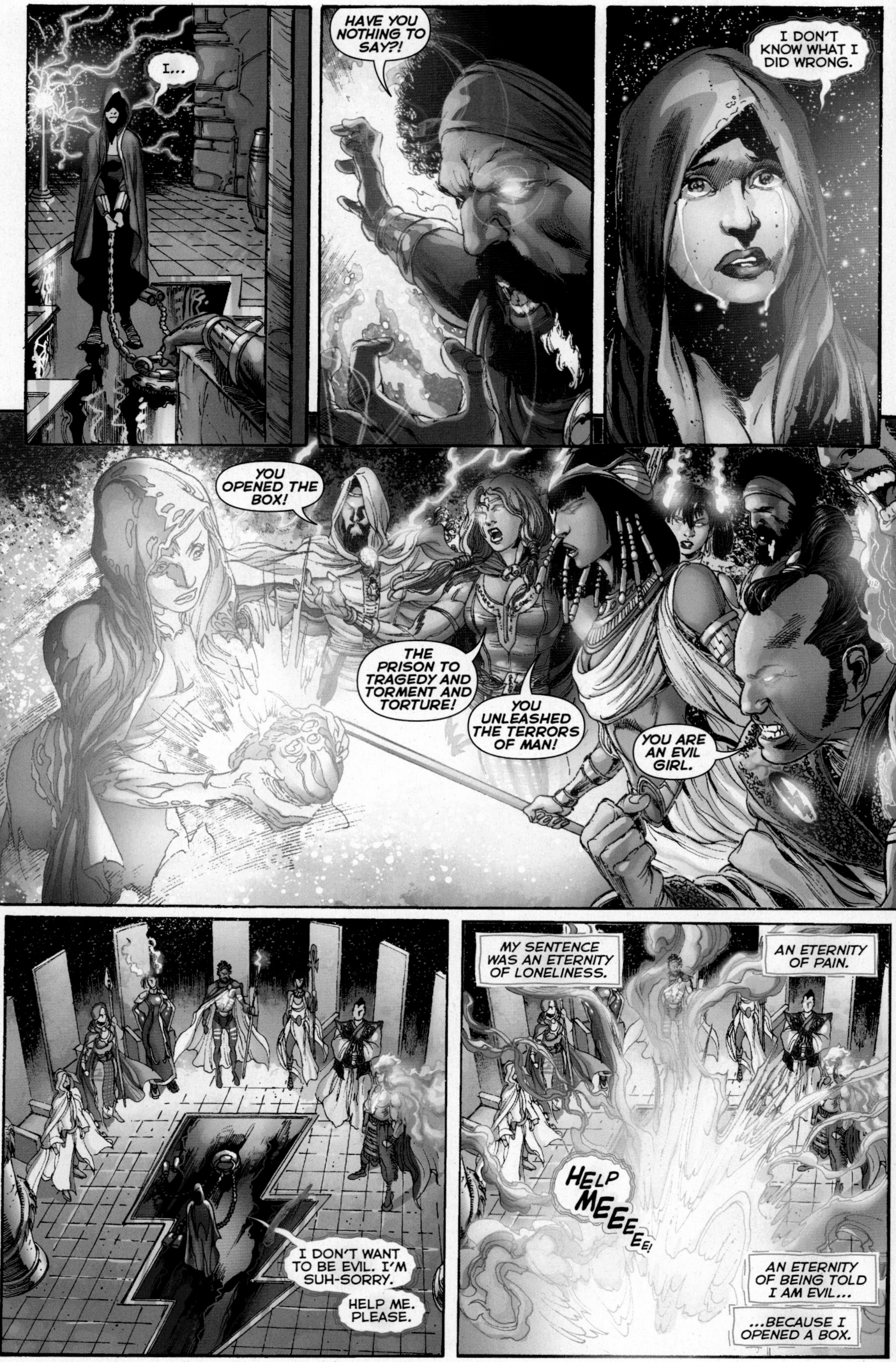

I...
HAVE YOU NOTHING TO SAY?!
I DON'T KNOW WHAT I DID WRONG.
YOU OPENED THE BOX!
THE PRISON TO TRAGEDY AND TORMENT AND TORTURE!
YOU UNLEASHED THE TERRORS OF MAN!
YOU ARE AN EVIL GIRL.
I DON'T WANT TO BE EVIL. I'M SUH-SORRY.
HELP ME. PLEASE.
MY SENTENCE WAS AN ETERNITY OF LONELINESS.
AN ETERNITY OF PAIN.
HELP MEEEEE!
AN ETERNITY OF BEING TOLD I AM EVIL...
...BECAUSE I OPENED A BOX.

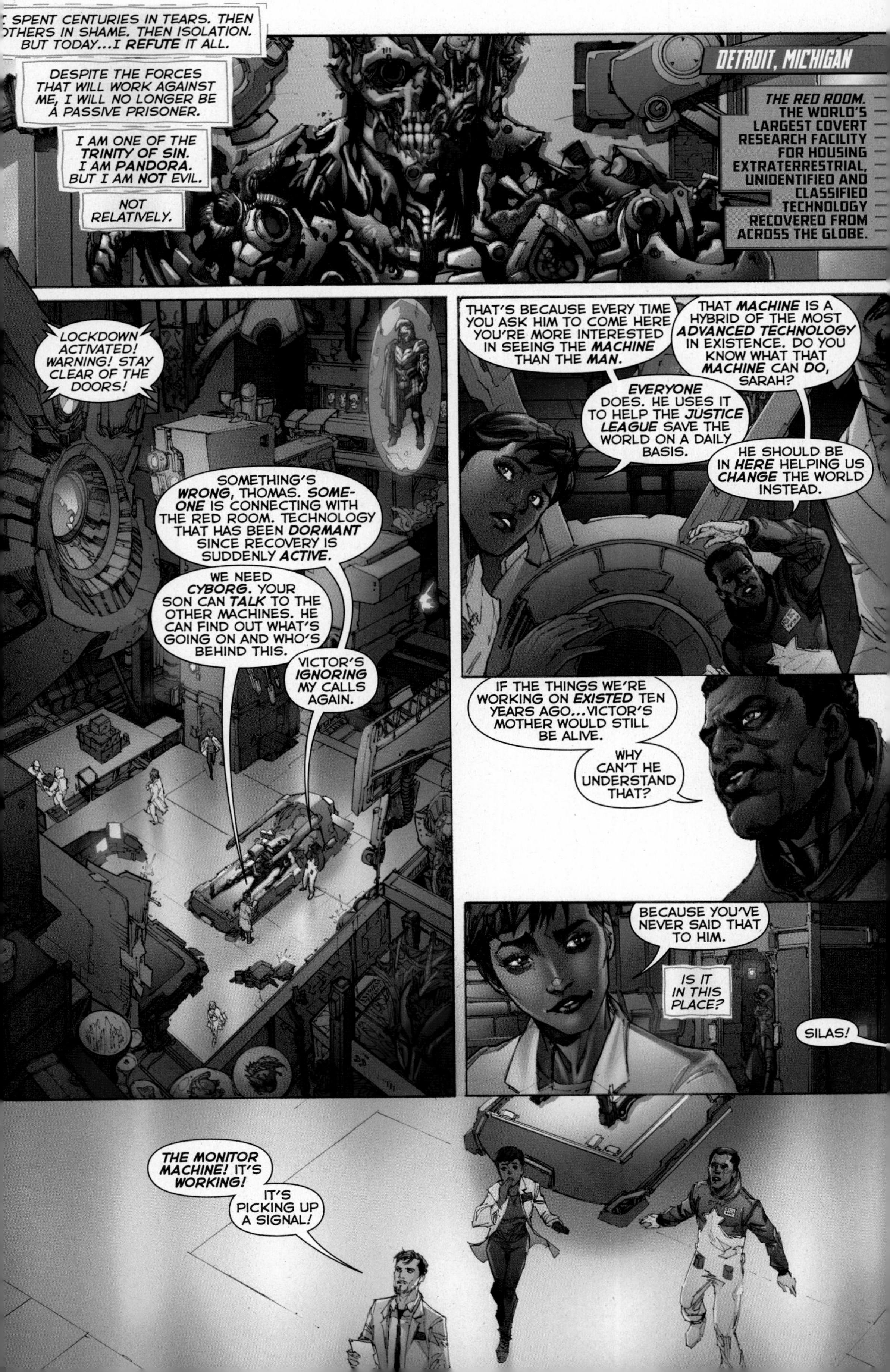

I SPENT CENTURIES IN TEARS. THEN OTHERS IN SHAME. THEN ISOLATION. BUT TODAY...I REFUTE IT ALL.
DESPITE THE FORCES THAT WILL WORK AGAINST ME, I WILL NO LONGER BE A PASSIVE PRISONER.
I AM ONE OF THE TRINITY OF SIN. I AM PANDORA. BUT I AM NOT EVIL.
NOT RELATIVELY.
DETROIT, MICHIGAN
THE RED ROOM. THE WORLD'S LARGEST COVERT RESEARCH FACILITY FOR HOUSING EXTRATERRESTRIAL, UNIDENTIFIED AND CLASSIFIED TECHNOLOGY RECOVERED FROM ACROSS THE GLOBE.
LOCKDOWN ACTIVATED! WARNING! STAY CLEAR OF THE DOORS!
SOMETHING'S WRONG, THOMAS. SOMEONE IS CONNECTING WITH THE RED ROOM. TECHNOLOGY THAT HAS BEEN DORMANT SINCE RECOVERY IS SUDDENLY ACTIVE.
WE NEED CYBORG. YOUR SON CAN TALK TO THE OTHER MACHINES. HE CAN FIND OUT WHAT'S GOING ON AND WHO'S BEHIND THIS.
VICTOR'S IGNORING MY CALLS AGAIN.
THAT'S BECAUSE EVERY TIME YOU ASK HIM TO COME HERE YOU'RE MORE INTERESTED IN SEEING THE MACHINE THAN THE MAN.
THAT MACHINE IS A HYBRID OF THE MOST ADVANCED TECHNOLOGY IN EXISTENCE. DO YOU KNOW WHAT THAT MACHINE CAN DO, SARAH?
EVERYONE DOES. HE USES IT TO HELP THE JUSTICE LEAGUE SAVE THE WORLD ON A DAILY BASIS.
HE SHOULD BE IN HERE HELPING US CHANGE THE WORLD INSTEAD.
IF THE THINGS WE'RE WORKING ON EXISTED TEN YEARS AGO...VICTOR'S MOTHER WOULD STILL BE ALIVE.
WHY CAN'T HE UNDERSTAND THAT?
BECAUSE YOU'VE NEVER SAID THAT TO HIM.
IS IT IN THIS PLACE?
SILAS!
THE MONITOR MACHINE! IT'S WORKING!
IT'S PICKING UP A SIGNAL!

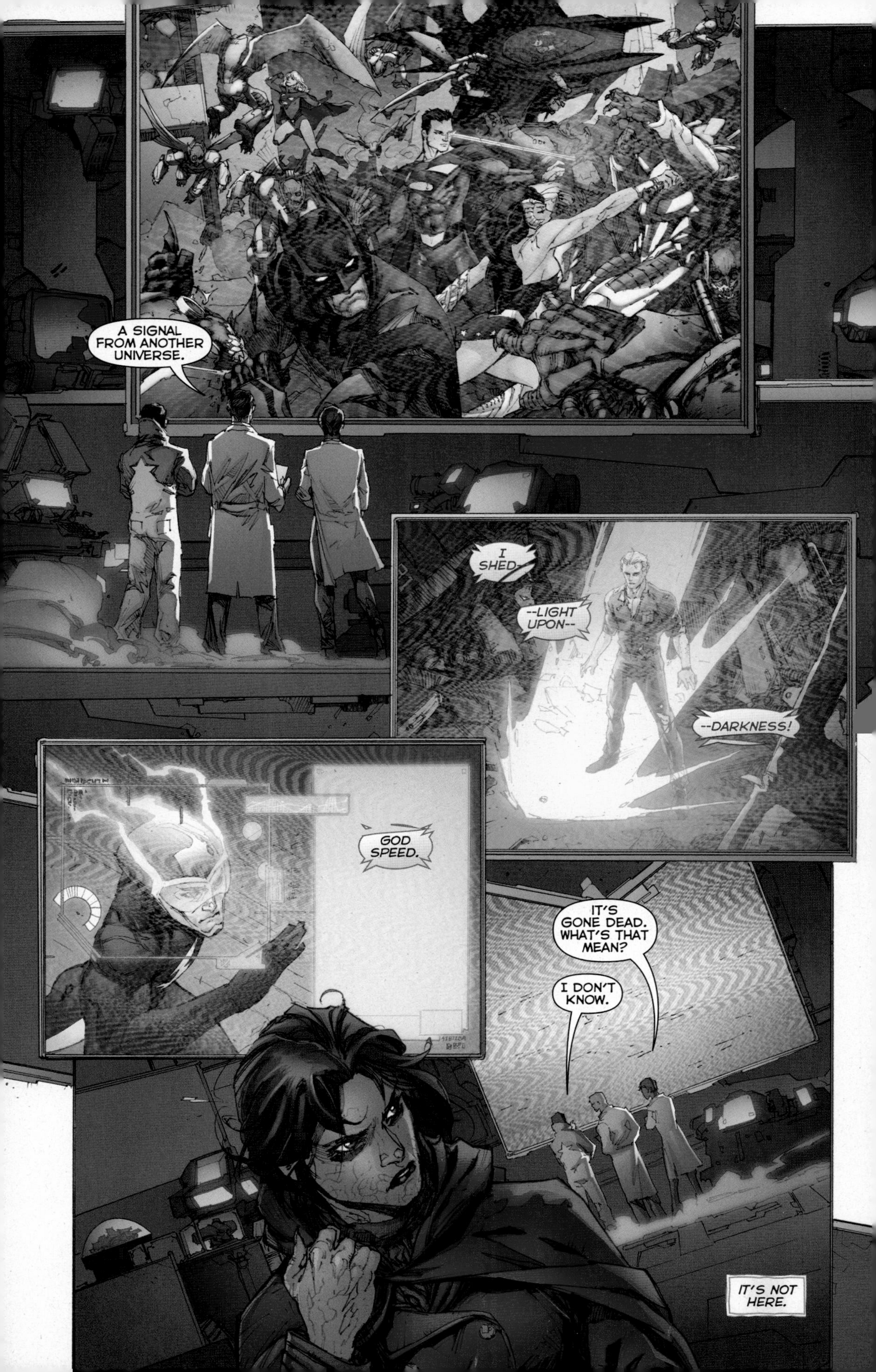
A SIGNAL FROM ANOTHER UNIVERSE.
I SHED--
--LIGHT UPON--
--DARKNESS!
GOD SPEED.
IT'S GONE DEAD. WHAT'S THAT MEAN?
I DON'T KNOW.
IT'S NOT HERE.

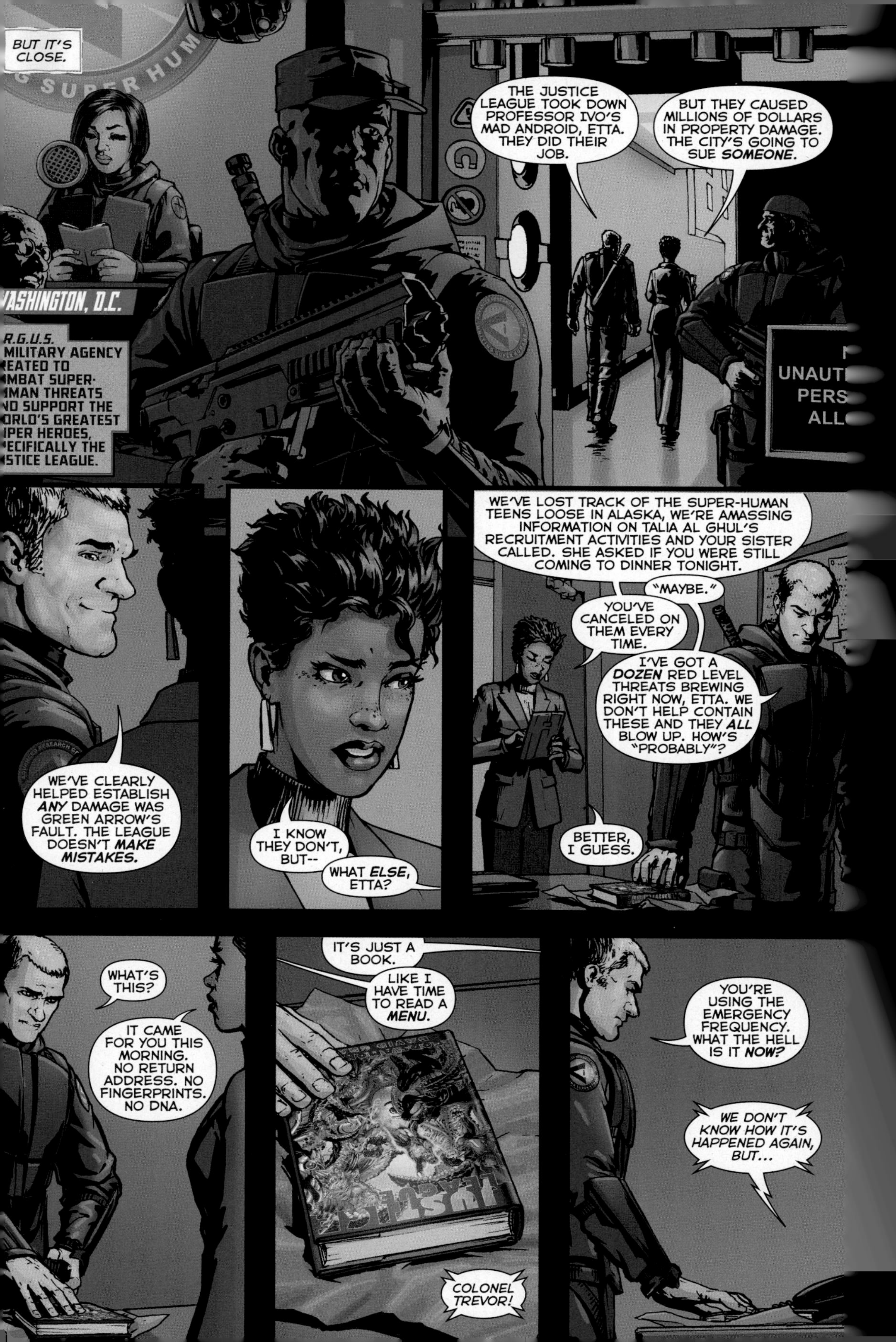
BUT IT'S CLOSE.
VASHINGTON, D.C.
R.G.U.S.
MILITARY AGENCY
REATED TO
MBAT SUPER-
MAN THREATS
ND SUPPORT THE
ORLD'S GREATEST
UPER HEROES,
ECIFICALLY THE
STICE LEAGUE.
THE JUSTICE LEAGUE TOOK DOWN PROFESSOR IVO'S MAD ANDROID, ETTA. THEY DID THEIR JOB.
BUT THEY CAUSED MILLIONS OF DOLLARS IN PROPERTY DAMAGE. THE CITY'S GOING TO SUE SOMEONE.
UNAUT
PERS
ALL
WE'VE CLEARLY HELPED ESTABLISH ANY DAMAGE WAS GREEN ARROW'S FAULT. THE LEAGUE DOESN'T MAKE MISTAKES.
I KNOW THEY DON'T, BUT--
WHAT ELSE, ETTA?
WE'VE LOST TRACK OF THE SUPER-HUMAN TEENS LOOSE IN ALASKA, WE'RE AMASSING INFORMATION ON TALIA AL GHUL'S RECRUITMENT ACTIVITIES AND YOUR SISTER CALLED. SHE ASKED IF YOU WERE STILL COMING TO DINNER TONIGHT.
"MAYBE."
YOU'VE CANCELED ON THEM EVERY TIME.
I'VE GOT A DOZEN RED LEVEL THREATS BREWING RIGHT NOW, ETTA. WE DON'T HELP CONTAIN THESE AND THEY ALL BLOW UP. HOW'S "PROBABLY"?
BETTER, I GUESS.
WHAT'S THIS?
IT CAME FOR YOU THIS MORNING. NO RETURN ADDRESS. NO FINGERPRINTS. NO DNA.
IT'S JUST A BOOK.
LIKE I HAVE TIME TO READ A MENU.
COLONEL TREVOR!
YOU'RE USING THE EMERGENCY FREQUENCY. WHAT THE HELL IS IT NOW?
WE DON'T KNOW HOW IT'S HAPPENED AGAIN, BUT...

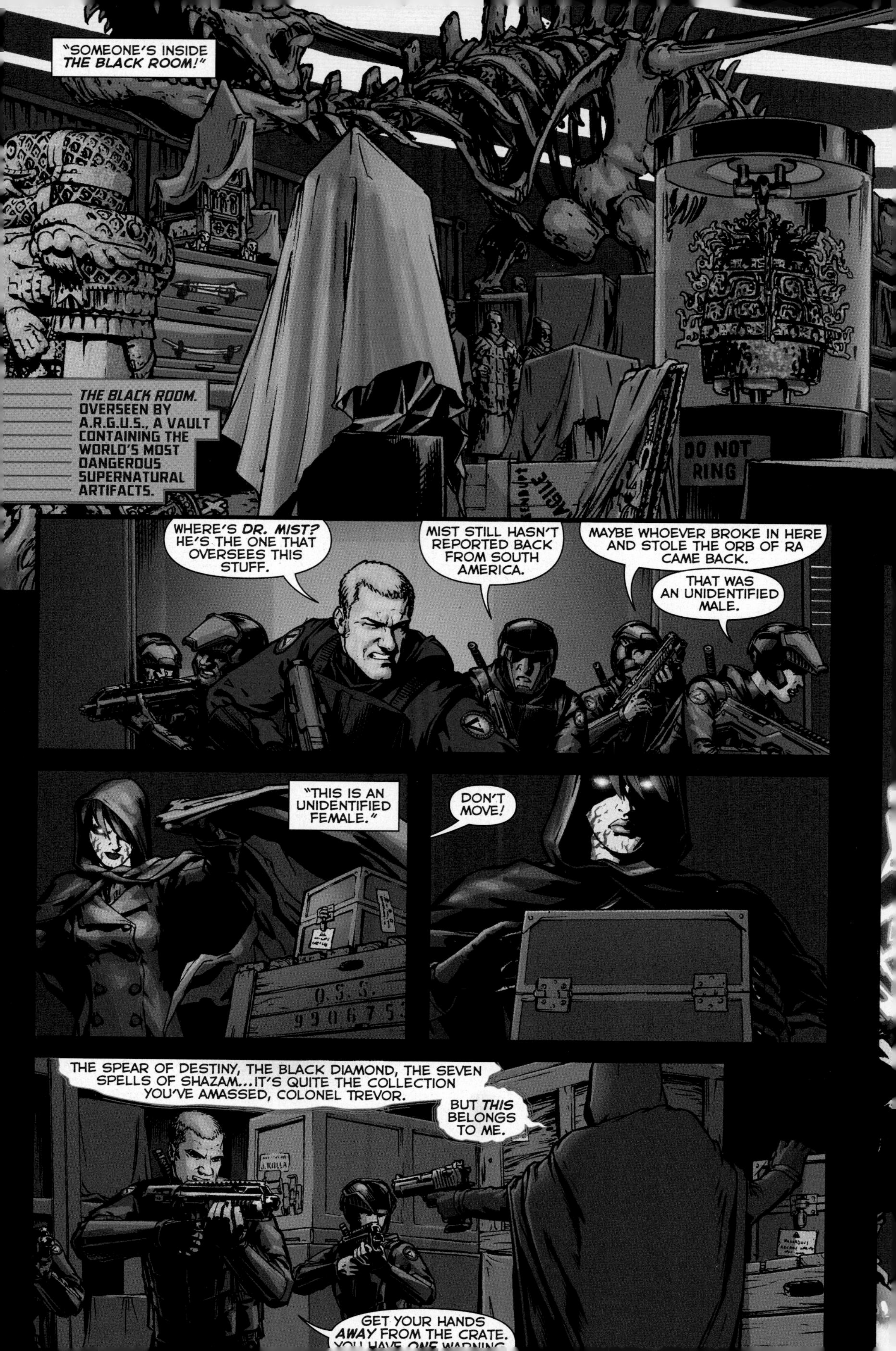
"SOMEONE'S INSIDE THE BLACK ROOM!"
THE BLACK ROOM. OVERSEEN BY A.R.G.U.S., A VAULT CONTAINING THE WORLD'S MOST DANGEROUS SUPERNATURAL ARTIFACTS.
DO NOT RING
FRAGILE
WHERE'S DR. MIST? HE'S THE ONE THAT OVERSEES THIS STUFF.
MIST STILL HASN'T REPORTED BACK FROM SOUTH AMERICA.
MAYBE WHOEVER BROKE IN HERE AND STOLE THE ORB OF RA CAME BACK.
THAT WAS AN UNIDENTIFIED MALE.
"THIS IS AN UNIDENTIFIED FEMALE."
O.S.S.
DON'T MOVE!
THE SPEAR OF DESTINY, THE BLACK DIAMOND, THE SEVEN SPELLS OF SHAZAM...IT'S QUITE THE COLLECTION YOU'VE AMASSED, COLONEL TREVOR.
BUT THIS BELONGS TO ME.
GET YOUR HANDS AWAY FROM THE CRATE.

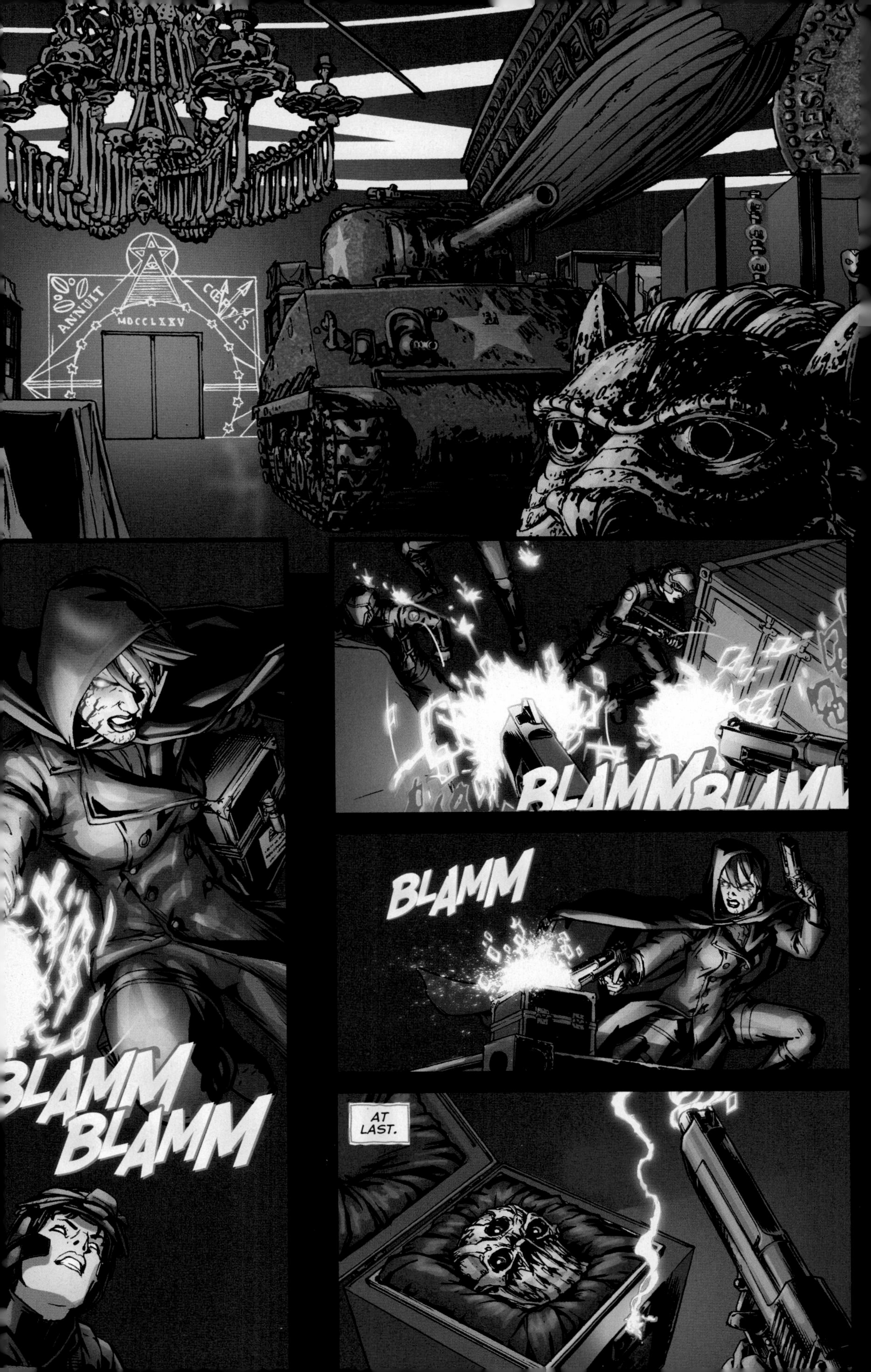
ANNUIT
COEPTIS
MDCCLXXV
CAESAR
BLAMM BLAMM
BLAMM
BLAMM
BLAMM
AT LAST.

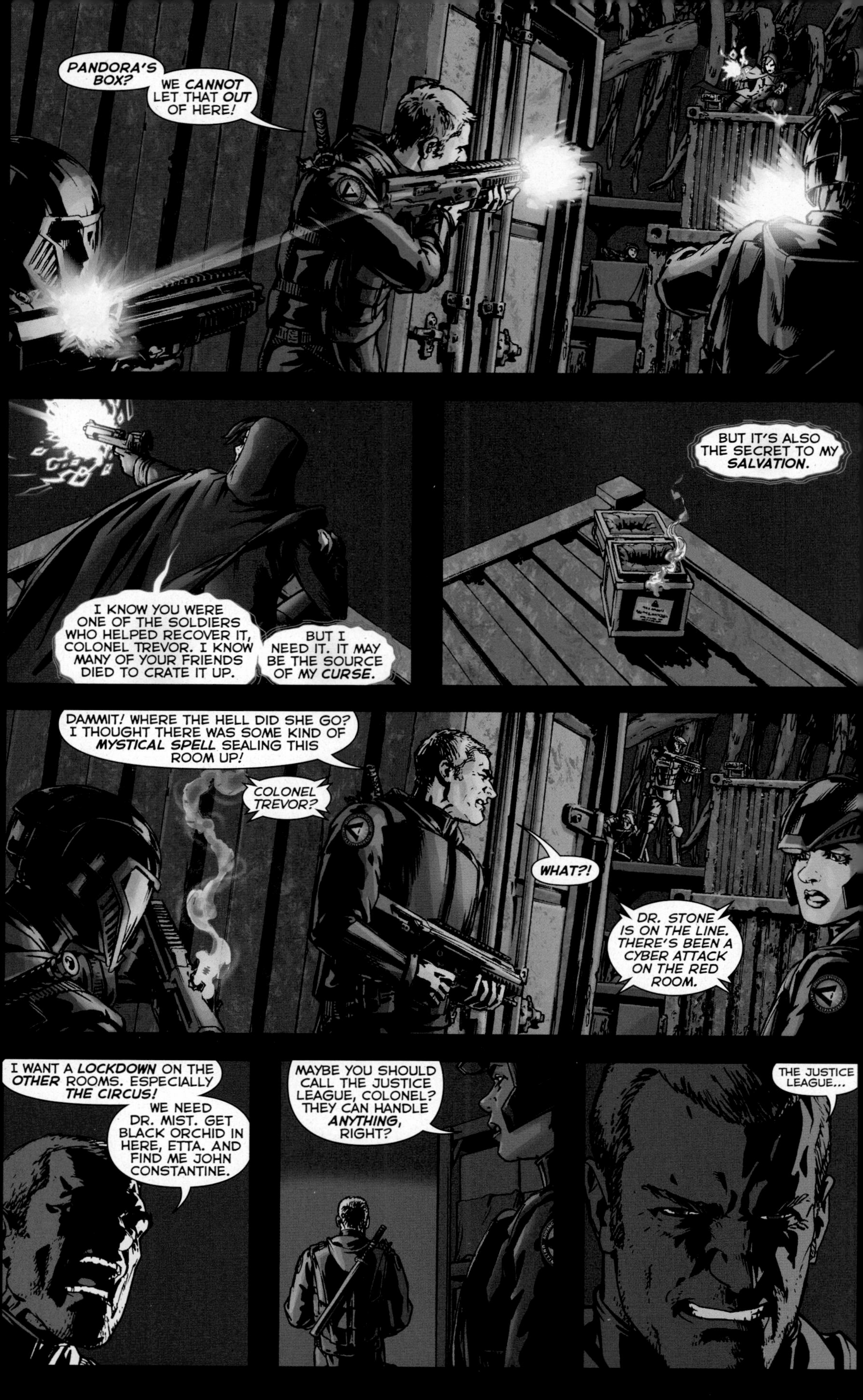
PANDORA'S BOX?
WE CANNOT LET THAT OUT OF HERE!
I KNOW YOU WERE ONE OF THE SOLDIERS WHO HELPED RECOVER IT, COLONEL TREVOR. I KNOW MANY OF YOUR FRIENDS DIED TO CRATE IT UP.
BUT I NEED IT. IT MAY BE THE SOURCE OF MY CURSE.
BUT IT'S ALSO THE SECRET TO MY SALVATION.
DAMMIT! WHERE THE HELL DID SHE GO? I THOUGHT THERE WAS SOME KIND OF MYSTICAL SPELL SEALING THIS ROOM UP!
COLONEL TREVOR?
WHAT?!
DR. STONE IS ON THE LINE. THERE'S BEEN A CYBER ATTACK ON THE RED ROOM.
I WANT A LOCKDOWN ON THE OTHER ROOMS. ESPECIALLY THE CIRCUS!
WE NEED DR. MIST. GET BLACK ORCHID IN HERE, ETTA. AND FIND ME JOHN CONSTANTINE.
MAYBE YOU SHOULD CALL THE JUSTICE LEAGUE, COLONEL? THEY CAN HANDLE ANYTHING, RIGHT?
THE JUSTICE LEAGUE...

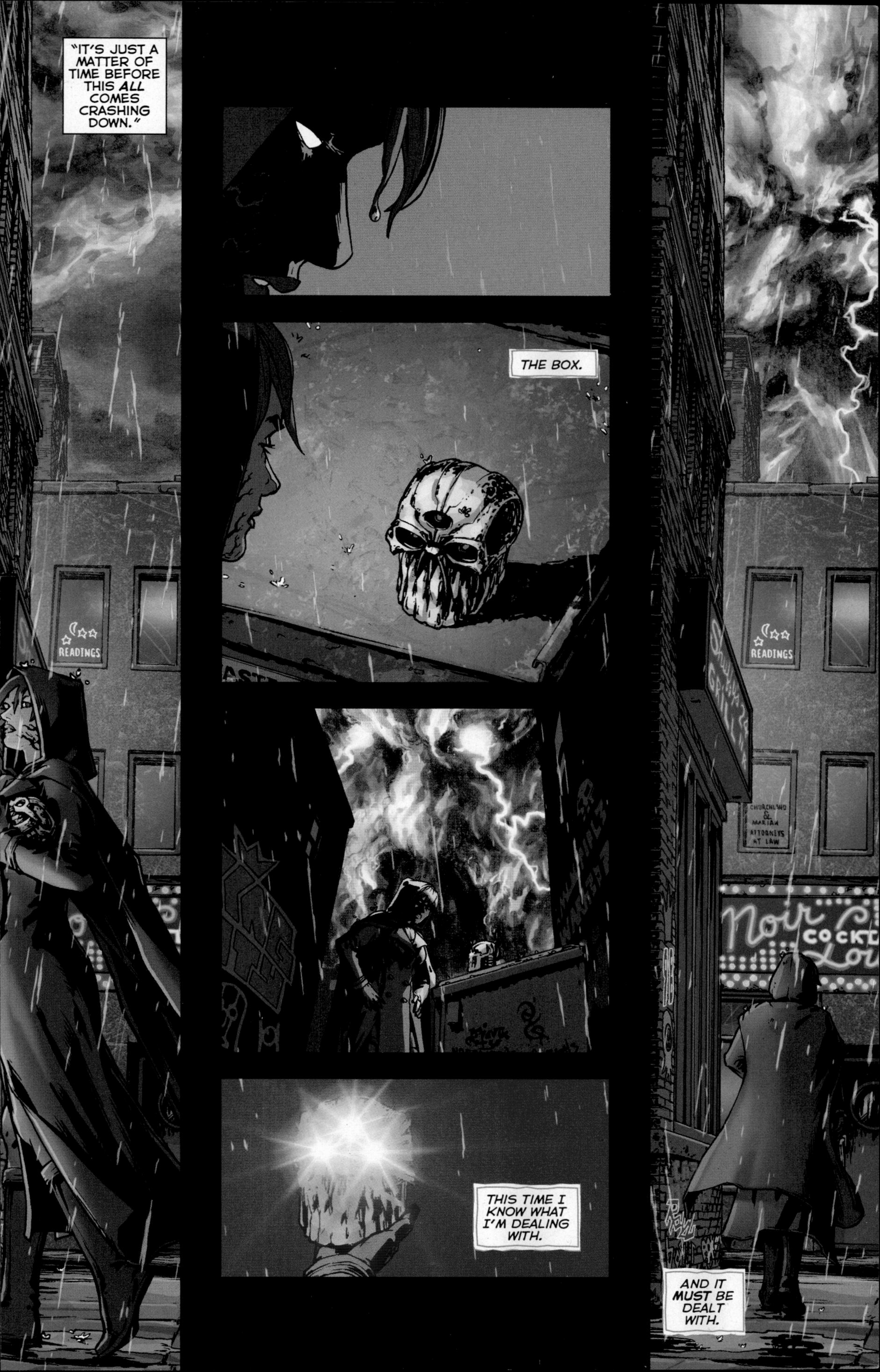
"IT'S JUST A MATTER OF TIME BEFORE THIS *ALL* COMES CRASHING DOWN."
THE BOX.
THIS TIME I KNOW WHAT I'M DEALING WITH.
AND IT *MUST* BE DEALT WITH.
READINGS
READINGS
Noir

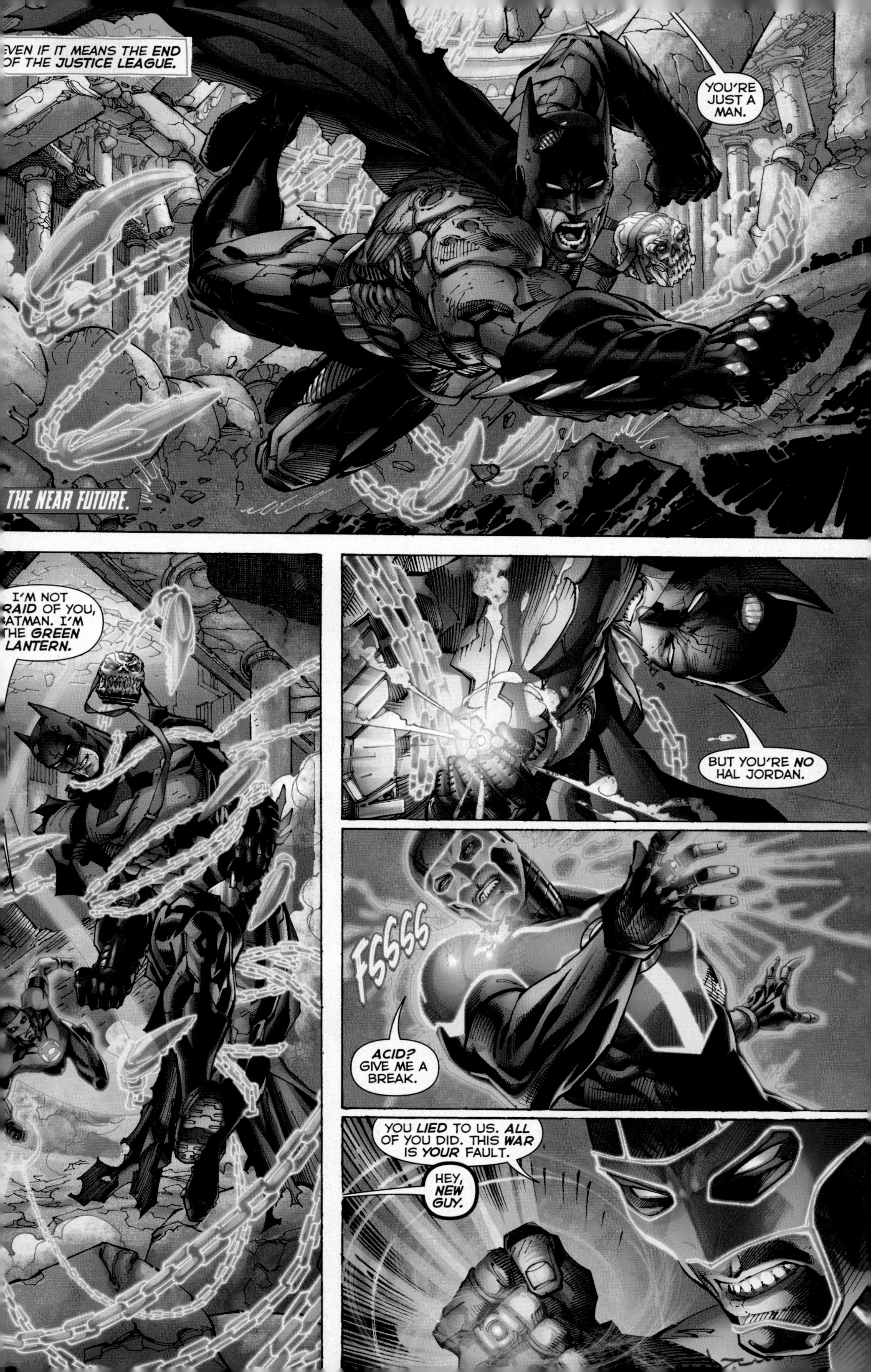
EVEN IF IT MEANS THE END OF THE JUSTICE LEAGUE.
YOU'RE JUST A MAN.
THE NEAR FUTURE.
I'M NOT RAID OF YOU, BATMAN. I'M THE GREEN LANTERN.
BUT YOU'RE NO HAL JORDAN.
FSSSS
ACID? GIVE ME A BREAK.
YOU LIED TO US. ALL OF YOU DID. THIS WAR IS YOUR FAULT.
HEY, NEW GUY.

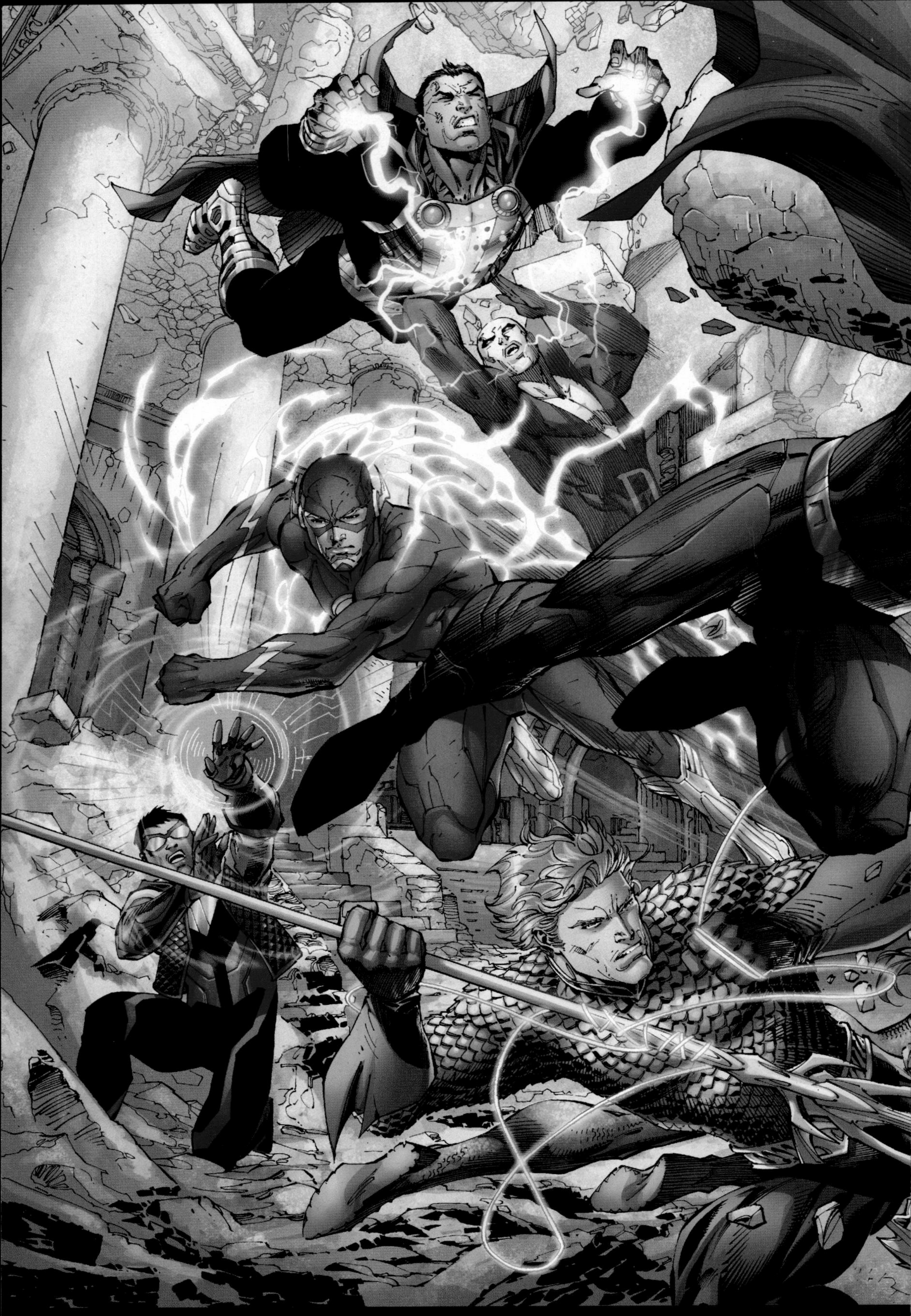

GEOFF JOHNS WRITER
JIM LEE PENCILS 12-16 AND COVER
SCOTT WILLIAMS INKS 12-16 AND COVE
ALEX SINCLAIR COLOR 12-16 AND COVE

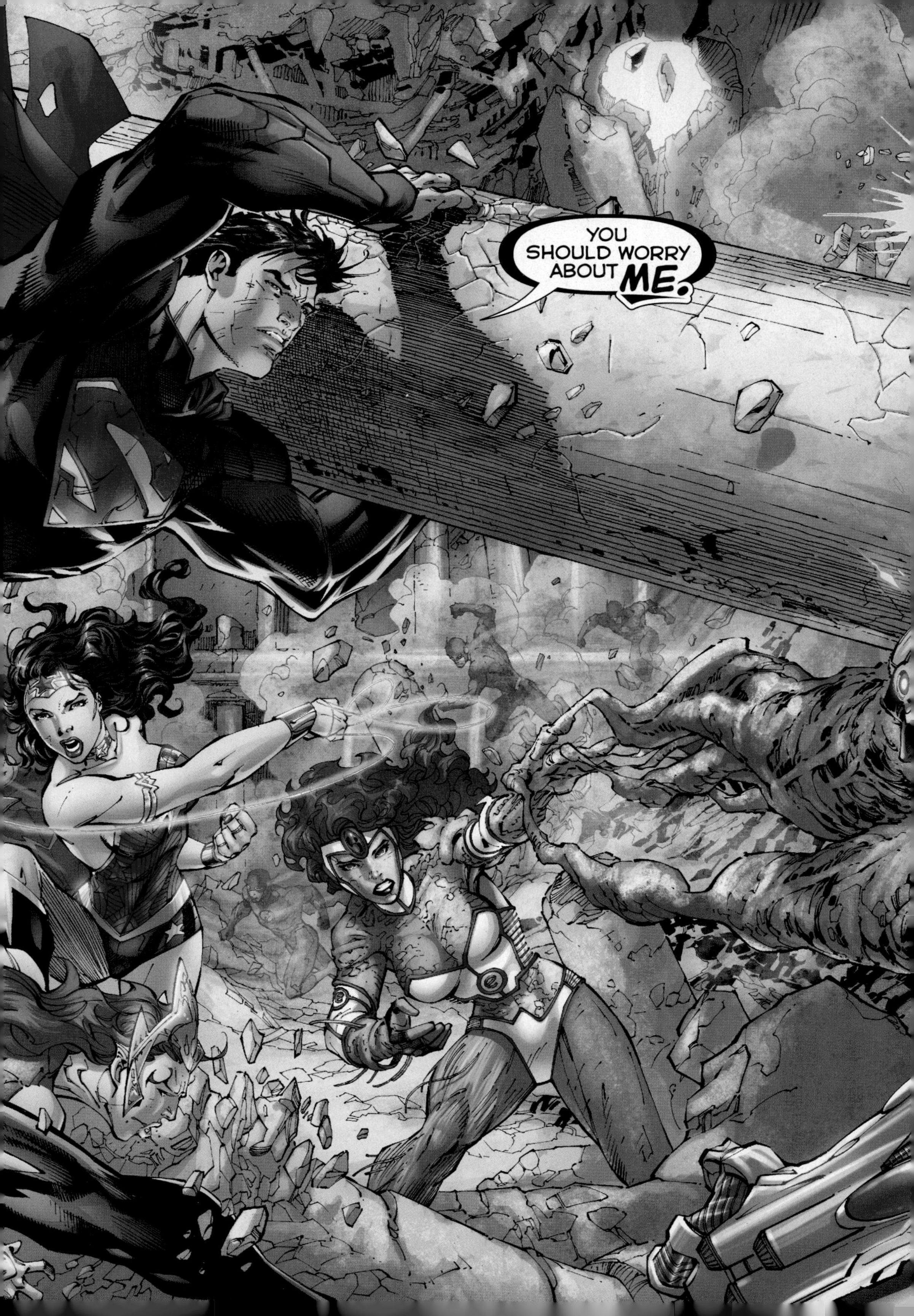
YOU SHOULD WORRY ABOUT ME.

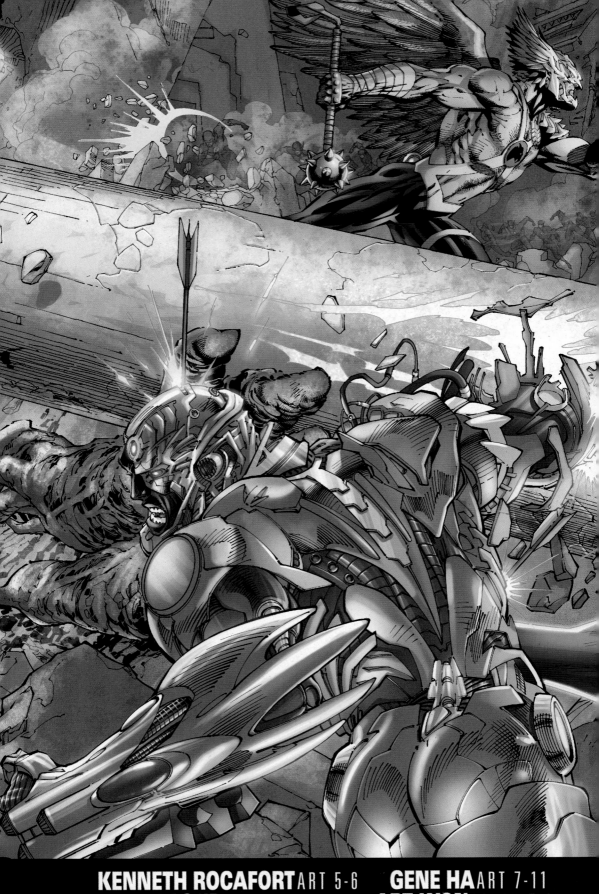

KENNETH ROCAFORT ART 5-6
BLOND COLOR 5-6

GENE HA ART 7-11
ART LYON COLOR 7-11

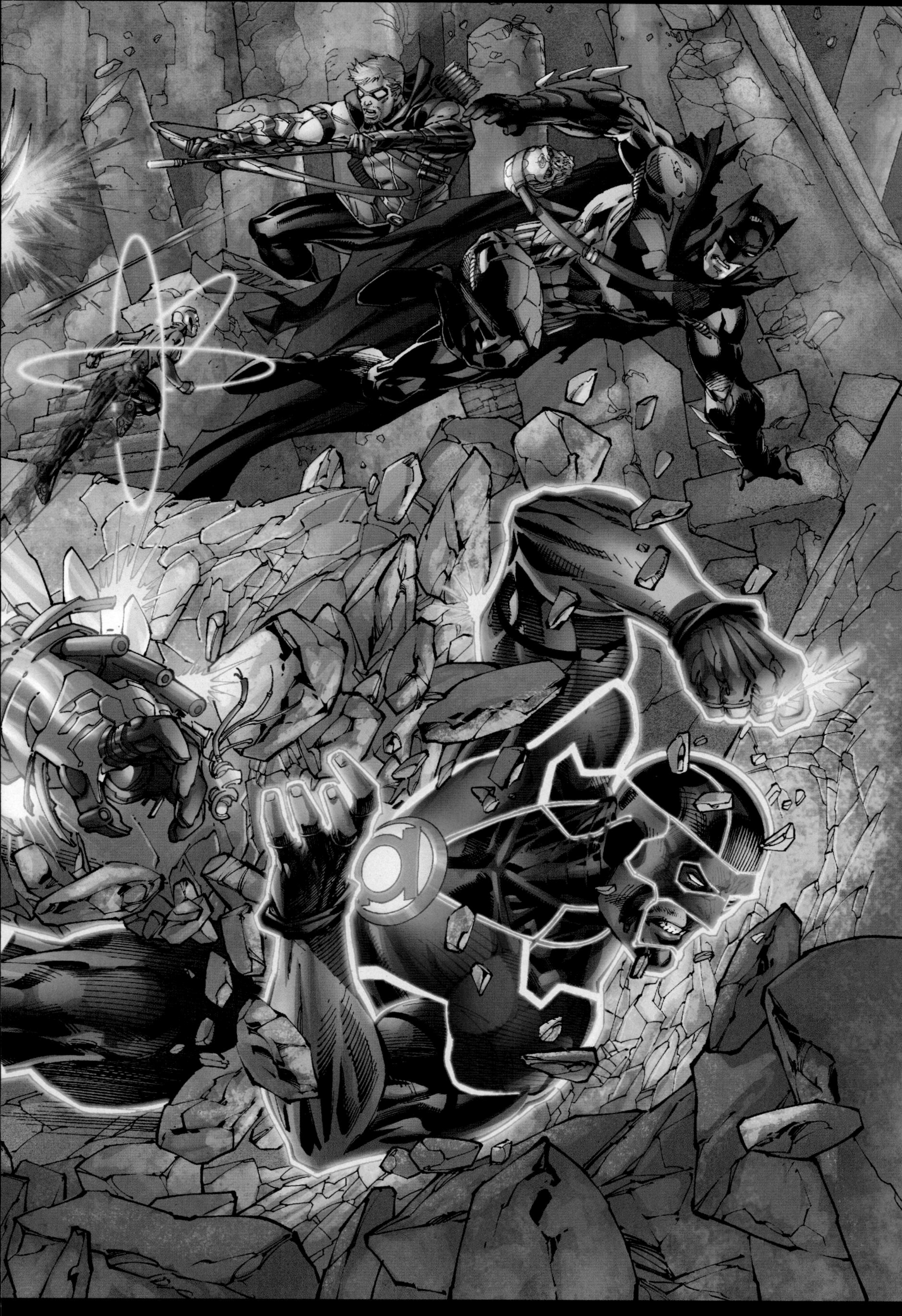

SAL CIPRIANO LETTERER

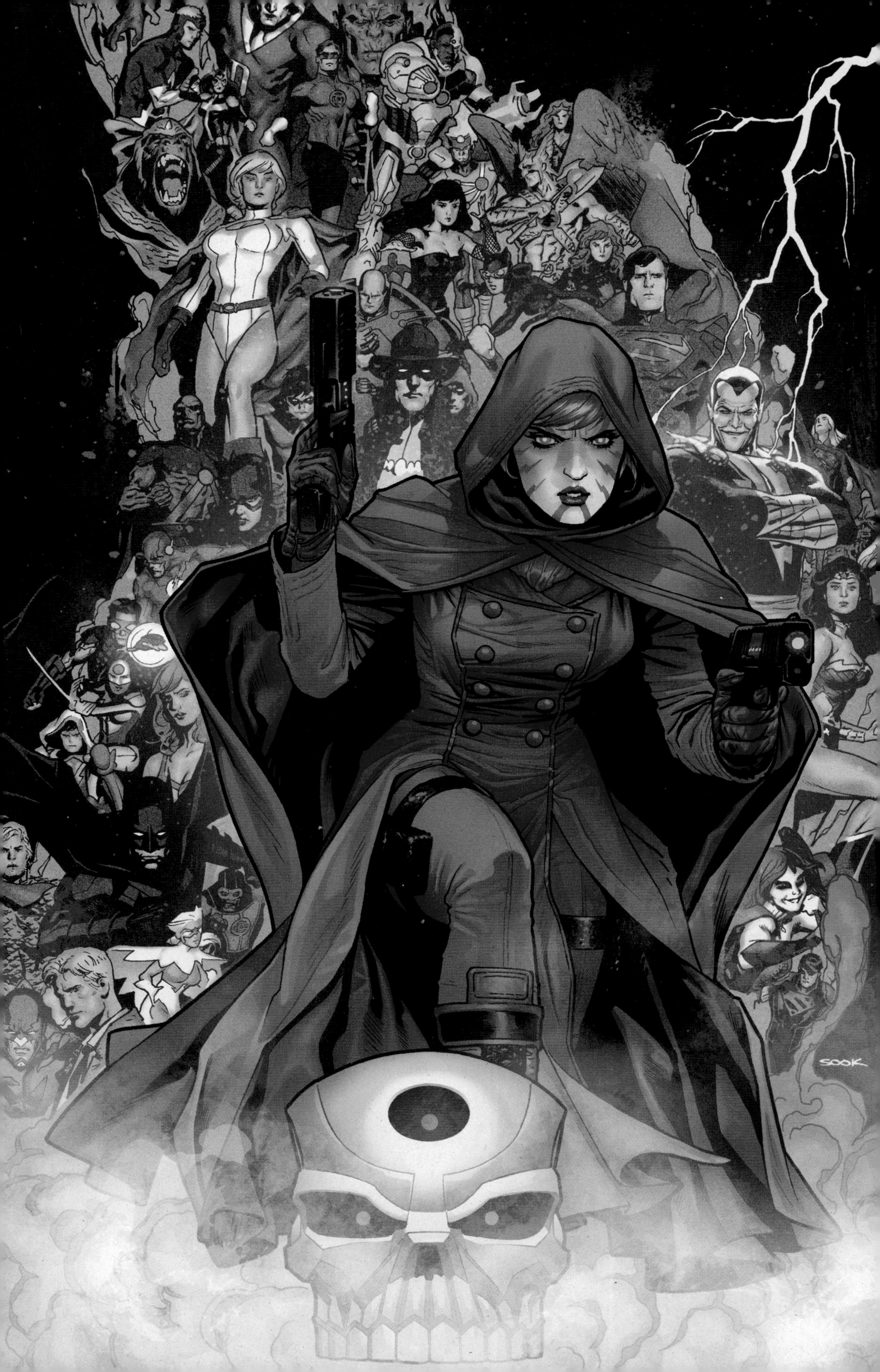
SOOK

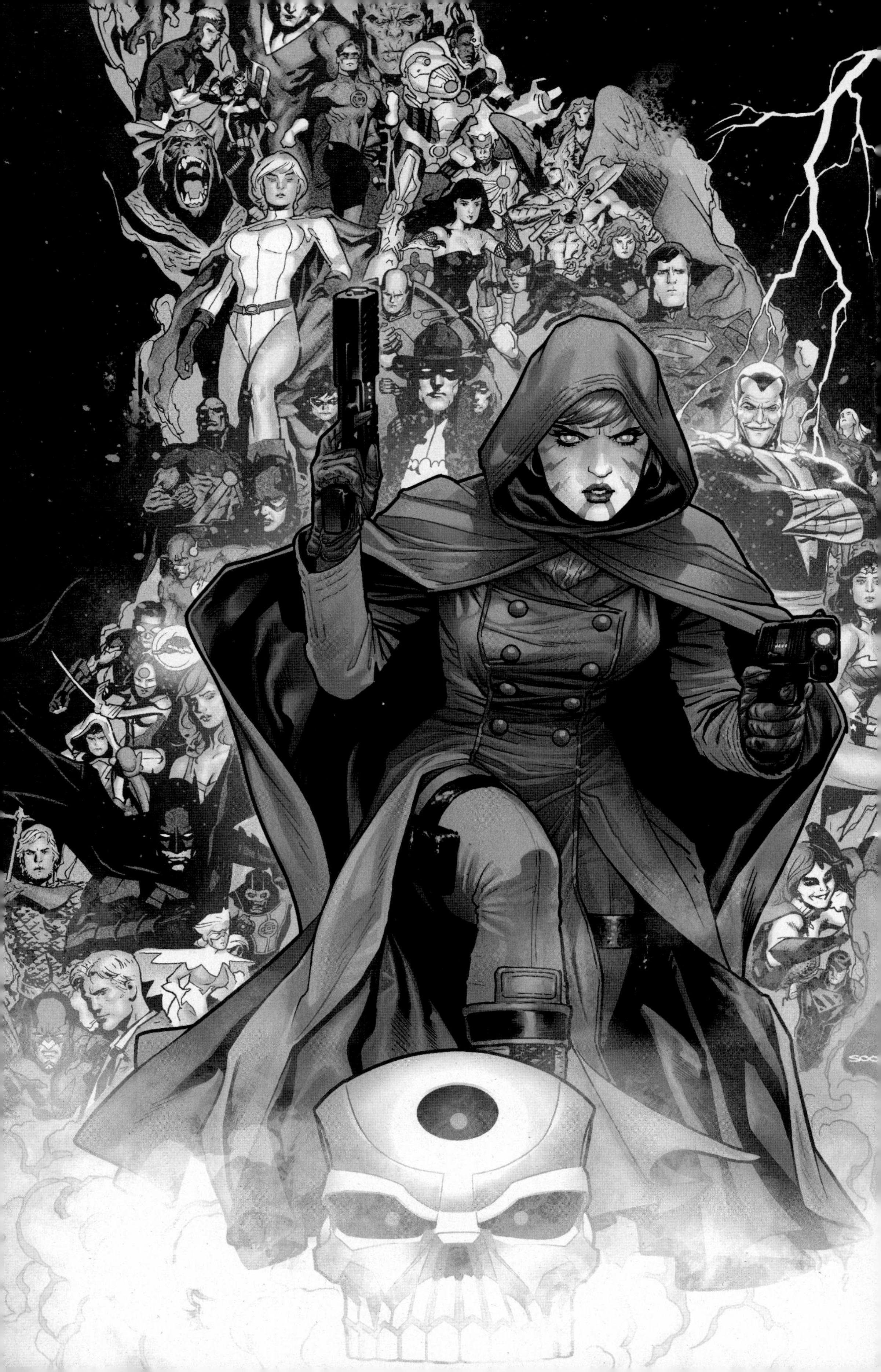

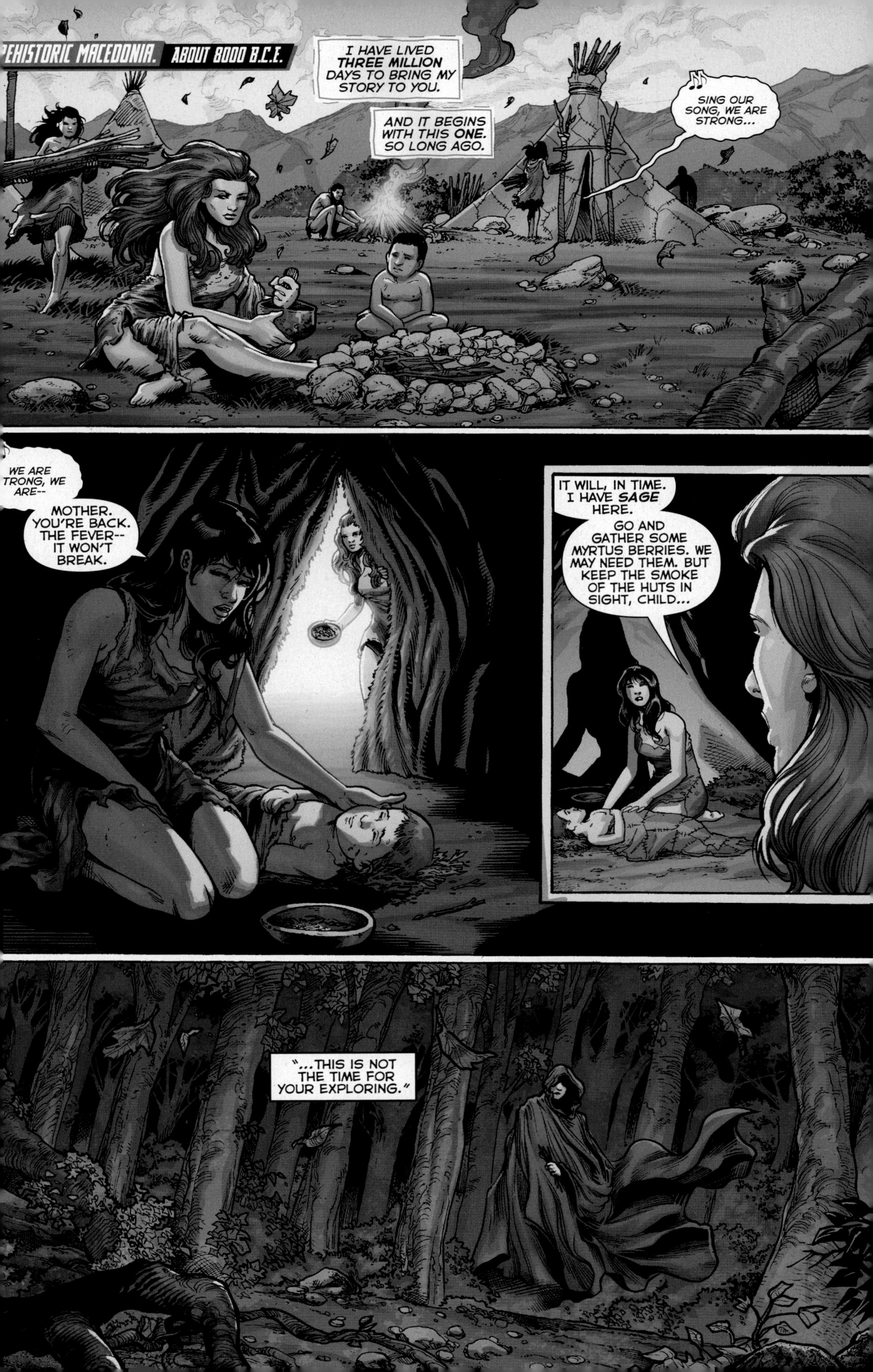
PREHISTORIC MACEDONIA. ABOUT 8000 B.C.E.
I HAVE LIVED THREE MILLION DAYS TO BRING MY STORY TO YOU.
AND IT BEGINS WITH THIS ONE. SO LONG AGO.
SING OUR SONG, WE ARE STRONG...
WE ARE STRONG, WE ARE--
MOTHER. YOU'RE BACK. THE FEVER-- IT WON'T BREAK.
IT WILL, IN TIME. I HAVE SAGE HERE.
GO AND GATHER SOME MYRTUS BERRIES. WE MAY NEED THEM. BUT KEEP THE SMOKE OF THE HUTS IN SIGHT, CHILD...
"...THIS IS NOT THE TIME FOR YOUR EXPLORING."

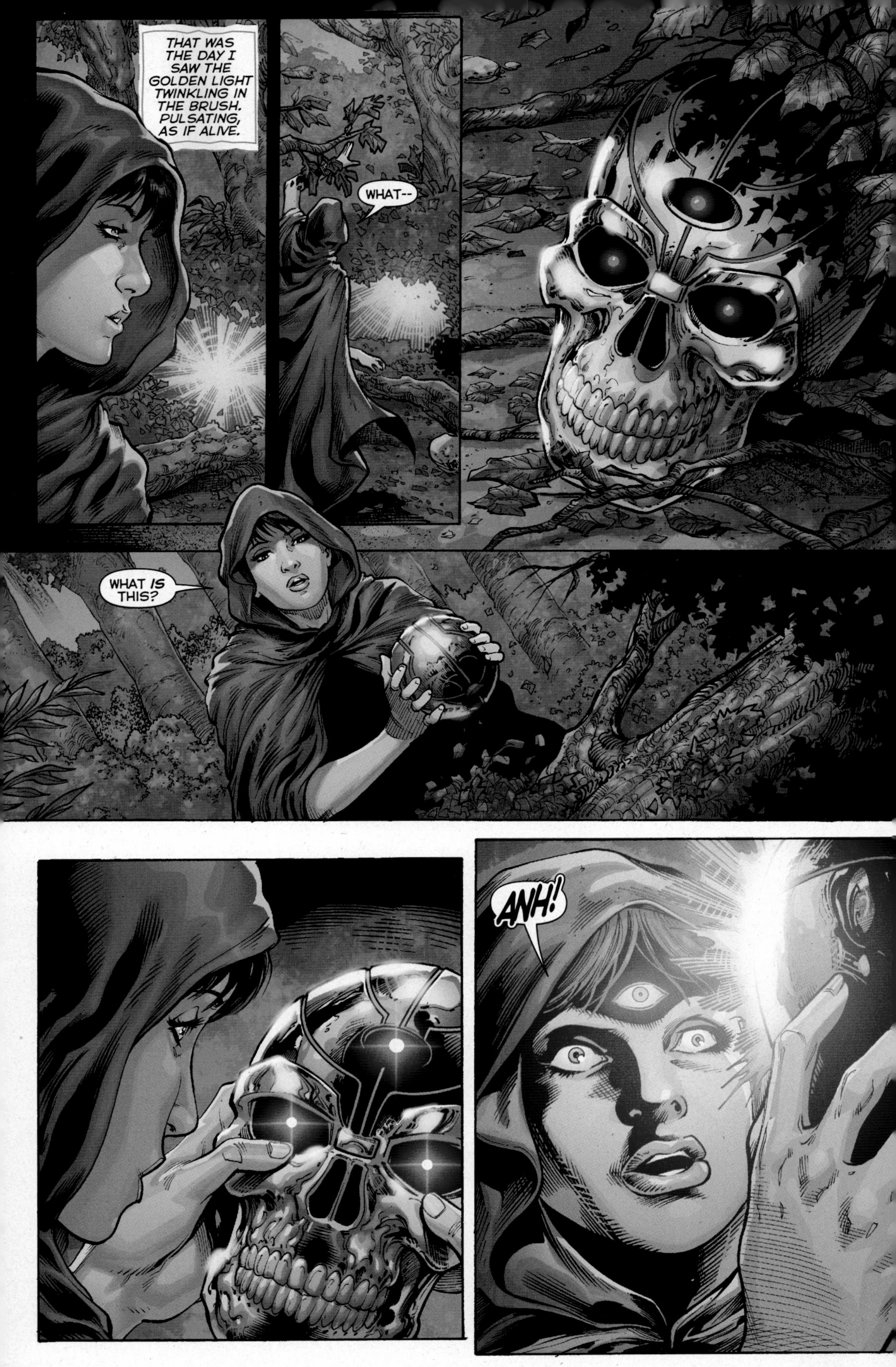
THAT WAS THE DAY I SAW THE GOLDEN LIGHT TWINKLING IN THE BRUSH. PULSATING, AS IF ALIVE.
WHAT--
WHAT *IS* THIS?
ANH!

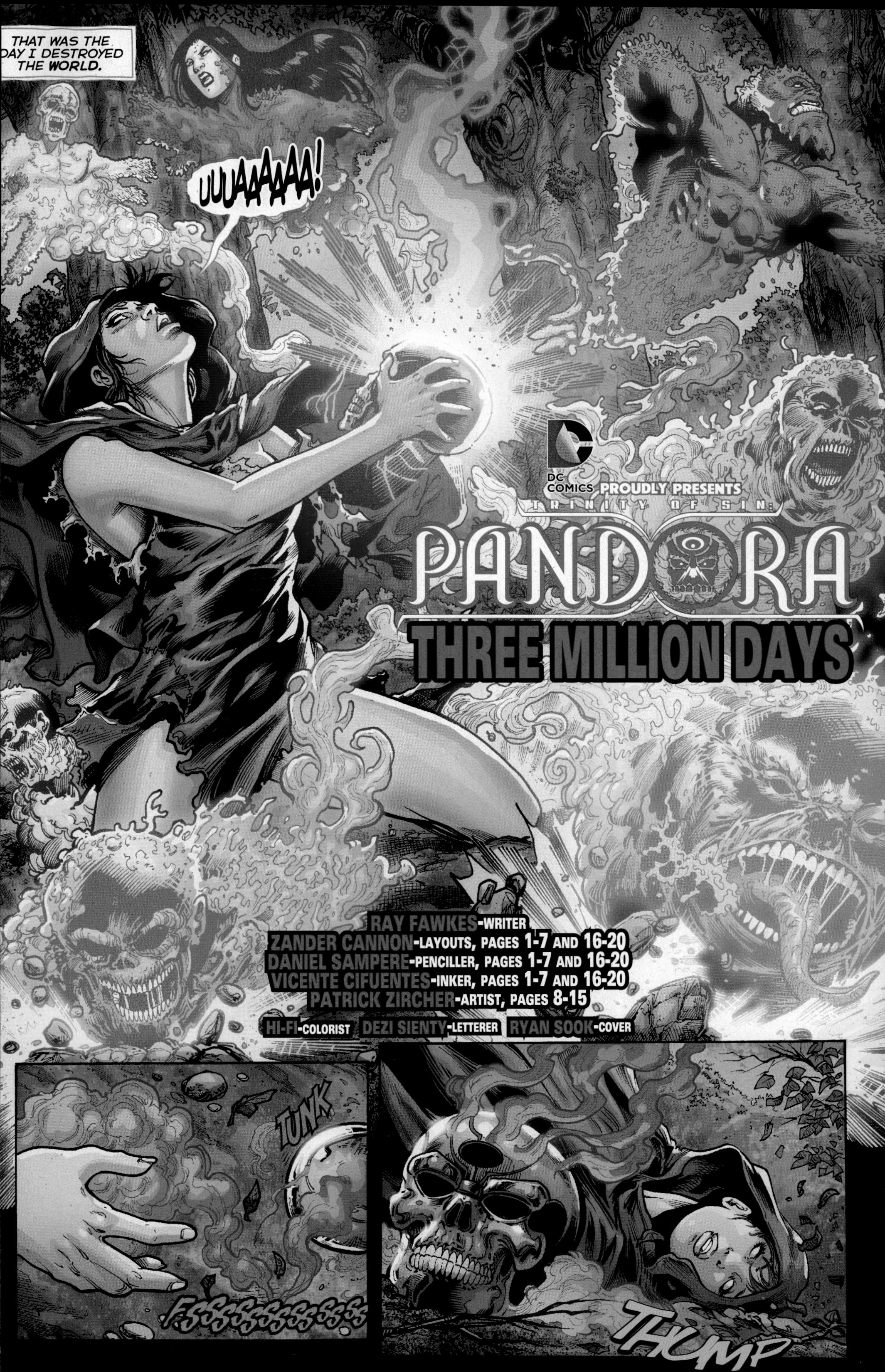
THAT WAS THE DAY I DESTROYED THE WORLD.
UUUAAAAAA!
DC COMICS PROUDLY PRESENTS
TRINITY OF SIN:
PANDORA
THREE MILLION DAYS
RAY FAWKES-WRITER
ZANDER CANNON-LAYOUTS, PAGES 1-7 AND 16-20
DANIEL SAMPERE-PENCILLER, PAGES 1-7 AND 16-20
VICENTE CIFUENTES-INKER, PAGES 1-7 AND 16-20
PATRICK ZIRCHER-ARTIST, PAGES 8-15
HI-FI-COLORIST DEZI SIENTY-LETTERER RYAN SOOK-COVER
TUNK
FSSSSSSSSSSS
THUMP

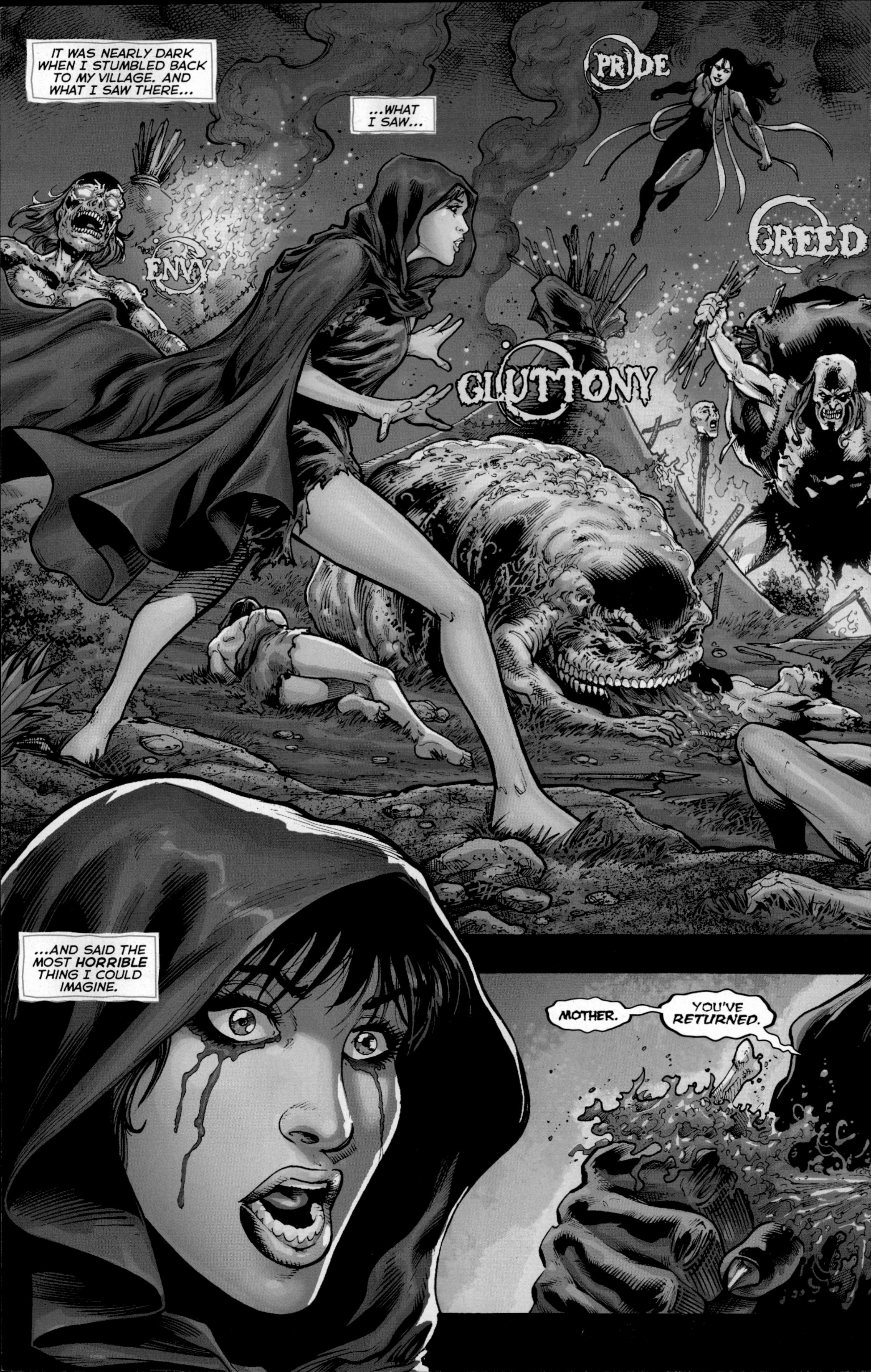

IT WAS NEARLY DARK WHEN I STUMBLED BACK TO MY VILLAGE. AND WHAT I SAW THERE...
...WHAT I SAW...
PRIDE
ENVY
GREED
GLUTTONY
...AND SAID THE MOST HORRIBLE THING I COULD IMAGINE.
MOTHER.
YOU'VE RETURNED.

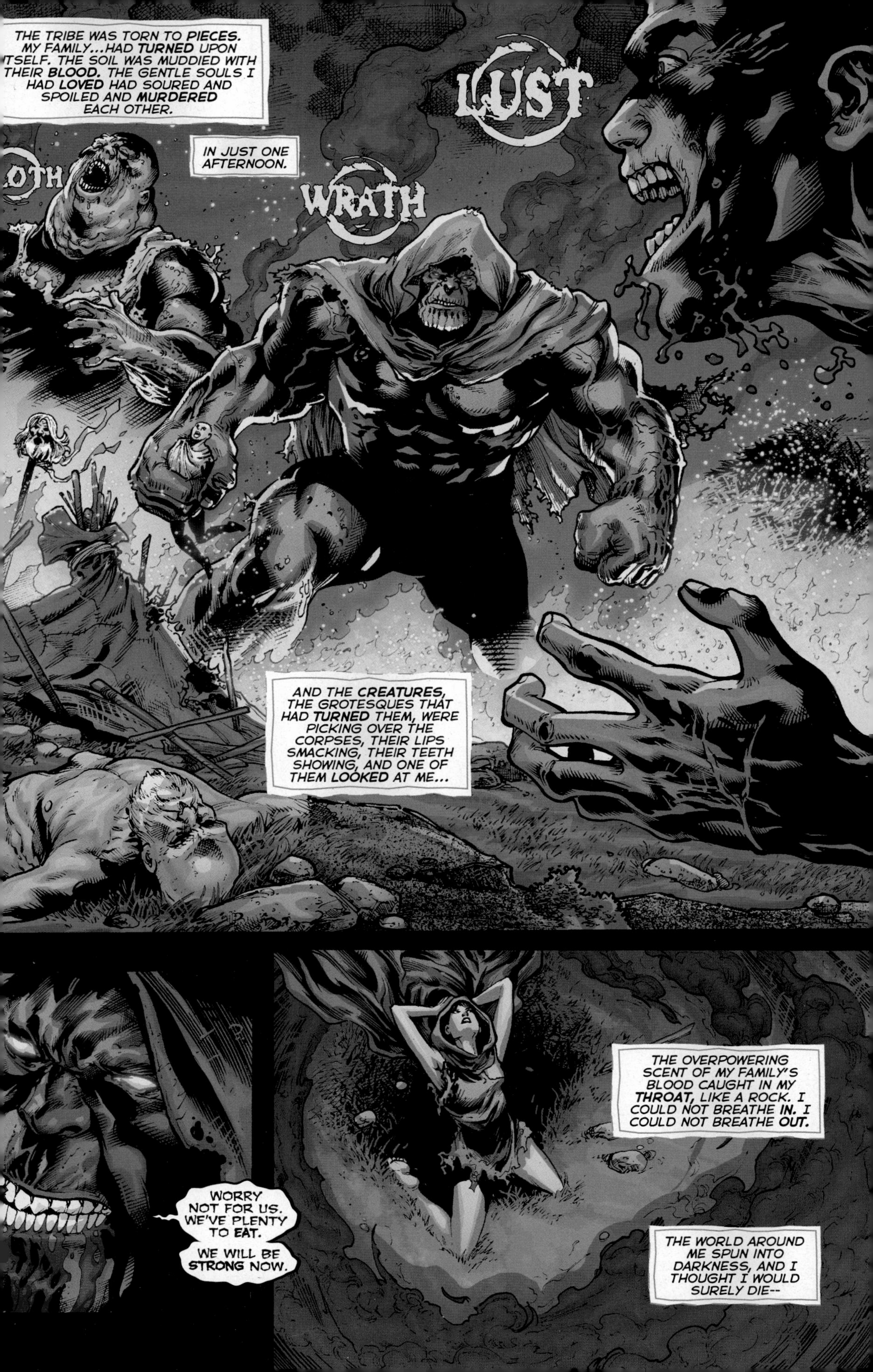
THE TRIBE WAS TORN TO PIECES. MY FAMILY...HAD TURNED UPON ITSELF. THE SOIL WAS MUDDIED WITH THEIR BLOOD. THE GENTLE SOULS I HAD LOVED HAD SOURED AND SPOILED AND MURDERED EACH OTHER.
LUST
IN JUST ONE AFTERNOON.
WRATH
AND THE CREATURES, THE GROTESQUES THAT HAD TURNED THEM, WERE PICKING OVER THE CORPSES, THEIR LIPS SMACKING, THEIR TEETH SHOWING, AND ONE OF THEM LOOKED AT ME...
WORRY NOT FOR US. WE'VE PLENTY TO EAT.
WE WILL BE STRONG NOW.
THE OVERPOWERING SCENT OF MY FAMILY'S BLOOD CAUGHT IN MY THROAT, LIKE A ROCK. I COULD NOT BREATHE IN. I COULD NOT BREATHE OUT.
THE WORLD AROUND ME SPUN INTO DARKNESS, AND I THOUGHT I WOULD SURELY DIE--

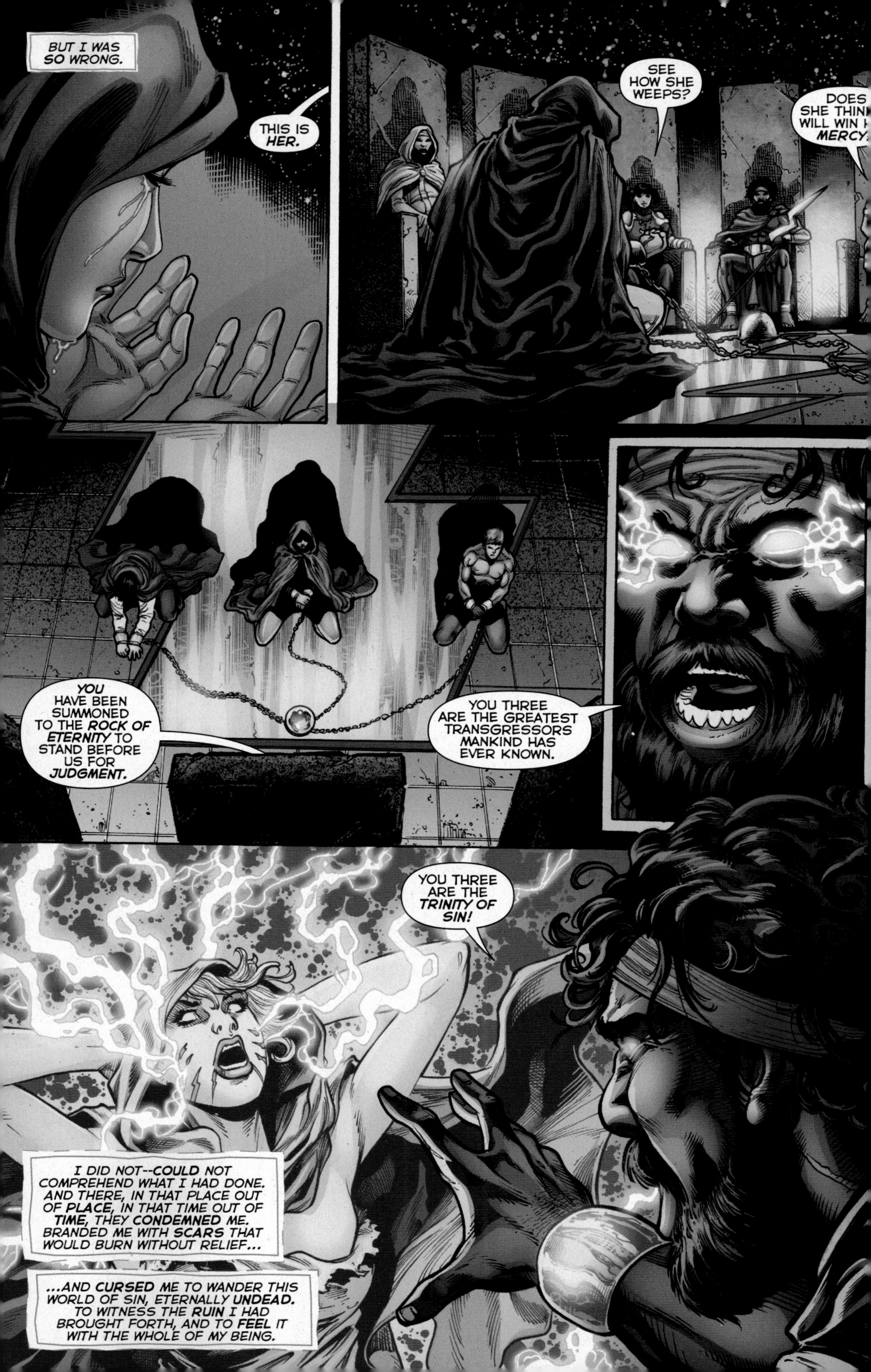
BUT I WAS SO WRONG.
THIS IS HER.
SEE HOW SHE WEEPS?
DOES SHE THINK WILL WIN MERCY
YOU HAVE BEEN SUMMONED TO THE ROCK OF ETERNITY TO STAND BEFORE US FOR JUDGMENT.
YOU THREE ARE THE GREATEST TRANSGRESSORS MANKIND HAS EVER KNOWN.
YOU THREE ARE THE TRINITY OF SIN!
I DID NOT--COULD NOT COMPREHEND WHAT I HAD DONE. AND THERE, IN THAT PLACE OUT OF PLACE, IN THAT TIME OUT OF TIME, THEY CONDEMNED ME. BRANDED ME WITH SCARS THAT WOULD BURN WITHOUT RELIEF...
...AND CURSED ME TO WANDER THIS WORLD OF SIN, ETERNALLY UNDEAD. TO WITNESS THE RUIN I HAD BROUGHT FORTH, AND TO FEEL IT WITH THE WHOLE OF MY BEING.

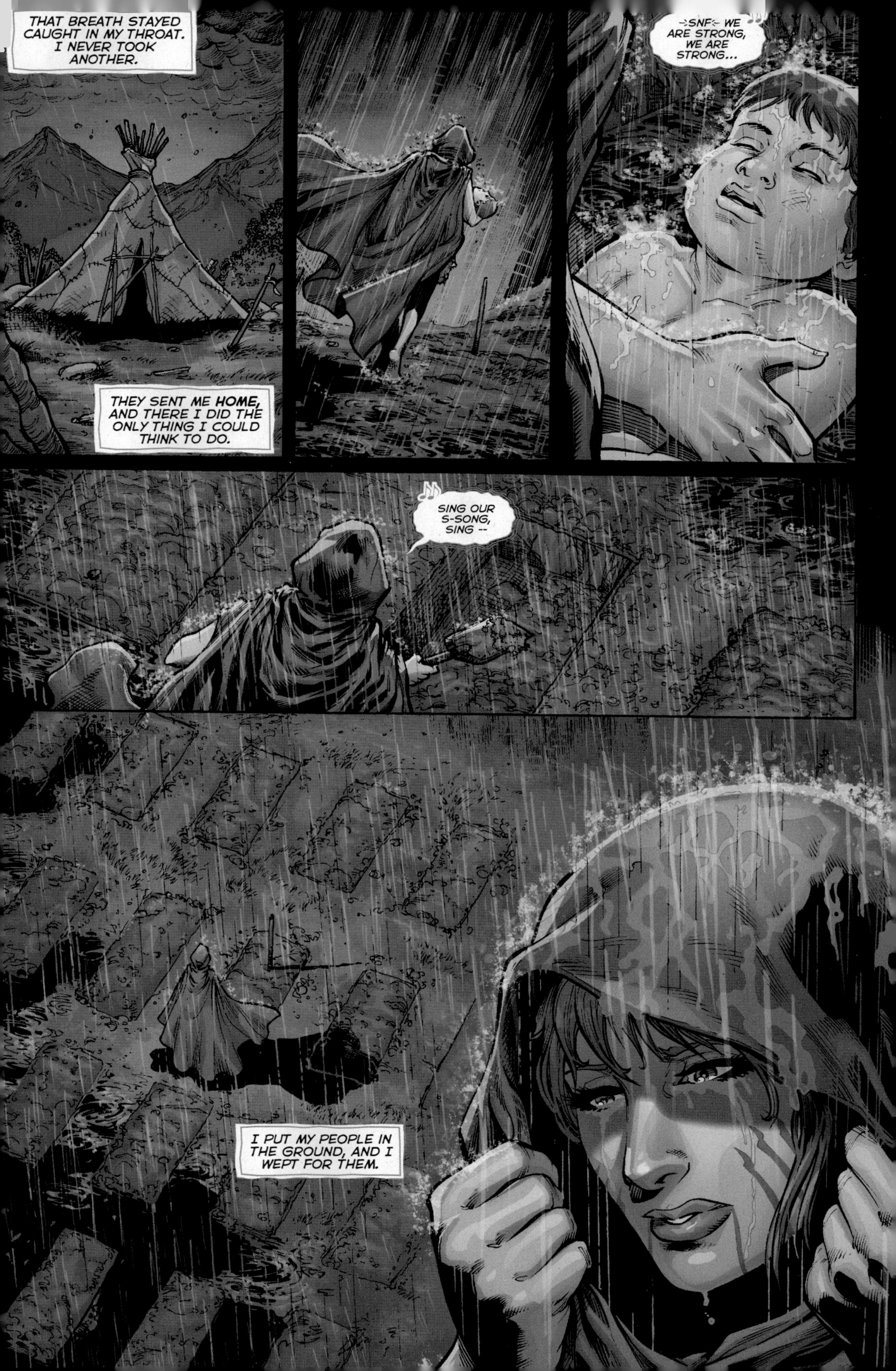
THAT BREATH STAYED CAUGHT IN MY THROAT. I NEVER TOOK ANOTHER.
THEY SENT ME HOME, AND THERE I DID THE ONLY THING I COULD THINK TO DO.
-SNF- WE ARE STRONG, WE ARE STRONG...
SING OUR S-SONG, SING --
I PUT MY PEOPLE IN THE GROUND, AND I WEPT FOR THEM.

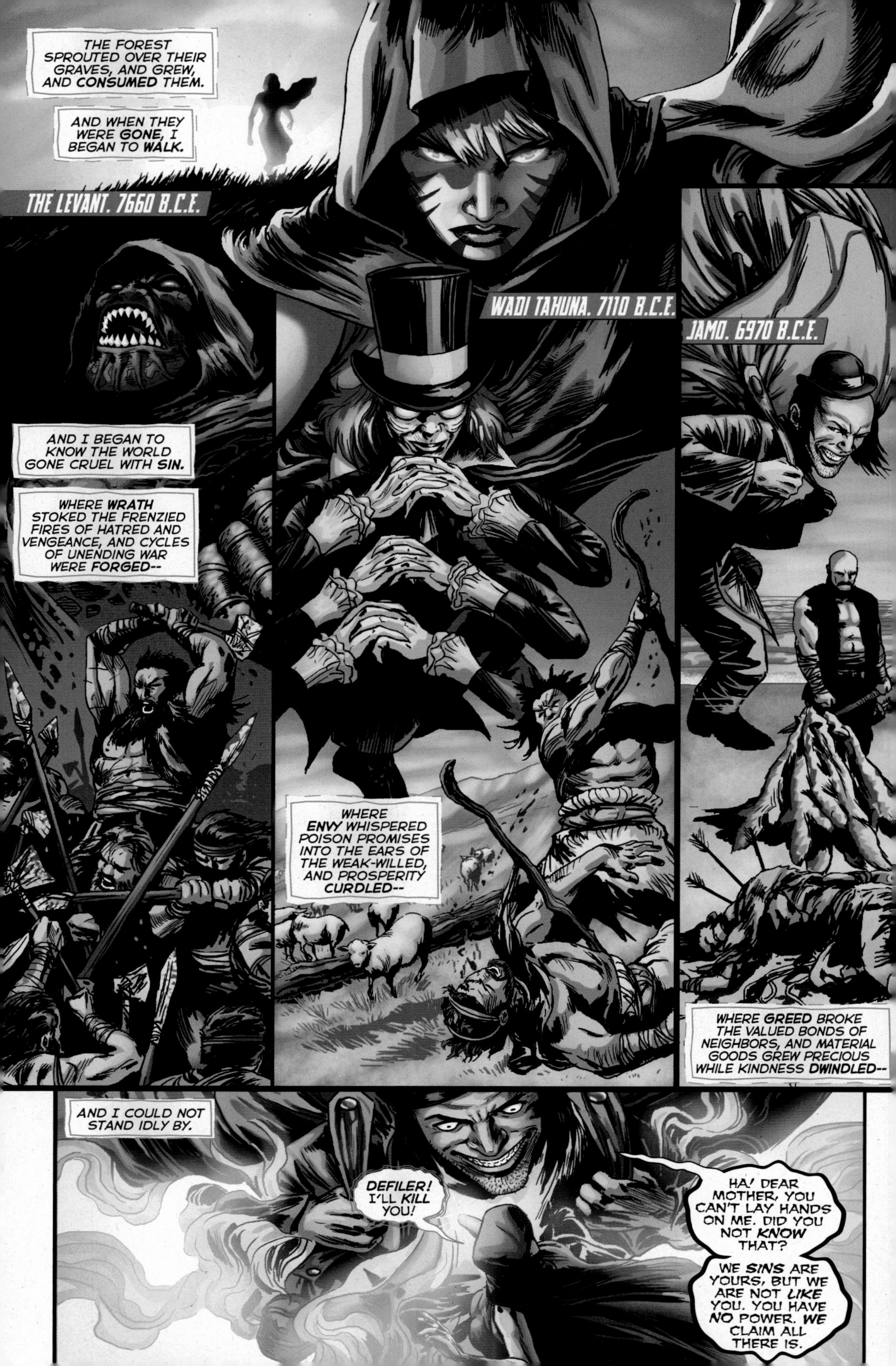
THE FOREST SPROUTED OVER THEIR GRAVES, AND GREW, AND CONSUMED THEM.
AND WHEN THEY WERE GONE, I BEGAN TO WALK.
THE LEVANT. 7660 B.C.E.
AND I BEGAN TO KNOW THE WORLD GONE CRUEL WITH SIN.
WHERE WRATH STOKED THE FRENZIED FIRES OF HATRED AND VENGEANCE, AND CYCLES OF UNENDING WAR WERE FORGED--
WADI TAHUNA. 7110 B.C.E.
WHERE ENVY WHISPERED POISON PROMISES INTO THE EARS OF THE WEAK-WILLED, AND PROSPERITY CURDLED--
JAMO. 6970 B.C.E.
WHERE GREED BROKE THE VALUED BONDS OF NEIGHBORS, AND MATERIAL GOODS GREW PRECIOUS WHILE KINDNESS DWINDLED--
AND I COULD NOT STAND IDLY BY.
DEFILER! I'LL KILL YOU!
HA! DEAR MOTHER, YOU CAN'T LAY HANDS ON ME. DID YOU NOT KNOW THAT?
WE SINS ARE YOURS, BUT WE ARE NOT LIKE YOU. YOU HAVE NO POWER. WE CLAIM ALL THERE IS.

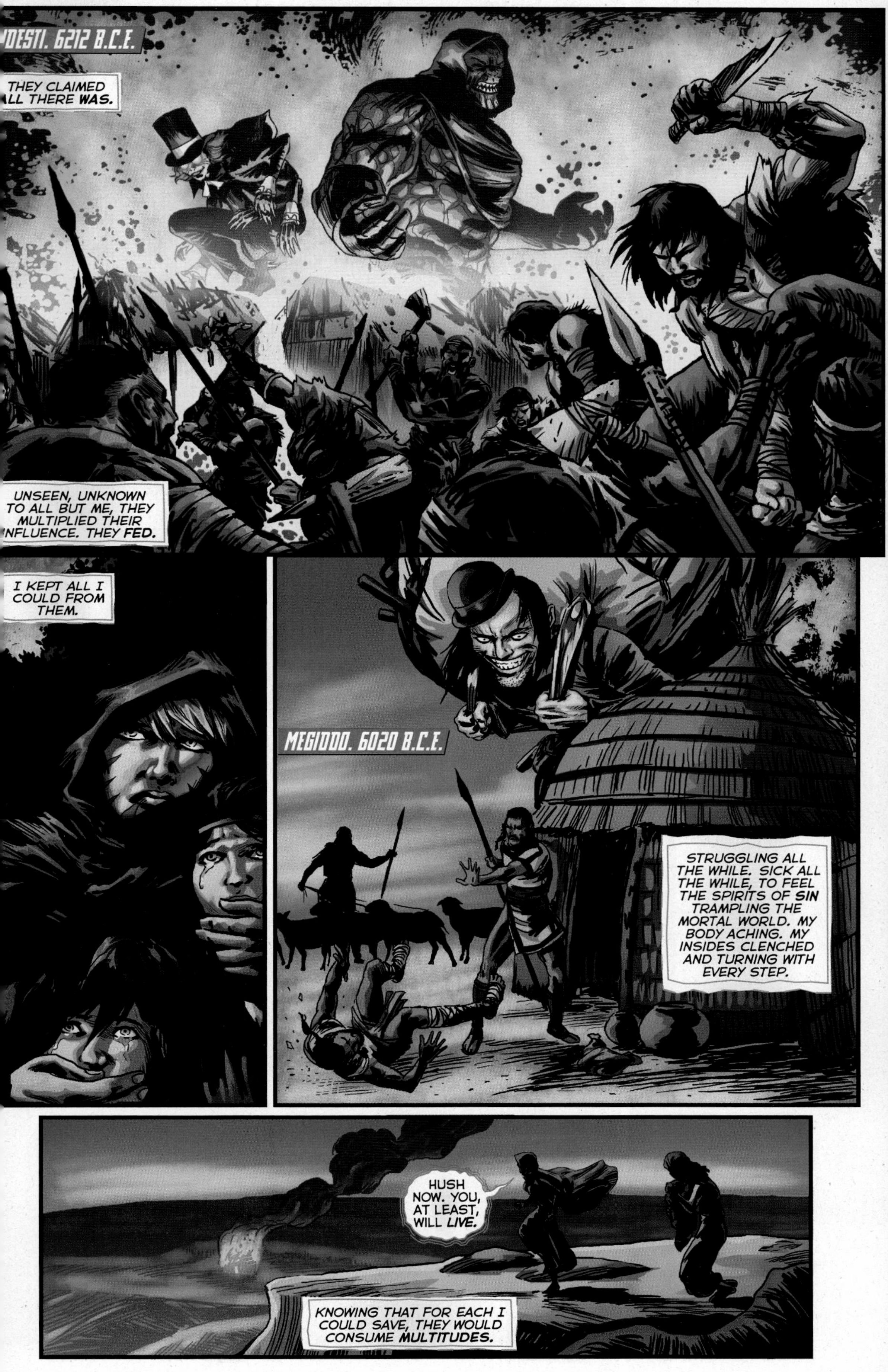
DESTI. 6212 B.C.E.
THEY CLAIMED LL THERE WAS.
UNSEEN, UNKNOWN TO ALL BUT ME, THEY MULTIPLIED THEIR NFLUENCE. THEY FED.
I KEPT ALL I COULD FROM THEM.
MEGIDDO. 6020 B.C.E.
STRUGGLING ALL THE WHILE. SICK ALL THE WHILE, TO FEEL THE SPIRITS OF SIN TRAMPLING THE MORTAL WORLD. MY BODY ACHING. MY INSIDES CLENCHED AND TURNING WITH EVERY STEP.
HUSH NOW. YOU, AT LEAST, WILL LIVE.
KNOWING THAT FOR EACH I COULD SAVE, THEY WOULD CONSUME MULTITUDES.

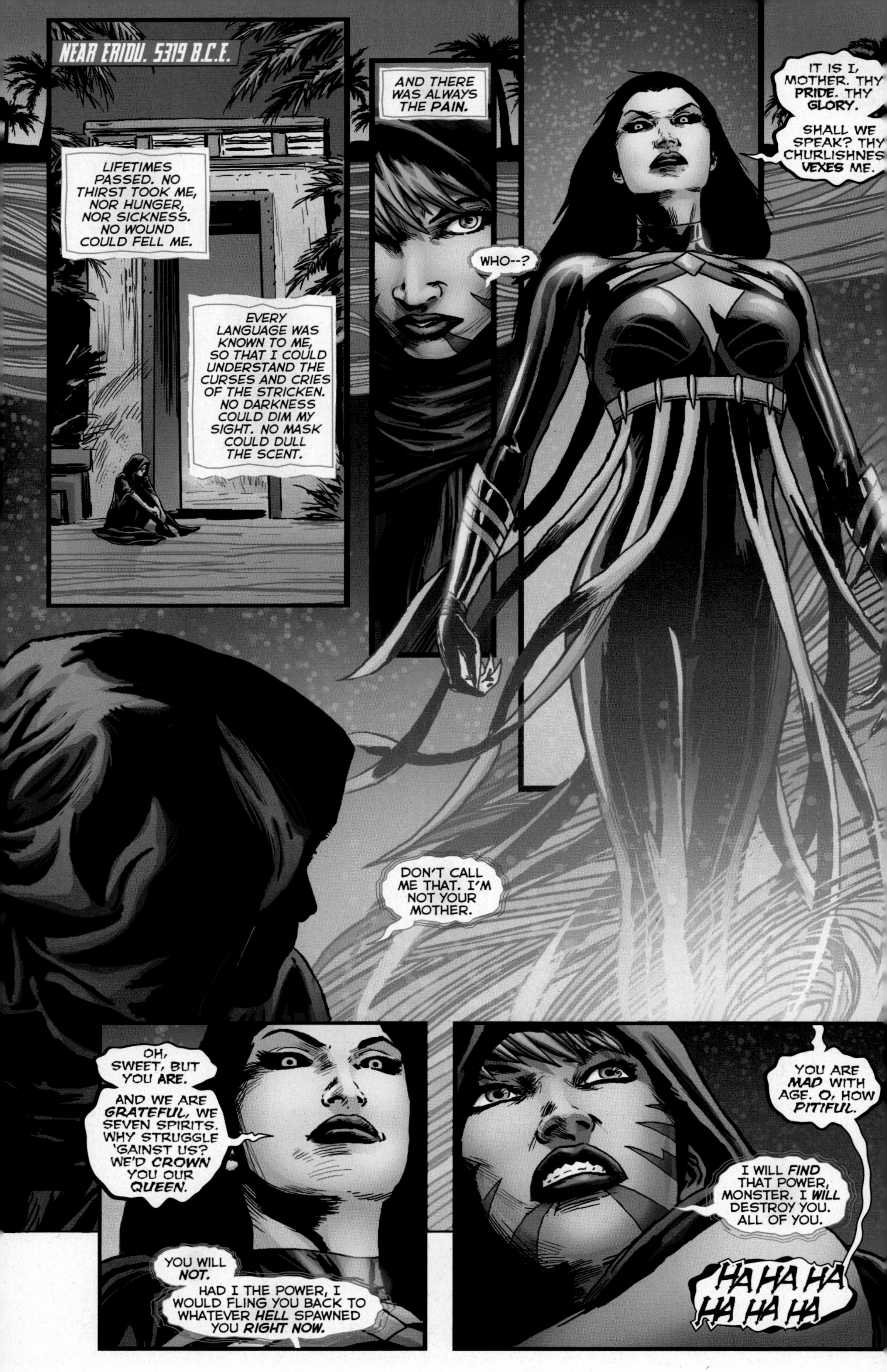
NEAR ERIDU. 5319 B.C.E.
LIFETIMES PASSED. NO THIRST TOOK ME, NOR HUNGER, NOR SICKNESS. NO WOUND COULD FELL ME.
EVERY LANGUAGE WAS KNOWN TO ME, SO THAT I COULD UNDERSTAND THE CURSES AND CRIES OF THE STRICKEN. NO DARKNESS COULD DIM MY SIGHT. NO MASK COULD DULL THE SCENT.
AND THERE WAS ALWAYS THE PAIN.
WHO--?
IT IS I, MOTHER. THY PRIDE. THY GLORY.
SHALL WE SPEAK? THY CHURLISHNES VEXES ME.
DON'T CALL ME THAT. I'M NOT YOUR MOTHER.
OH, SWEET, BUT YOU ARE.
AND WE ARE GRATEFUL, WE SEVEN SPIRITS. WHY STRUGGLE 'GAINST US? WE'D CROWN YOU OUR QUEEN.
YOU WILL NOT.
HAD I THE POWER, I WOULD FLING YOU BACK TO WHATEVER HELL SPAWNED YOU RIGHT NOW.
YOU ARE MAD WITH AGE. O, HOW PITIFUL.
I WILL FIND THAT POWER, MONSTER. I WILL DESTROY YOU. ALL OF YOU.
HA HA HA HA HA HA

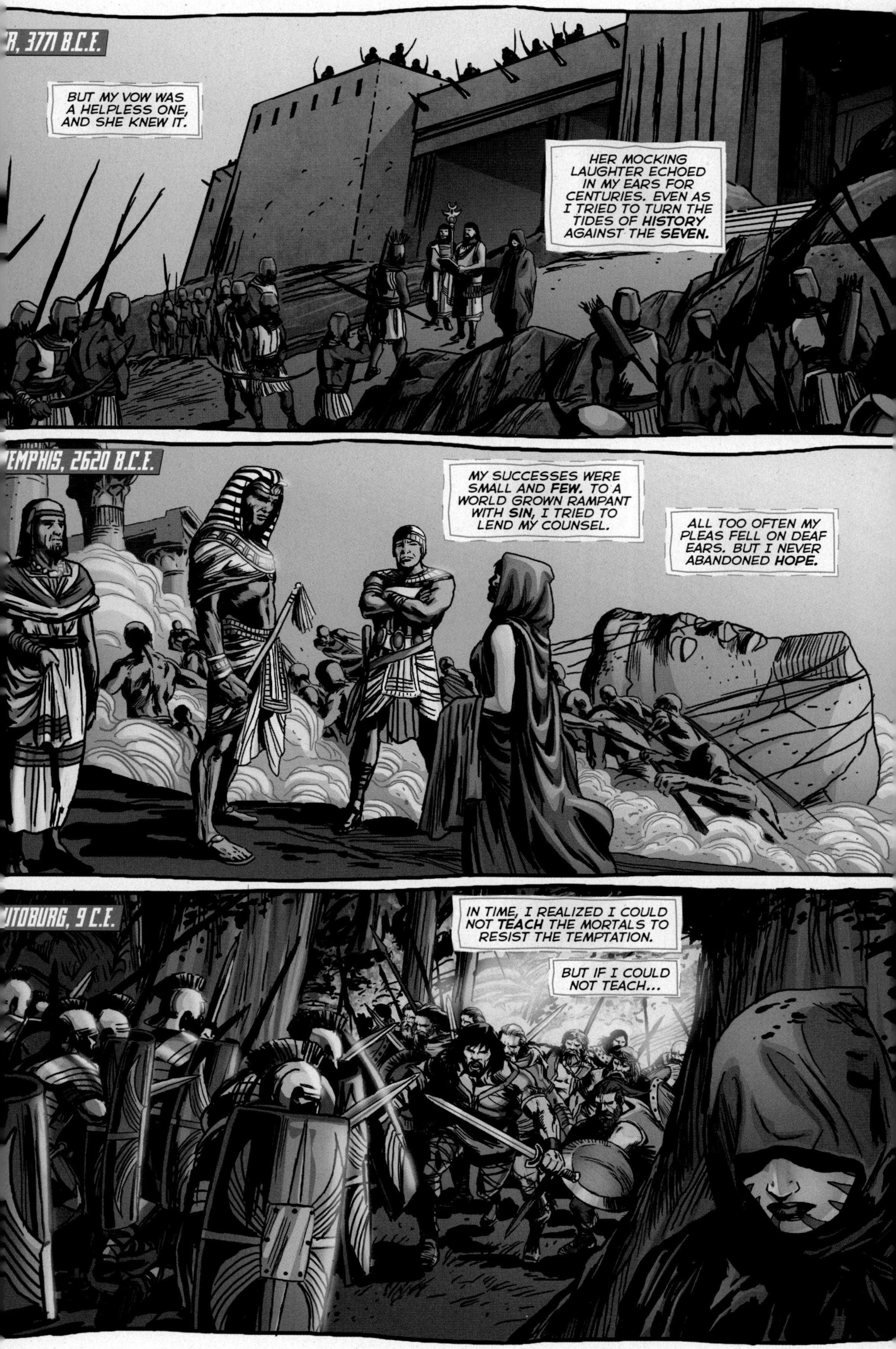
R, 3771 B.C.E.
BUT MY VOW WAS A HELPLESS ONE, AND SHE KNEW IT.
HER MOCKING LAUGHTER ECHOED IN MY EARS FOR CENTURIES. EVEN AS I TRIED TO TURN THE TIDES OF HISTORY AGAINST THE SEVEN.
EMPHIS, 2620 B.C.E.
MY SUCCESSES WERE SMALL AND FEW. TO A WORLD GROWN RAMPANT WITH SIN, I TRIED TO LEND MY COUNSEL.
ALL TOO OFTEN MY PLEAS FELL ON DEAF EARS. BUT I NEVER ABANDONED HOPE.
UTOBURG, 9 C.E.
IN TIME, I REALIZED I COULD NOT TEACH THE MORTALS TO RESIST THE TEMPTATION.
BUT IF I COULD NOT TEACH...

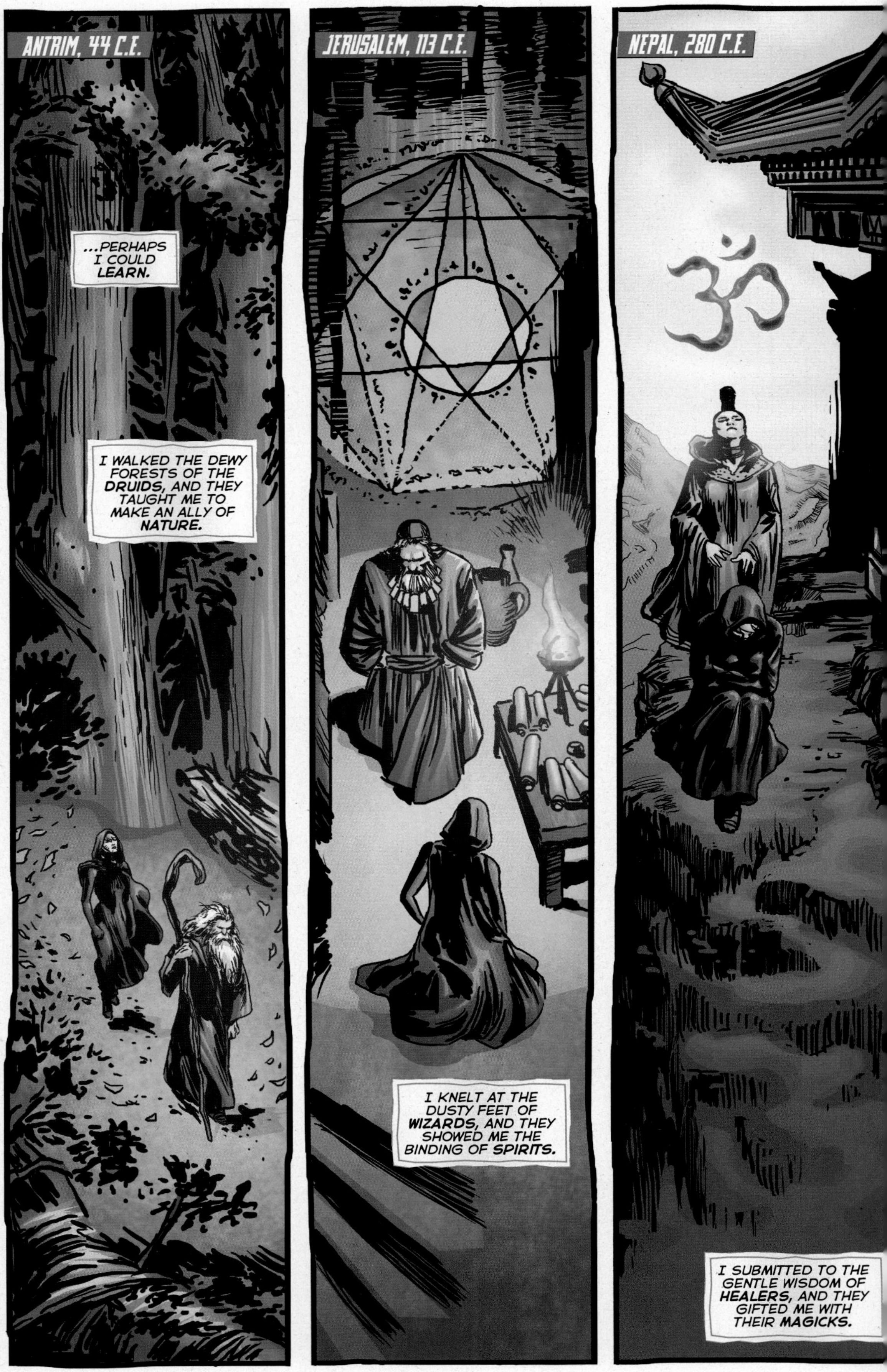
ANTRIM, 44 C.E.
...PERHAPS I COULD LEARN.
I WALKED THE DEWY FORESTS OF THE DRUIDS, AND THEY TAUGHT ME TO MAKE AN ALLY OF NATURE.
JERUSALEM, 113 C.E.
I KNELT AT THE DUSTY FEET OF WIZARDS, AND THEY SHOWED ME THE BINDING OF SPIRITS.
NEPAL, 280 C.E.
I SUBMITTED TO THE GENTLE WISDOM OF HEALERS, AND THEY GIFTED ME WITH THEIR MAGICKS.

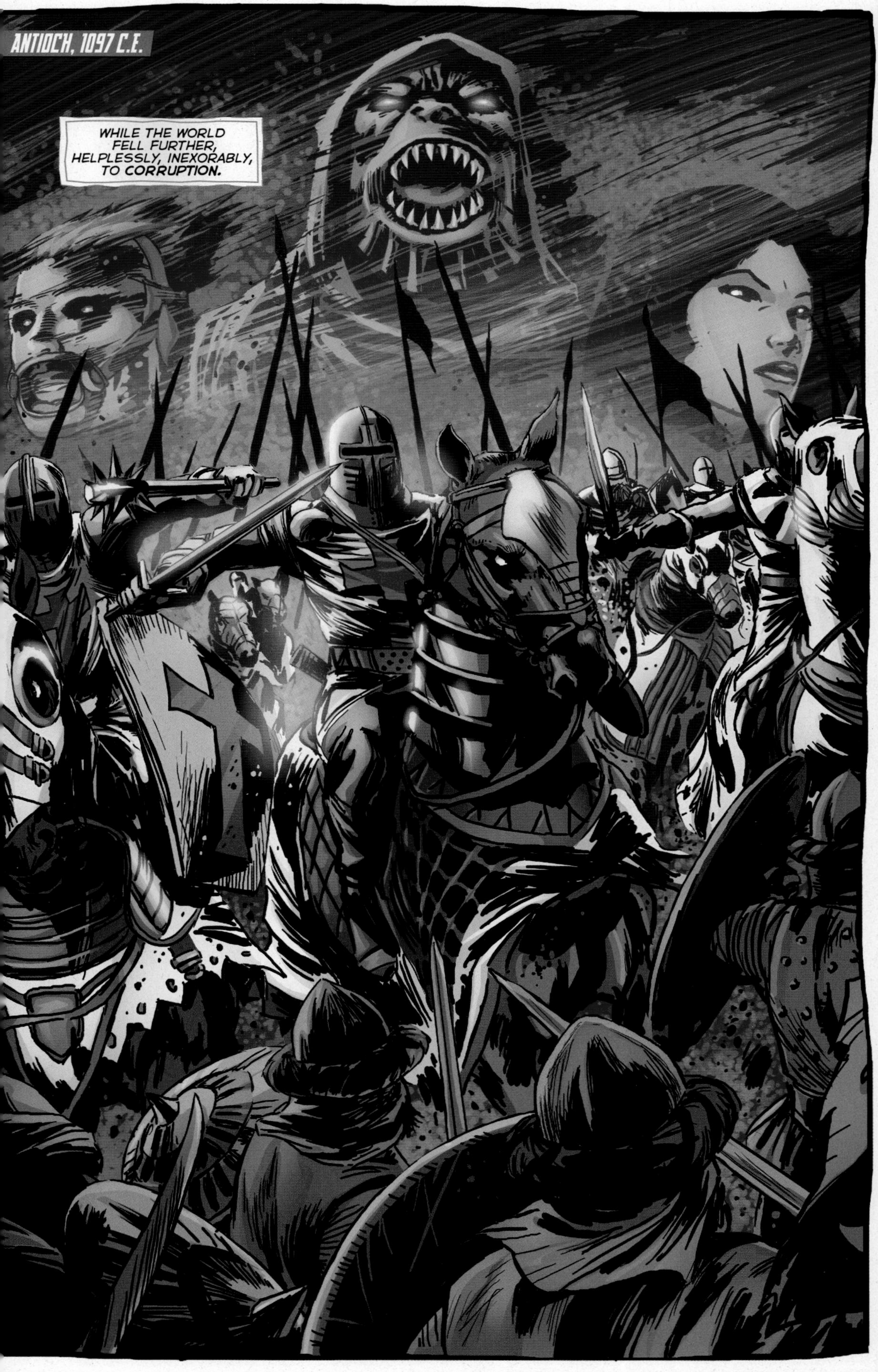
ANTIOCH, 1097 C.E.
WHILE THE WORLD FELL FURTHER, HELPLESSLY, INEXORABLY, TO CORRUPTION.

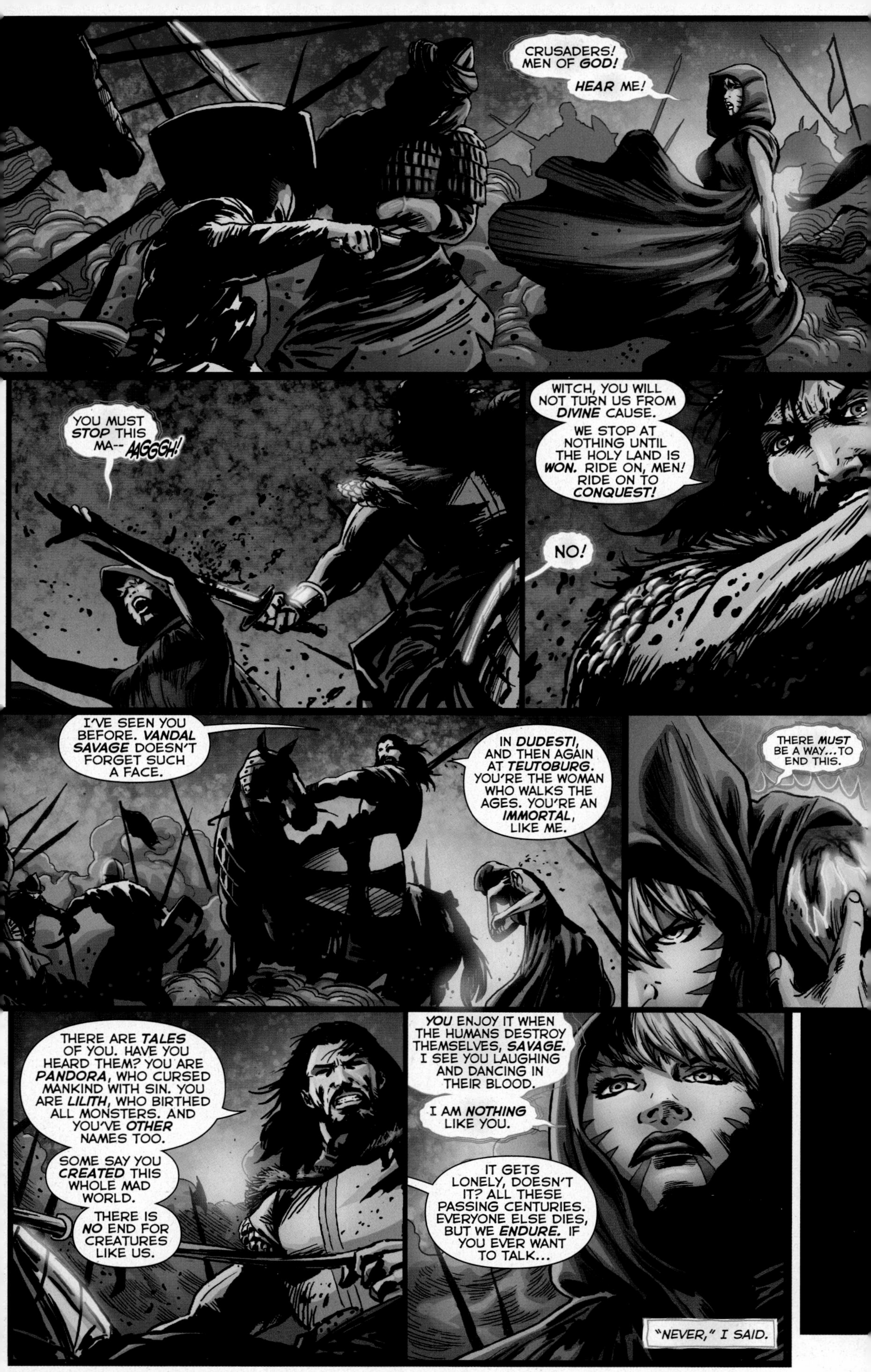

CRUSADERS! MEN OF GOD!
HEAR ME!
YOU MUST STOP THIS MA-- AAGGGH!
WITCH, YOU WILL NOT TURN US FROM DIVINE CAUSE.
WE STOP AT NOTHING UNTIL THE HOLY LAND IS WON. RIDE ON, MEN! RIDE ON TO CONQUEST!
NO!
I'VE SEEN YOU BEFORE. VANDAL SAVAGE DOESN'T FORGET SUCH A FACE.
IN DUDESTI, AND THEN AGAIN AT TEUTOBURG. YOU'RE THE WOMAN WHO WALKS THE AGES. YOU'RE AN IMMORTAL, LIKE ME.
THERE MUST BE A WAY...TO END THIS.
THERE ARE TALES OF YOU. HAVE YOU HEARD THEM? YOU ARE PANDORA, WHO CURSED MANKIND WITH SIN. YOU ARE LILITH, WHO BIRTHED ALL MONSTERS. AND YOU'VE OTHER NAMES TOO.
SOME SAY YOU CREATED THIS WHOLE MAD WORLD.
THERE IS NO END FOR CREATURES LIKE US.
YOU ENJOY IT WHEN THE HUMANS DESTROY THEMSELVES, SAVAGE. I SEE YOU LAUGHING AND DANCING IN THEIR BLOOD.
I AM NOTHING LIKE YOU.
IT GETS LONELY, DOESN'T IT? ALL THESE PASSING CENTURIES. EVERYONE ELSE DIES, BUT WE ENDURE. IF YOU EVER WANT TO TALK...
"NEVER," I SAID.

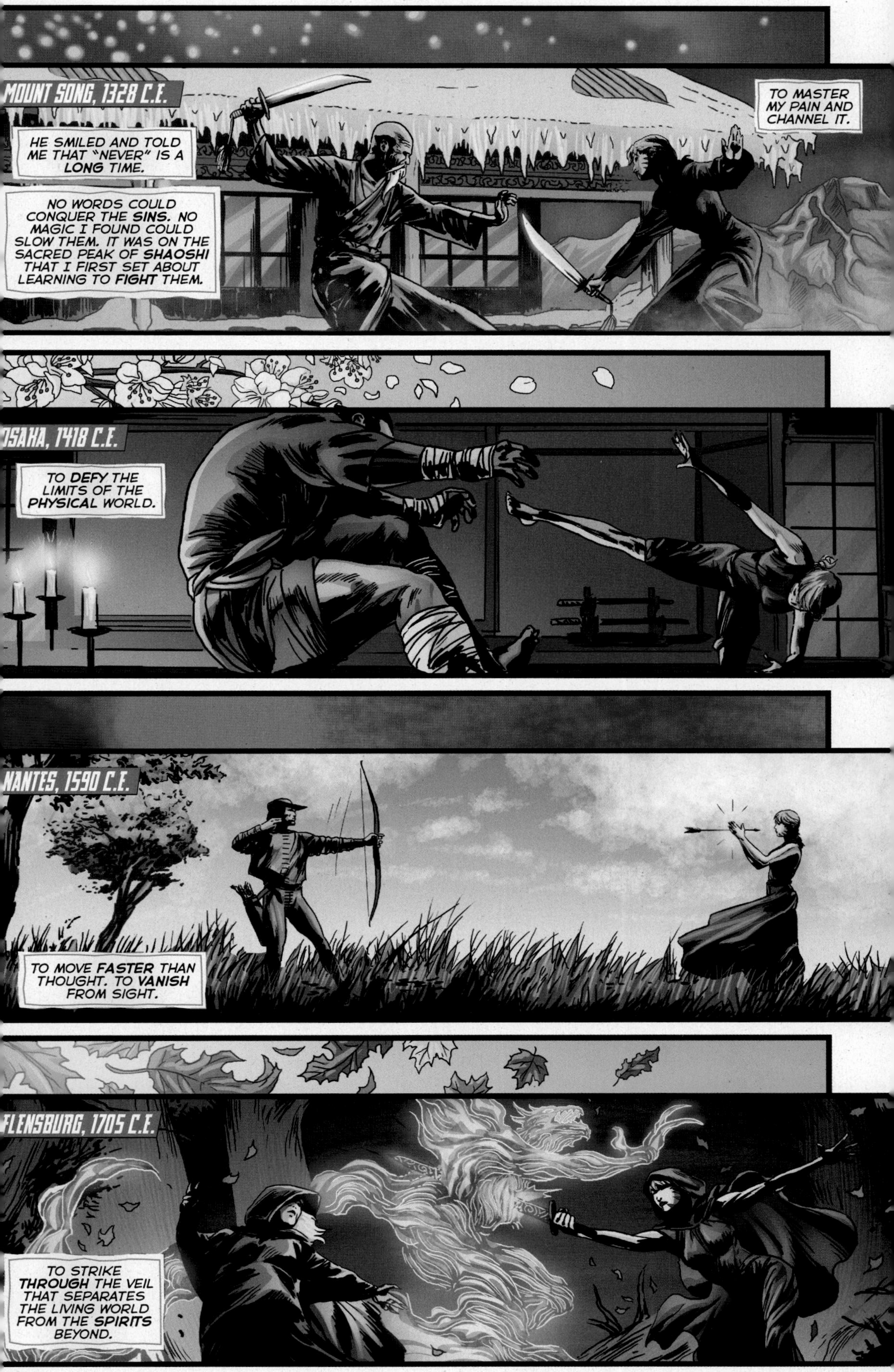
MOUNT SONG, 1328 C.E.
HE SMILED AND TOLD ME THAT "NEVER" IS A LONG TIME.
NO WORDS COULD CONQUER THE SINS. NO MAGIC I FOUND COULD SLOW THEM. IT WAS ON THE SACRED PEAK OF SHAOSHI THAT I FIRST SET ABOUT LEARNING TO FIGHT THEM.
TO MASTER MY PAIN AND CHANNEL IT.
OSAKA, 1418 C.E.
TO DEFY THE LIMITS OF THE PHYSICAL WORLD.
NANTES, 1590 C.E.
TO MOVE FASTER THAN THOUGHT. TO VANISH FROM SIGHT.
FLENSBURG, 1705 C.E.
TO STRIKE THROUGH THE VEIL THAT SEPARATES THE LIVING WORLD FROM THE SPIRITS BEYOND.

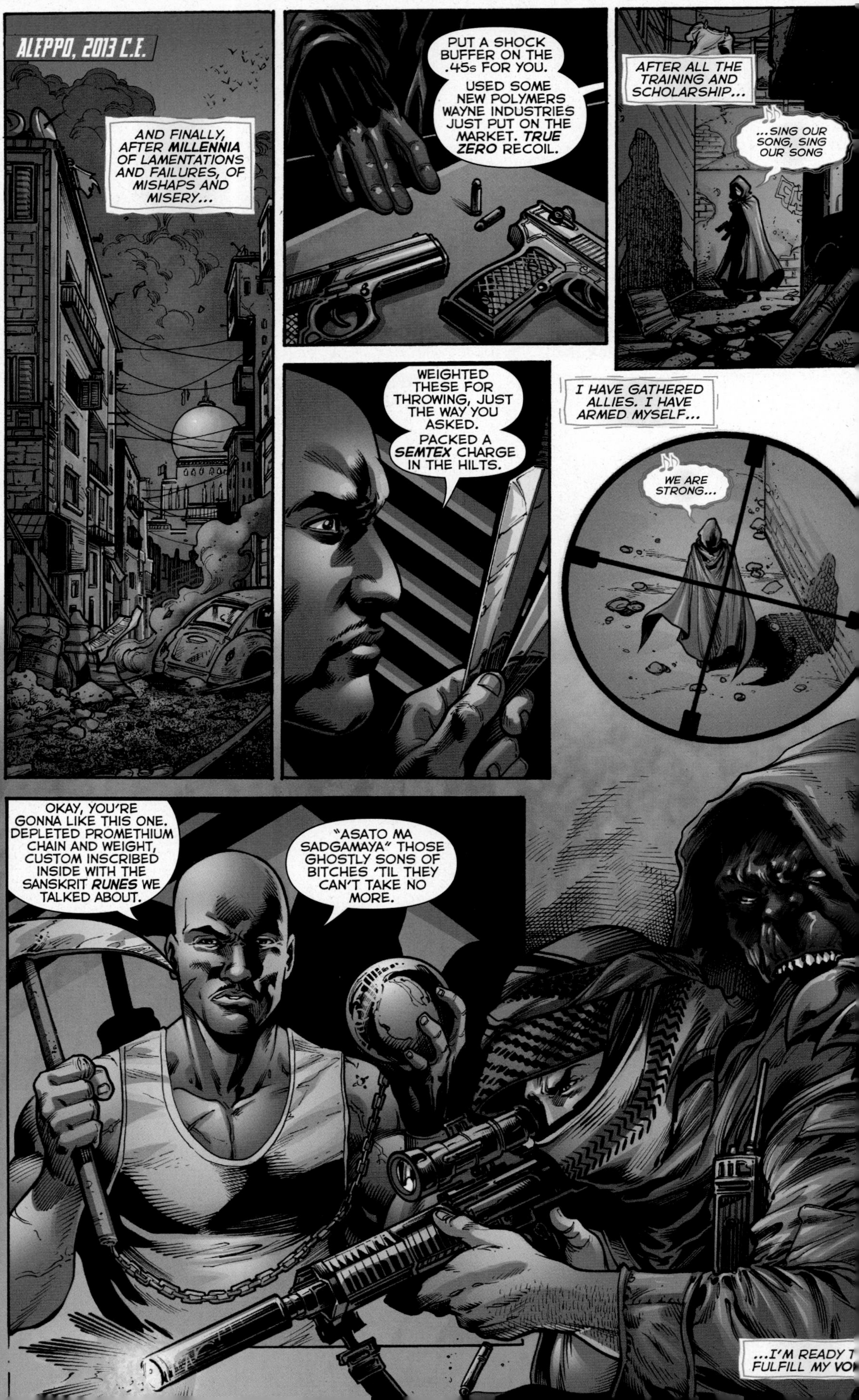

ALEPPO, 2013 C.E.
AND FINALLY, AFTER MILLENNIA OF LAMENTATIONS AND FAILURES, OF MISHAPS AND MISERY...
PUT A SHOCK BUFFER ON THE .45s FOR YOU.
USED SOME NEW POLYMERS WAYNE INDUSTRIES JUST PUT ON THE MARKET. TRUE ZERO RECOIL.
AFTER ALL THE TRAINING AND SCHOLARSHIP...
...SING OUR SONG, SING OUR SONG
WEIGHTED THESE FOR THROWING, JUST THE WAY YOU ASKED.
PACKED A SEMTEX CHARGE IN THE HILTS.
I HAVE GATHERED ALLIES. I HAVE ARMED MYSELF...
WE ARE STRONG...
OKAY, YOU'RE GONNA LIKE THIS ONE. DEPLETED PROMETHIUM CHAIN AND WEIGHT, CUSTOM INSCRIBED INSIDE WITH THE SANSKRIT RUNES WE TALKED ABOUT.
"ASATO MA SADGAMAYA" THOSE GHOSTLY SONS OF BITCHES 'TIL THEY CAN'T TAKE NO MORE.
...I'M READY T
FULFILL MY VO

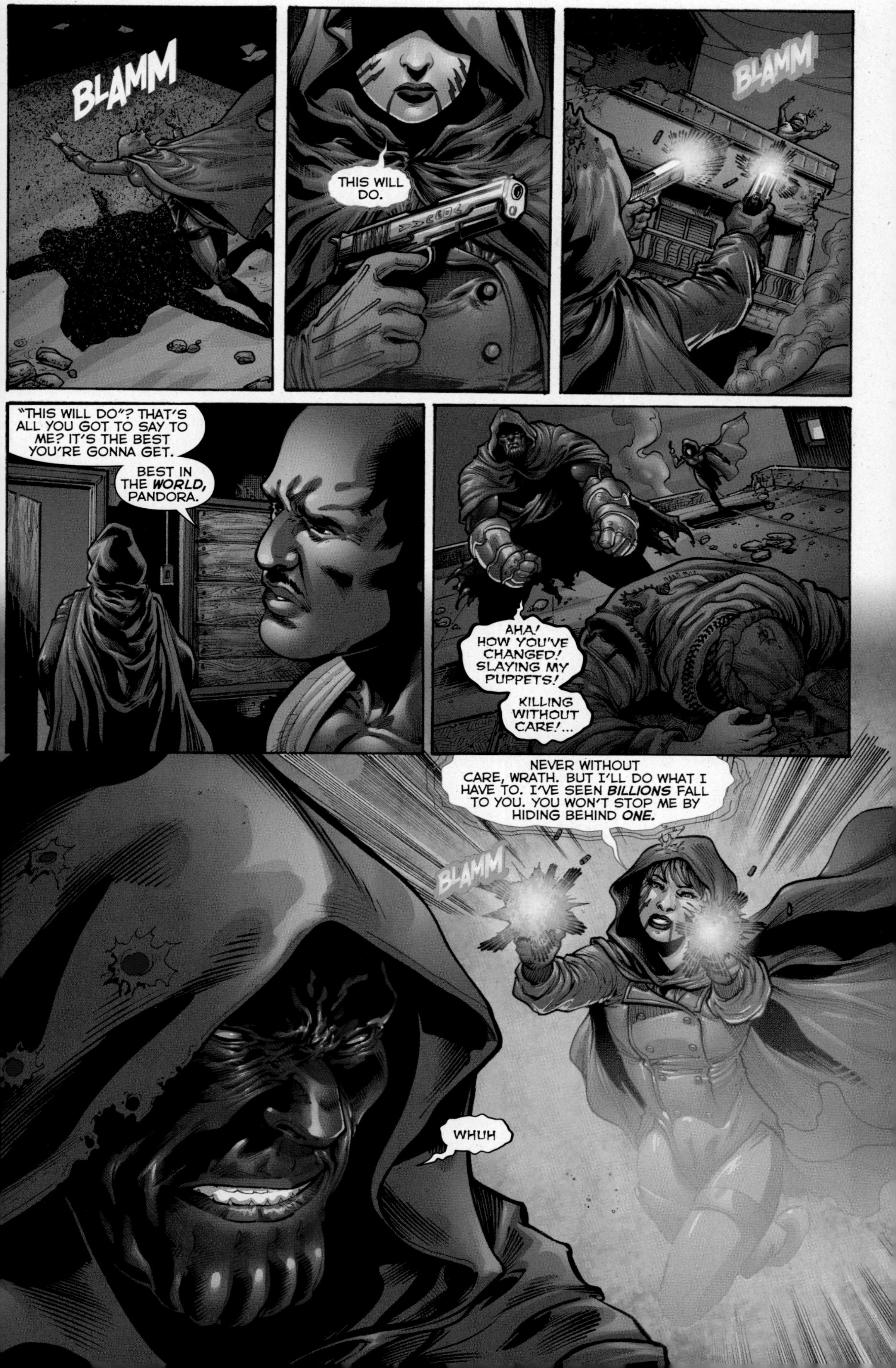
BLAMM
THIS WILL DO.
BLAMM
"THIS WILL DO"? THAT'S ALL YOU GOT TO SAY TO ME? IT'S THE BEST YOU'RE GONNA GET.
BEST IN THE *WORLD,* PANDORA.
AHA! HOW YOU'VE CHANGED! SLAYING MY PUPPETS!
KILLING WITHOUT CARE!...
NEVER WITHOUT CARE, WRATH. BUT I'LL DO WHAT I HAVE TO. I'VE SEEN *BILLIONS* FALL TO YOU. YOU WON'T STOP ME BY HIDING BEHIND *ONE.*
BLAMM
WHUH

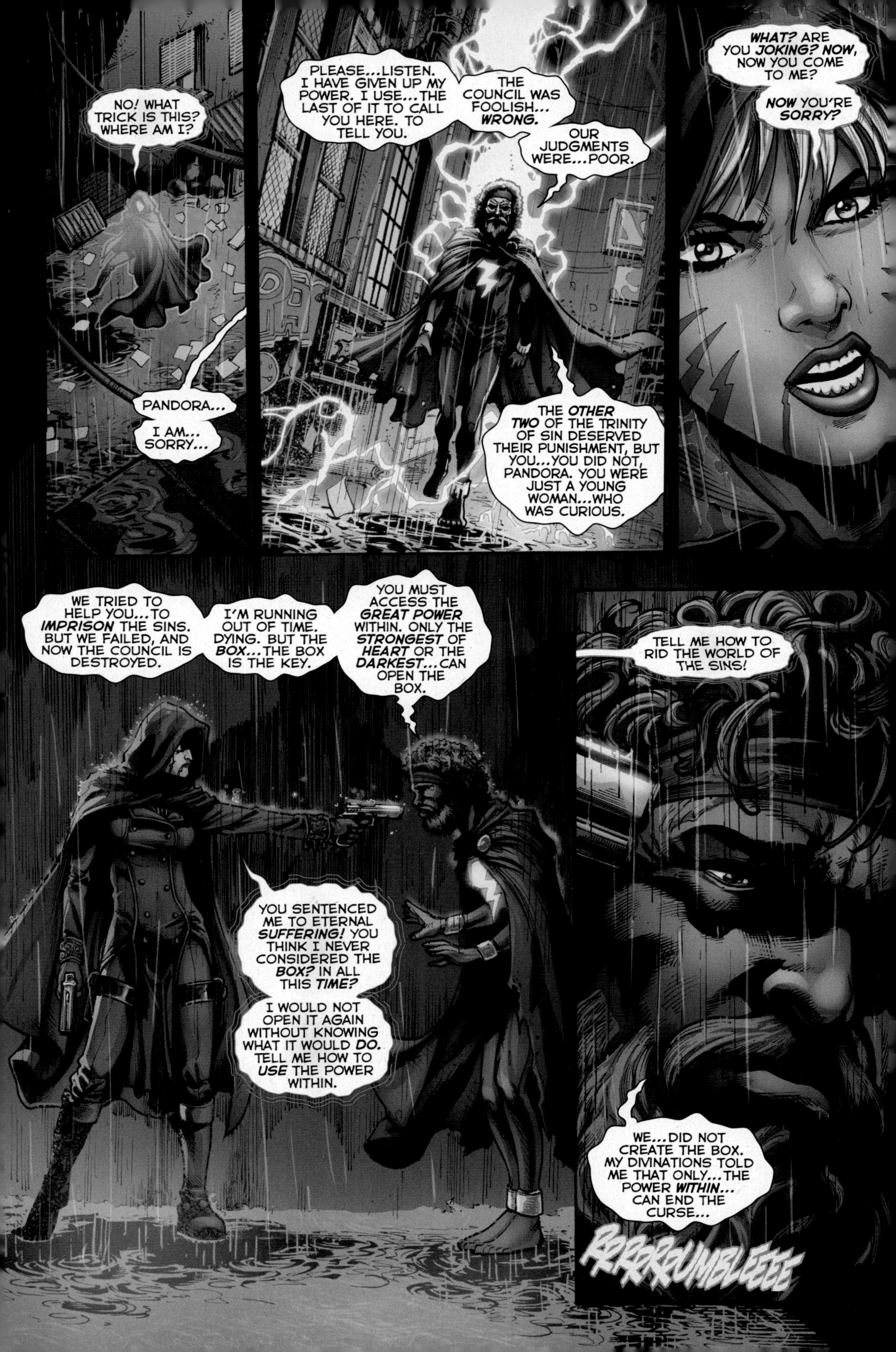
NO! WHAT TRICK IS THIS? WHERE AM I?
PANDORA...
I AM... SORRY...
PLEASE...LISTEN. I HAVE GIVEN UP MY POWER. I USE...THE LAST OF IT TO CALL YOU HERE. TO TELL YOU.
THE COUNCIL WAS FOOLISH... WRONG.
OUR JUDGMENTS WERE...POOR.
THE OTHER TWO OF THE TRINITY OF SIN DESERVED THEIR PUNISHMENT, BUT YOU...YOU DID NOT, PANDORA. YOU WERE JUST A YOUNG WOMAN...WHO WAS CURIOUS.
WHAT? ARE YOU JOKING? NOW, NOW YOU COME TO ME?
NOW YOU'RE SORRY?
WE TRIED TO HELP YOU...TO IMPRISON THE SINS. BUT WE FAILED, AND NOW THE COUNCIL IS DESTROYED.
I'M RUNNING OUT OF TIME. DYING. BUT THE BOX...THE BOX IS THE KEY.
YOU MUST ACCESS THE GREAT POWER WITHIN. ONLY THE STRONGEST OF HEART OR THE DARKEST...CAN OPEN THE BOX.
YOU SENTENCED ME TO ETERNAL SUFFERING! YOU THINK I NEVER CONSIDERED THE BOX? IN ALL THIS TIME?
I WOULD NOT OPEN IT AGAIN WITHOUT KNOWING WHAT IT WOULD DO. TELL ME HOW TO USE THE POWER WITHIN.
TELL ME HOW TO RID THE WORLD OF THE SINS!
WE...DID NOT CREATE THE BOX. MY DIVINATIONS TOLD ME THAT ONLY...THE POWER WITHIN... CAN END THE CURSE...
RRRRRUMBLEEEE

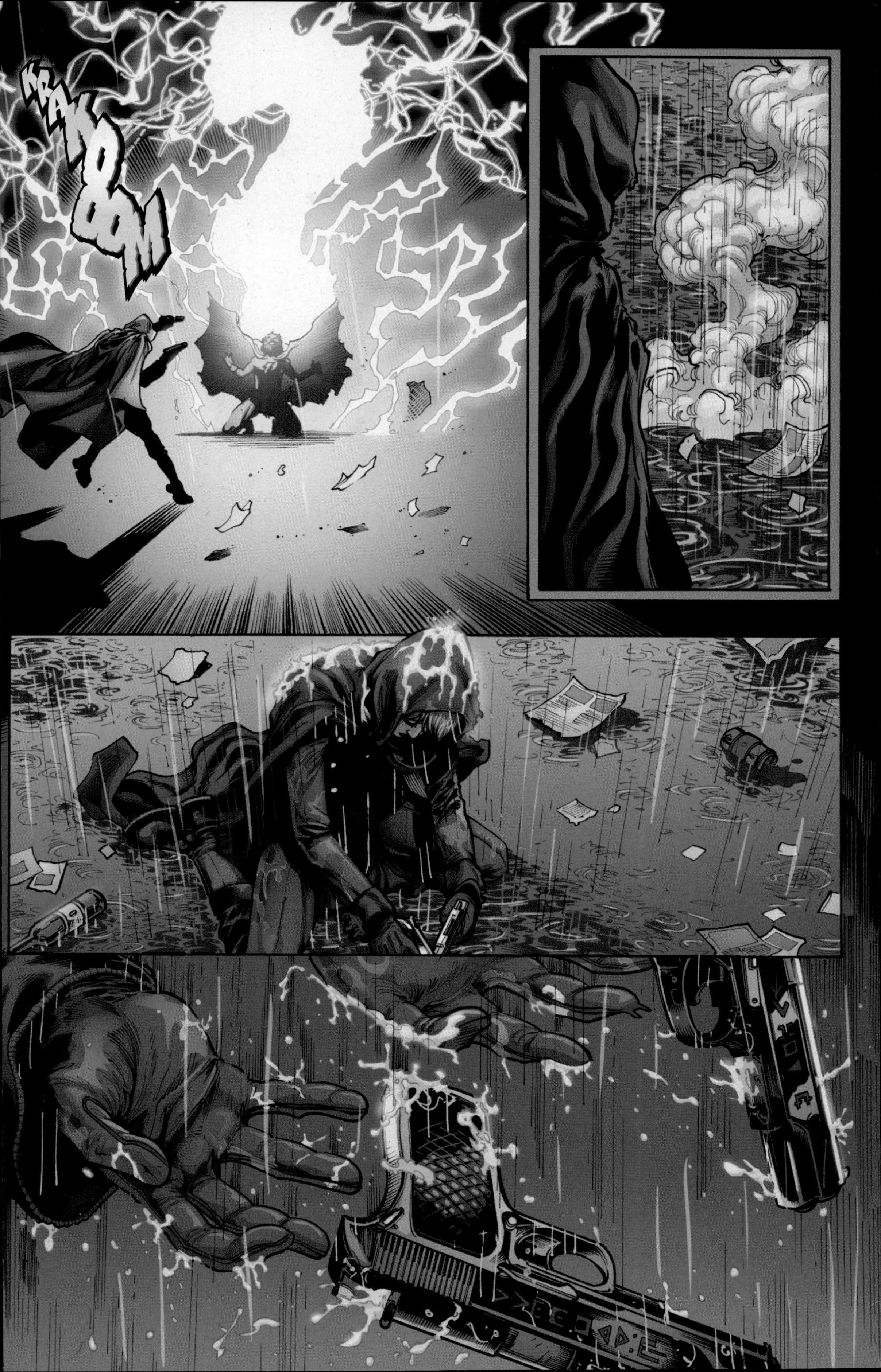
KRAKBOOM

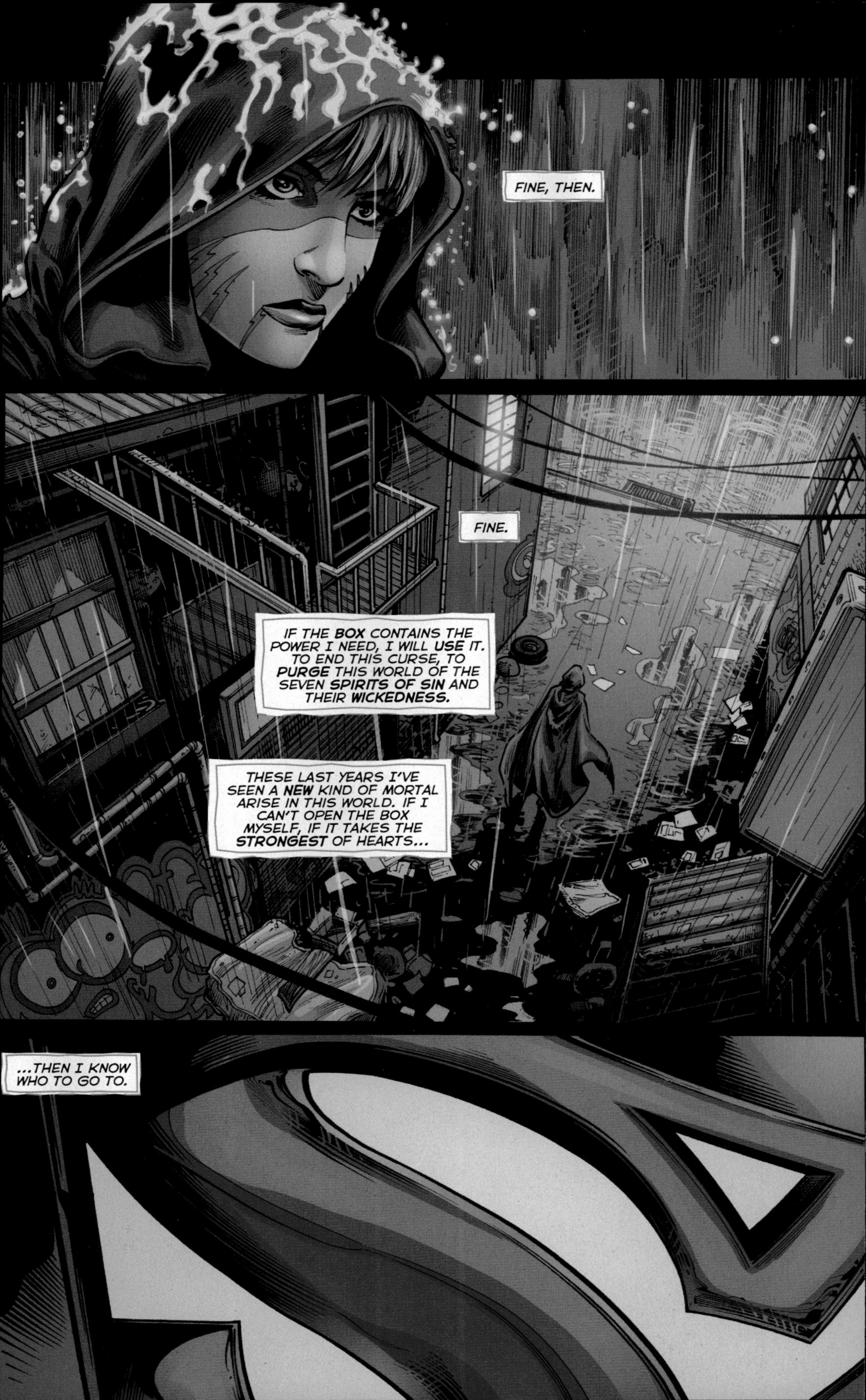
FINE, THEN.
FINE.
IF THE BOX CONTAINS THE POWER I NEED, I WILL USE IT. TO END THIS CURSE, TO PURGE THIS WORLD OF THE SEVEN SPIRITS OF SIN AND THEIR WICKEDNESS.
THESE LAST YEARS I'VE SEEN A NEW KIND OF MORTAL ARISE IN THIS WORLD. IF I CAN'T OPEN THE BOX MYSELF, IF IT TAKES THE STRONGEST OF HEARTS...
...THEN I KNOW WHO TO GO TO.

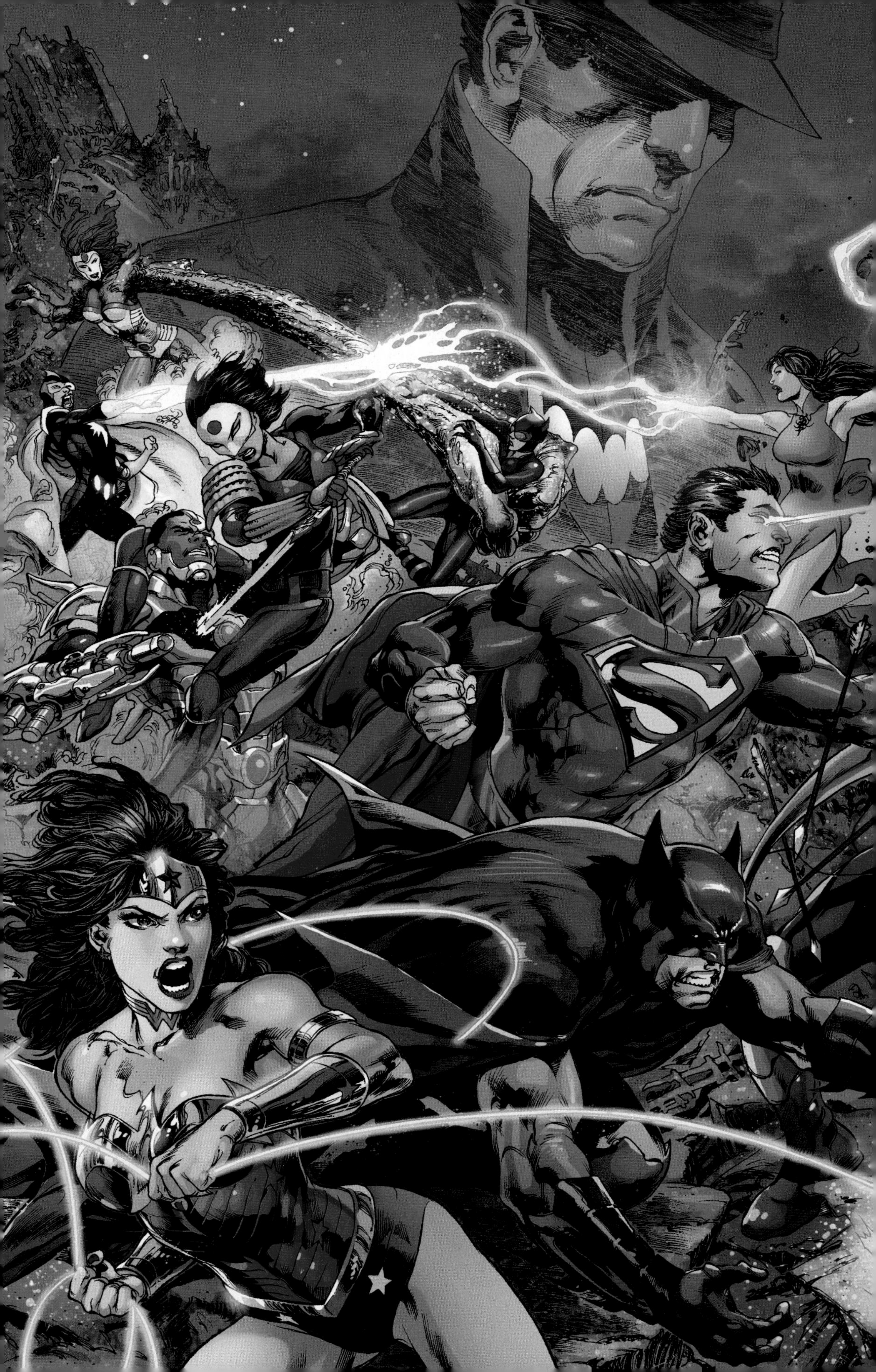

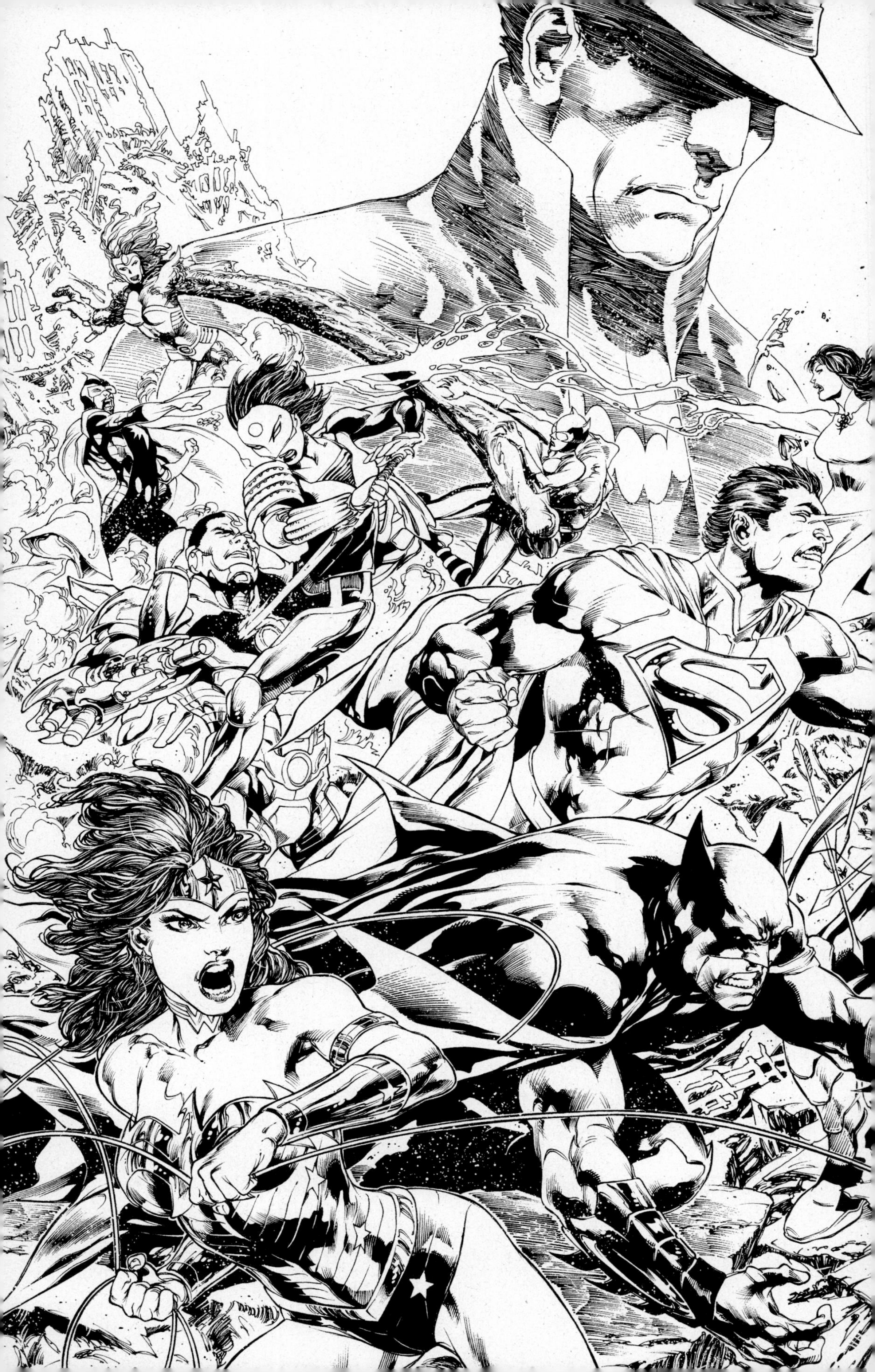

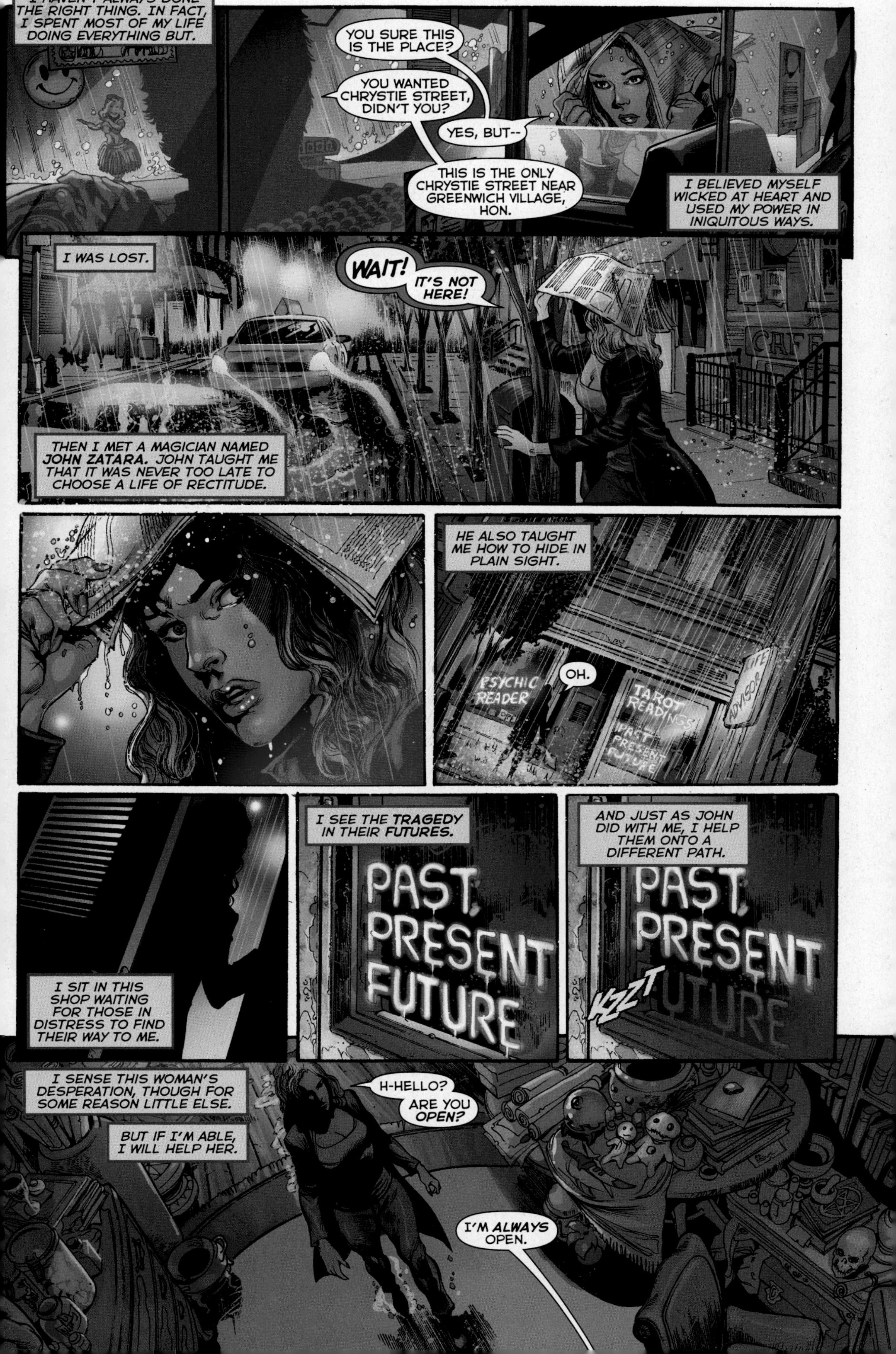
I HAVEN'T ALWAYS DONE THE RIGHT THING. IN FACT, I SPENT MOST OF MY LIFE DOING EVERYTHING BUT.
YOU SURE THIS IS THE PLACE?
YOU WANTED CHRYSTIE STREET, DIDN'T YOU?
YES, BUT--
THIS IS THE ONLY CHRYSTIE STREET NEAR GREENWICH VILLAGE, HON.
I BELIEVED MYSELF WICKED AT HEART AND USED MY POWER IN INIQUITOUS WAYS.
I WAS LOST.
WAIT!
IT'S NOT HERE!
THEN I MET A MAGICIAN NAMED JOHN ZATARA. JOHN TAUGHT ME THAT IT WAS NEVER TOO LATE TO CHOOSE A LIFE OF RECTITUDE.
HE ALSO TAUGHT ME HOW TO HIDE IN PLAIN SIGHT.
PSYCHIC READER
OH.
TAROT READINGS
PAST PRESENT FUTURE
LIFE ADVISOR
I SIT IN THIS SHOP WAITING FOR THOSE IN DISTRESS TO FIND THEIR WAY TO ME.
I SEE THE TRAGEDY IN THEIR FUTURES.
PAST PRESENT FUTURE
AND JUST AS JOHN DID WITH ME, I HELP THEM ONTO A DIFFERENT PATH.
PAST PRESENT FUTURE
KZZT
I SENSE THIS WOMAN'S DESPERATION, THOUGH FOR SOME REASON LITTLE ELSE.
BUT IF I'M ABLE, I WILL HELP HER.
H-HELLO?
ARE YOU OPEN?
I'M ALWAYS OPEN.

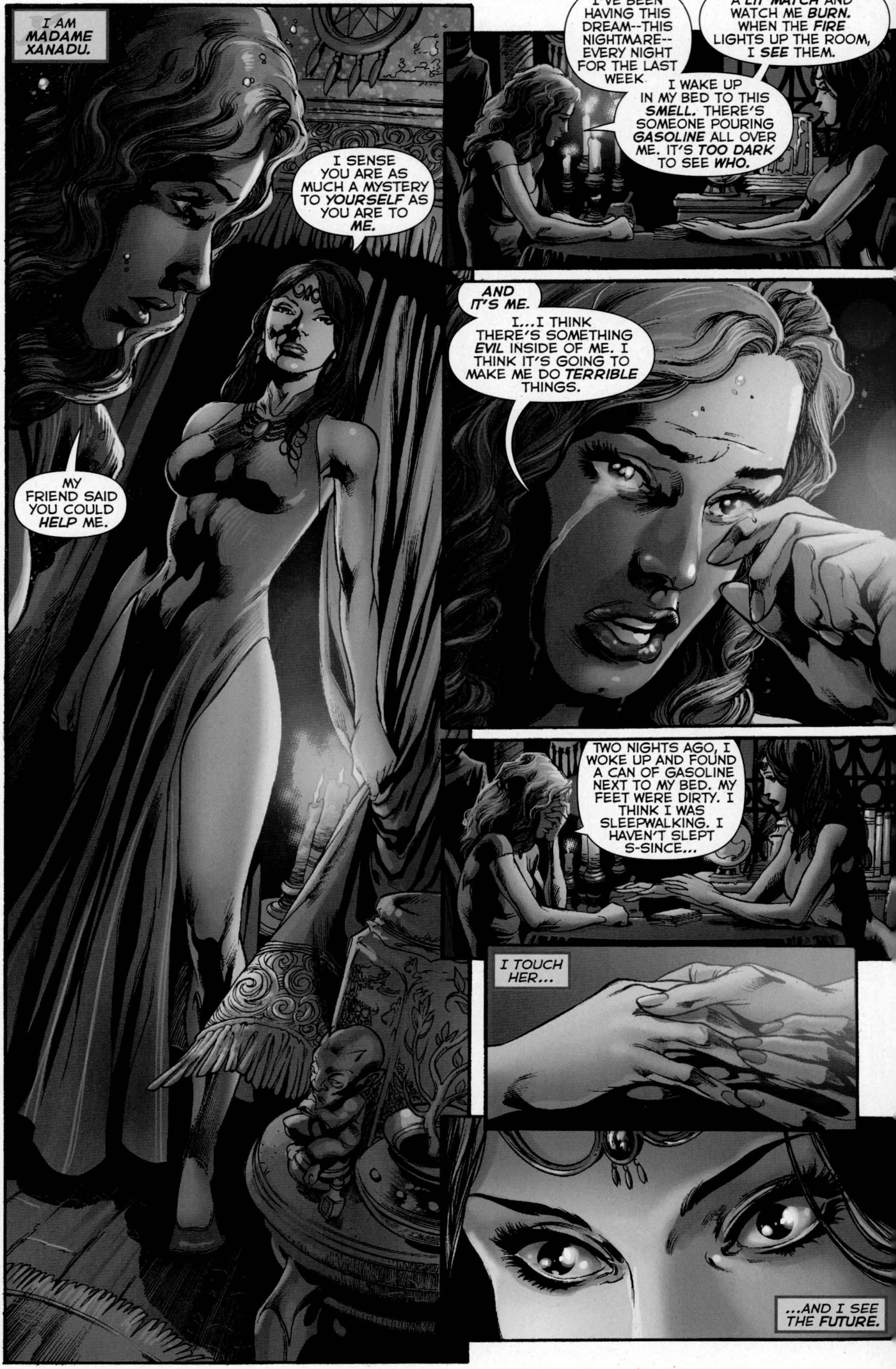
I AM MADAME XANADU.
I SENSE YOU ARE AS MUCH A MYSTERY TO YOURSELF AS YOU ARE TO ME.
MY FRIEND SAID YOU COULD HELP ME.
I'VE BEEN HAVING THIS DREAM--THIS NIGHTMARE--EVERY NIGHT FOR THE LAST WEEK.
I WAKE UP IN MY BED TO THIS SMELL. THERE'S SOMEONE POURING GASOLINE ALL OVER ME. IT'S TOO DARK TO SEE WHO.
THEY THROW A LIT MATCH AND WATCH ME BURN. WHEN THE FIRE LIGHTS UP THE ROOM, I SEE THEM.
AND IT'S ME.
I...I THINK THERE'S SOMETHING EVIL INSIDE OF ME. I THINK IT'S GOING TO MAKE ME DO TERRIBLE THINGS.
TWO NIGHTS AGO, I WOKE UP AND FOUND A CAN OF GASOLINE NEXT TO MY BED. MY FEET WERE DIRTY. I THINK I WAS SLEEPWALKING. I HAVEN'T SLEPT S-SINCE...
I TOUCH HER...
...AND I SEE THE FUTURE.

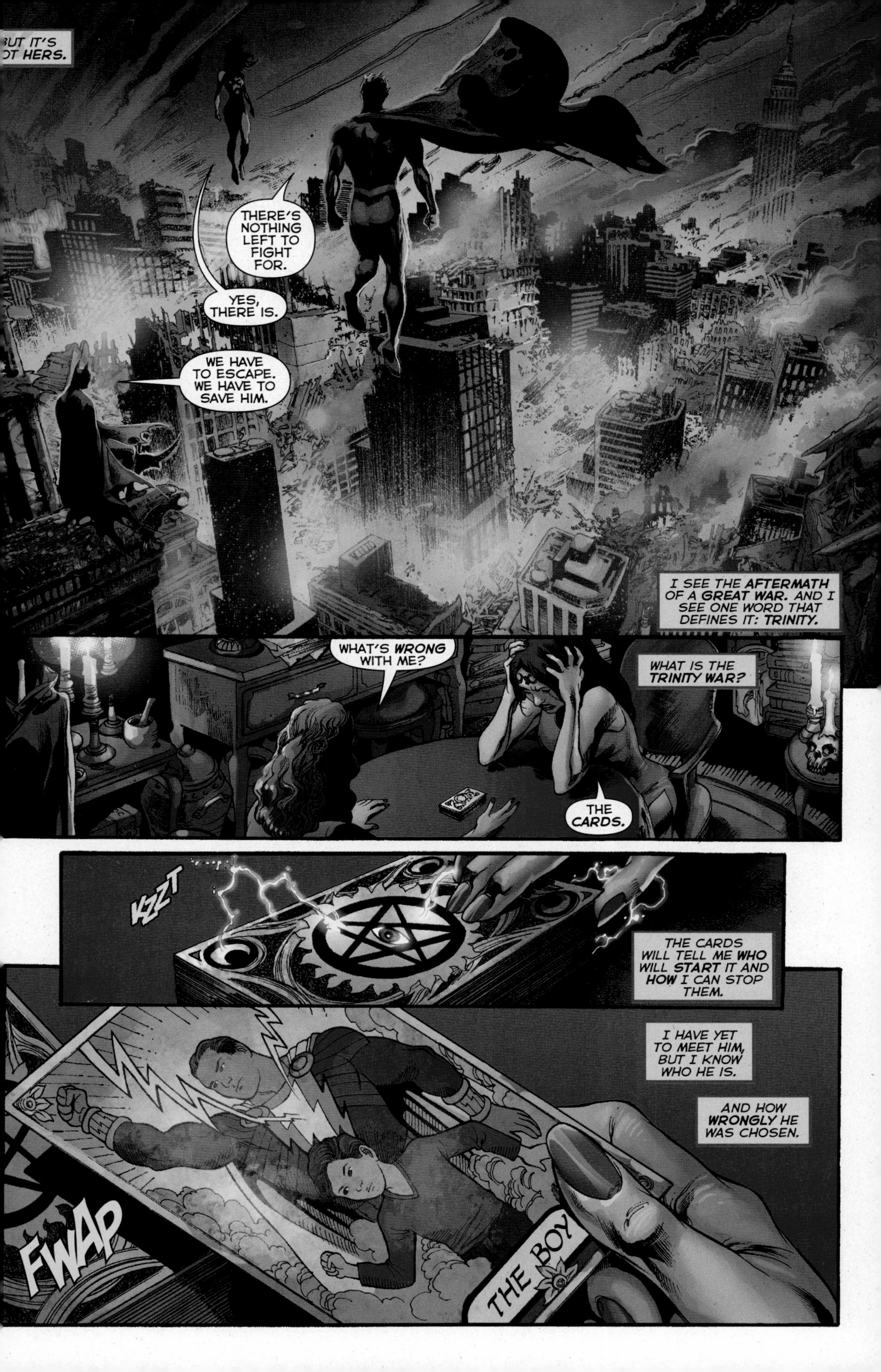
BUT IT'S
OT HERS.
THERE'S NOTHING LEFT TO FIGHT FOR.
YES, THERE IS.
WE HAVE TO ESCAPE. WE HAVE TO SAVE HIM.
I SEE THE AFTERMATH OF A GREAT WAR. AND I SEE ONE WORD THAT DEFINES IT: TRINITY.
WHAT'S WRONG WITH ME?
WHAT IS THE TRINITY WAR?
THE CARDS.
KZZT
THE CARDS WILL TELL ME WHO WILL START IT AND HOW I CAN STOP THEM.
I HAVE YET TO MEET HIM, BUT I KNOW WHO HE IS.
AND HOW WRONGLY HE WAS CHOSEN.
FWAP
THE BOY

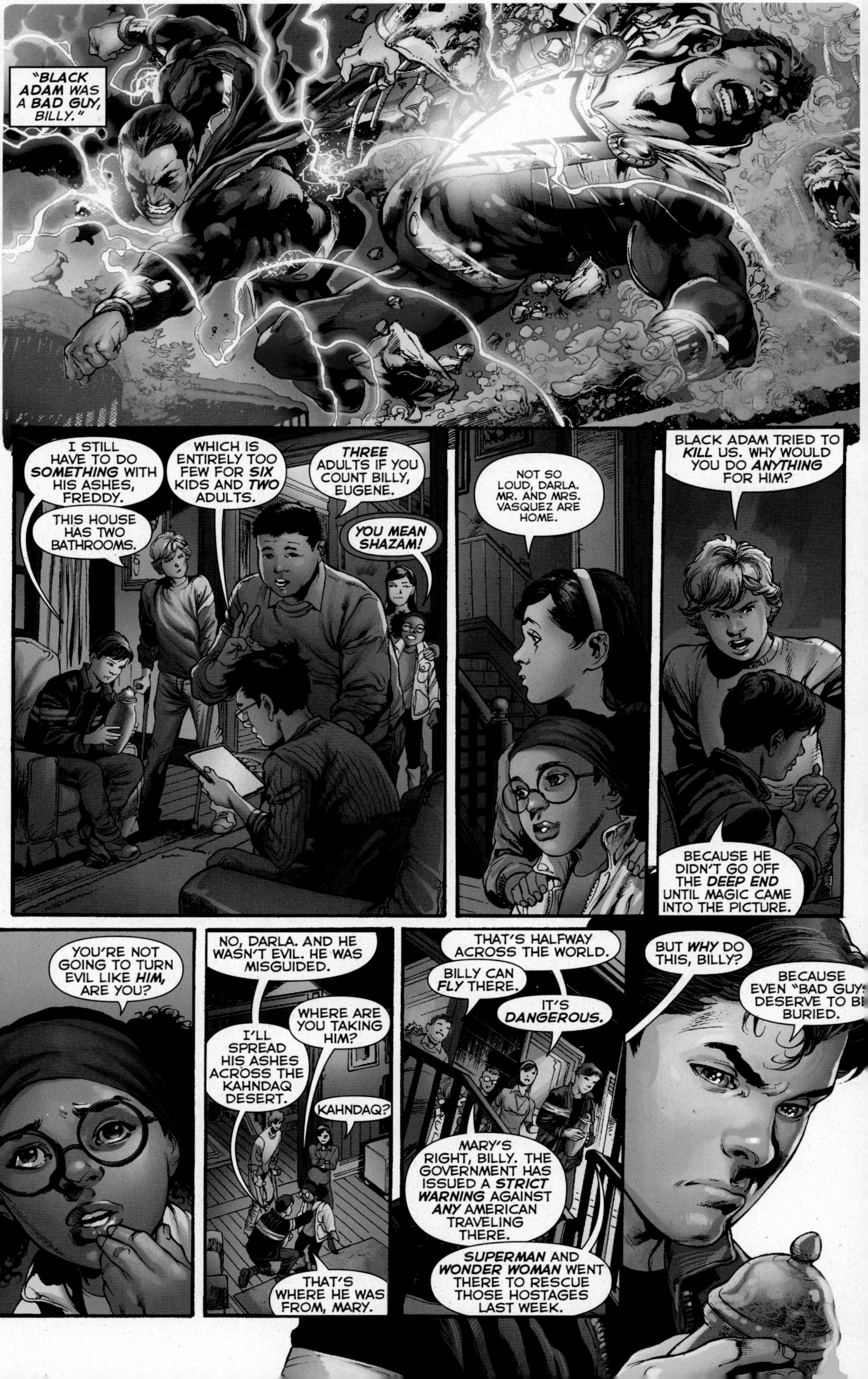
"BLACK ADAM WAS A BAD GUY, BILLY."
I STILL HAVE TO DO SOMETHING WITH HIS ASHES, FREDDY.
THIS HOUSE HAS TWO BATHROOMS.
WHICH IS ENTIRELY TOO FEW FOR SIX KIDS AND TWO ADULTS.
THREE ADULTS IF YOU COUNT BILLY, EUGENE.
YOU MEAN SHAZAM!
NOT SO LOUD, DARLA. MR. AND MRS. VASQUEZ ARE HOME.
BLACK ADAM TRIED TO KILL US. WHY WOULD YOU DO ANYTHING FOR HIM?
BECAUSE HE DIDN'T GO OFF THE DEEP END UNTIL MAGIC CAME INTO THE PICTURE.
YOU'RE NOT GOING TO TURN EVIL LIKE HIM, ARE YOU?
NO, DARLA. AND HE WASN'T EVIL. HE WAS MISGUIDED.
WHERE ARE YOU TAKING HIM?
I'LL SPREAD HIS ASHES ACROSS THE KAHNDAQ DESERT.
KAHNDAQ?
THAT'S WHERE HE WAS FROM, MARY.
THAT'S HALFWAY ACROSS THE WORLD.
BILLY CAN FLY THERE.
IT'S DANGEROUS.
MARY'S RIGHT, BILLY. THE GOVERNMENT HAS ISSUED A STRICT WARNING AGAINST ANY AMERICAN TRAVELING THERE.
SUPERMAN AND WONDER WOMAN WENT THERE TO RESCUE THOSE HOSTAGES LAST WEEK.
BUT WHY DO THIS, BILLY?
BECAUSE EVEN "BAD GUYS DESERVE TO BE BURIED.

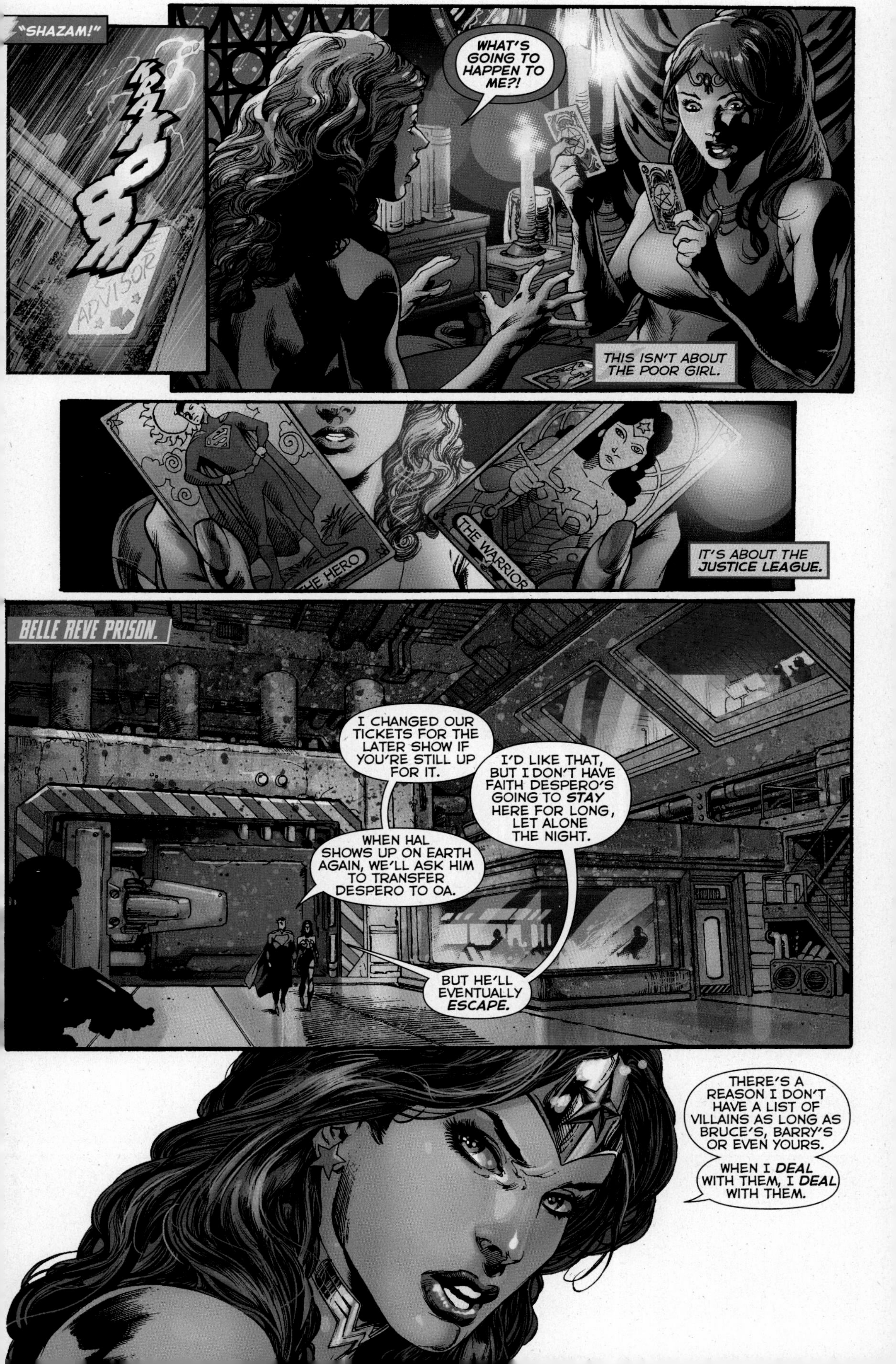
"SHAZAM!"
KRAKOOOM
ADVISOR
WHAT'S GOING TO HAPPEN TO ME?!
THIS ISN'T ABOUT THE POOR GIRL.
THE HERO
THE WARRIOR
IT'S ABOUT THE JUSTICE LEAGUE.
BELLE REVE PRISON.
I CHANGED OUR TICKETS FOR THE LATER SHOW IF YOU'RE STILL UP FOR IT.
I'D LIKE THAT, BUT I DON'T HAVE FAITH DESPERO'S GOING TO STAY HERE FOR LONG, LET ALONE THE NIGHT.
WHEN HAL SHOWS UP ON EARTH AGAIN, WE'LL ASK HIM TO TRANSFER DESPERO TO OA.
BUT HE'LL EVENTUALLY ESCAPE.
THERE'S A REASON I DON'T HAVE A LIST OF VILLAINS AS LONG AS BRUCE'S, BARRY'S OR EVEN YOURS.
WHEN I DEAL WITH THEM, I DEAL WITH THEM.

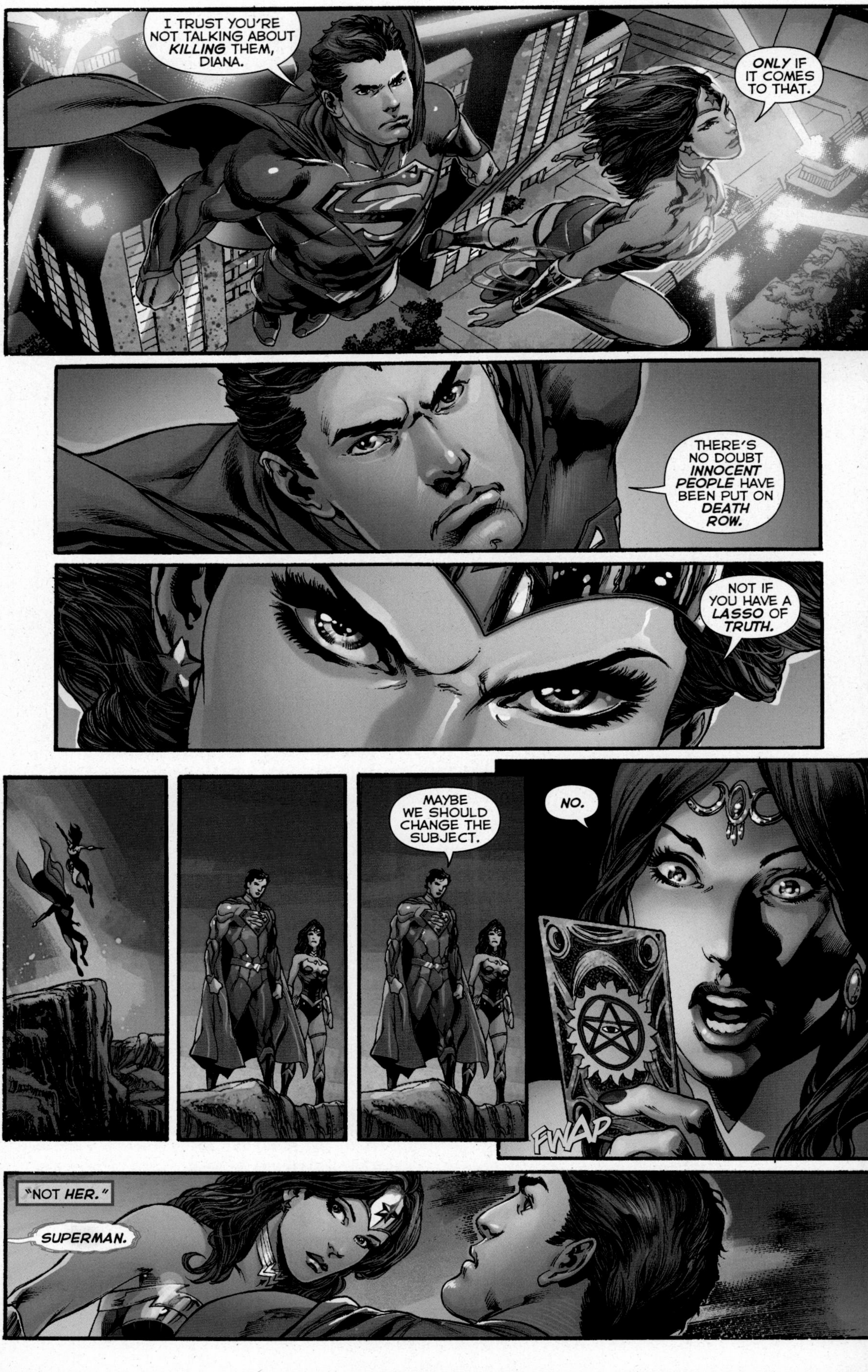
I TRUST YOU'RE NOT TALKING ABOUT *KILLING* THEM, DIANA.
ONLY IF IT COMES TO THAT.
THERE'S NO DOUBT *INNOCENT PEOPLE* HAVE BEEN PUT ON *DEATH ROW.*
NOT IF YOU HAVE A *LASSO* OF *TRUTH.*
MAYBE WE SHOULD CHANGE THE SUBJECT.
NO.
FWAP
"NOT *HER.*"
SUPERMAN.

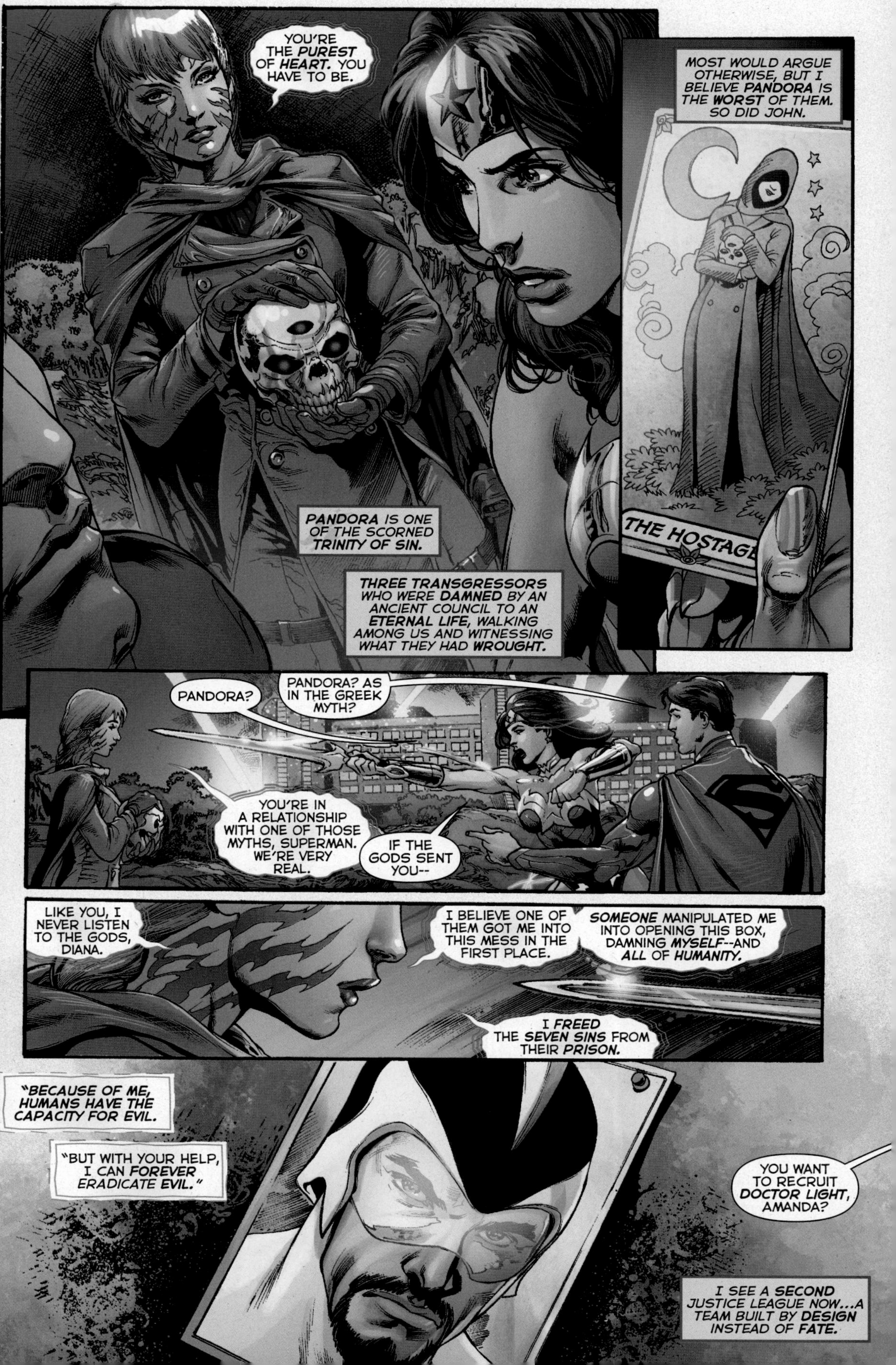
YOU'RE THE PUREST OF HEART. YOU HAVE TO BE.
MOST WOULD ARGUE OTHERWISE, BUT I BELIEVE PANDORA IS THE WORST OF THEM. SO DID JOHN.
THE HOSTAGE
PANDORA IS ONE OF THE SCORNED TRINITY OF SIN.
THREE TRANSGRESSORS WHO WERE DAMNED BY AN ANCIENT COUNCIL TO AN ETERNAL LIFE, WALKING AMONG US AND WITNESSING WHAT THEY HAD WROUGHT.
PANDORA?
PANDORA? AS IN THE GREEK MYTH?
YOU'RE IN A RELATIONSHIP WITH ONE OF THOSE MYTHS, SUPERMAN. WE'RE VERY REAL.
IF THE GODS SENT YOU--
LIKE YOU, I NEVER LISTEN TO THE GODS, DIANA.
I BELIEVE ONE OF THEM GOT ME INTO THIS MESS IN THE FIRST PLACE.
SOMEONE MANIPULATED ME INTO OPENING THIS BOX, DAMNING MYSELF--AND ALL OF HUMANITY.
I FREED THE SEVEN SINS FROM THEIR PRISON.
"BECAUSE OF ME, HUMANS HAVE THE CAPACITY FOR EVIL.
"BUT WITH YOUR HELP, I CAN FOREVER ERADICATE EVIL."
YOU WANT TO RECRUIT DOCTOR LIGHT, AMANDA?
I SEE A SECOND JUSTICE LEAGUE NOW...A TEAM BUILT BY DESIGN INSTEAD OF FATE.

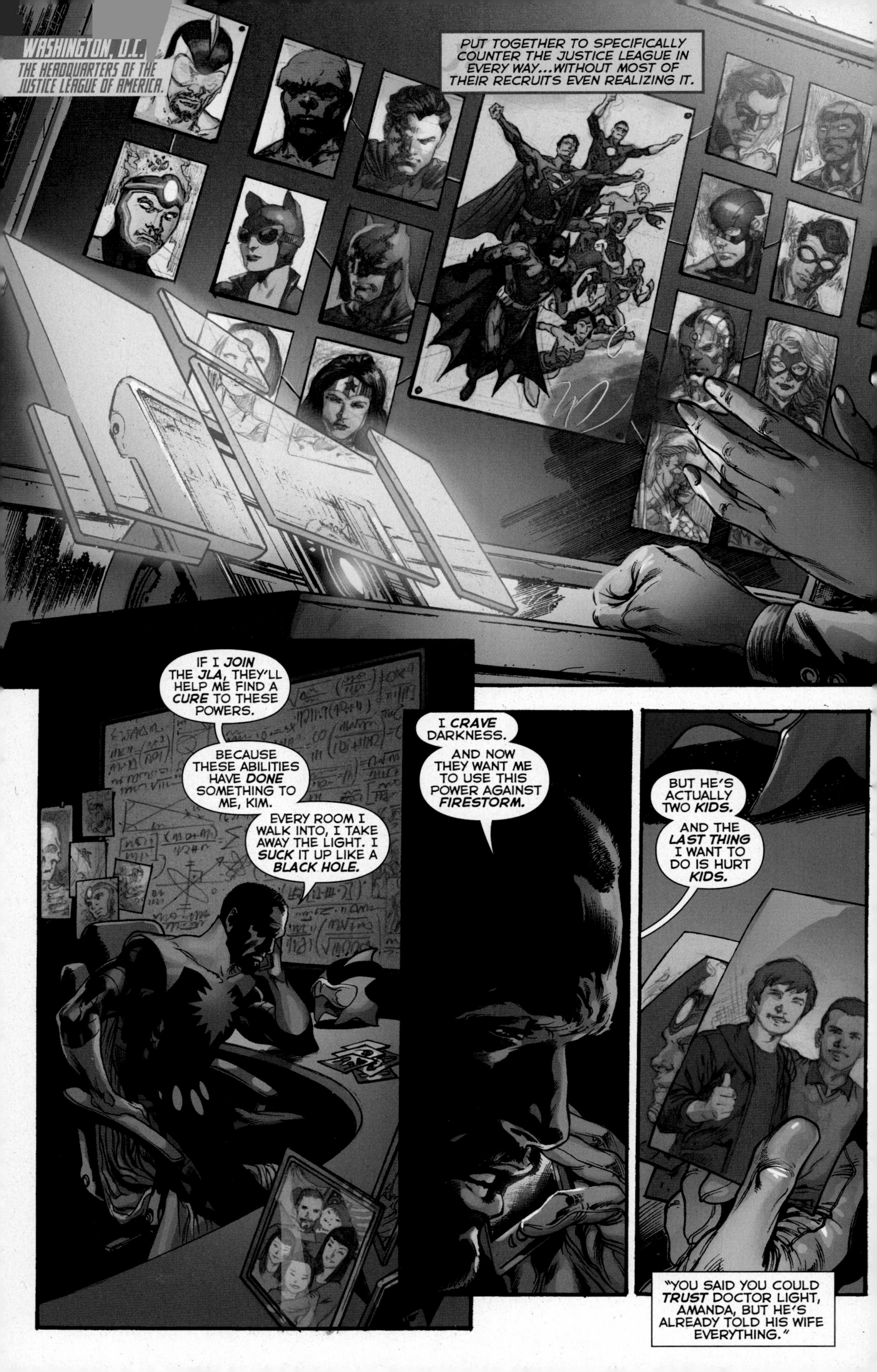
WASHINGTON, D.C.
THE HEADQUARTERS OF THE JUSTICE LEAGUE OF AMERICA.
PUT TOGETHER TO SPECIFICALLY COUNTER THE JUSTICE LEAGUE IN EVERY WAY...WITHOUT MOST OF THEIR RECRUITS EVEN REALIZING IT.
IF I JOIN THE JLA, THEY'LL HELP ME FIND A CURE TO THESE POWERS.
BECAUSE THESE ABILITIES HAVE DONE SOMETHING TO ME, KIM.
EVERY ROOM I WALK INTO, I TAKE AWAY THE LIGHT. I SUCK IT UP LIKE A BLACK HOLE.
I CRAVE DARKNESS.
AND NOW THEY WANT ME TO USE THIS POWER AGAINST FIRESTORM.
BUT HE'S ACTUALLY TWO KIDS.
AND THE LAST THING I WANT TO DO IS HURT KIDS.
"YOU SAID YOU COULD TRUST DOCTOR LIGHT, AMANDA, BUT HE'S ALREADY TOLD HIS WIFE EVERYTHING."

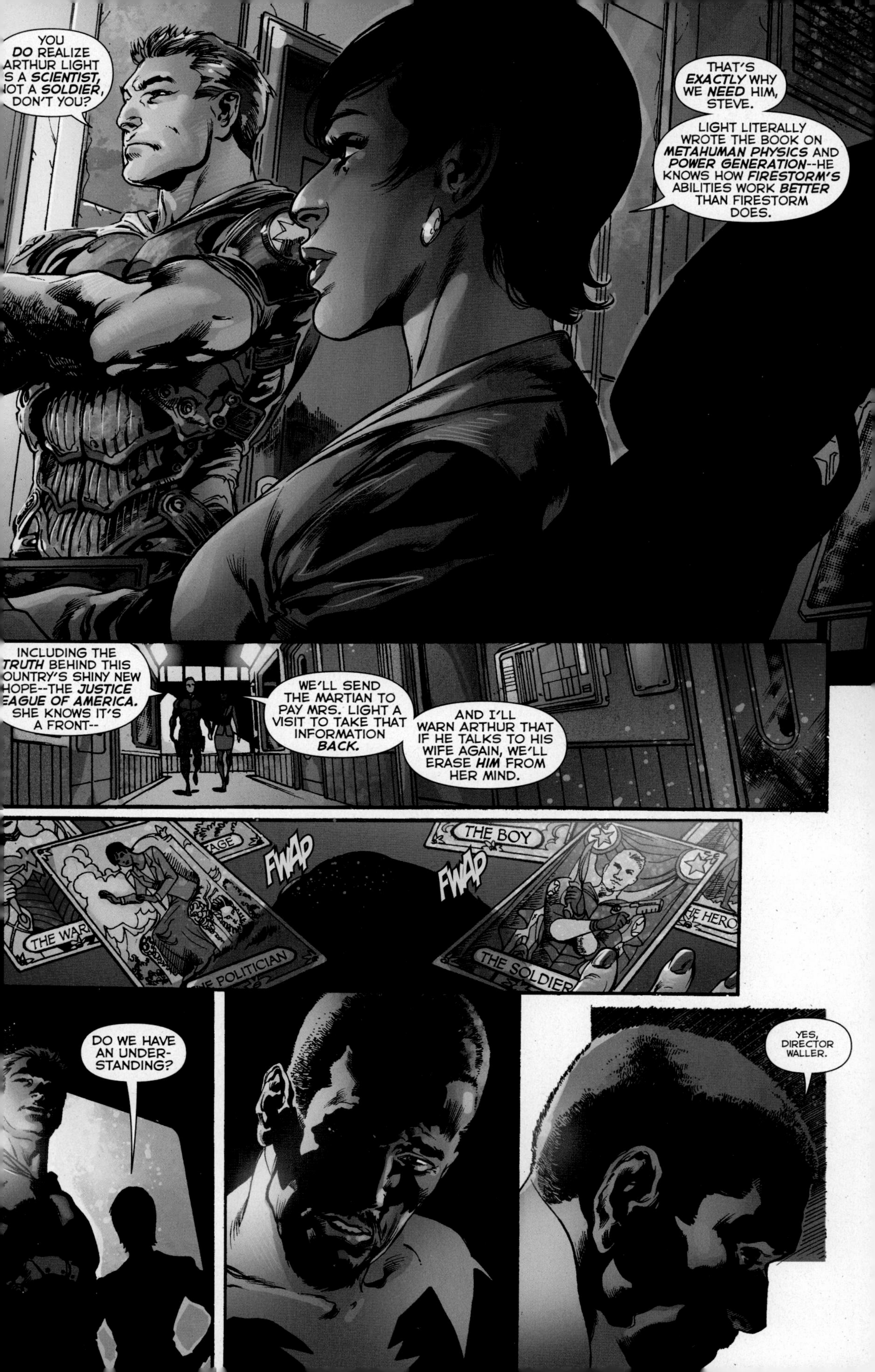

YOU DO REALIZE ARTHUR LIGHT IS A SCIENTIST, NOT A SOLDIER, DON'T YOU?
THAT'S EXACTLY WHY WE NEED HIM, STEVE.
LIGHT LITERALLY WROTE THE BOOK ON METAHUMAN PHYSICS AND POWER GENERATION--HE KNOWS HOW FIRESTORM'S ABILITIES WORK BETTER THAN FIRESTORM DOES.
INCLUDING THE TRUTH BEHIND THIS COUNTRY'S SHINY NEW HOPE--THE JUSTICE LEAGUE OF AMERICA. SHE KNOWS IT'S A FRONT--
WE'LL SEND THE MARTIAN TO PAY MRS. LIGHT A VISIT TO TAKE THAT INFORMATION BACK.
AND I'LL WARN ARTHUR THAT IF HE TALKS TO HIS WIFE AGAIN, WE'LL ERASE HIM FROM HER MIND.
THE BOY
FWAP
FWAP
THE POLITICIAN
THE SOLDIER
DO WE HAVE AN UNDER-STANDING?
YES, DIRECTOR WALLER.

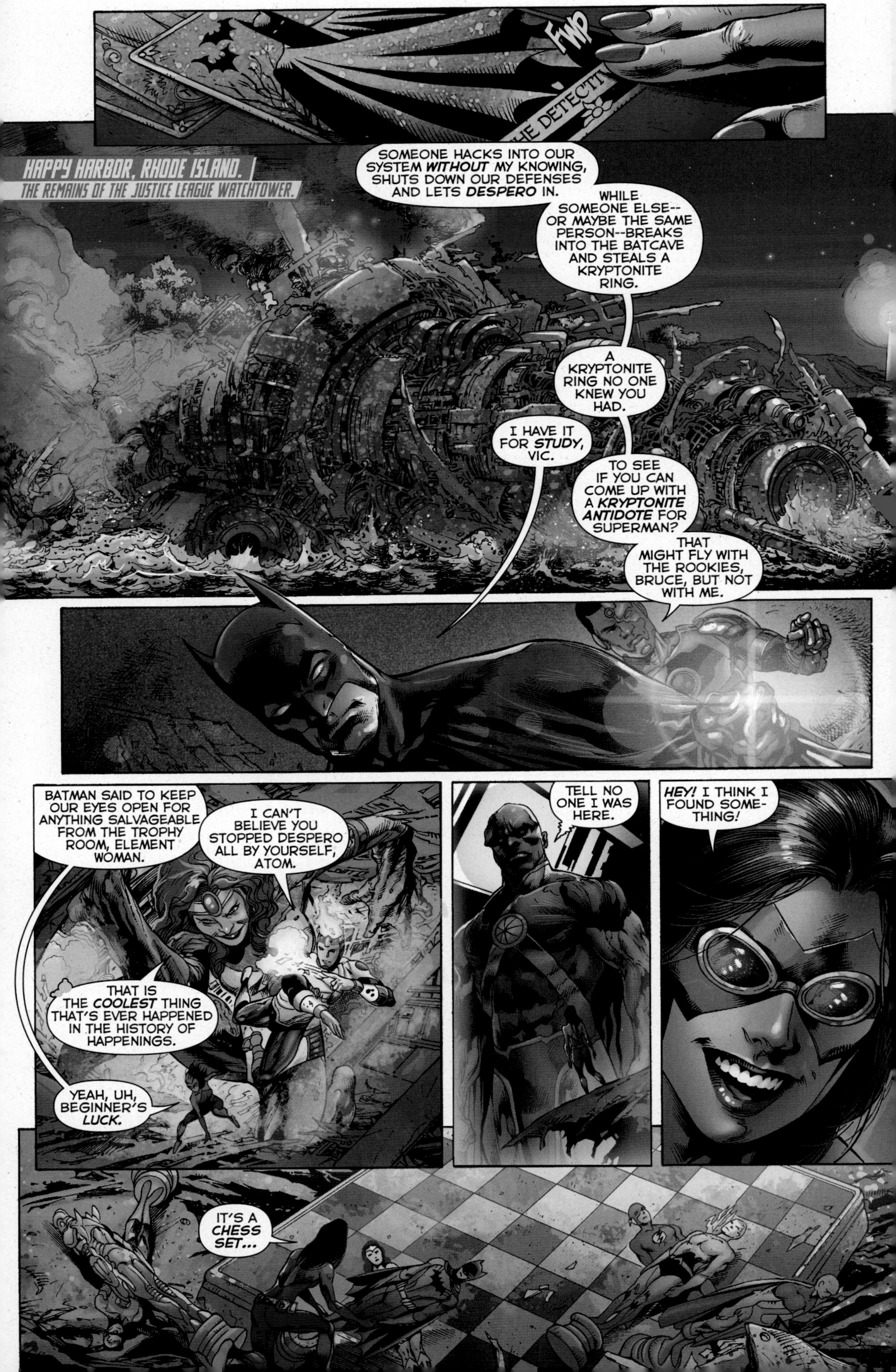

FWP
THE DETECTI
HAPPY HARBOR, RHODE ISLAND.
THE REMAINS OF THE JUSTICE LEAGUE WATCHTOWER.
SOMEONE HACKS INTO OUR SYSTEM WITHOUT MY KNOWING, SHUTS DOWN OUR DEFENSES AND LETS DESPERO IN.
WHILE SOMEONE ELSE-- OR MAYBE THE SAME PERSON--BREAKS INTO THE BATCAVE AND STEALS A KRYPTONITE RING.
A KRYPTONITE RING NO ONE KNEW YOU HAD.
I HAVE IT FOR STUDY, VIC.
TO SEE IF YOU CAN COME UP WITH A KRYPTONITE ANTIDOTE FOR SUPERMAN?
THAT MIGHT FLY WITH THE ROOKIES, BRUCE, BUT NOT WITH ME.
BATMAN SAID TO KEEP OUR EYES OPEN FOR ANYTHING SALVAGEABLE FROM THE TROPHY ROOM, ELEMENT WOMAN.
I CAN'T BELIEVE YOU STOPPED DESPERO ALL BY YOURSELF, ATOM.
THAT IS THE COOLEST THING THAT'S EVER HAPPENED IN THE HISTORY OF HAPPENINGS.
YEAH, UH, BEGINNER'S LUCK.
TELL NO ONE I WAS HERE.
HEY! I THINK I FOUND SOME-THING!
IT'S A CHESS SET...

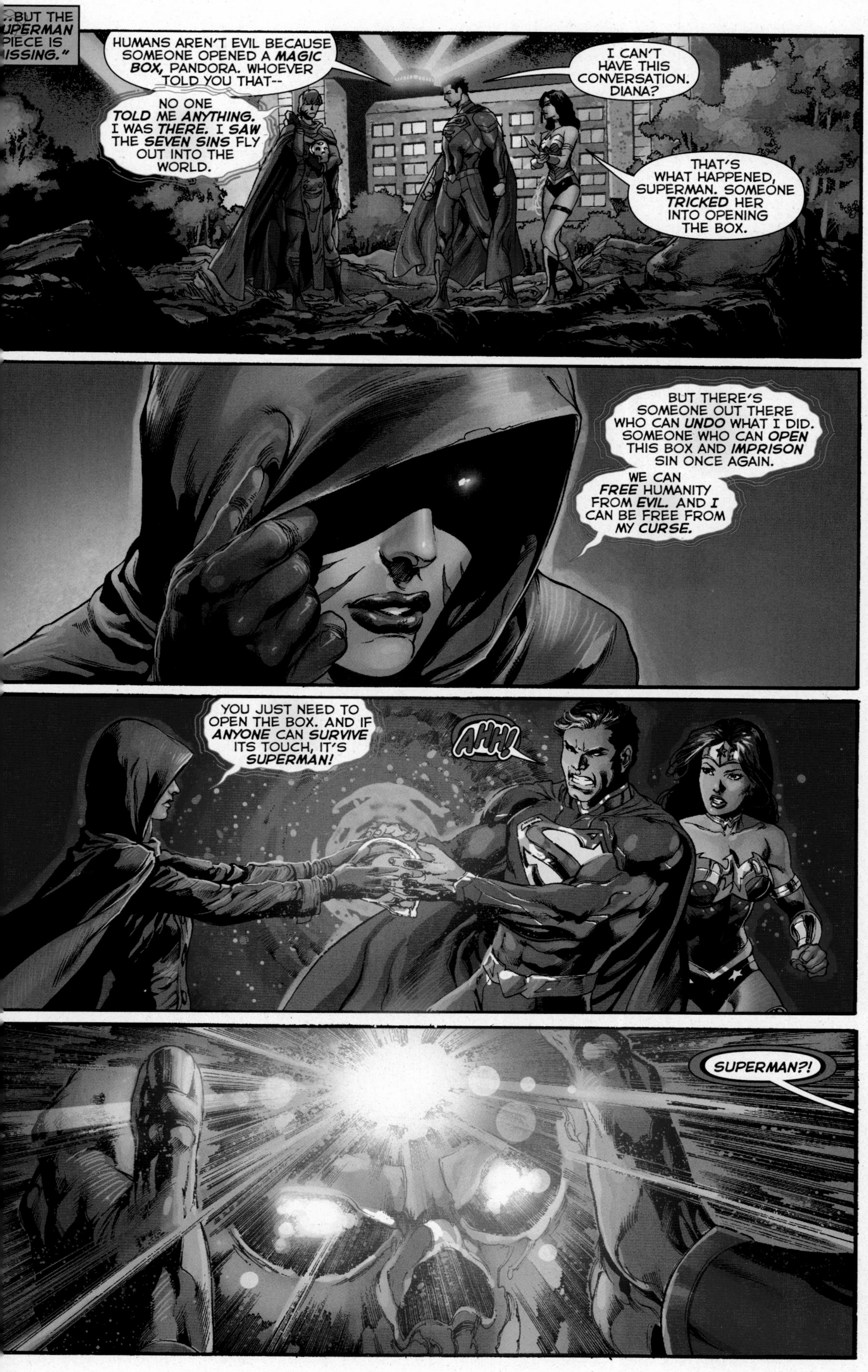

"...BUT THE SUPERMAN PIECE IS MISSING."
HUMANS AREN'T EVIL BECAUSE SOMEONE OPENED A MAGIC BOX, PANDORA. WHOEVER TOLD YOU THAT--
NO ONE TOLD ME ANYTHING. I WAS THERE. I SAW THE SEVEN SINS FLY OUT INTO THE WORLD.
I CAN'T HAVE THIS CONVERSATION. DIANA?
THAT'S WHAT HAPPENED, SUPERMAN. SOMEONE TRICKED HER INTO OPENING THE BOX.
BUT THERE'S SOMEONE OUT THERE WHO CAN UNDO WHAT I DID. SOMEONE WHO CAN OPEN THIS BOX AND IMPRISON SIN ONCE AGAIN.
WE CAN FREE HUMANITY FROM EVIL. AND I CAN BE FREE FROM MY CURSE.
YOU JUST NEED TO OPEN THE BOX. AND IF ANYONE CAN SURVIVE ITS TOUCH, IT'S SUPERMAN!
AHH!
SUPERMAN?!

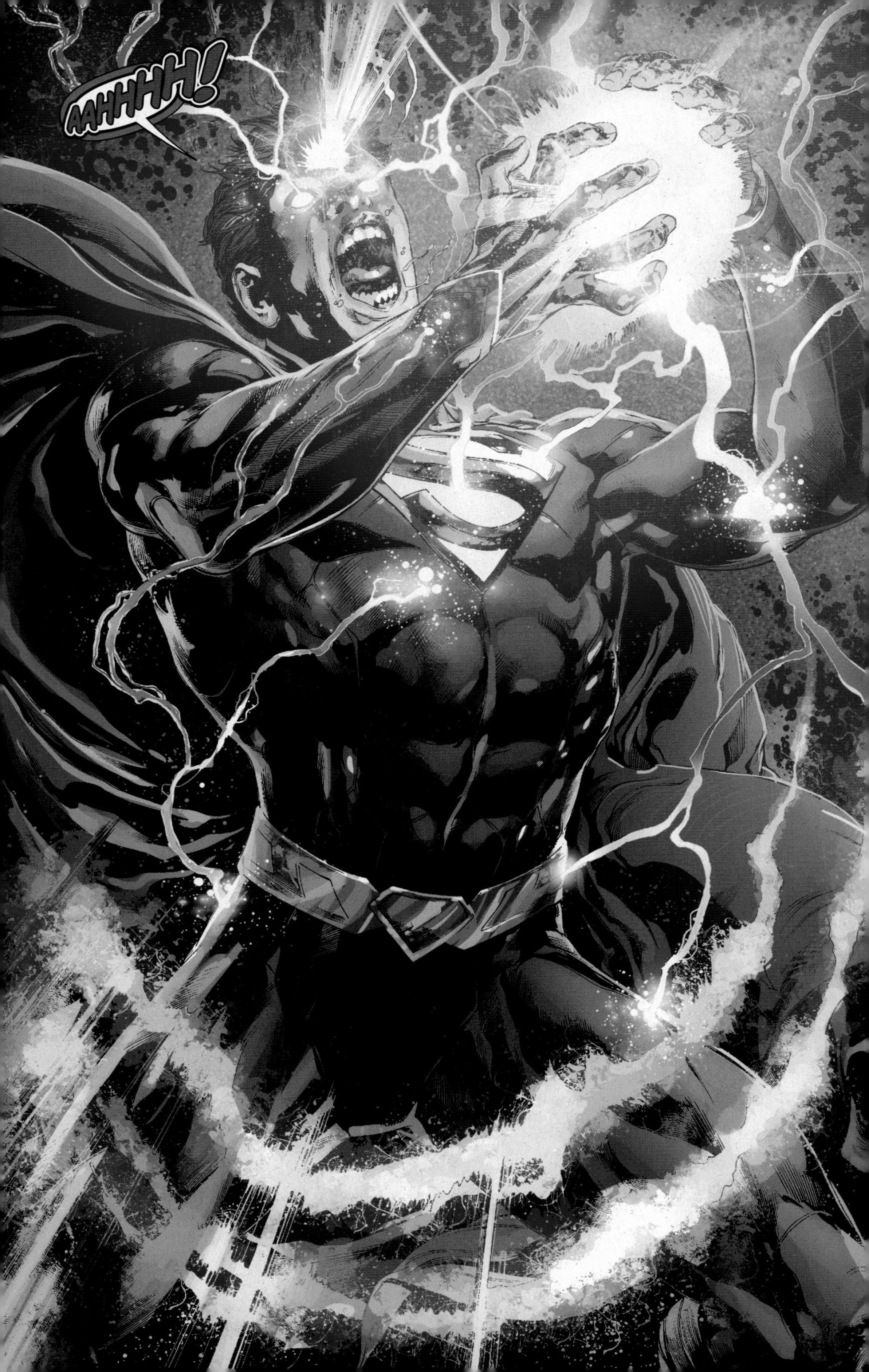
AAHHHH!

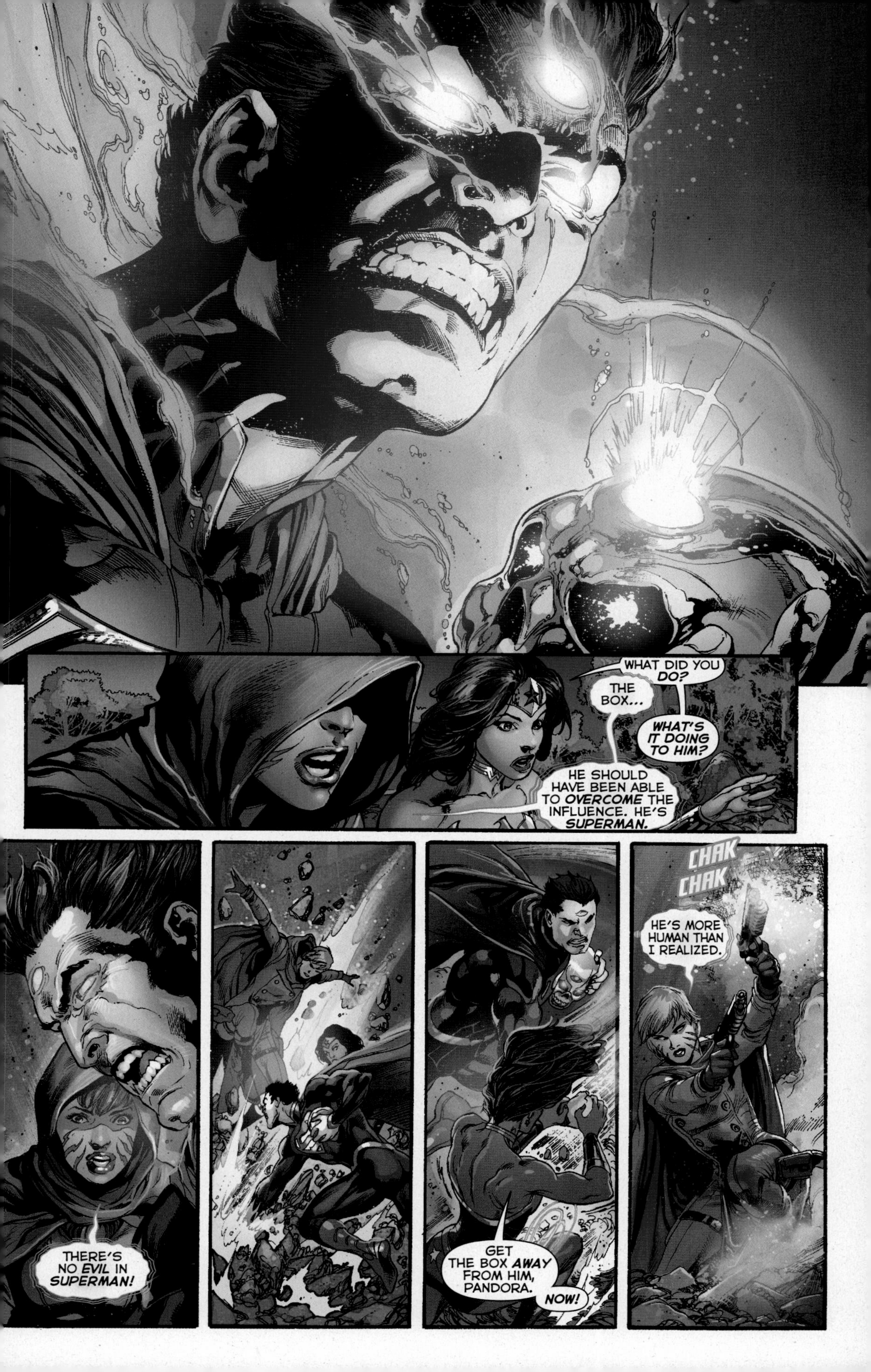

WHAT DID YOU DO?
THE BOX...
WHAT'S IT DOING TO HIM?
HE SHOULD HAVE BEEN ABLE TO OVERCOME THE INFLUENCE. HE'S SUPERMAN.
THERE'S NO EVIL IN SUPERMAN!
GET THE BOX AWAY FROM HIM, PANDORA.
NOW!
CHAK
CHAK
HE'S MORE HUMAN THAN I REALIZED.

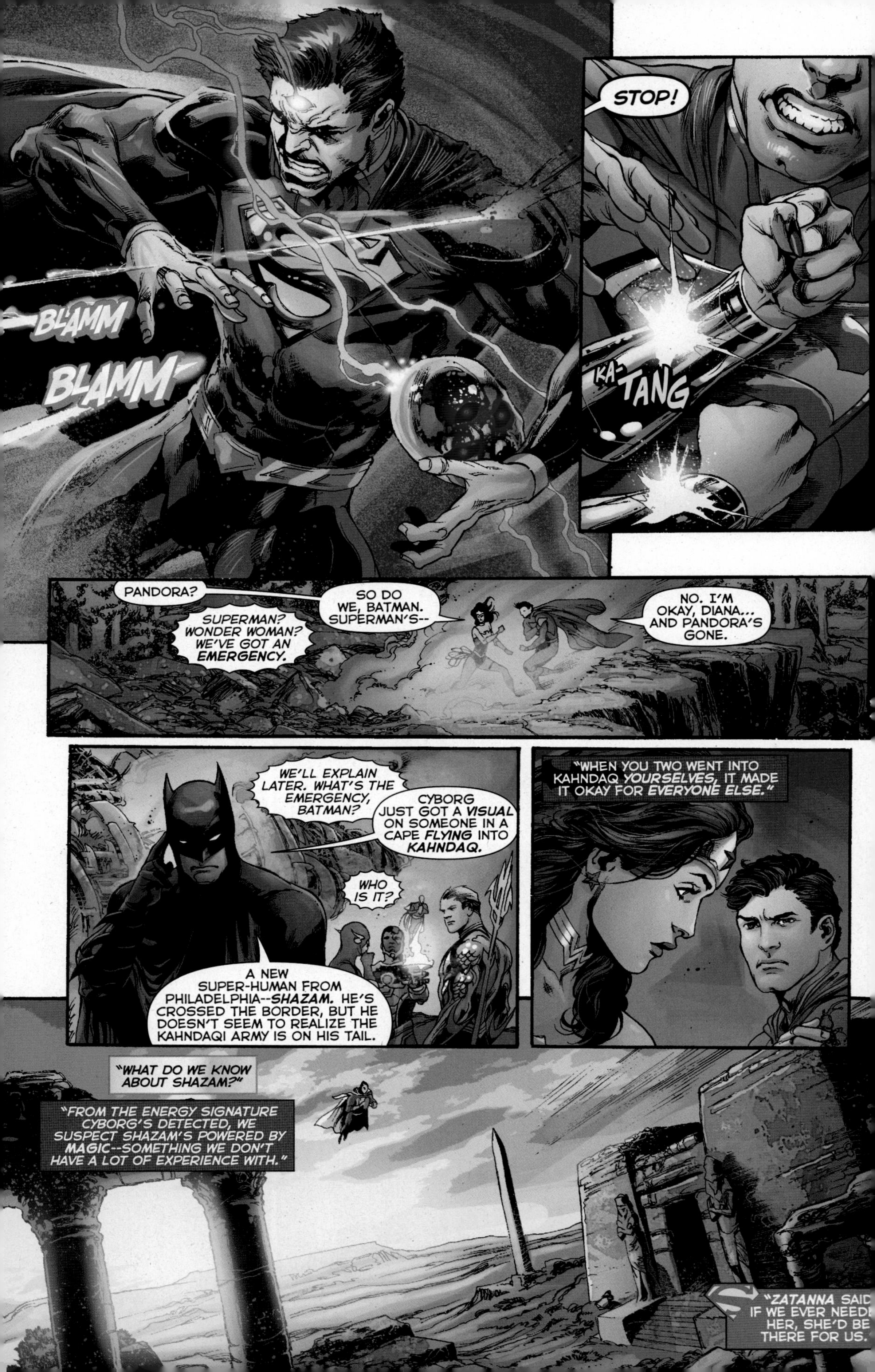
STOP!
BLAMM
BLAMM-
KA-TANG
PANDORA?
SUPERMAN? WONDER WOMAN? WE'VE GOT AN EMERGENCY.
SO DO WE, BATMAN. SUPERMAN'S--
NO. I'M OKAY, DIANA... AND PANDORA'S GONE.
WE'LL EXPLAIN LATER. WHAT'S THE EMERGENCY, BATMAN?
CYBORG JUST GOT A VISUAL ON SOMEONE IN A CAPE FLYING INTO KAHNDAQ.
WHO IS IT?
A NEW SUPER-HUMAN FROM PHILADELPHIA--SHAZAM. HE'S CROSSED THE BORDER, BUT HE DOESN'T SEEM TO REALIZE THE KAHNDAQI ARMY IS ON HIS TAIL.
"WHEN YOU TWO WENT INTO KAHNDAQ YOURSELVES, IT MADE IT OKAY FOR EVERYONE ELSE."
"WHAT DO WE KNOW ABOUT SHAZAM?"
"FROM THE ENERGY SIGNATURE CYBORG'S DETECTED, WE SUSPECT SHAZAM'S POWERED BY MAGIC--SOMETHING WE DON'T HAVE A LOT OF EXPERIENCE WITH."
"ZATANNA SAID IF WE EVER NEED HER, SHE'D BE THERE FOR US.

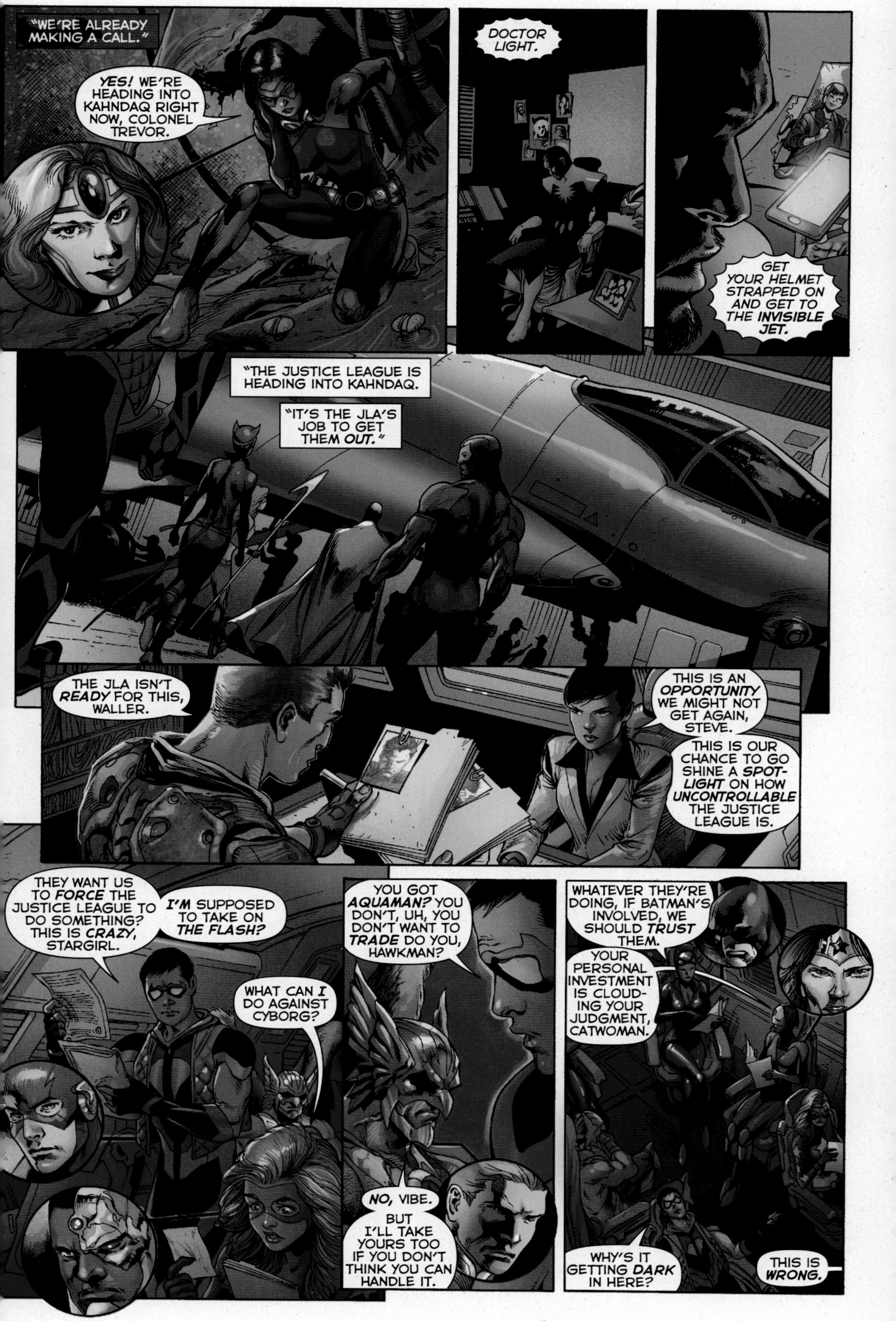
"WE'RE ALREADY MAKING A CALL."
YES! WE'RE HEADING INTO KAHNDAQ RIGHT NOW, COLONEL TREVOR.
DOCTOR LIGHT.
GET YOUR HELMET STRAPPED ON AND GET TO THE INVISIBLE JET.
"THE JUSTICE LEAGUE IS HEADING INTO KAHNDAQ.
"IT'S THE JLA'S JOB TO GET THEM OUT."
THE JLA ISN'T READY FOR THIS, WALLER.
THIS IS AN OPPORTUNITY WE MIGHT NOT GET AGAIN, STEVE.
THIS IS OUR CHANCE TO GO SHINE A SPOT-LIGHT ON HOW UNCONTROLLABLE THE JUSTICE LEAGUE IS.
THEY WANT US TO FORCE THE JUSTICE LEAGUE TO DO SOMETHING? THIS IS CRAZY, STARGIRL.
I'M SUPPOSED TO TAKE ON THE FLASH?
WHAT CAN I DO AGAINST CYBORG?
YOU GOT AQUAMAN? YOU DON'T, UH, YOU DON'T WANT TO TRADE DO YOU, HAWKMAN?
NO, VIBE.
BUT I'LL TAKE YOURS TOO IF YOU DON'T THINK YOU CAN HANDLE IT.
WHATEVER THEY'RE DOING, IF BATMAN'S INVOLVED, WE SHOULD TRUST THEM.
YOUR PERSONAL INVESTMENT IS CLOUD-ING YOUR JUDGMENT, CATWOMAN.
WHY'S IT GETTING DARK IN HERE?
THIS IS WRONG.

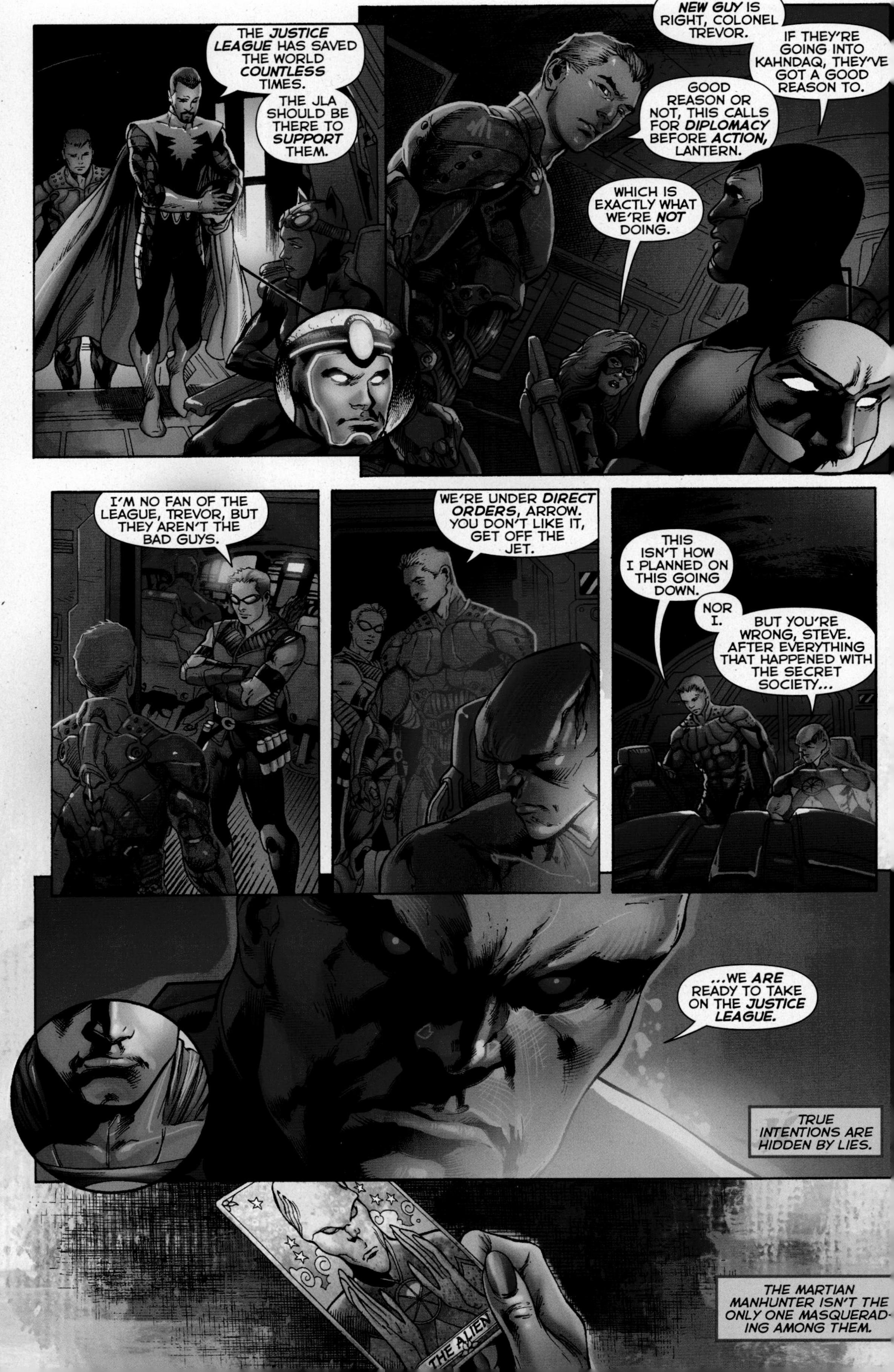
THE JUSTICE LEAGUE HAS SAVED THE WORLD COUNTLESS TIMES.
THE JLA SHOULD BE THERE TO SUPPORT THEM.
THE NEW GUY IS RIGHT, COLONEL TREVOR.
IF THEY'RE GOING INTO KAHNDAQ, THEY'VE GOT A GOOD REASON TO.
GOOD REASON OR NOT, THIS CALLS FOR DIPLOMACY BEFORE ACTION, LANTERN.
WHICH IS EXACTLY WHAT WE'RE NOT DOING.
I'M NO FAN OF THE LEAGUE, TREVOR, BUT THEY AREN'T THE BAD GUYS.
WE'RE UNDER DIRECT ORDERS, ARROW. YOU DON'T LIKE IT, GET OFF THE JET.
THIS ISN'T HOW I PLANNED ON THIS GOING DOWN.
NOR I.
BUT YOU'RE WRONG, STEVE. AFTER EVERYTHING THAT HAPPENED WITH THE SECRET SOCIETY...
...WE ARE READY TO TAKE ON THE JUSTICE LEAGUE.
TRUE INTENTIONS ARE HIDDEN BY LIES.
THE ALIEN
THE MARTIAN MANHUNTER ISN'T THE ONLY ONE MASQUERAD-ING AMONG THEM.

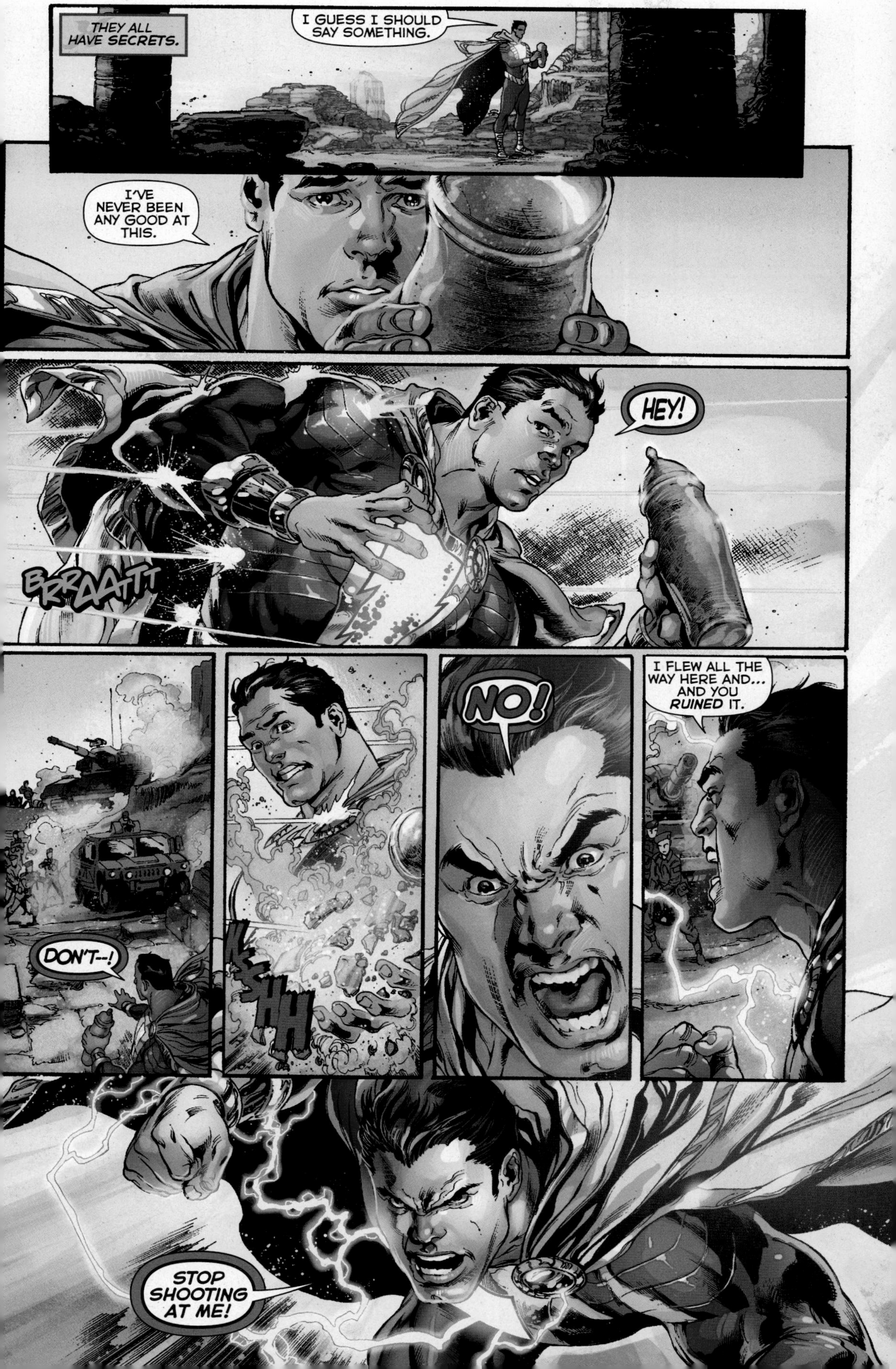
THEY ALL HAVE SECRETS.
I GUESS I SHOULD SAY SOMETHING.
I'VE NEVER BEEN ANY GOOD AT THIS.
HEY!
BRRAATTT
DON'T--!
KRSHH
NO!
I FLEW ALL THE WAY HERE AND... AND YOU RUINED IT.
STOP SHOOTING AT ME!

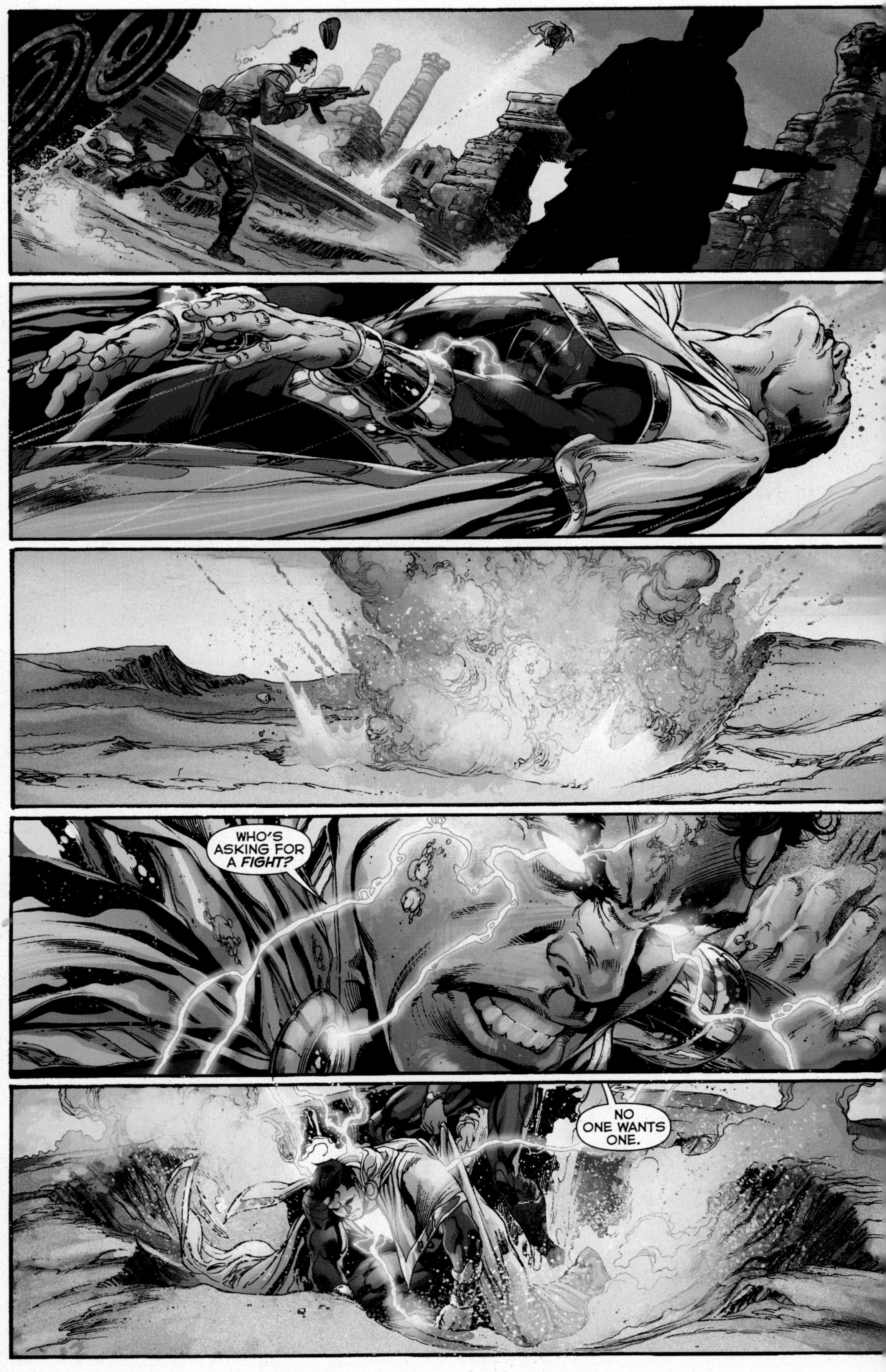
WHO'S ASKING FOR A *FIGHT?*
NO ONE WANTS ONE.

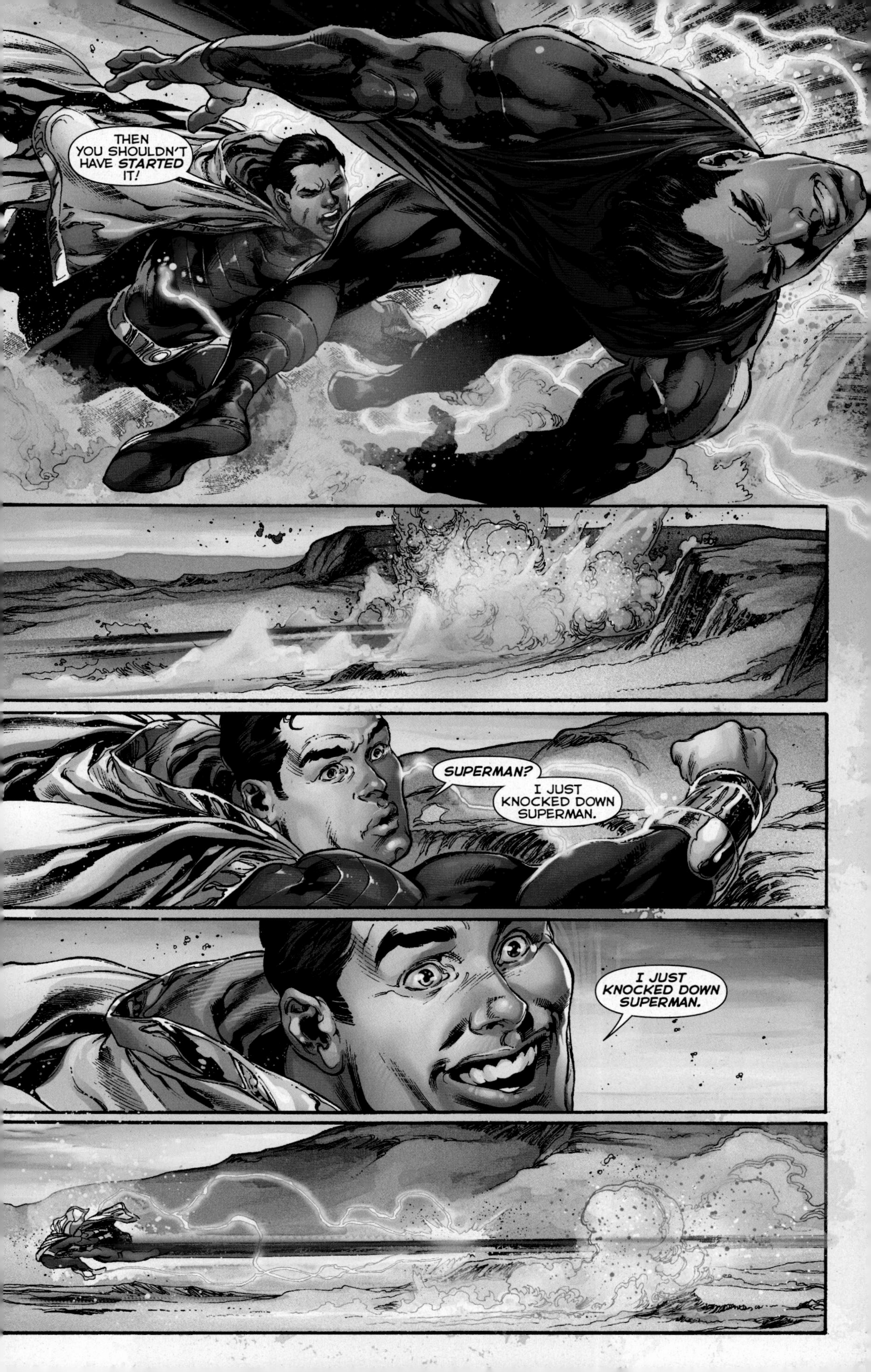
THEN YOU SHOULDN'T HAVE STARTED IT!
SUPERMAN?
I JUST KNOCKED DOWN SUPERMAN.
I JUST KNOCKED DOWN SUPERMAN.

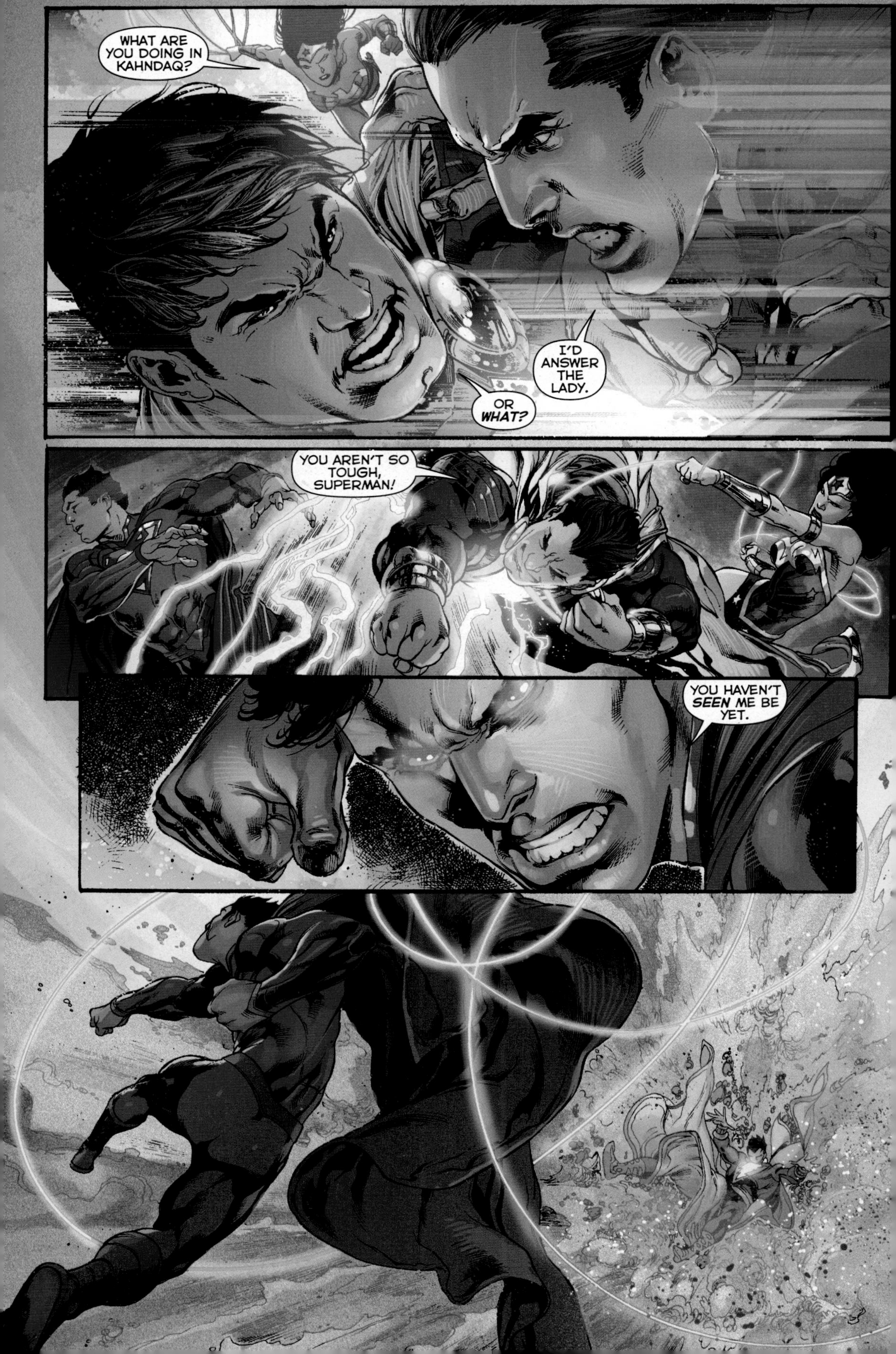
WHAT ARE YOU DOING IN KAHNDAQ?
I'D ANSWER THE LADY.
OR WHAT?
YOU AREN'T SO TOUGH, SUPERMAN!
YOU HAVEN'T SEEN ME BE YET.

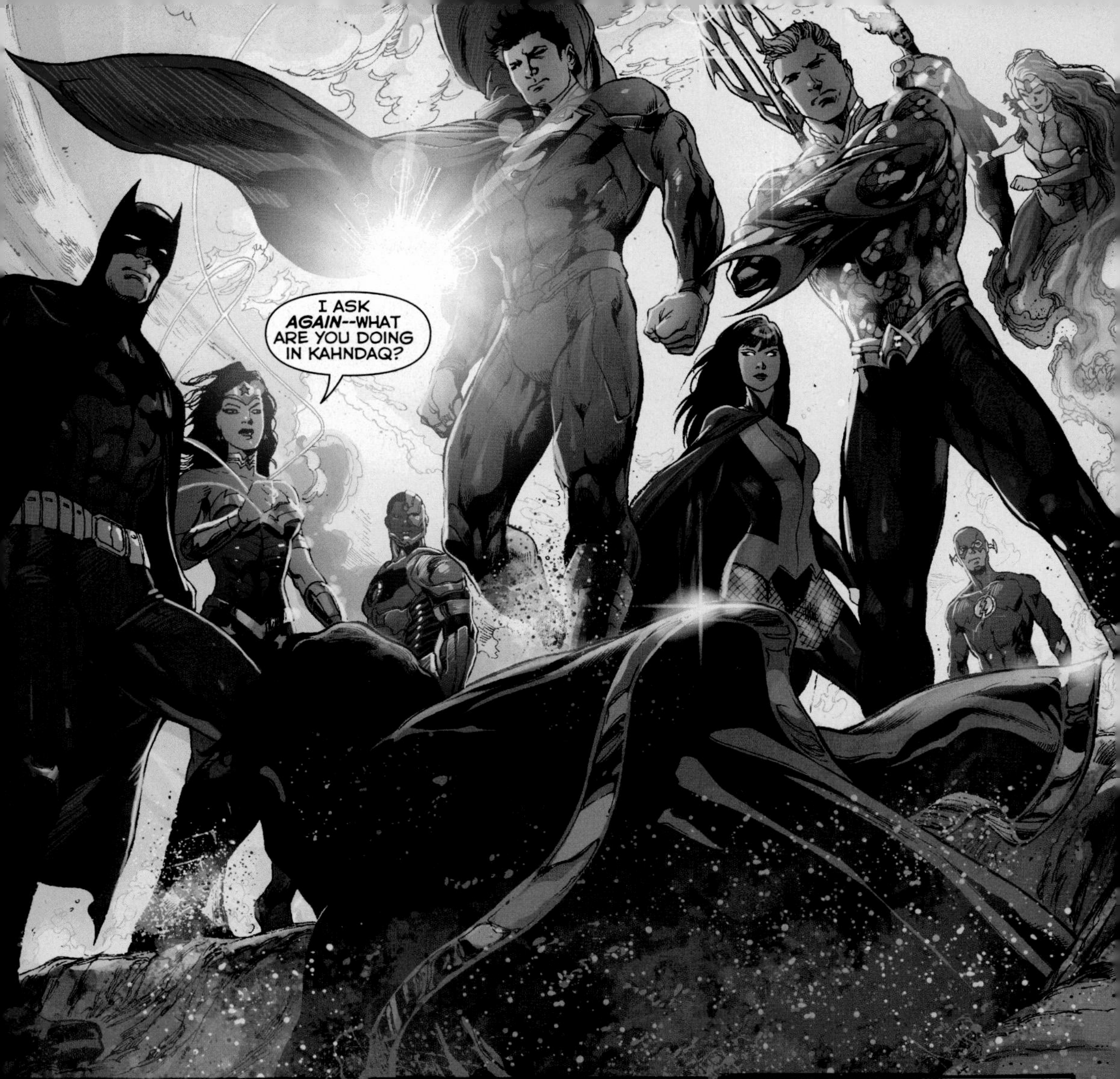
I ASK AGAIN--WHAT ARE YOU DOING IN KAHNDAQ?

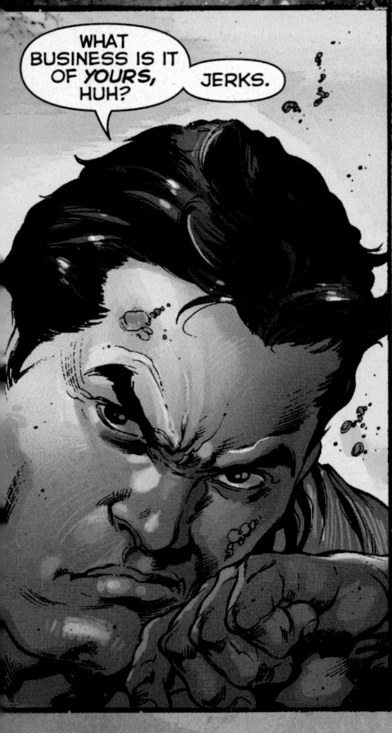
WHAT BUSINESS IS IT OF YOURS, HUH?
JERKS.

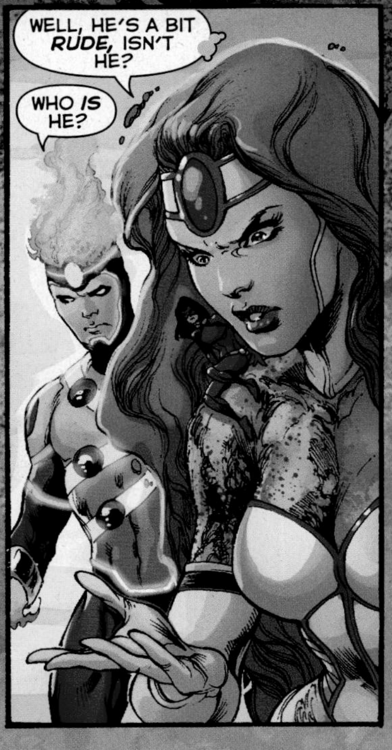
WELL, HE'S A BIT RUDE, ISN'T HE?
WHO IS HE?

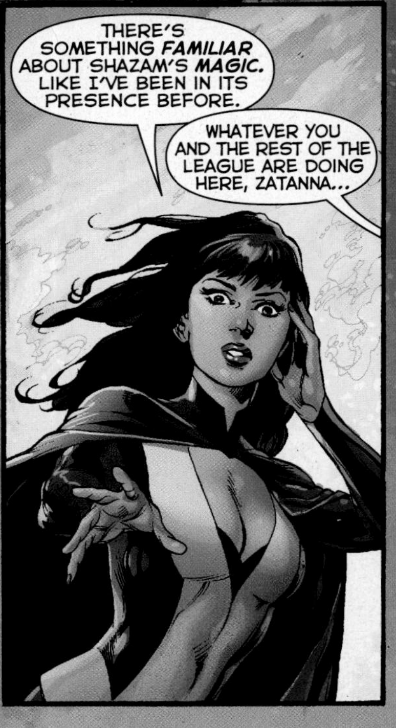
THERE'S SOMETHING FAMILIAR ABOUT SHAZAM'S MAGIC. LIKE I'VE BEEN IN ITS PRESENCE BEFORE.
WHATEVER YOU AND THE REST OF THE LEAGUE ARE DOING HERE, ZATANNA...

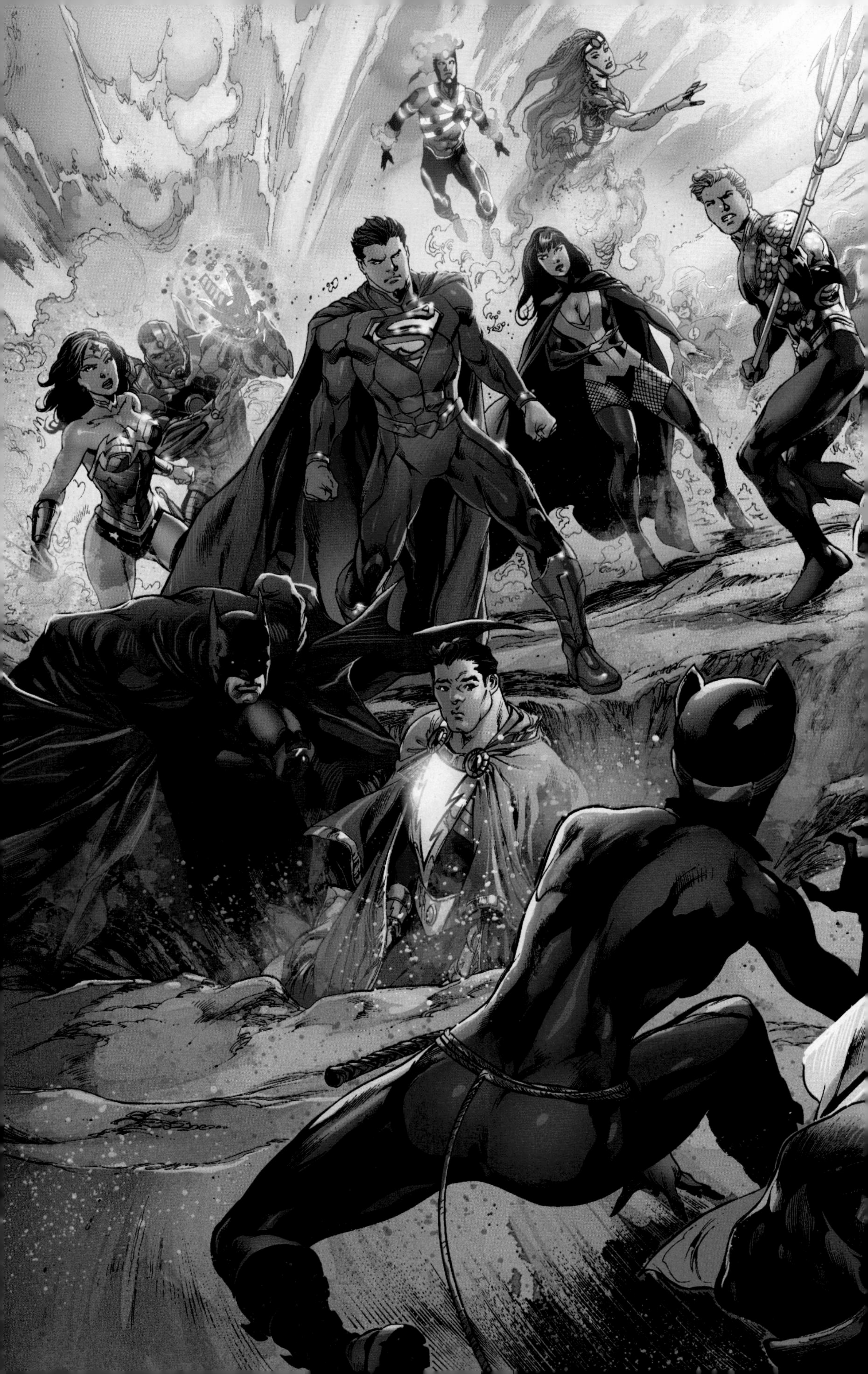

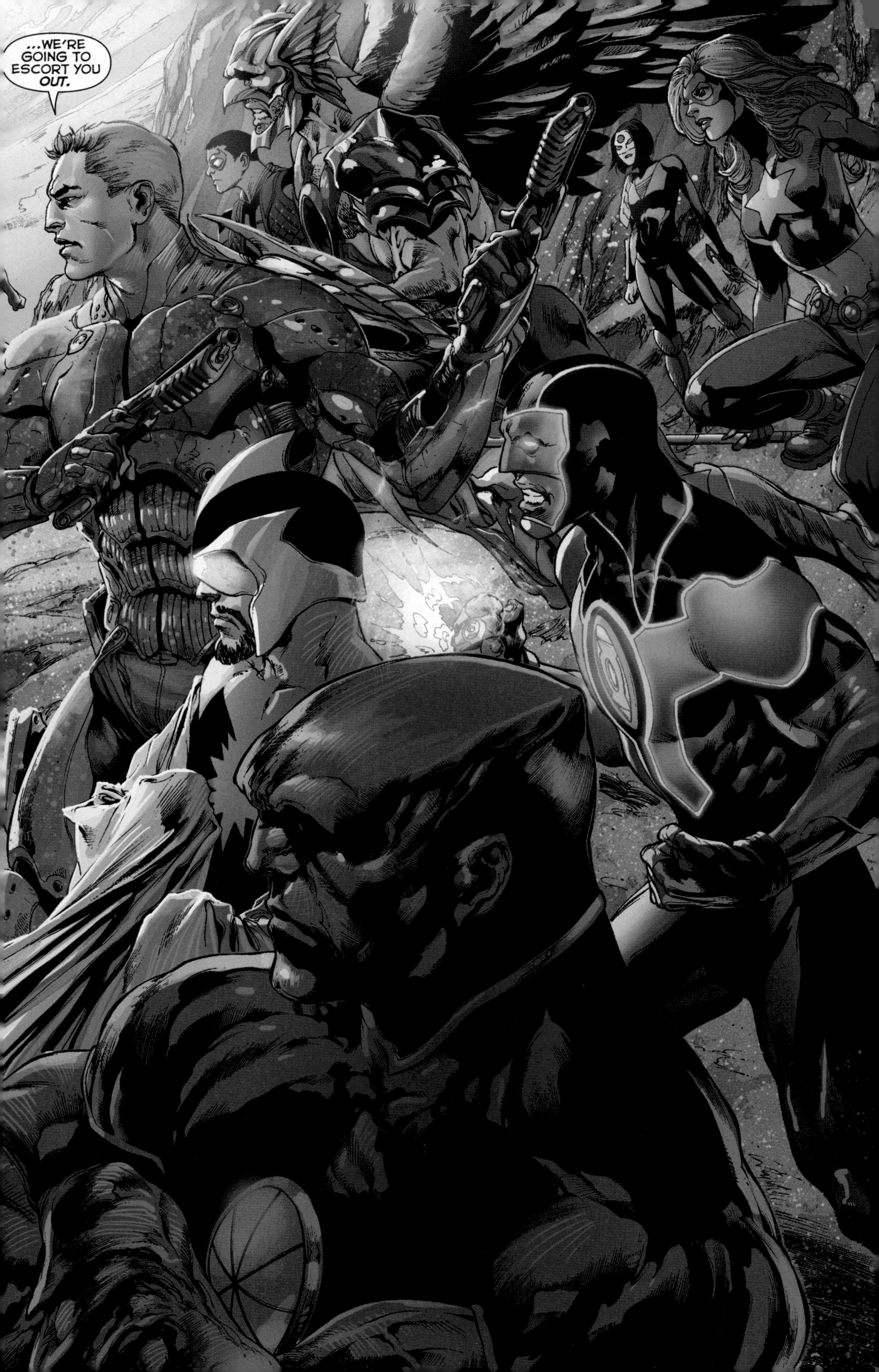
...WE'RE GOING TO ESCORT YOU *OUT*.

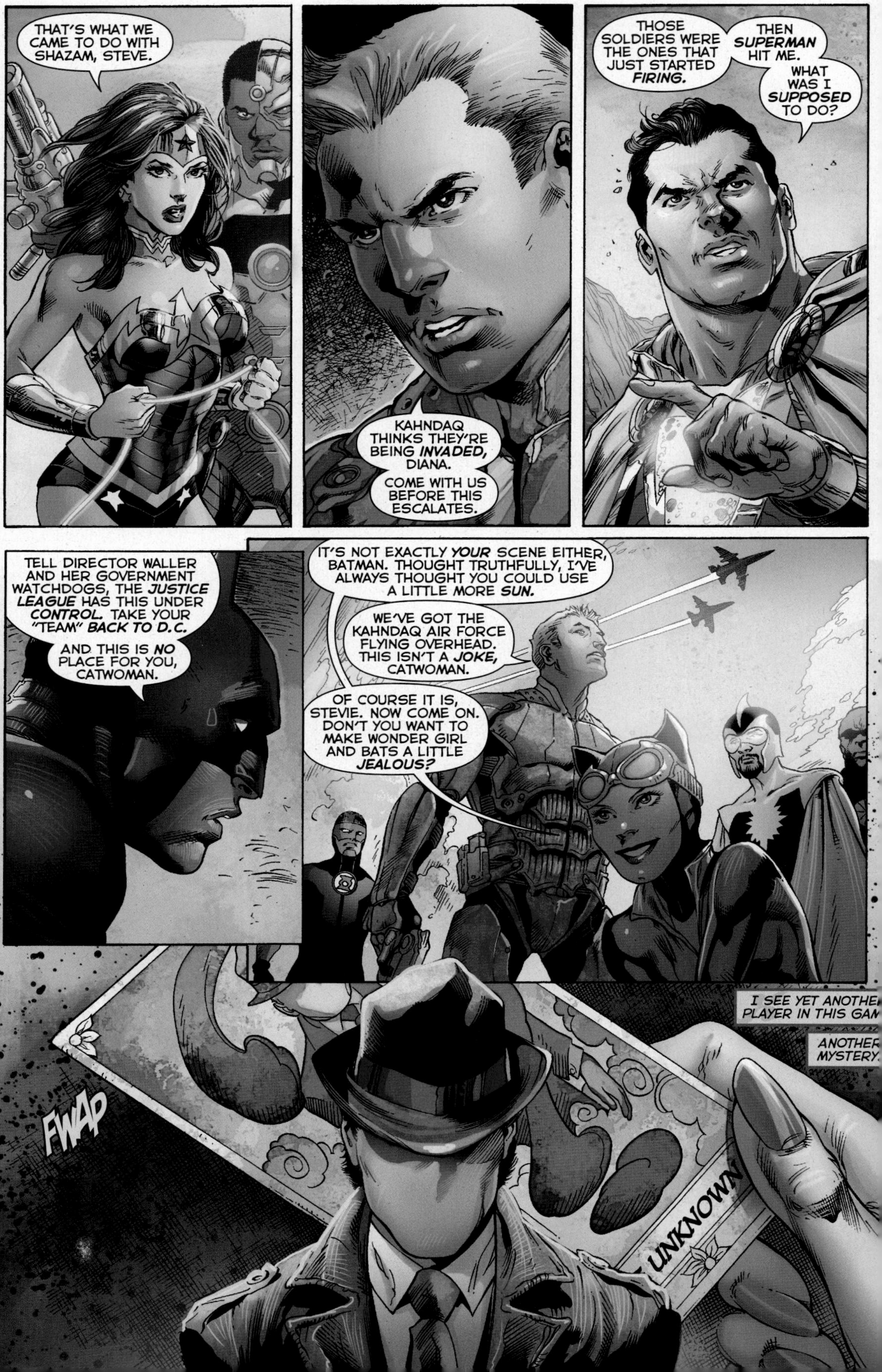
THAT'S WHAT WE CAME TO DO WITH SHAZAM, STEVE.
KAHNDAQ THINKS THEY'RE BEING INVADED, DIANA.
COME WITH US BEFORE THIS ESCALATES.
THOSE SOLDIERS WERE THE ONES THAT JUST STARTED FIRING.
THEN SUPERMAN HIT ME.
WHAT WAS I SUPPOSED TO DO?
TELL DIRECTOR WALLER AND HER GOVERNMENT WATCHDOGS, THE JUSTICE LEAGUE HAS THIS UNDER CONTROL. TAKE YOUR "TEAM" BACK TO D.C.
AND THIS IS NO PLACE FOR YOU, CATWOMAN.
IT'S NOT EXACTLY YOUR SCENE EITHER, BATMAN. THOUGHT TRUTHFULLY, I'VE ALWAYS THOUGHT YOU COULD USE A LITTLE MORE SUN.
WE'VE GOT THE KAHNDAQ AIR FORCE FLYING OVERHEAD. THIS ISN'T A JOKE, CATWOMAN.
OF COURSE IT IS, STEVIE. NOW COME ON. DON'T YOU WANT TO MAKE WONDER GIRL AND BATS A LITTLE JEALOUS?
I SEE YET ANOTHE PLAYER IN THIS GAM
ANOTHER MYSTERY.
FWAP
UNKNOWN

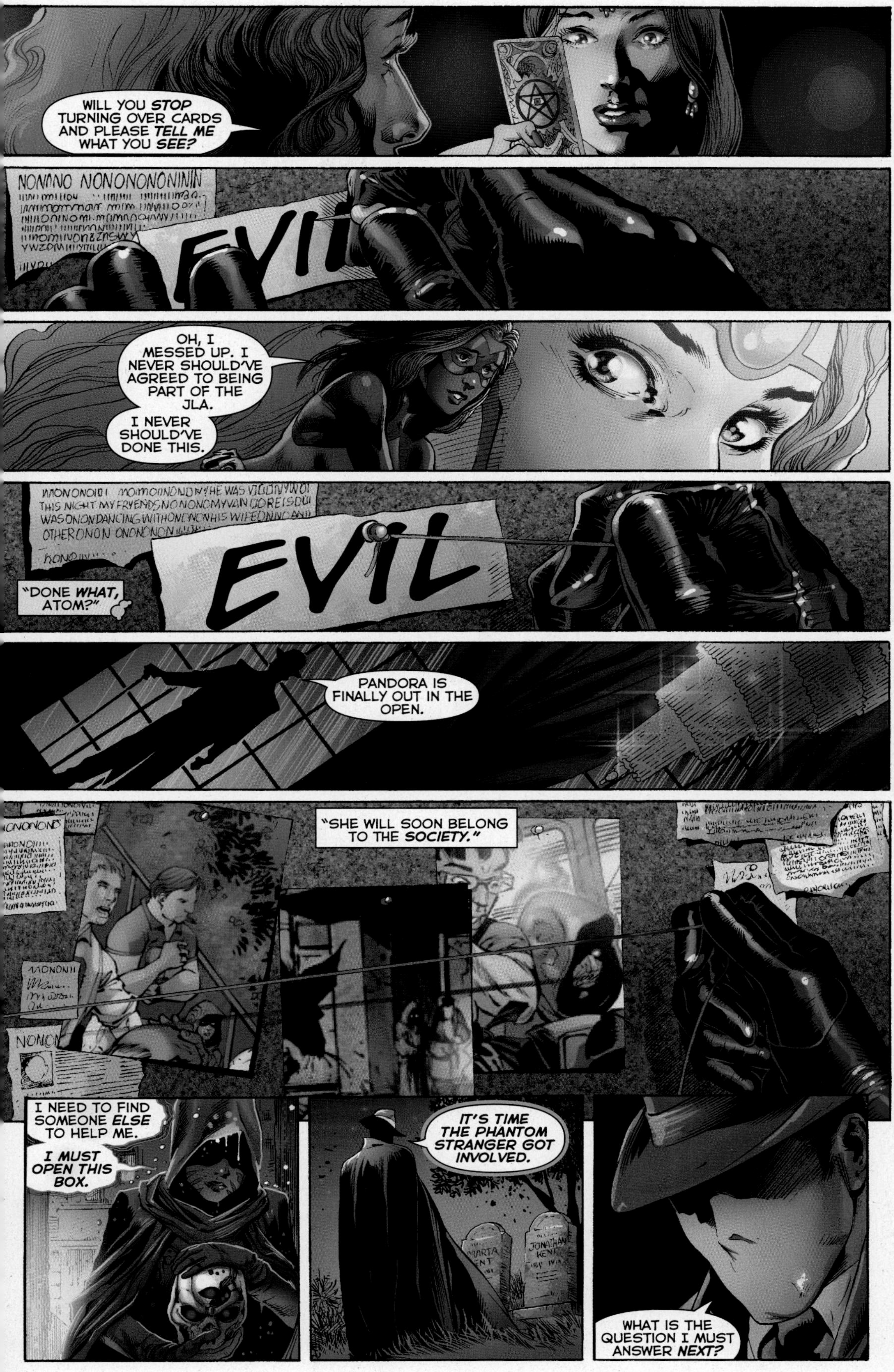

WILL YOU STOP TURNING OVER CARDS AND PLEASE TELL ME WHAT YOU SEE?
NONONO NONONONONINIIN
EVIL
OH, I MESSED UP. I NEVER SHOULD'VE AGREED TO BEING PART OF THE JLA.
I NEVER SHOULD'VE DONE THIS.
THIS NIGHT MY FRYENDS
EVIL
"DONE WHAT, ATOM?"
PANDORA IS FINALLY OUT IN THE OPEN.
"SHE WILL SOON BELONG TO THE SOCIETY."
I NEED TO FIND SOMEONE ELSE TO HELP ME.
I MUST OPEN THIS BOX.
IT'S TIME THE PHANTOM STRANGER GOT INVOLVED.
MARTA KENT
JONATHAN KENT
WHAT IS THE QUESTION I MUST ANSWER NEXT?

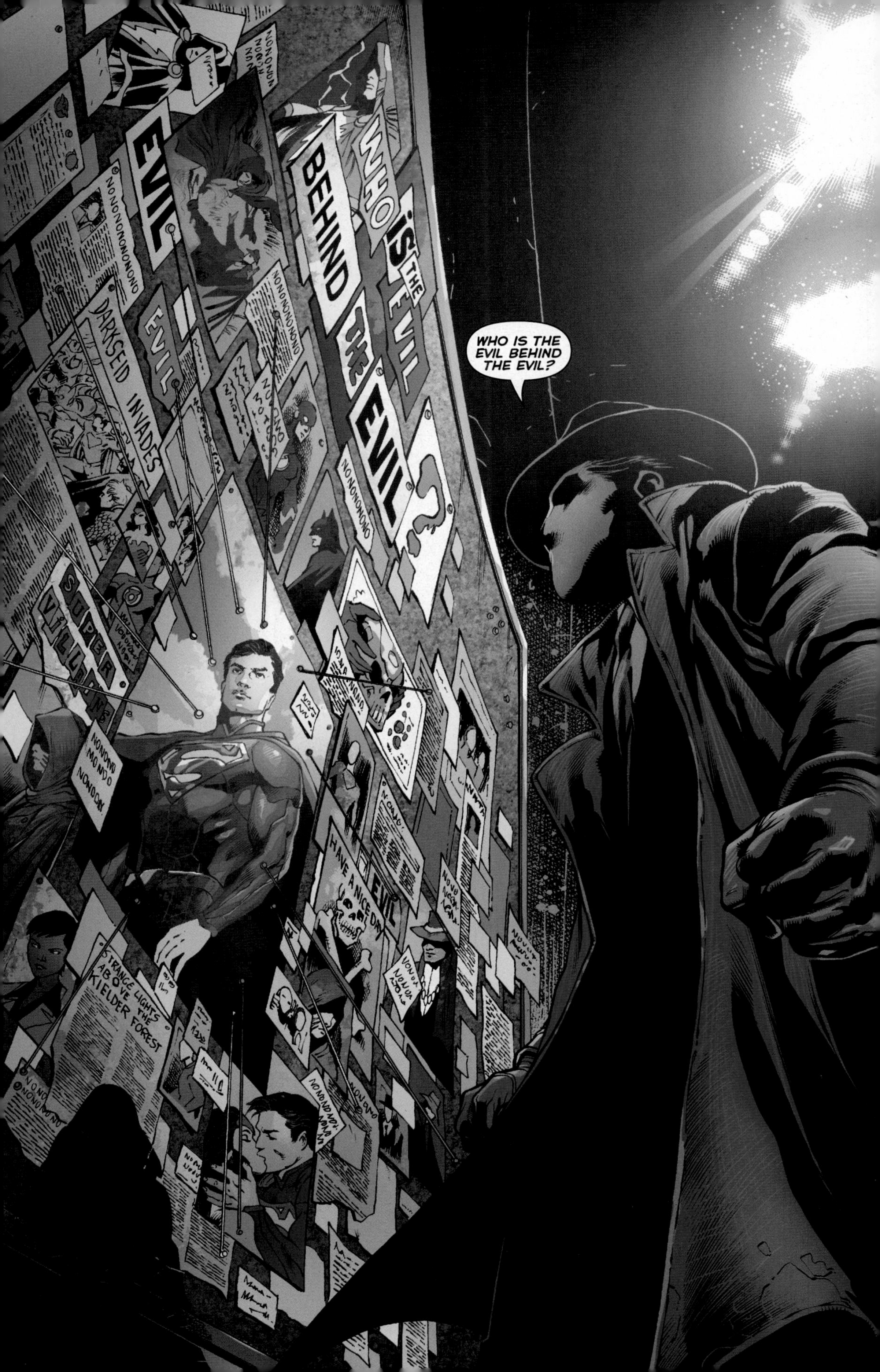
WHO IS THE EVIL BEHIND THE EVIL?
WHO IS THE EVIL BEHIND THE EVIL
EVIL
EVIL
DARKSEID INVADES
SUPER VILLAINS
HAVE A NICE DAY
EVIL
STRANGE LIGHTS ABOVE THE KIELDER FOREST

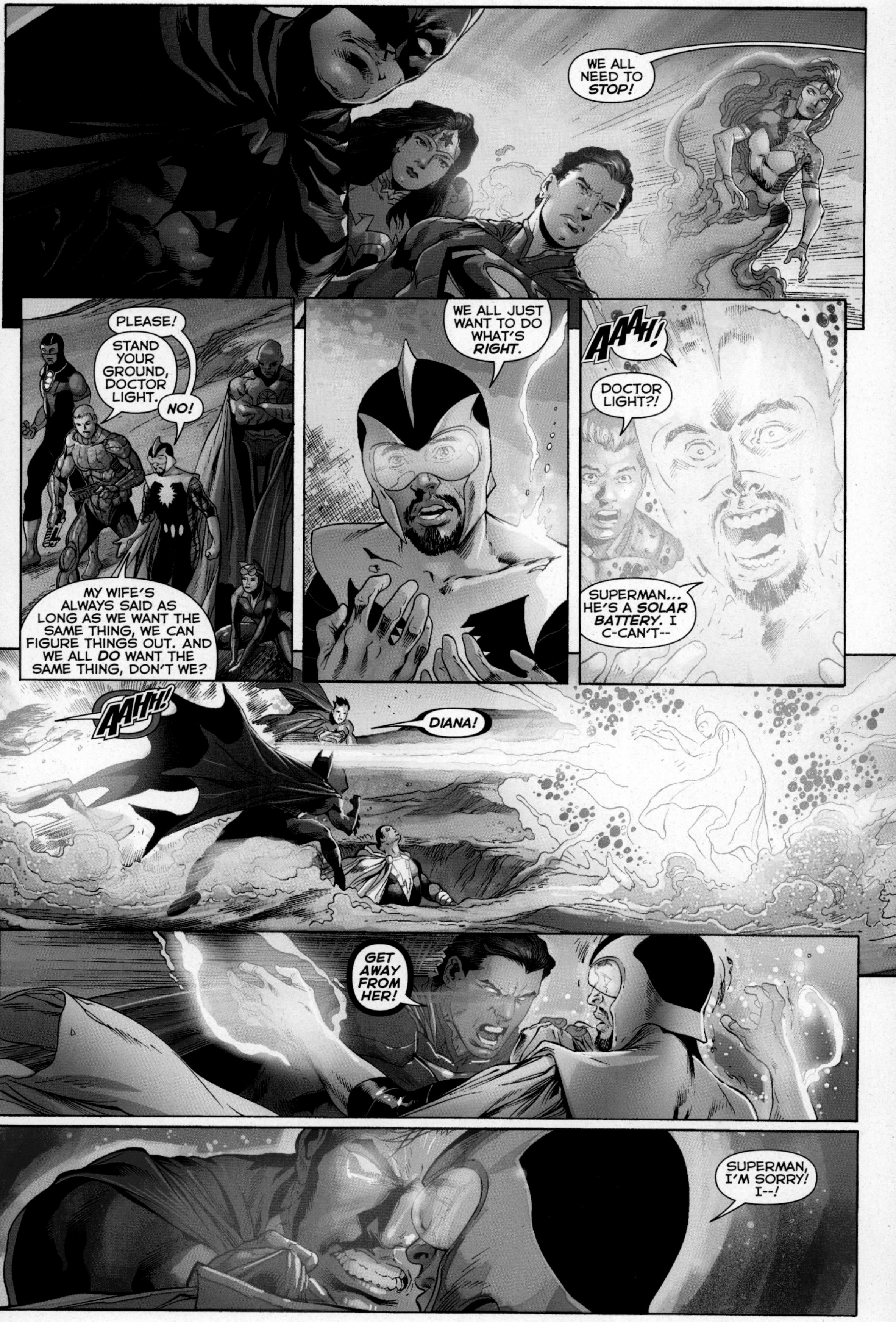
WE ALL NEED TO STOP!
PLEASE!
STAND YOUR GROUND, DOCTOR LIGHT.
NO!
MY WIFE'S ALWAYS SAID AS LONG AS WE WANT THE SAME THING, WE CAN FIGURE THINGS OUT. AND WE ALL DO WANT THE SAME THING, DON'T WE?
WE ALL JUST WANT TO DO WHAT'S RIGHT.
AAAH!
DOCTOR LIGHT?!
SUPERMAN... HE'S A SOLAR BATTERY. I C-CAN'T--
AAHH!
DIANA!
GET AWAY FROM HER!
SUPERMAN, I'M SORRY! I--!

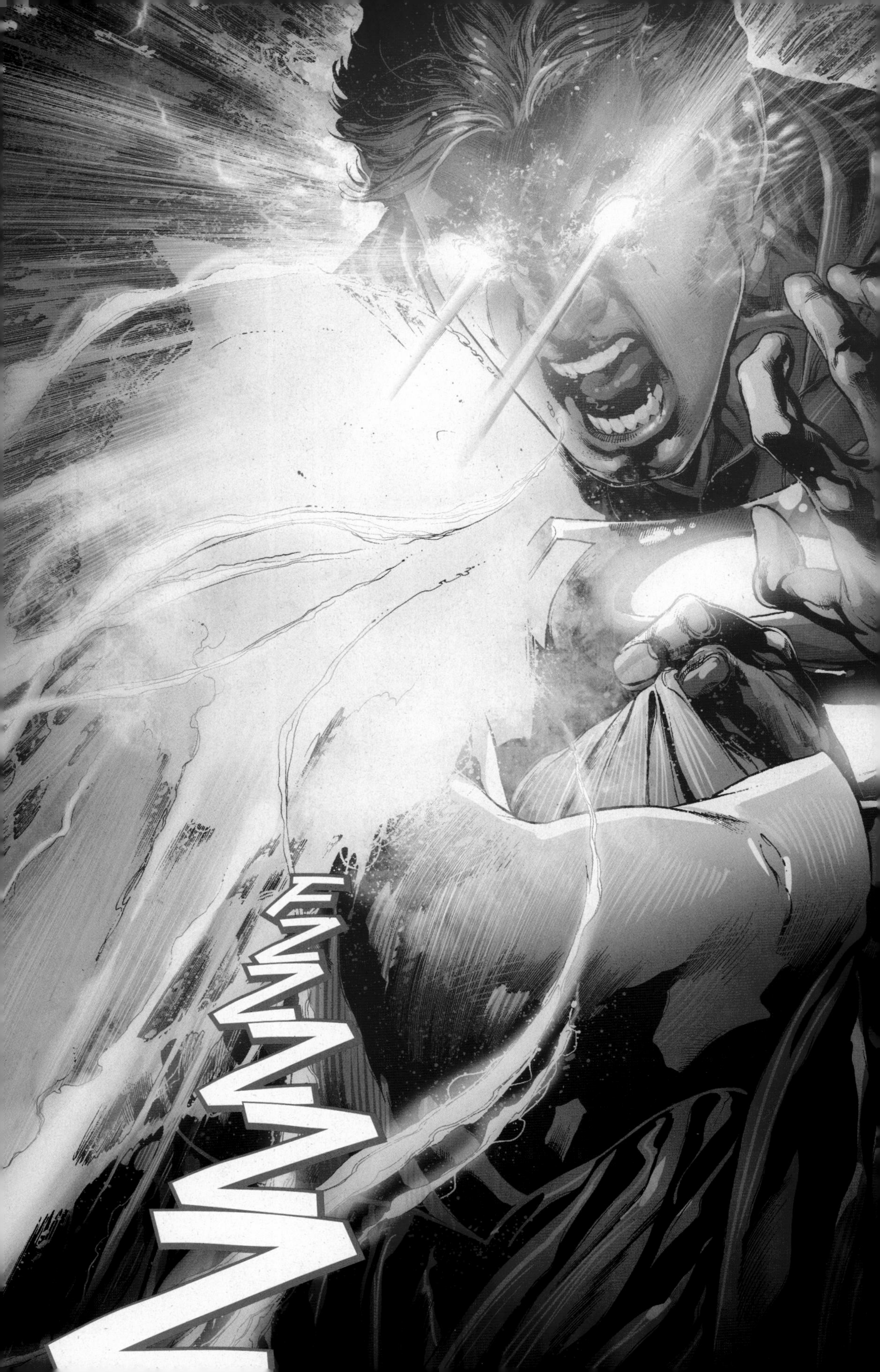

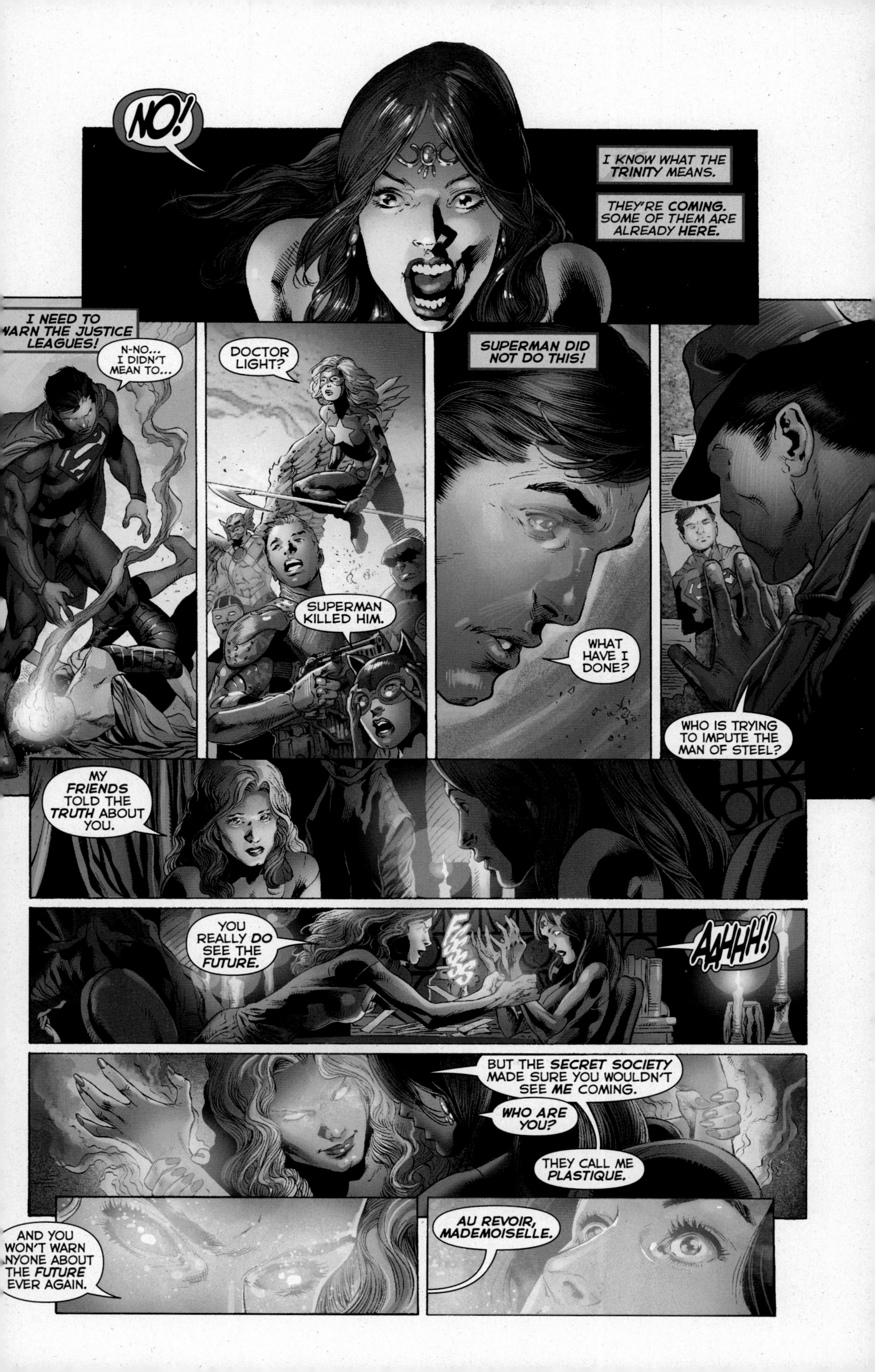
NO!
I KNOW WHAT THE TRINITY MEANS.
THEY'RE COMING. SOME OF THEM ARE ALREADY HERE.
I NEED TO WARN THE JUSTICE LEAGUES!
N-NO... I DIDN'T MEAN TO...
DOCTOR LIGHT?
SUPERMAN KILLED HIM.
SUPERMAN DID NOT DO THIS!
WHAT HAVE I DONE?
WHO IS TRYING TO IMPUTE THE MAN OF STEEL?
MY FRIENDS TOLD THE TRUTH ABOUT YOU.
YOU REALLY DO SEE THE FUTURE.
AAHHH!
BUT THE SECRET SOCIETY MADE SURE YOU WOULDN'T SEE ME COMING.
WHO ARE YOU?
THEY CALL ME PLASTIQUE.
AND YOU WON'T WARN ANYONE ABOUT THE FUTURE EVER AGAIN.
AU REVOIR, MADEMOISELLE.

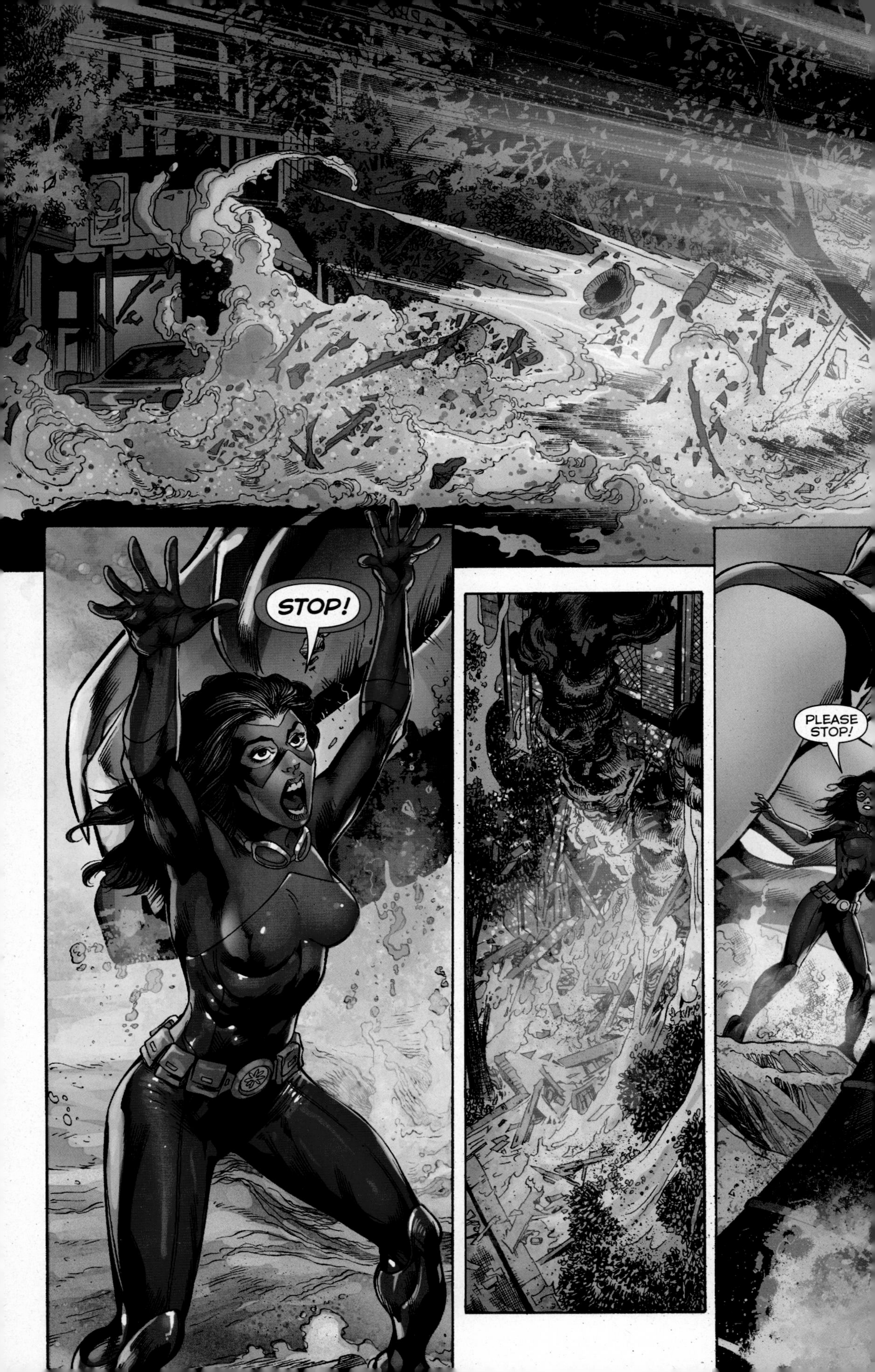
STOP!
PLEASE STOP!

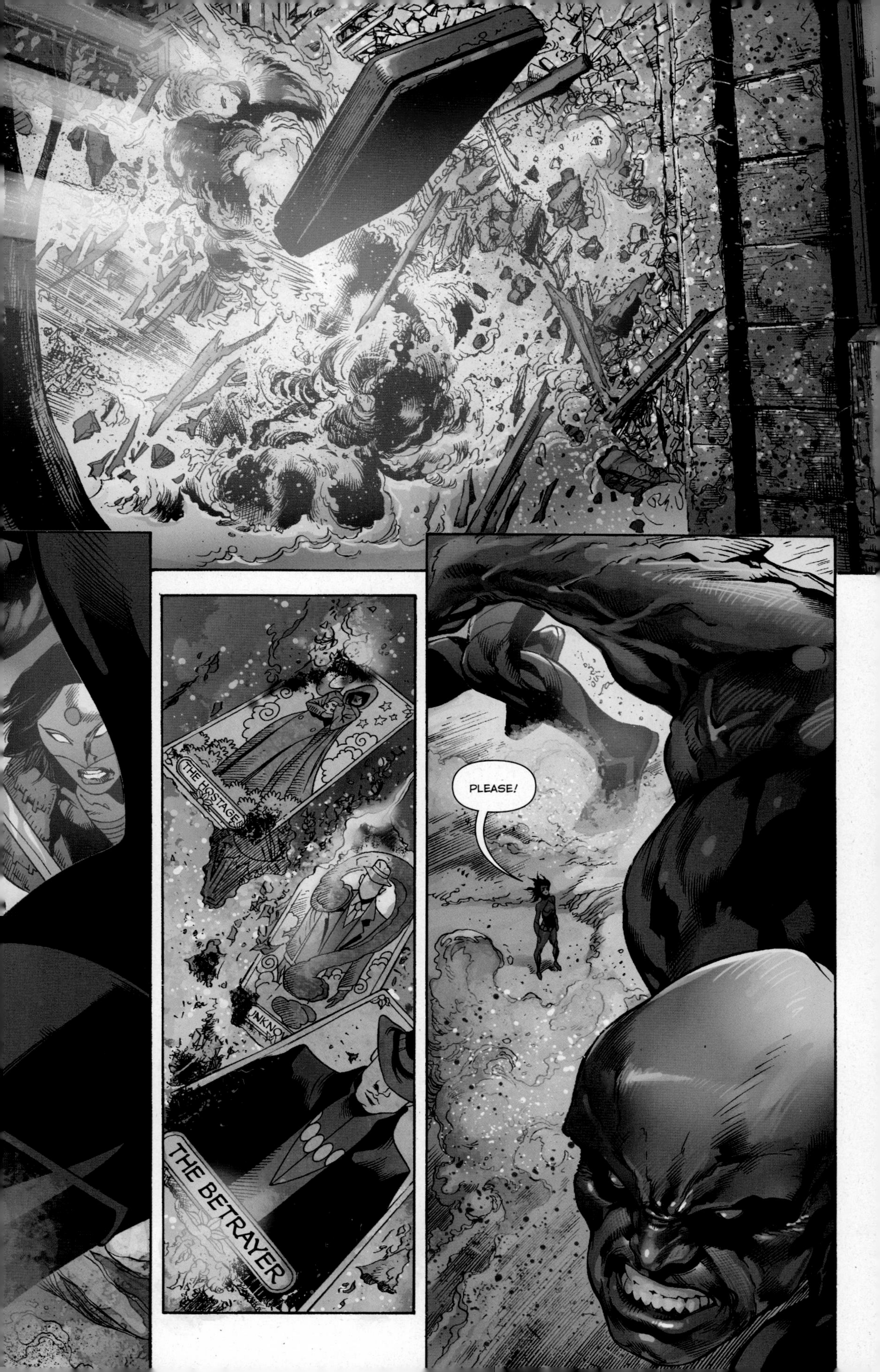
THE HOSTAGE
THE BETRAYER
PLEASE!

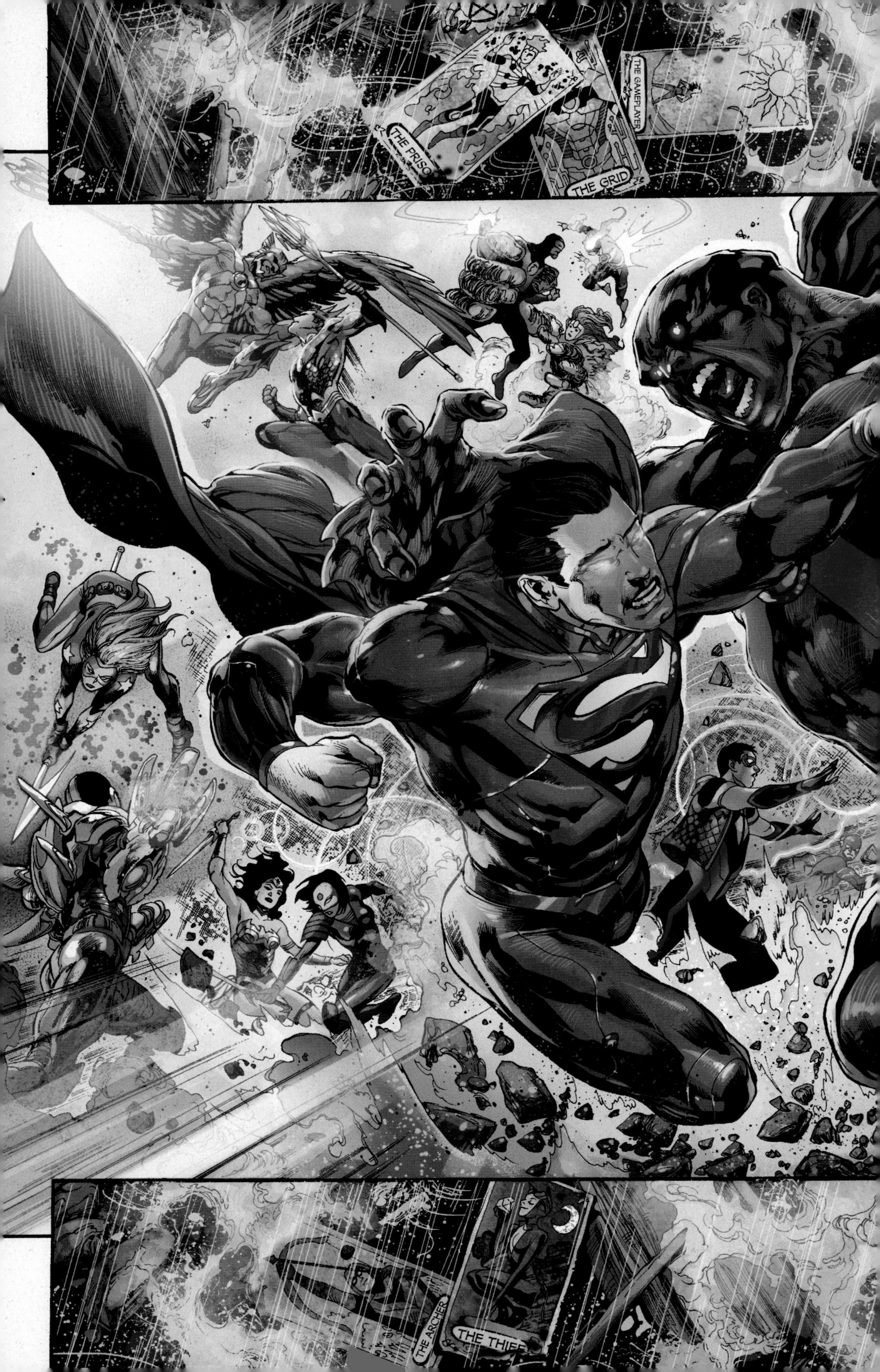
THE GAMEPLAYER
THE PRISO
THE GRID
THE ARCHER
THE THIEF

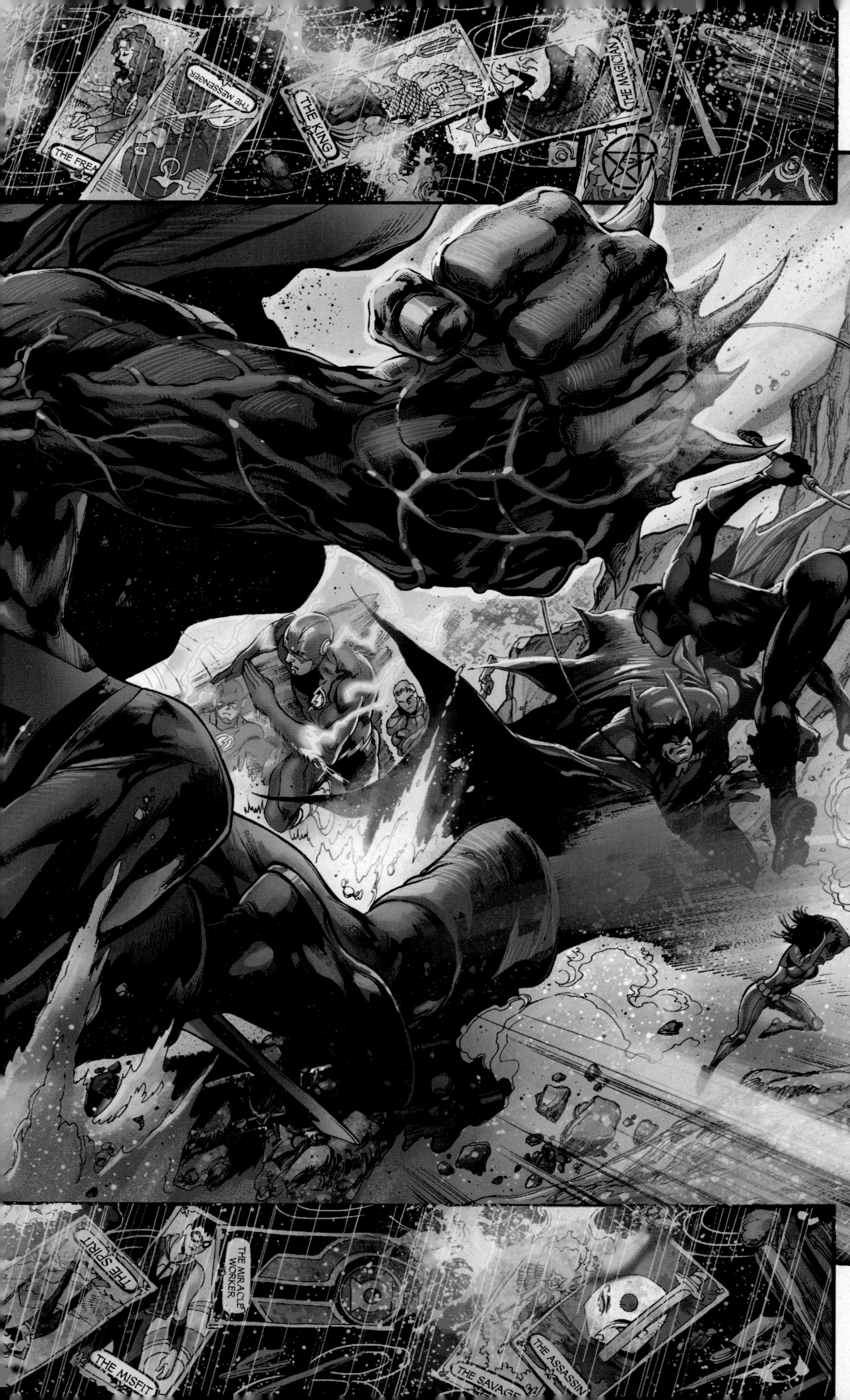
THE FREA
THE MESSENGER
THE KING
THE MAGICIAN
THE SPIRIT
THE MIRACLE WORKER
THE MISFIT
THE SAVAGE
THE ASSASSIN

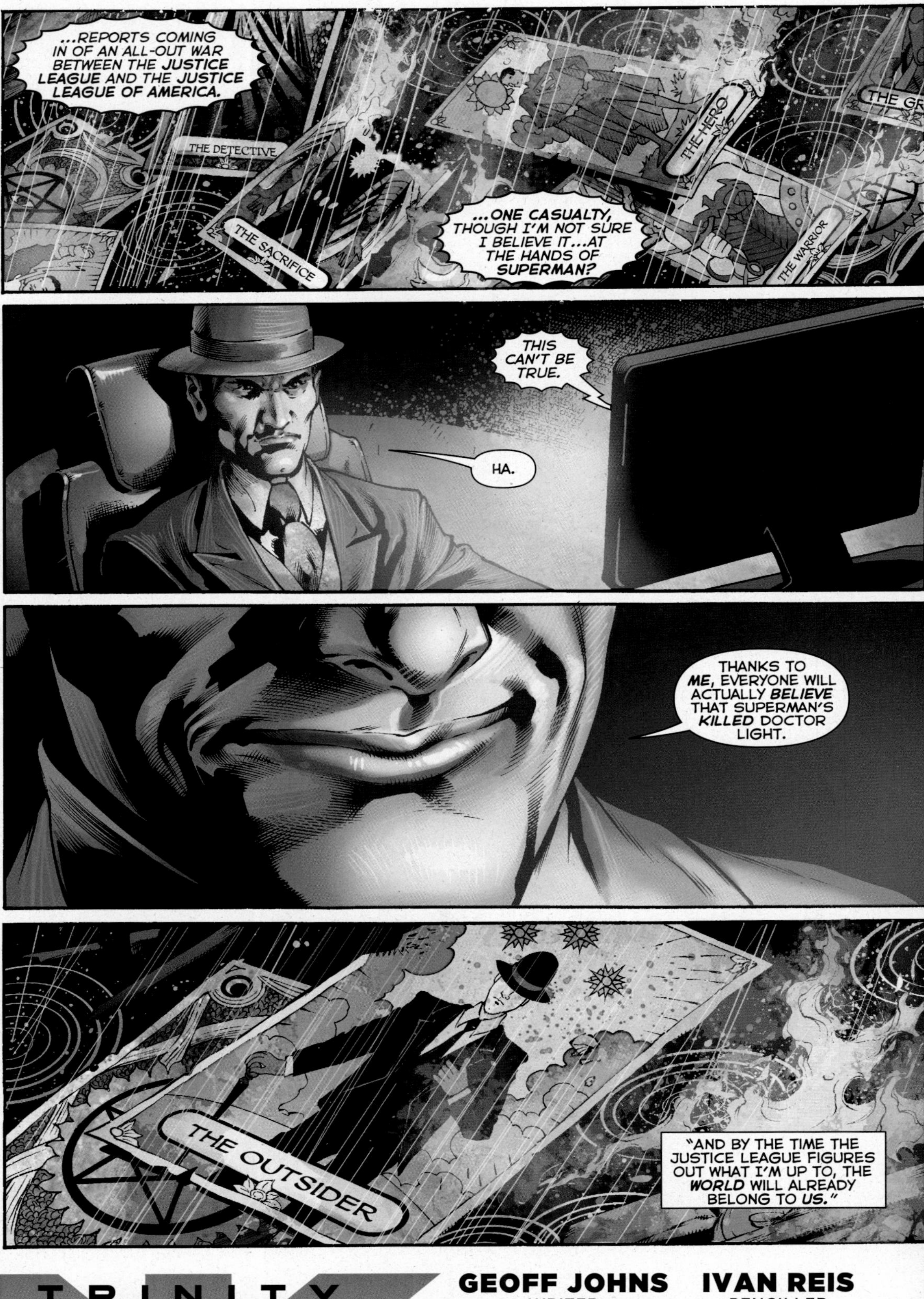
...REPORTS COMING IN OF AN ALL-OUT WAR BETWEEN THE JUSTICE LEAGUE AND THE JUSTICE LEAGUE OF AMERICA.
THE DETECTIVE
THE HERO
...ONE CASUALTY, THOUGH I'M NOT SURE I BELIEVE IT...AT THE HANDS OF SUPERMAN?
THE SACRIFICE
THE WARRIOR
THIS CAN'T BE TRUE.
HA.
THANKS TO ME, EVERYONE WILL ACTUALLY BELIEVE THAT SUPERMAN'S KILLED DOCTOR LIGHT.
THE OUTSIDER
"AND BY THE TIME THE JUSTICE LEAGUE FIGURES OUT WHAT I'M UP TO, THE WORLD WILL ALREADY BELONG TO US."

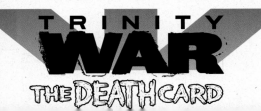

TRINITY WAR
THE DEATH CARD

GEOFF JOHNS WRITER
IVAN REIS PENCILLER
JOE PRADO & **OCLAIR ALBERT** INKERS
ROD REIS COLORS • **DC LETTERING** LETTERS
IVAN REIS, JOE PRADO & **ROD REIS** COVER

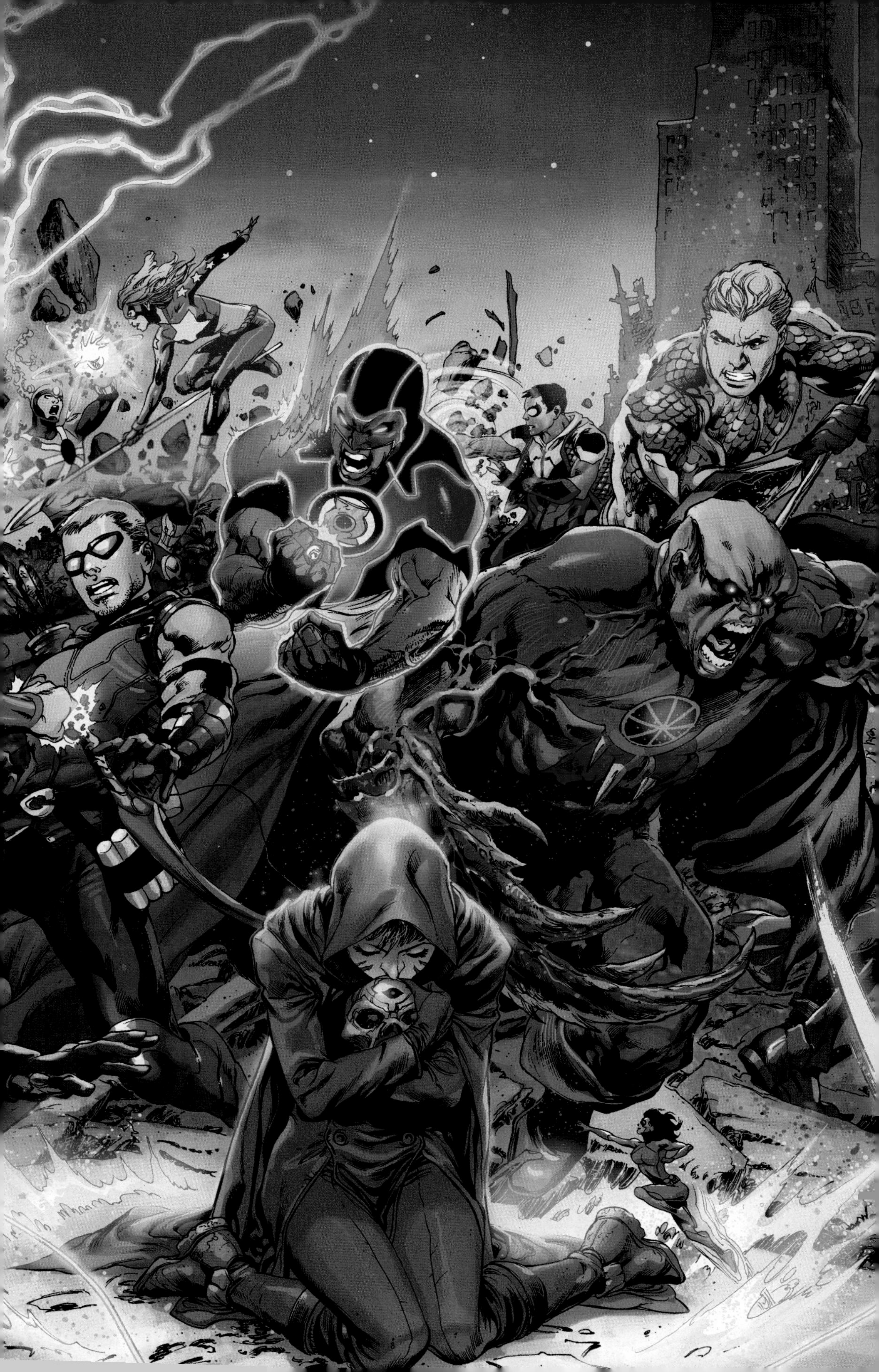

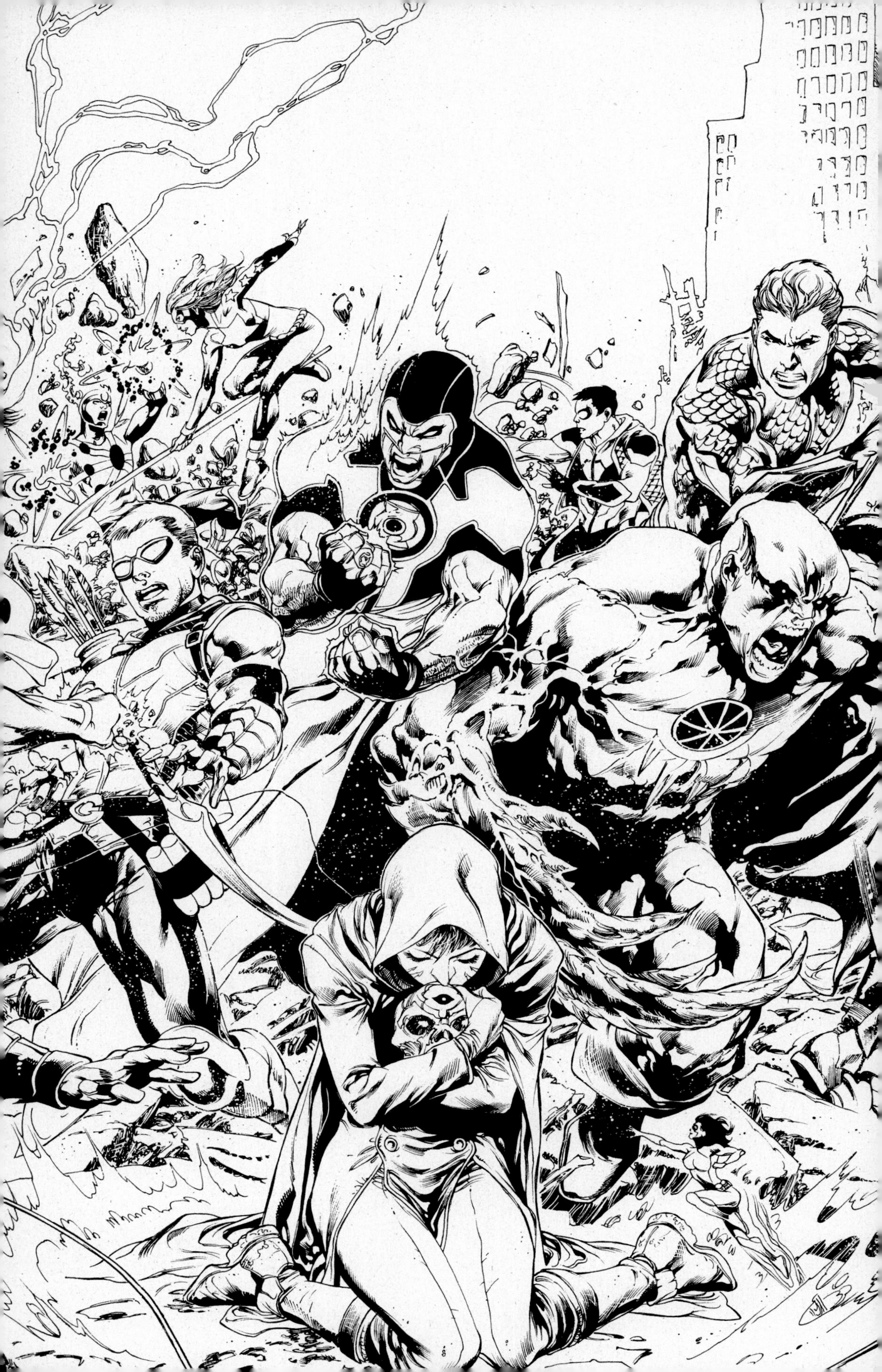

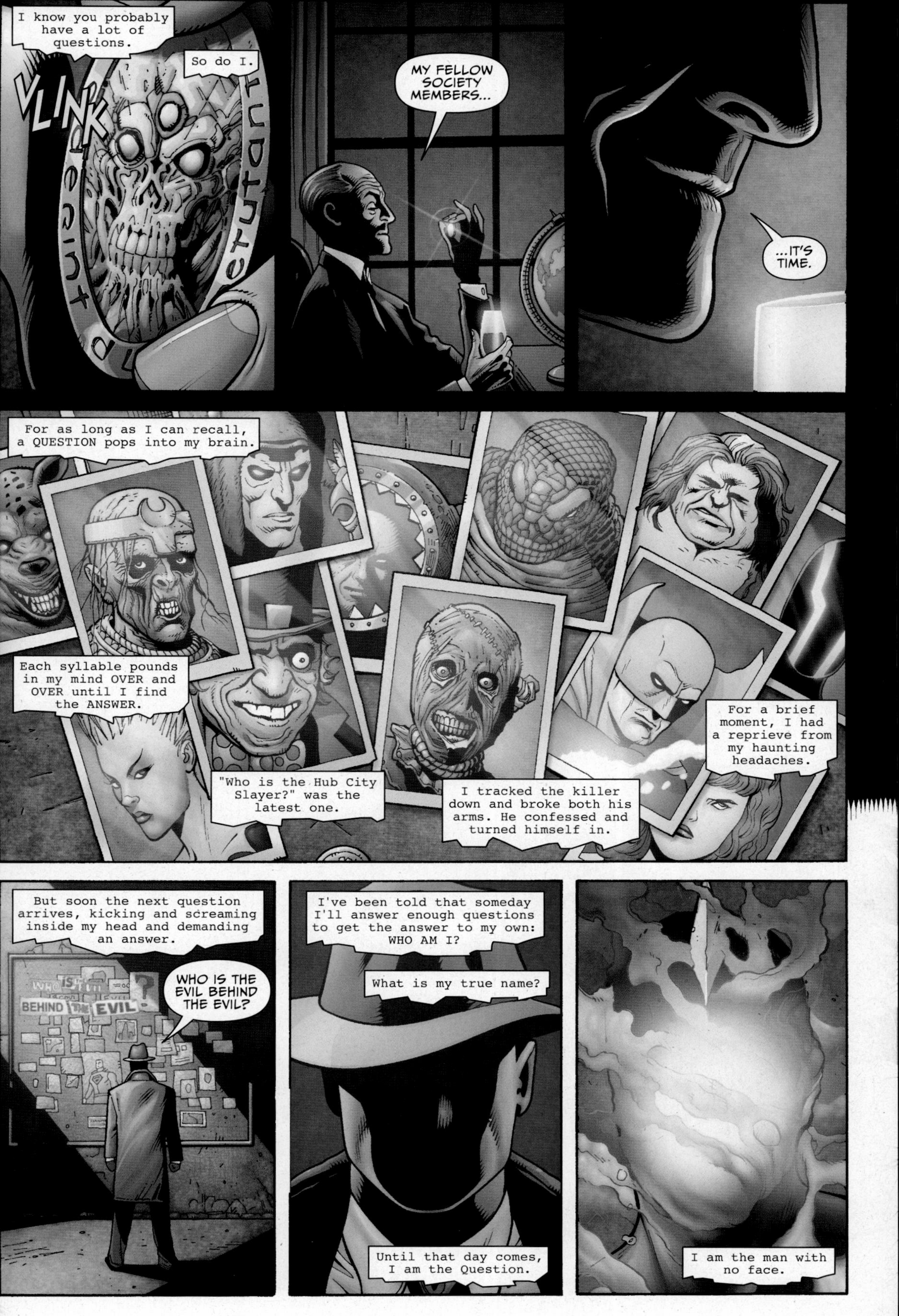
I know you probably have a lot of questions.
So do I.
VLINK
MY FELLOW SOCIETY MEMBERS...
...IT'S TIME.
For as long as I can recall, a QUESTION pops into my brain.
Each syllable pounds in my mind OVER and OVER until I find the ANSWER.
"Who is the Hub City Slayer?" was the latest one.
I tracked the killer down and broke both his arms. He confessed and turned himself in.
For a brief moment, I had a reprieve from my haunting headaches.
But soon the next question arrives, kicking and screaming inside my head and demanding an answer.
BEHIND THE EVIL
WHO IS THE EVIL BEHIND THE EVIL?
I've been told that someday I'll answer enough questions to get the answer to my own: WHO AM I?
What is my true name?
Until that day comes, I am the Question.
I am the man with no face.

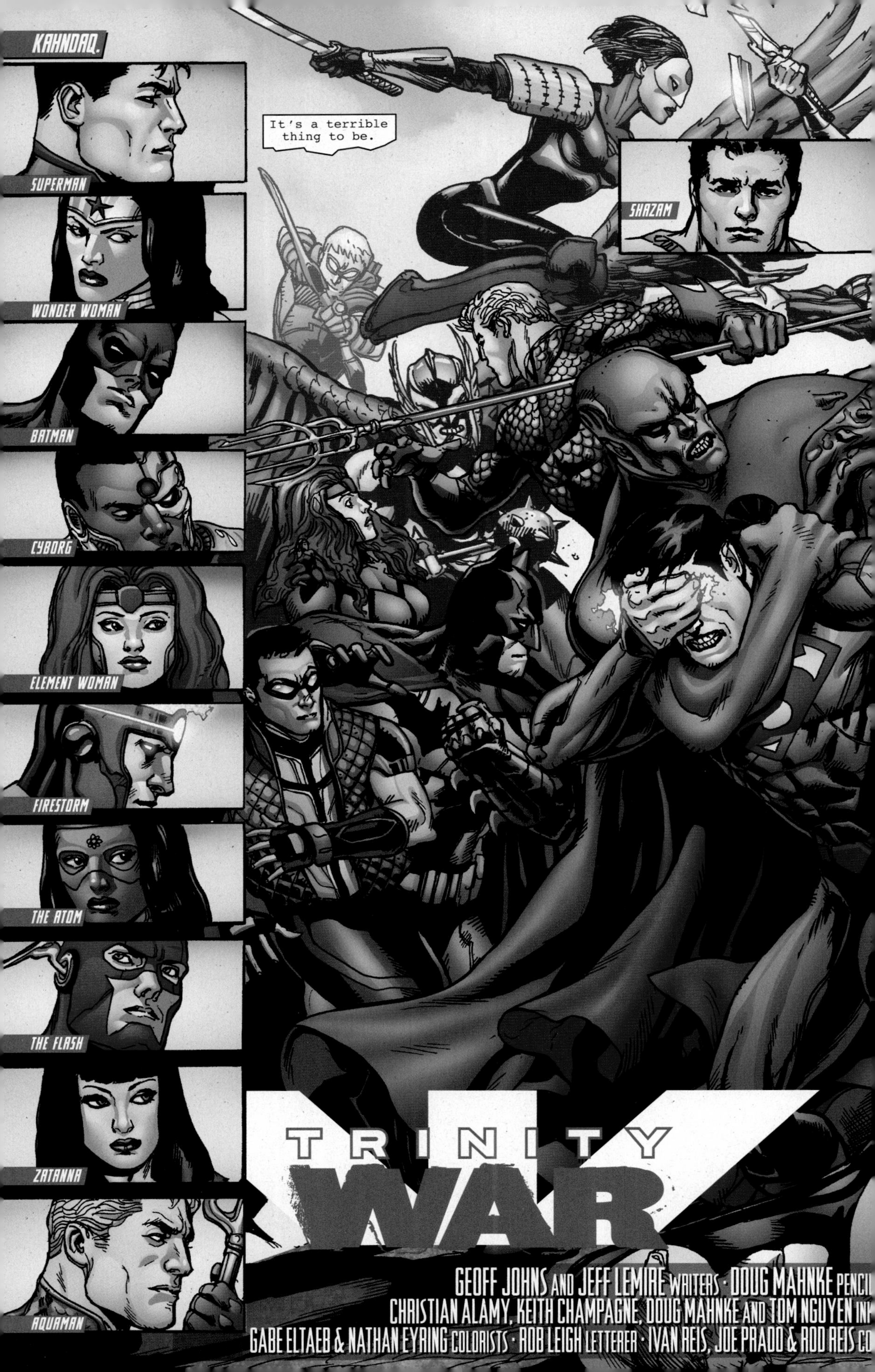
KAHNDAQ.
It's a terrible thing to be.
SUPERMAN
WONDER WOMAN
BATMAN
CYBORG
ELEMENT WOMAN
FIRESTORM
THE ATOM
THE FLASH
ZATANNA
AQUAMAN
SHAZAM
TRINITY
WAR
GEOFF JOHNS AND JEFF LEMIRE WRITERS · DOUG MAHNKE PENCI
CHRISTIAN ALAMY, KEITH CHAMPAGNE, DOUG MAHNKE AND TOM NGUYEN INK
GABE ELTAEB & NATHAN EYRING COLORISTS · ROB LEIGH LETTERER · IVAN REIS, JOE PRADO & ROD REIS CO

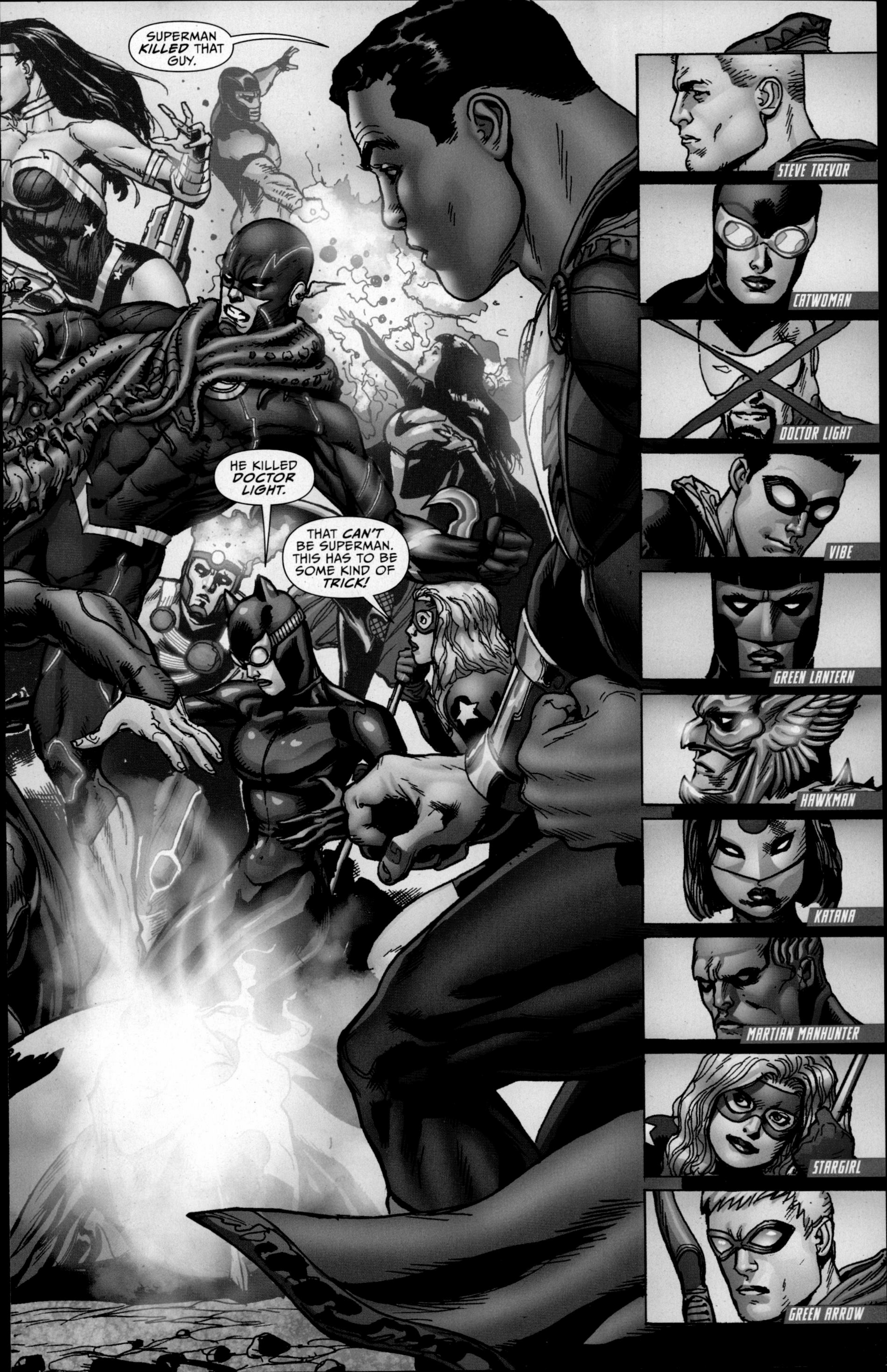
SUPERMAN KILLED THAT GUY.
HE KILLED DOCTOR LIGHT.
THAT CAN'T BE SUPERMAN. THIS HAS TO BE SOME KIND OF TRICK!
STEVE TREVOR
CATWOMAN
DOCTOR LIGHT
VIBE
GREEN LANTERN
HAWKMAN
KATANA
MARTIAN MANHUNTER
STARGIRL
GREEN ARROW

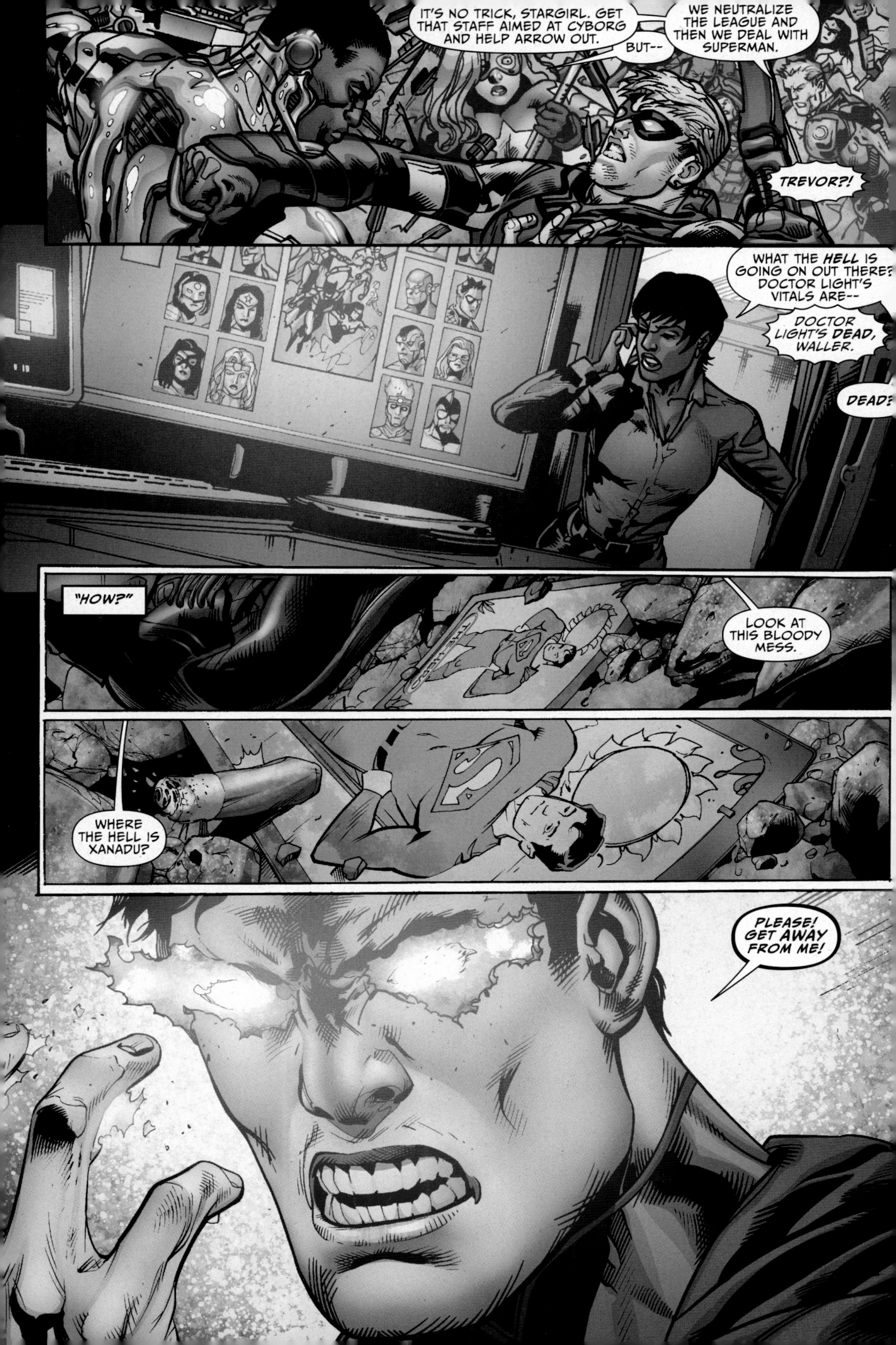

IT'S NO TRICK, STARGIRL. GET THAT STAFF AIMED AT CYBORG AND HELP ARROW OUT.
BUT--
WE NEUTRALIZE THE LEAGUE AND THEN WE DEAL WITH SUPERMAN.
TREVOR?!
WHAT THE HELL IS GOING ON OUT THERE? DOCTOR LIGHT'S VITALS ARE--
DOCTOR LIGHT'S DEAD, WALLER.
DEAD?
"HOW?"
LOOK AT THIS BLOODY MESS.
WHERE THE HELL IS XANADU?
PLEASE! GET AWAY FROM ME!

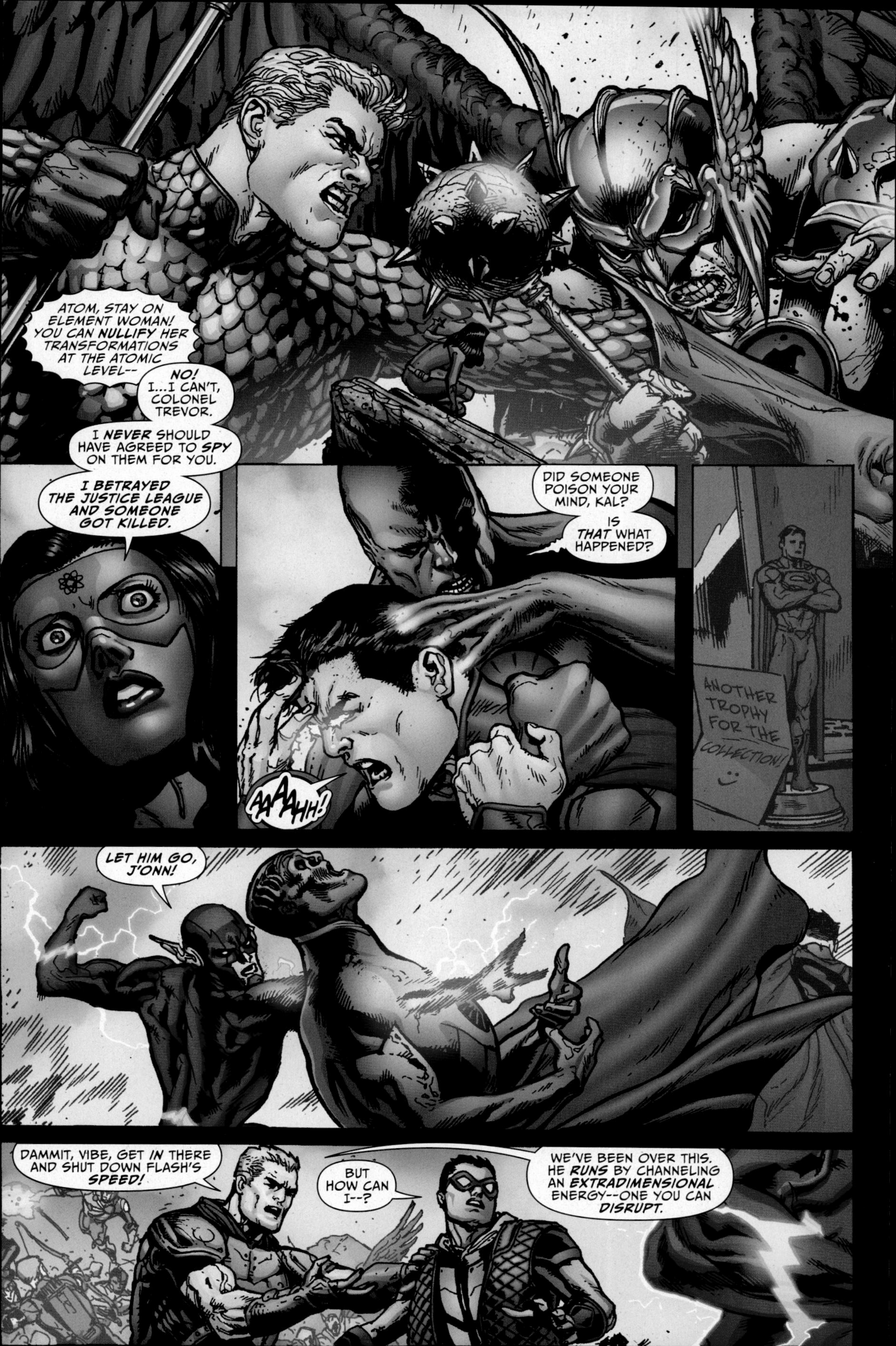

ATOM, STAY ON ELEMENT WOMAN! YOU CAN NULLIFY HER TRANSFORMATIONS AT THE ATOMIC LEVEL--
NO! I...I CAN'T, COLONEL TREVOR.
I NEVER SHOULD HAVE AGREED TO SPY ON THEM FOR YOU.
I BETRAYED THE JUSTICE LEAGUE AND SOMEONE GOT KILLED.
DID SOMEONE POISON YOUR MIND, KAL?
IS THAT WHAT HAPPENED?
AAAAHH!
ANOTHER TROPHY FOR THE COLLECTION!
LET HIM GO, J'ONN!
DAMMIT, VIBE, GET IN THERE AND SHUT DOWN FLASH'S SPEED!
BUT HOW CAN I--?
WE'VE BEEN OVER THIS. HE RUNS BY CHANNELING AN EXTRADIMENSIONAL ENERGY--ONE YOU CAN DISRUPT.

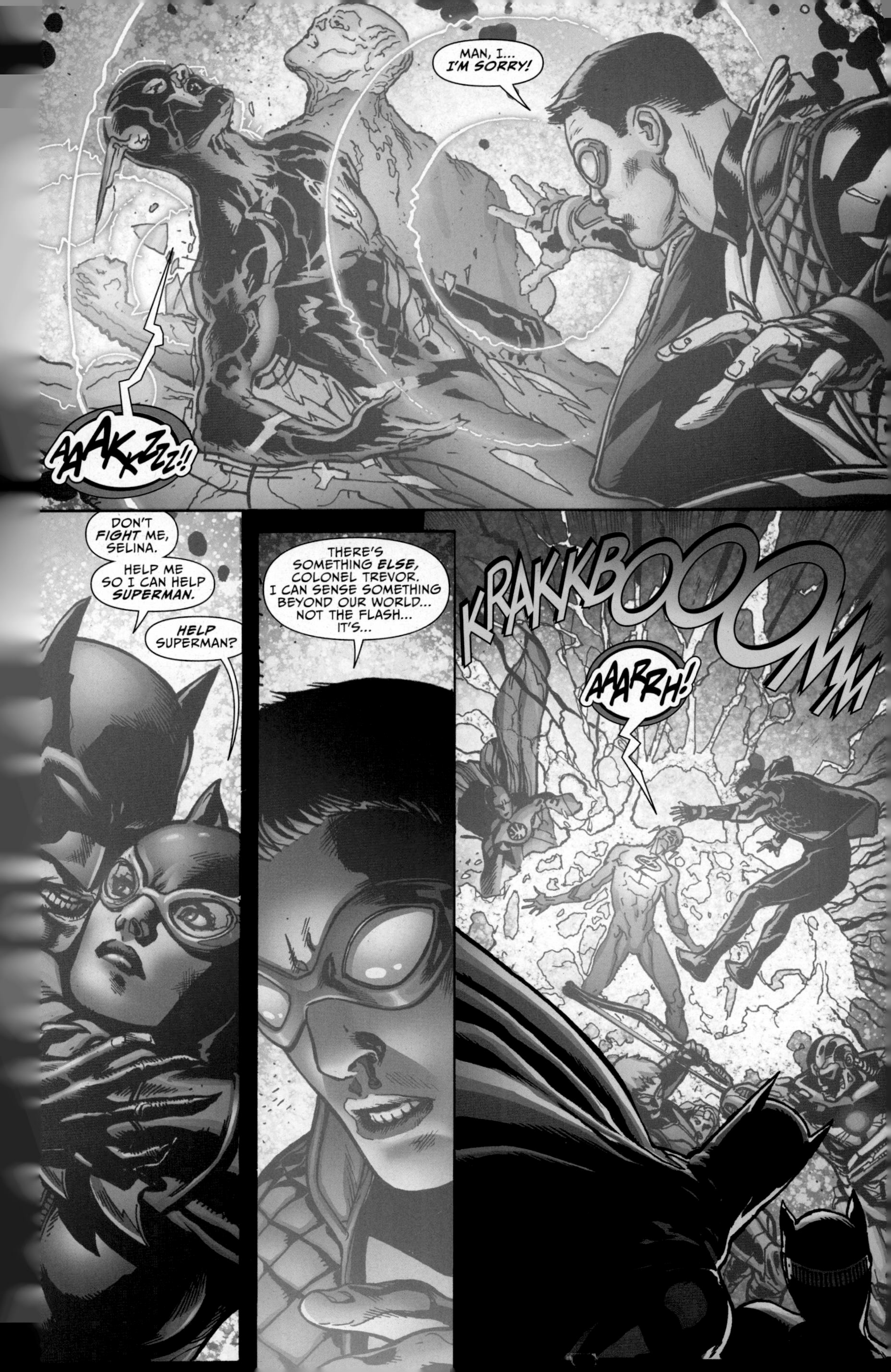

MAN, I... I'M SORRY!
AAAKXZZZZ!!
DON'T FIGHT ME, SELINA.
HELP ME SO I CAN HELP SUPERMAN.
HELP SUPERMAN?
THERE'S SOMETHING ELSE, COLONEL TREVOR. I CAN SENSE SOMETHING BEYOND OUR WORLD... NOT THE FLASH... IT'S...
KRAKKBOOOOM
AAARRH!

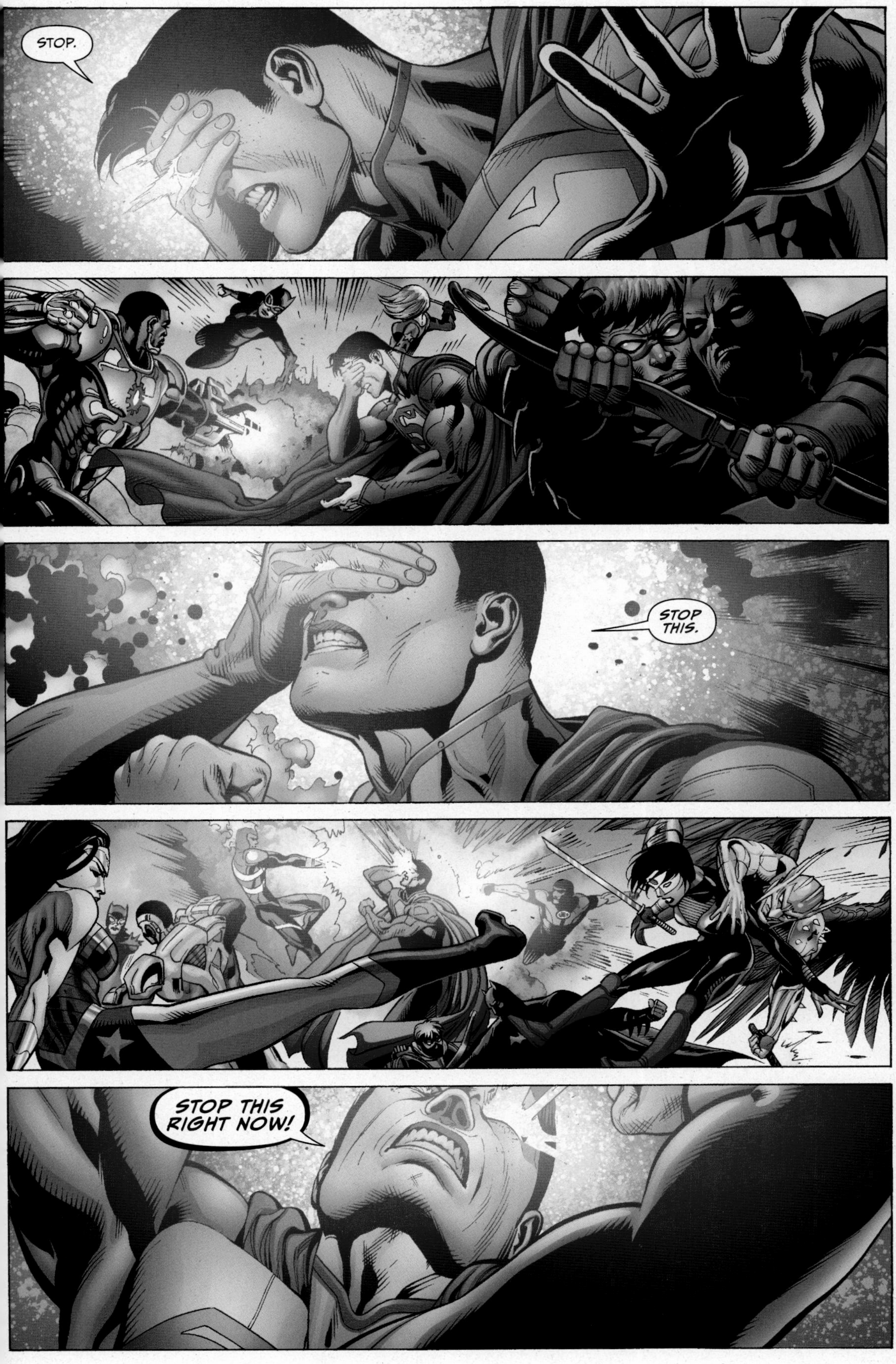
STOP.
STOP THIS.
STOP THIS RIGHT NOW!

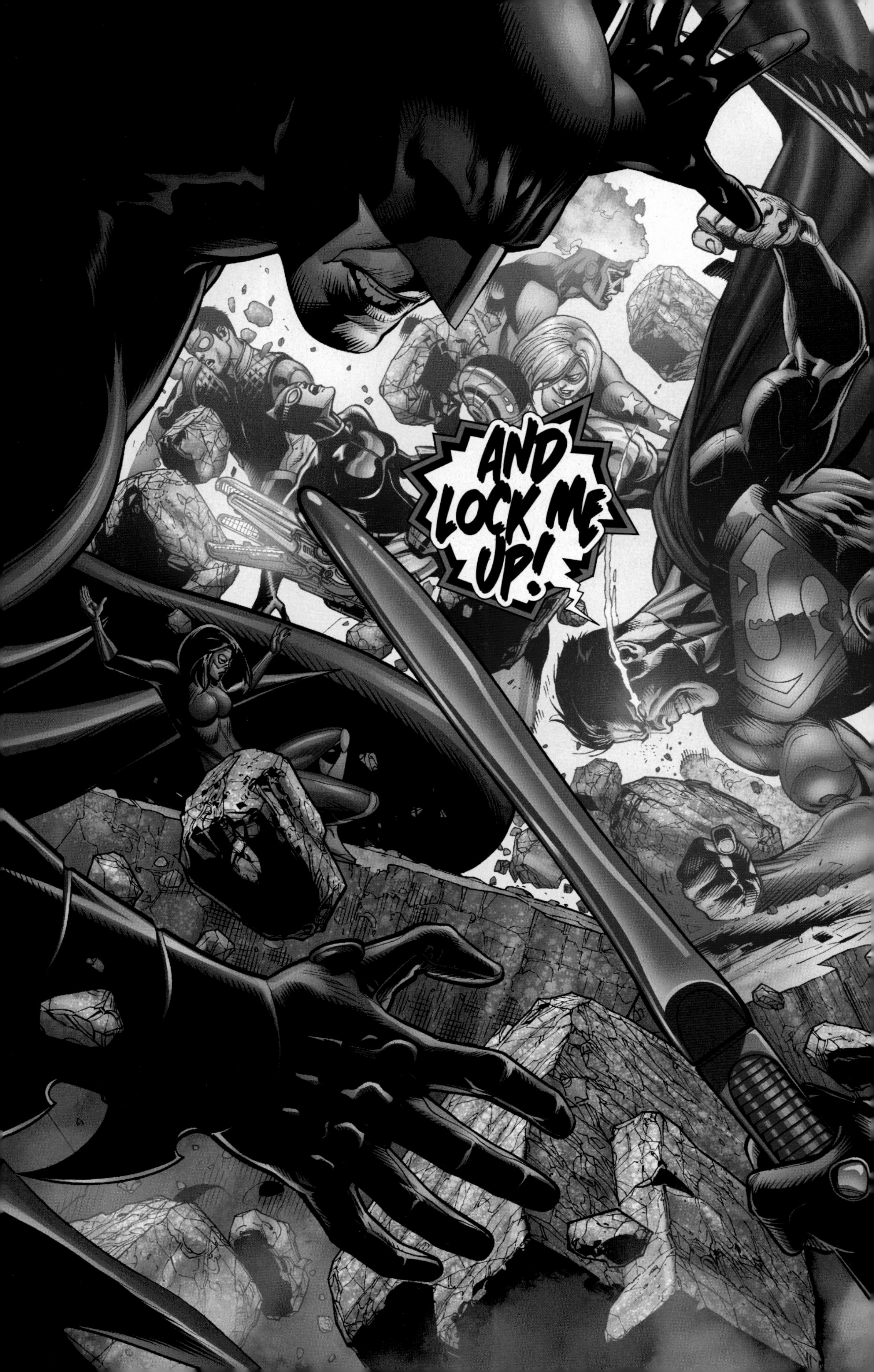
AND LOCK ME UP!

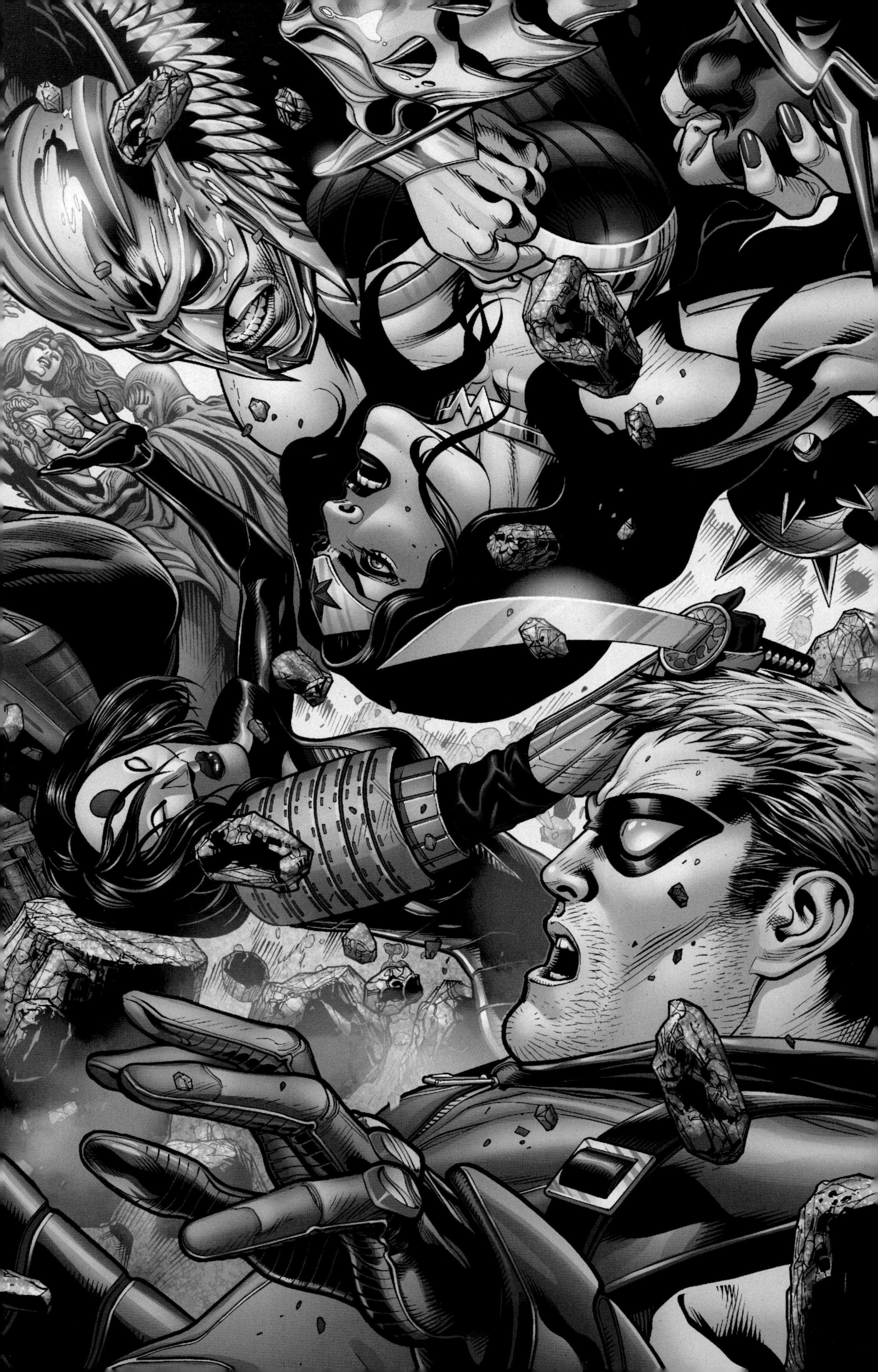

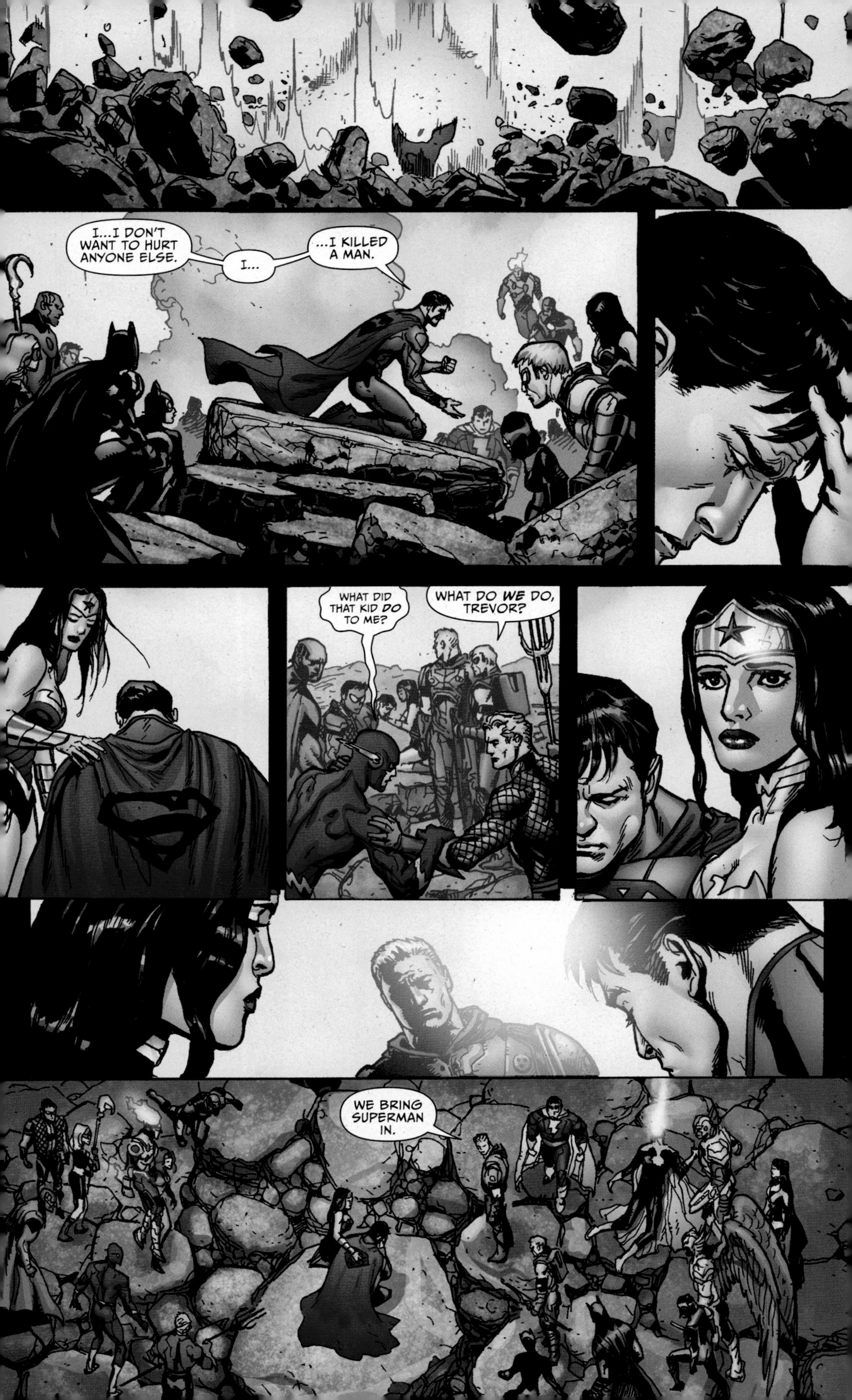
I...I DON'T WANT TO HURT ANYONE ELSE.
I...
...I KILLED A MAN.
WHAT DID THAT KID DO TO ME?
WHAT DO WE DO, TREVOR?
WE BRING SUPERMAN IN.

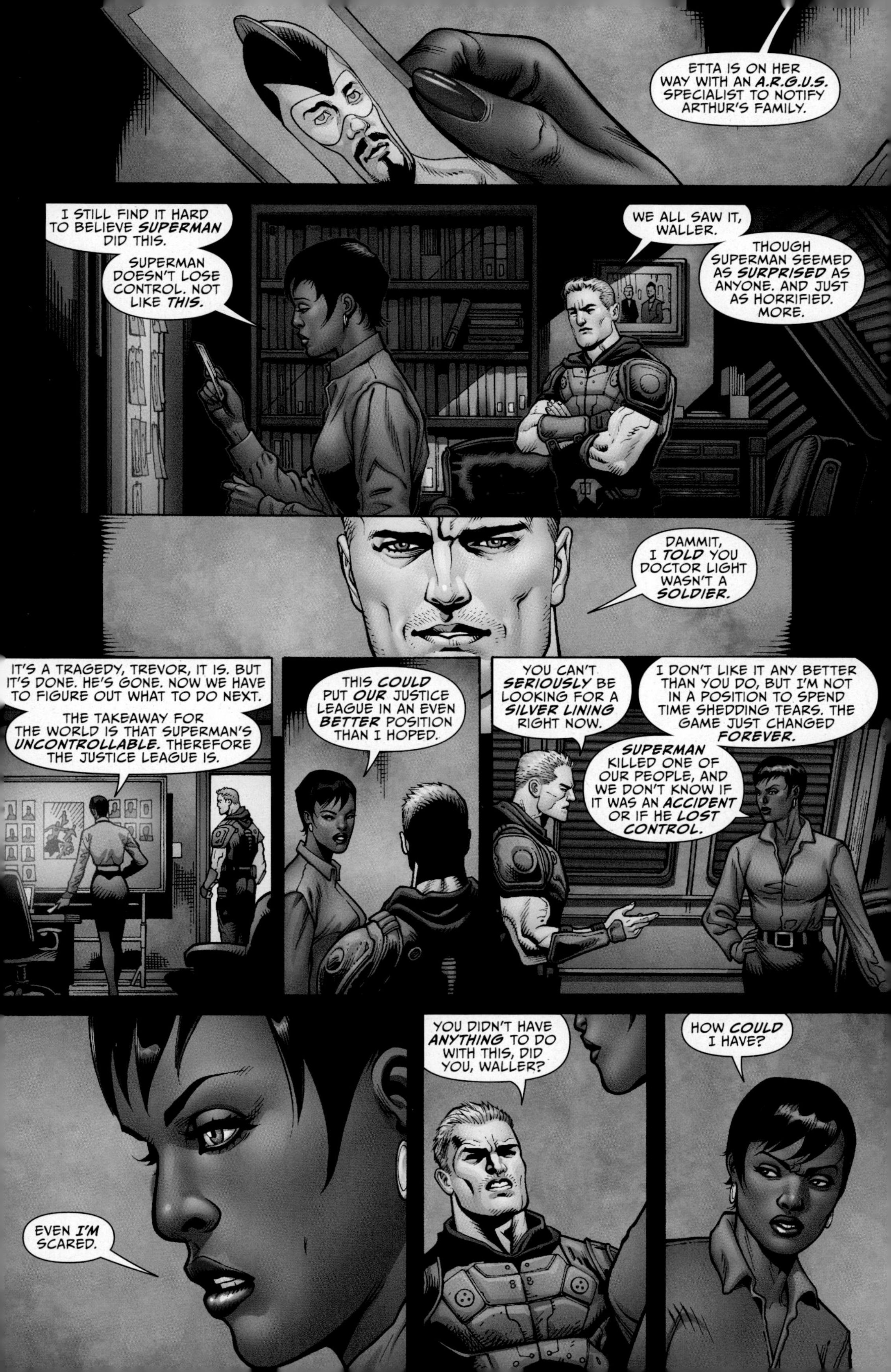
ETTA IS ON HER WAY WITH AN A.R.G.U.S. SPECIALIST TO NOTIFY ARTHUR'S FAMILY.
I STILL FIND IT HARD TO BELIEVE SUPERMAN DID THIS.
SUPERMAN DOESN'T LOSE CONTROL. NOT LIKE THIS.
WE ALL SAW IT, WALLER.
THOUGH SUPERMAN SEEMED AS SURPRISED AS ANYONE. AND JUST AS HORRIFIED. MORE.
DAMMIT, I TOLD YOU DOCTOR LIGHT WASN'T A SOLDIER.
IT'S A TRAGEDY, TREVOR, IT IS. BUT IT'S DONE. HE'S GONE. NOW WE HAVE TO FIGURE OUT WHAT TO DO NEXT.
THE TAKEAWAY FOR THE WORLD IS THAT SUPERMAN'S UNCONTROLLABLE. THEREFORE THE JUSTICE LEAGUE IS.
THIS COULD PUT OUR JUSTICE LEAGUE IN AN EVEN BETTER POSITION THAN I HOPED.
YOU CAN'T SERIOUSLY BE LOOKING FOR A SILVER LINING RIGHT NOW.
I DON'T LIKE IT ANY BETTER THAN YOU DO, BUT I'M NOT IN A POSITION TO SPEND TIME SHEDDING TEARS. THE GAME JUST CHANGED FOREVER.
SUPERMAN KILLED ONE OF OUR PEOPLE, AND WE DON'T KNOW IF IT WAS AN ACCIDENT OR IF HE LOST CONTROL.
EVEN I'M SCARED.
YOU DIDN'T HAVE ANYTHING TO DO WITH THIS, DID YOU, WALLER?
HOW COULD I HAVE?

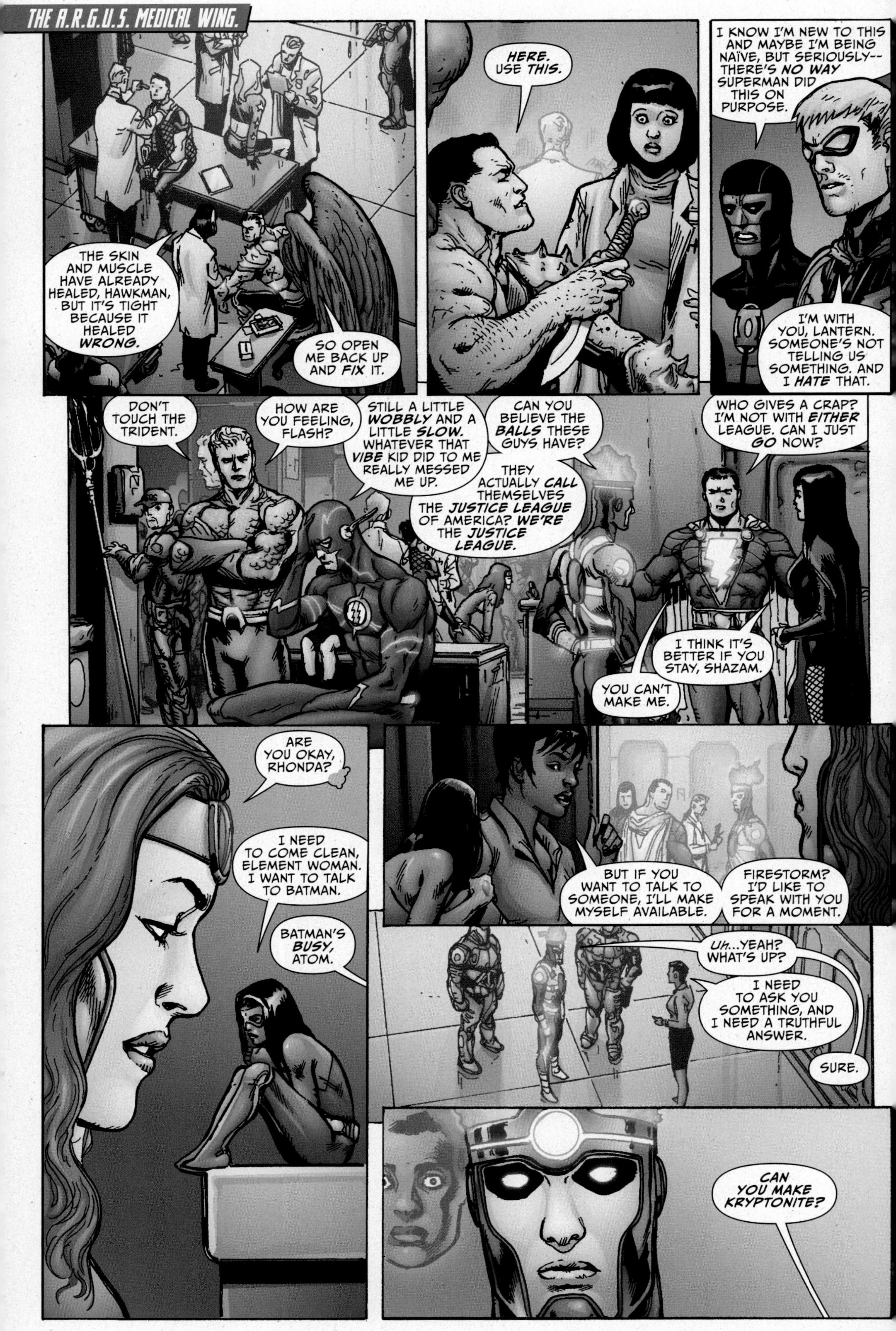
THE A.R.G.U.S. MEDICAL WING.
THE SKIN AND MUSCLE HAVE ALREADY HEALED, HAWKMAN, BUT IT'S TIGHT BECAUSE IT HEALED WRONG.
SO OPEN ME BACK UP AND FIX IT.
HERE. USE THIS.
I KNOW I'M NEW TO THIS AND MAYBE I'M BEING NAÏVE, BUT SERIOUSLY-- THERE'S NO WAY SUPERMAN DID THIS ON PURPOSE.
I'M WITH YOU, LANTERN. SOMEONE'S NOT TELLING US SOMETHING. AND I HATE THAT.
DON'T TOUCH THE TRIDENT.
HOW ARE YOU FEELING, FLASH?
STILL A LITTLE WOBBLY AND A LITTLE SLOW. WHATEVER THAT VIBE KID DID TO ME REALLY MESSED ME UP.
CAN YOU BELIEVE THE BALLS THESE GUYS HAVE?
THEY ACTUALLY CALL THEMSELVES THE JUSTICE LEAGUE OF AMERICA? WE'RE THE JUSTICE LEAGUE.
WHO GIVES A CRAP? I'M NOT WITH EITHER LEAGUE. CAN I JUST GO NOW?
I THINK IT'S BETTER IF YOU STAY, SHAZAM.
YOU CAN'T MAKE ME.
ARE YOU OKAY, RHONDA?
I NEED TO COME CLEAN, ELEMENT WOMAN. I WANT TO TALK TO BATMAN.
BATMAN'S BUSY, ATOM.
BUT IF YOU WANT TO TALK TO SOMEONE, I'LL MAKE MYSELF AVAILABLE.
FIRESTORM? I'D LIKE TO SPEAK WITH YOU FOR A MOMENT.
Uh...YEAH? WHAT'S UP?
I NEED TO ASK YOU SOMETHING, AND I NEED A TRUTHFUL ANSWER.
SURE.
CAN YOU MAKE KRYPTONITE?

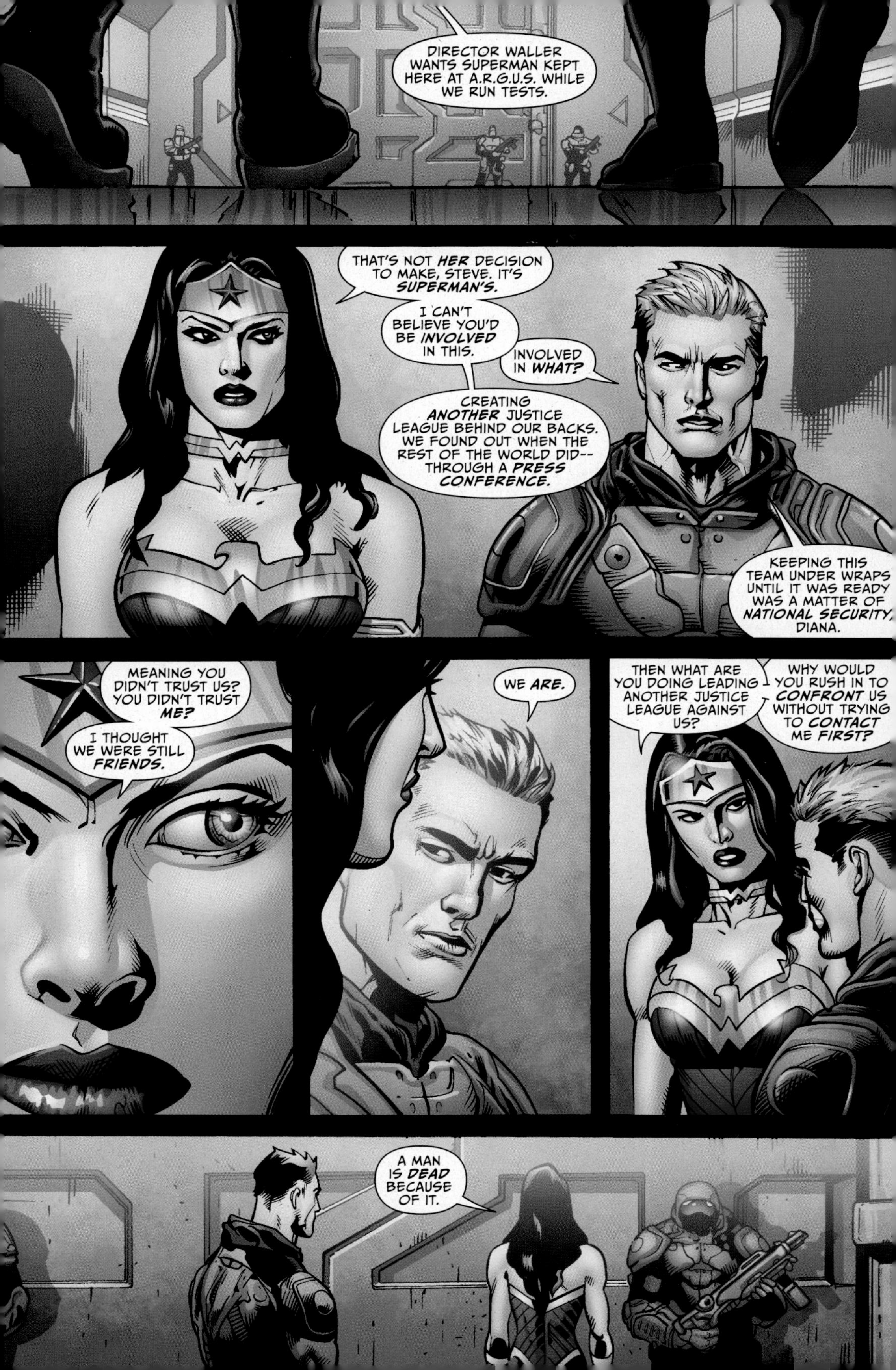
DIRECTOR WALLER WANTS SUPERMAN KEPT HERE AT A.R.G.U.S. WHILE WE RUN TESTS.
THAT'S NOT HER DECISION TO MAKE, STEVE. IT'S SUPERMAN'S.
I CAN'T BELIEVE YOU'D BE INVOLVED IN THIS.
INVOLVED IN WHAT?
CREATING ANOTHER JUSTICE LEAGUE BEHIND OUR BACKS. WE FOUND OUT WHEN THE REST OF THE WORLD DID-- THROUGH A PRESS CONFERENCE.
KEEPING THIS TEAM UNDER WRAPS UNTIL IT WAS READY WAS A MATTER OF NATIONAL SECURITY, DIANA.
MEANING YOU DIDN'T TRUST US? YOU DIDN'T TRUST ME?
I THOUGHT WE WERE STILL FRIENDS.
WE ARE.
THEN WHAT ARE YOU DOING LEADING ANOTHER JUSTICE LEAGUE AGAINST US?
WHY WOULD YOU RUSH IN TO CONFRONT US WITHOUT TRYING TO CONTACT ME FIRST?
A MAN IS DEAD BECAUSE OF IT.

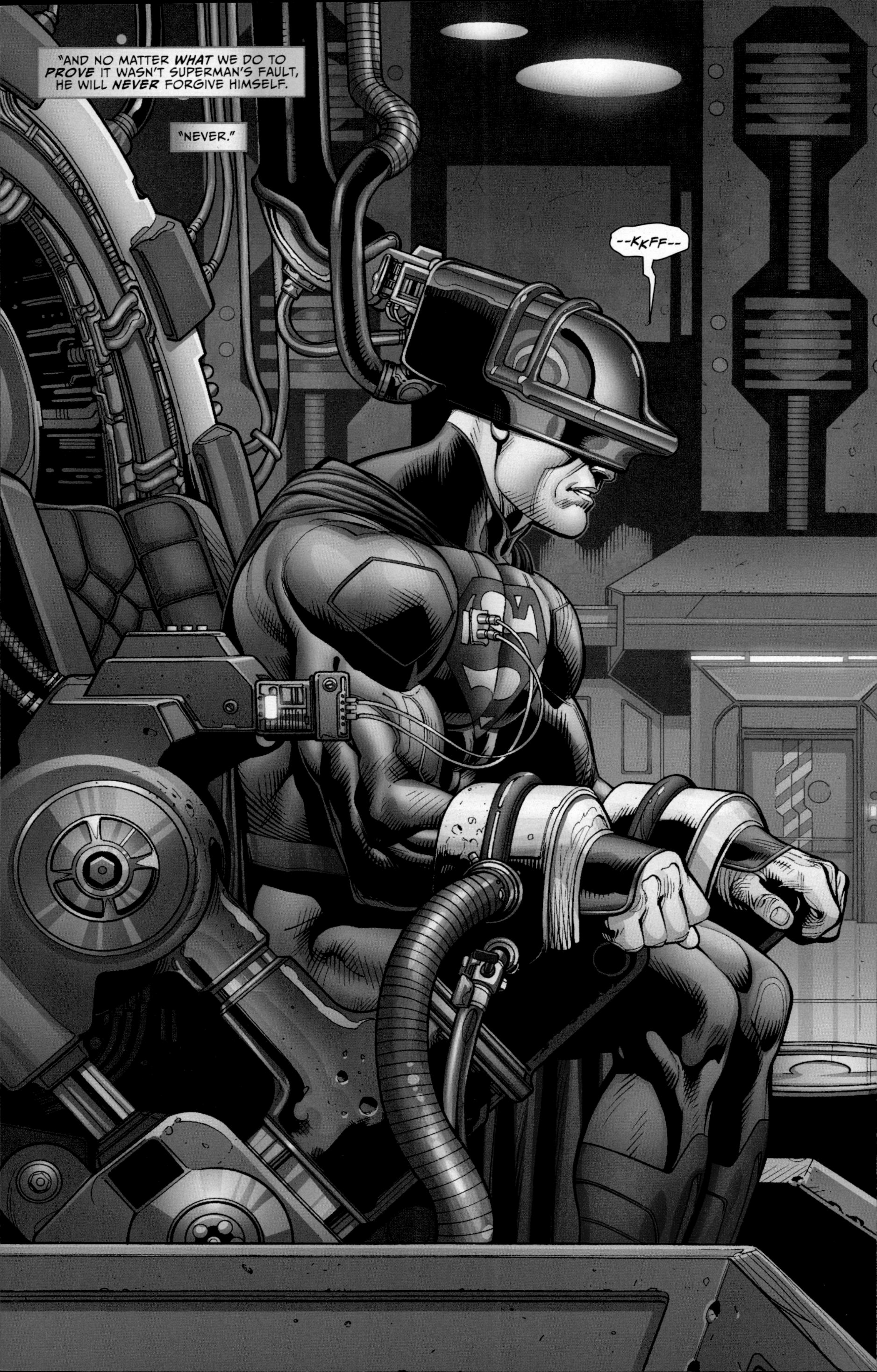
"AND NO MATTER WHAT WE DO TO PROVE IT WASN'T SUPERMAN'S FAULT, HE WILL NEVER FORGIVE HIMSELF.
"NEVER."
--KKFF--

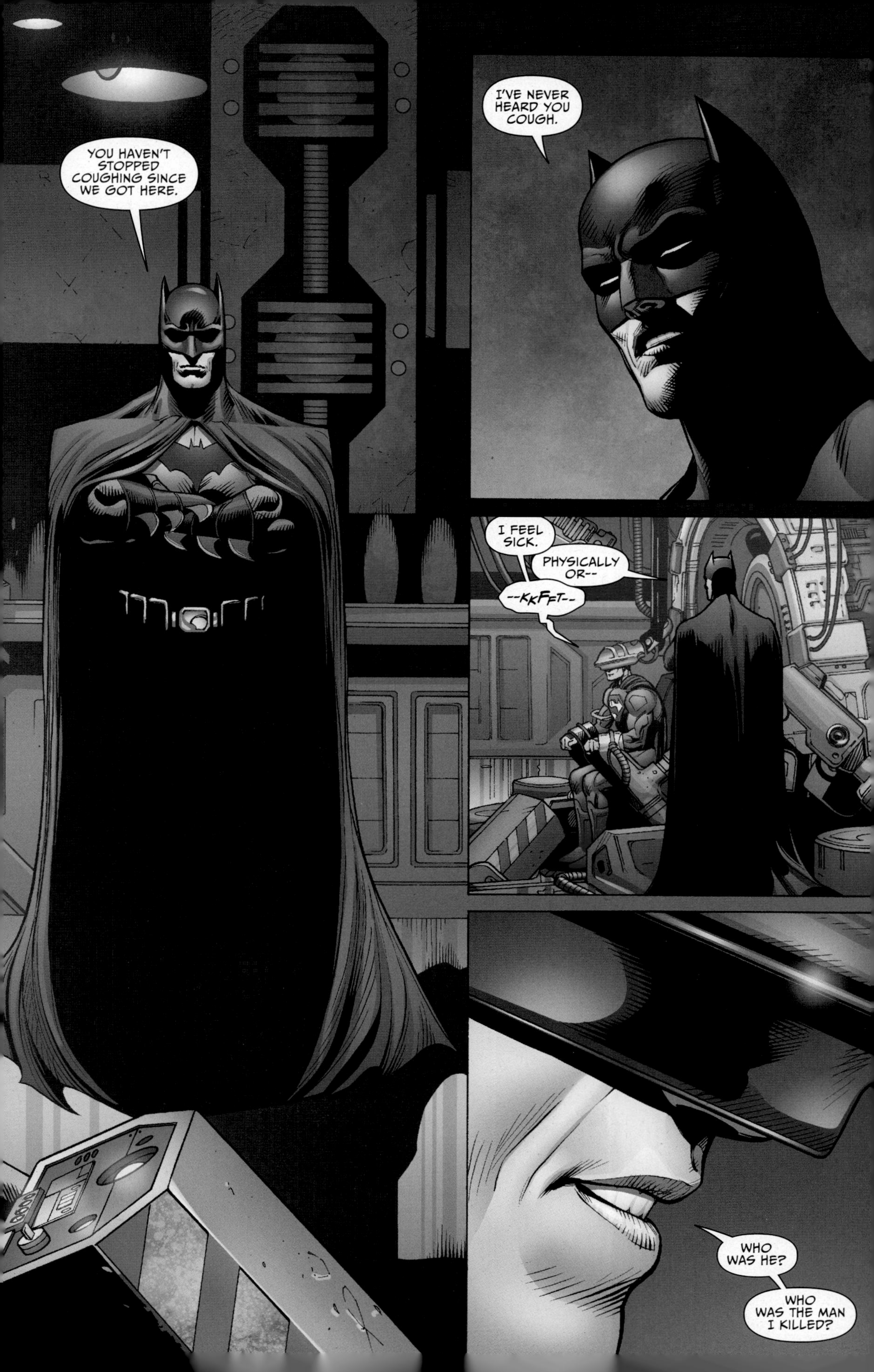
YOU HAVEN'T STOPPED COUGHING SINCE WE GOT HERE.
I'VE NEVER HEARD YOU COUGH.
I FEEL SICK.
PHYSICALLY OR--
--KKFFT--
WHO WAS HE?
WHO WAS THE MAN I KILLED?

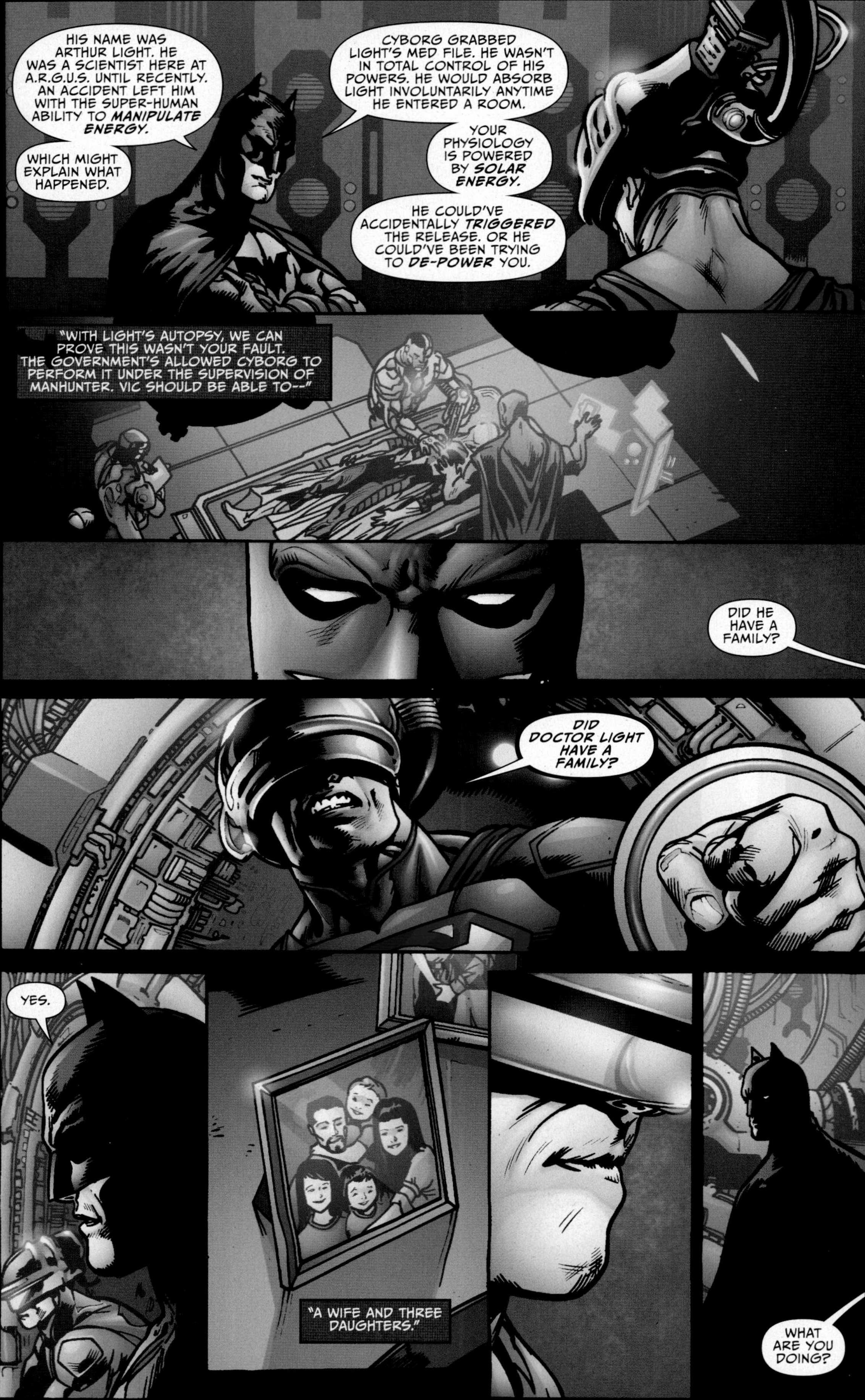
HIS NAME WAS ARTHUR LIGHT. HE WAS A SCIENTIST HERE AT A.R.G.U.S. UNTIL RECENTLY. AN ACCIDENT LEFT HIM WITH THE SUPER-HUMAN ABILITY TO MANIPULATE ENERGY.
WHICH MIGHT EXPLAIN WHAT HAPPENED.
CYBORG GRABBED LIGHT'S MED FILE. HE WASN'T IN TOTAL CONTROL OF HIS POWERS. HE WOULD ABSORB LIGHT INVOLUNTARILY ANYTIME HE ENTERED A ROOM.
YOUR PHYSIOLOGY IS POWERED BY SOLAR ENERGY.
HE COULD'VE ACCIDENTALLY TRIGGERED THE RELEASE. OR HE COULD'VE BEEN TRYING TO DE-POWER YOU.
"WITH LIGHT'S AUTOPSY, WE CAN PROVE THIS WASN'T YOUR FAULT. THE GOVERNMENT'S ALLOWED CYBORG TO PERFORM IT UNDER THE SUPERVISION OF MANHUNTER. VIC SHOULD BE ABLE TO--"
DID HE HAVE A FAMILY?
DID DOCTOR LIGHT HAVE A FAMILY?
YES.
"A WIFE AND THREE DAUGHTERS."
WHAT ARE YOU DOING?

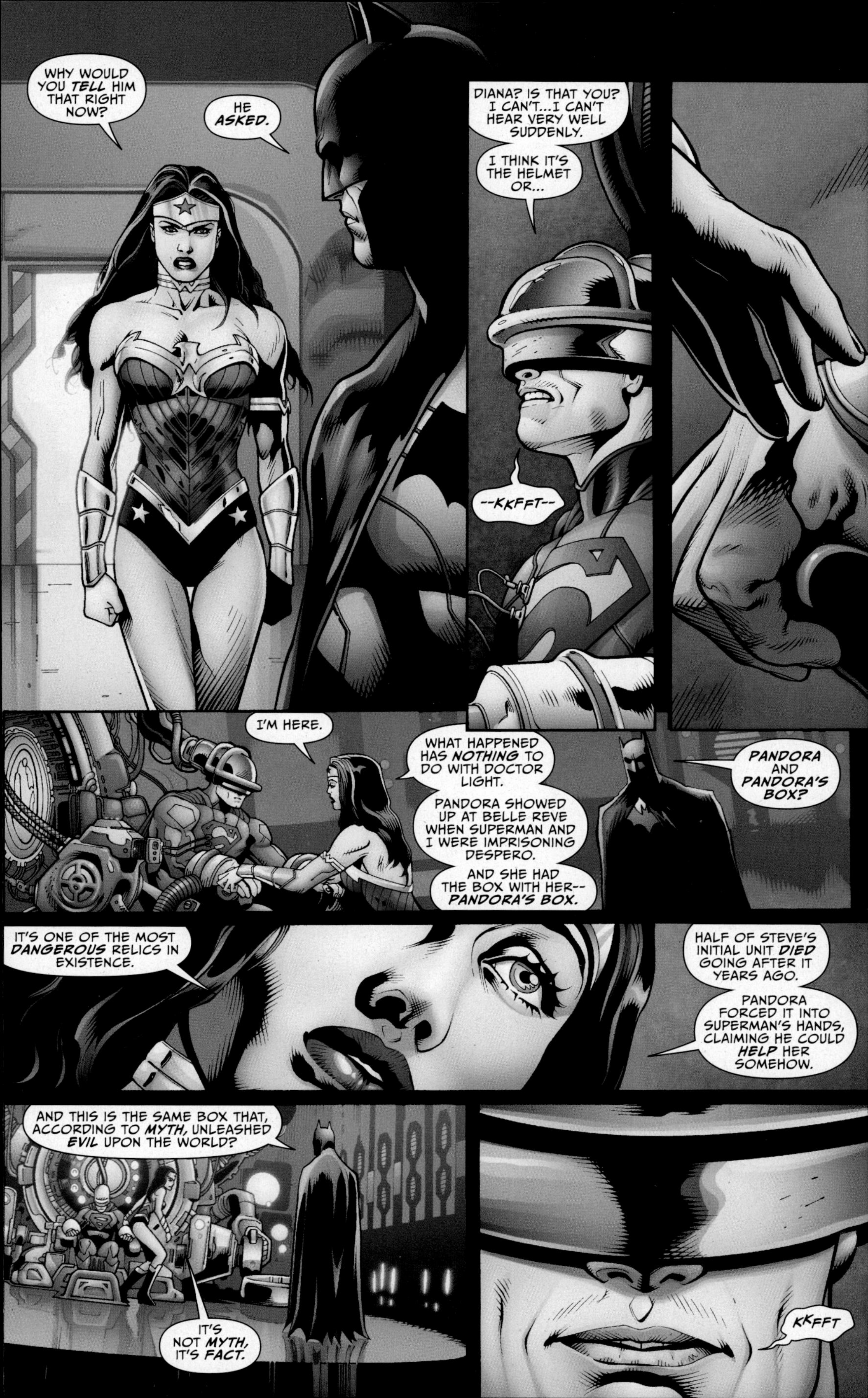
WHY WOULD YOU TELL HIM THAT RIGHT NOW?
HE ASKED.
DIANA? IS THAT YOU? I CAN'T...I CAN'T HEAR VERY WELL SUDDENLY.
I THINK IT'S THE HELMET OR...
--KKFFT--
I'M HERE.
WHAT HAPPENED HAS NOTHING TO DO WITH DOCTOR LIGHT.
PANDORA SHOWED UP AT BELLE REVE WHEN SUPERMAN AND I WERE IMPRISONING DESPERO.
AND SHE HAD THE BOX WITH HER-- PANDORA'S BOX.
PANDORA AND PANDORA'S BOX?
IT'S ONE OF THE MOST DANGEROUS RELICS IN EXISTENCE.
HALF OF STEVE'S INITIAL UNIT DIED GOING AFTER IT YEARS AGO.
PANDORA FORCED IT INTO SUPERMAN'S HANDS, CLAIMING HE COULD HELP HER SOMEHOW.
AND THIS IS THE SAME BOX THAT, ACCORDING TO MYTH, UNLEASHED EVIL UPON THE WORLD?
IT'S NOT MYTH, IT'S FACT.
KKFFT

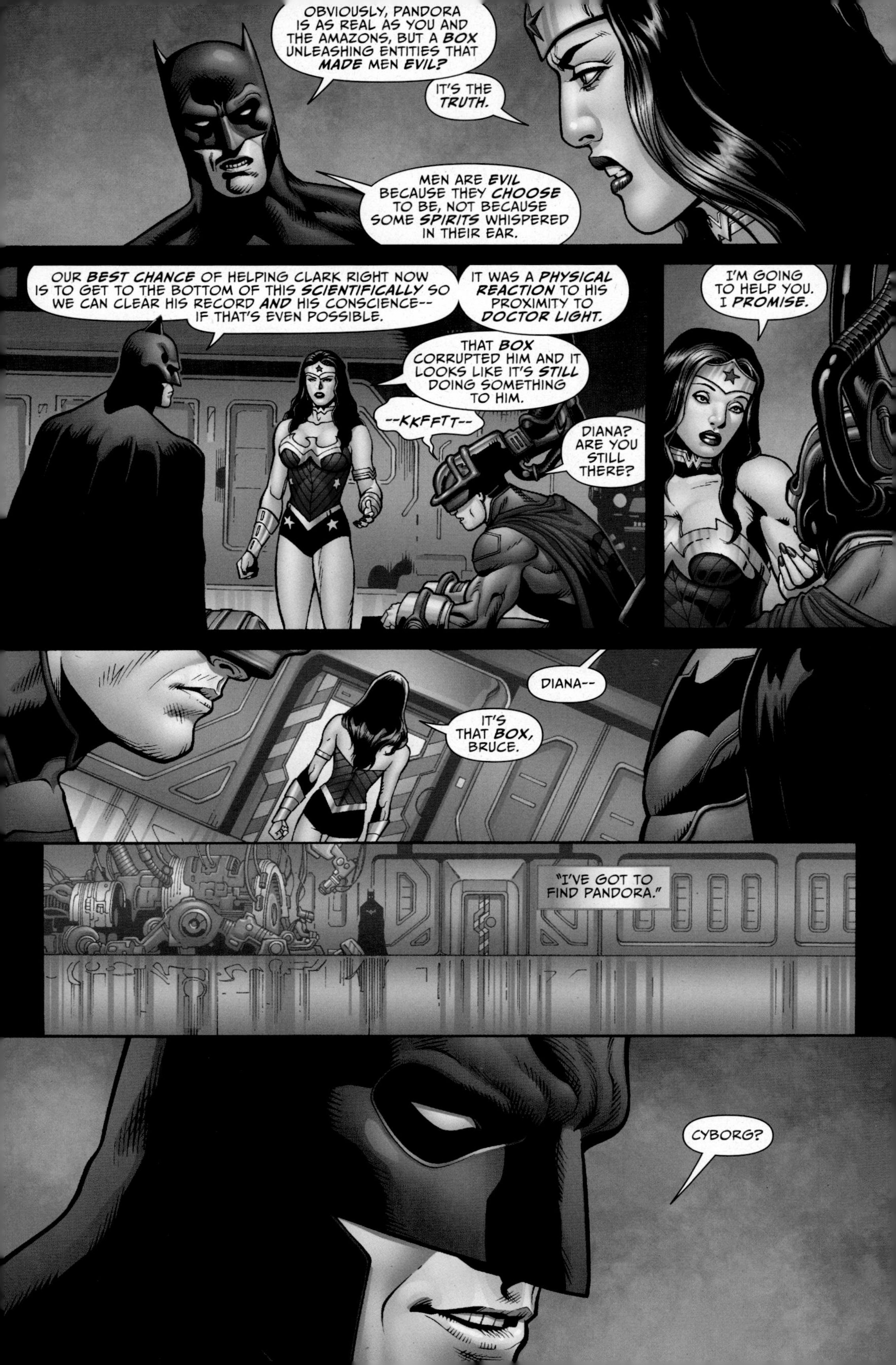
OBVIOUSLY, PANDORA IS AS REAL AS YOU AND THE AMAZONS, BUT A BOX UNLEASHING ENTITIES THAT MADE MEN EVIL?
IT'S THE TRUTH.
MEN ARE EVIL BECAUSE THEY CHOOSE TO BE, NOT BECAUSE SOME SPIRITS WHISPERED IN THEIR EAR.
OUR BEST CHANCE OF HELPING CLARK RIGHT NOW IS TO GET TO THE BOTTOM OF THIS SCIENTIFICALLY SO WE CAN CLEAR HIS RECORD AND HIS CONSCIENCE-- IF THAT'S EVEN POSSIBLE.
IT WAS A PHYSICAL REACTION TO HIS PROXIMITY TO DOCTOR LIGHT.
THAT BOX CORRUPTED HIM AND IT LOOKS LIKE IT'S STILL DOING SOMETHING TO HIM.
--KKFFTT--
DIANA? ARE YOU STILL THERE?
I'M GOING TO HELP YOU. I PROMISE.
DIANA--
IT'S THAT BOX, BRUCE.
"I'VE GOT TO FIND PANDORA."
CYBORG?

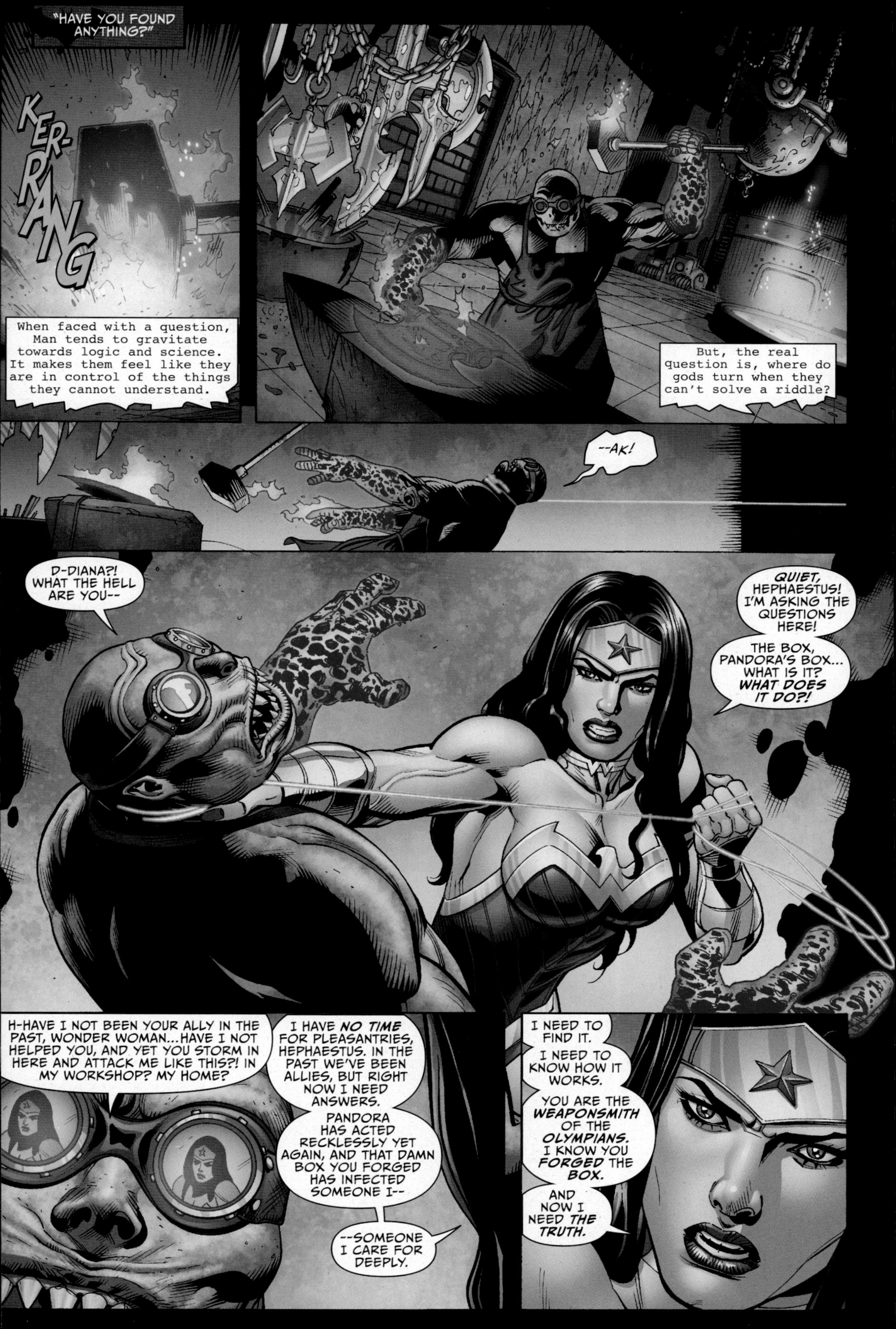
"HAVE YOU FOUND ANYTHING?"
KER-RANG
When faced with a question, Man tends to gravitate towards logic and science. It makes them feel like they are in control of the things they cannot understand.
But, the real question is, where do gods turn when they can't solve a riddle?
--AK!
D-DIANA?! WHAT THE HELL ARE YOU--
QUIET, HEPHAESTUS! I'M ASKING THE QUESTIONS HERE!
THE BOX, PANDORA'S BOX... WHAT IS IT? WHAT DOES IT DO?!
H-HAVE I NOT BEEN YOUR ALLY IN THE PAST, WONDER WOMAN...HAVE I NOT HELPED YOU, AND YET YOU STORM IN HERE AND ATTACK ME LIKE THIS?! IN MY WORKSHOP? MY HOME?
I HAVE NO TIME FOR PLEASANTRIES, HEPHAESTUS. IN THE PAST WE'VE BEEN ALLIES, BUT RIGHT NOW I NEED ANSWERS.
PANDORA HAS ACTED RECKLESSLY YET AGAIN, AND THAT DAMN BOX YOU FORGED HAS INFECTED SOMEONE I--
--SOMEONE I CARE FOR DEEPLY.
I NEED TO FIND IT.
I NEED TO KNOW HOW IT WORKS.
YOU ARE THE WEAPONSMITH OF THE OLYMPIANS. I KNOW YOU FORGED THE BOX.
AND NOW I NEED THE TRUTH.

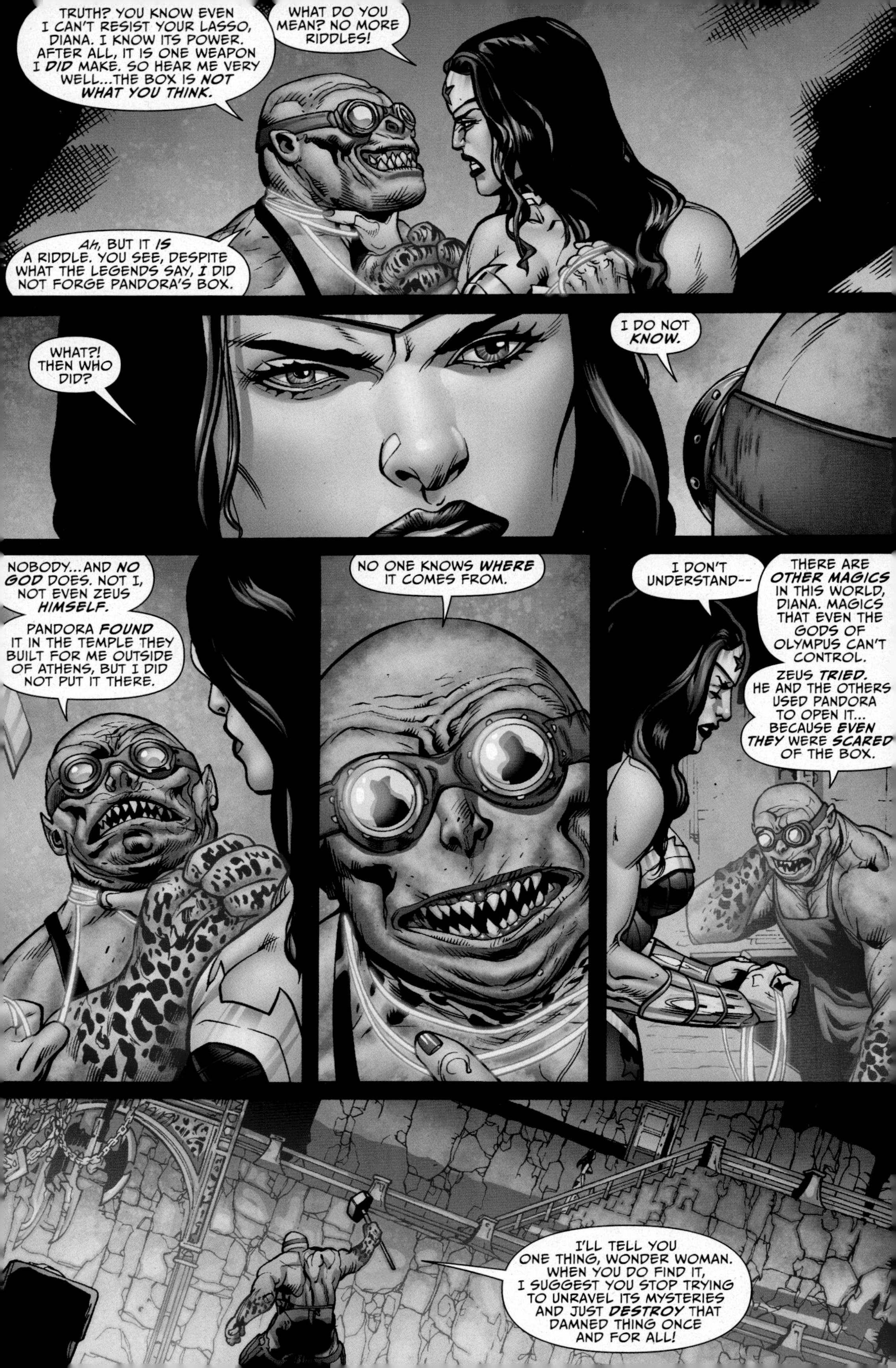
TRUTH? YOU KNOW EVEN I CAN'T RESIST YOUR LASSO, DIANA. I KNOW ITS POWER. AFTER ALL, IT IS ONE WEAPON I *DID* MAKE. SO HEAR ME VERY WELL...THE BOX IS *NOT WHAT YOU THINK.*
WHAT DO YOU MEAN? NO MORE RIDDLES!
Ah, BUT IT *IS* A RIDDLE. YOU SEE, DESPITE WHAT THE LEGENDS SAY, *I* DID NOT FORGE PANDORA'S BOX.
WHAT?! THEN WHO DID?
I DO NOT *KNOW.*
NOBODY...AND *NO GOD* DOES. NOT I, NOT EVEN ZEUS *HIMSELF.*
PANDORA *FOUND* IT IN THE TEMPLE THEY BUILT FOR ME OUTSIDE OF ATHENS, BUT I DID NOT PUT IT THERE.
NO ONE KNOWS *WHERE* IT COMES FROM.
I DON'T UNDERSTAND--
THERE ARE *OTHER MAGICS* IN THIS WORLD, DIANA. MAGICS THAT EVEN THE GODS OF OLYMPUS CAN'T CONTROL.
ZEUS *TRIED.* HE AND THE OTHERS USED PANDORA TO OPEN IT... BECAUSE *EVEN THEY* WERE *SCARED* OF THE BOX.
I'LL TELL YOU ONE THING, WONDER WOMAN. WHEN YOU DO FIND IT, I SUGGEST YOU STOP TRYING TO UNRAVEL ITS MYSTERIES AND JUST *DESTROY* THAT DAMNED THING ONCE AND FOR ALL!

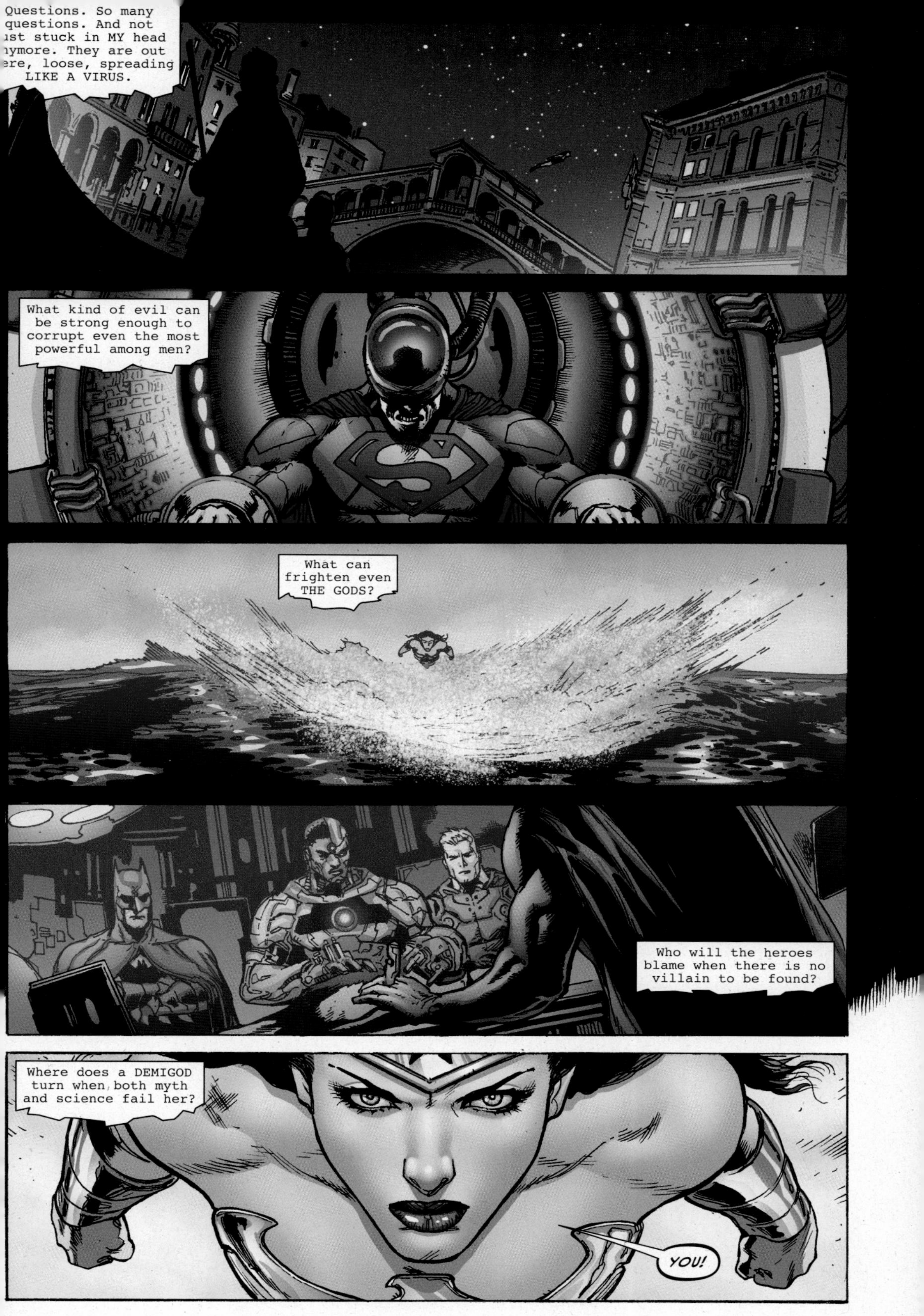

Questions. So many questions. And not ıst stuck in MY head ıymore. They are out ere, loose, spreading LIKE A VIRUS.
What kind of evil can be strong enough to corrupt even the most powerful among men?
What can frighten even THE GODS?
Who will the heroes blame when there is no villain to be found?
Where does a DEMIGOD turn when both myth and science fail her?
YOU!

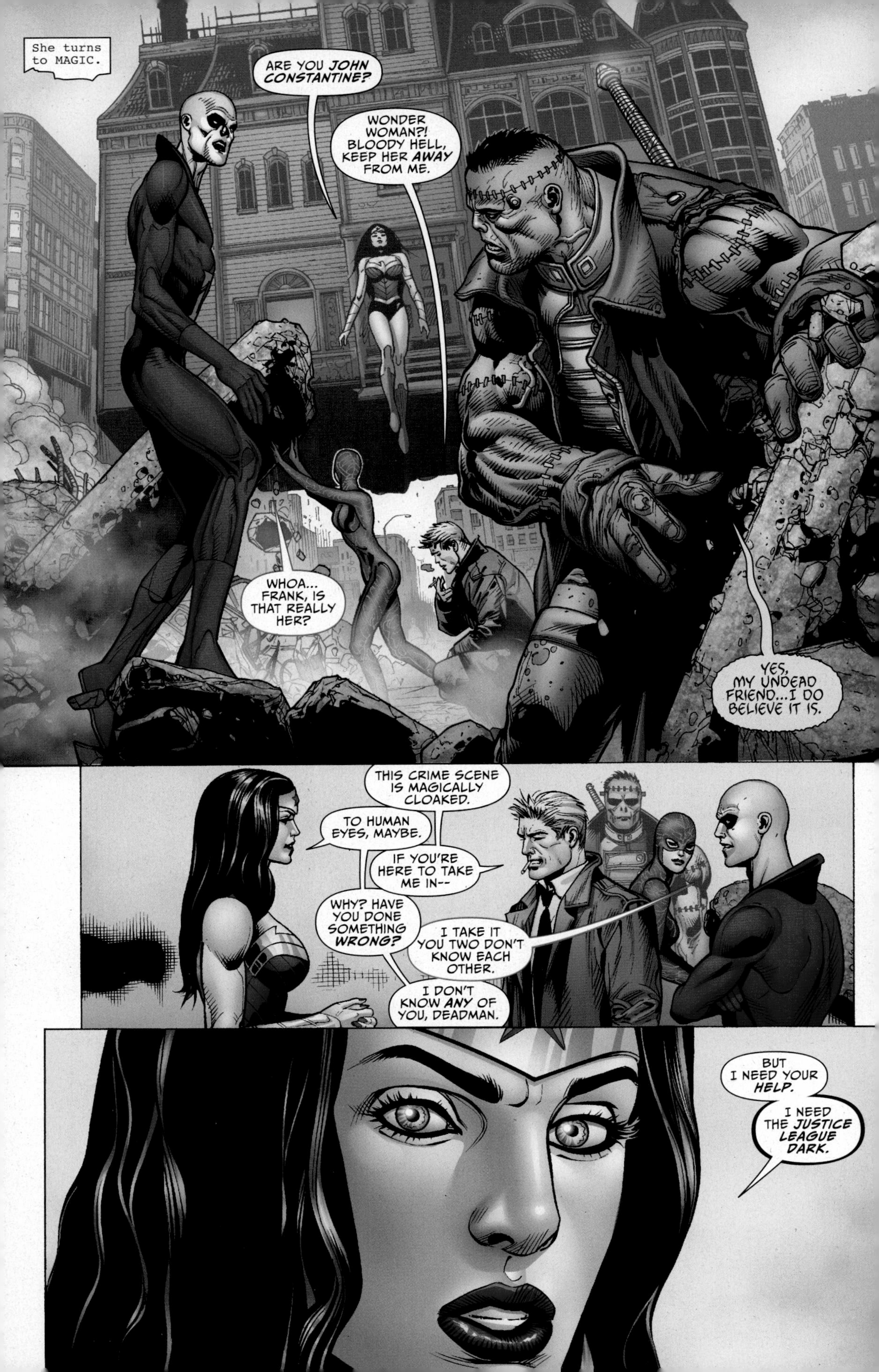
She turns to MAGIC.
ARE YOU JOHN CONSTANTINE?
WONDER WOMAN?! BLOODY HELL, KEEP HER AWAY FROM ME.
WHOA... FRANK, IS THAT REALLY HER?
YES, MY UNDEAD FRIEND...I DO BELIEVE IT IS.
THIS CRIME SCENE IS MAGICALLY CLOAKED.
TO HUMAN EYES, MAYBE.
IF YOU'RE HERE TO TAKE ME IN--
WHY? HAVE YOU DONE SOMETHING WRONG?
I TAKE IT YOU TWO DON'T KNOW EACH OTHER.
I DON'T KNOW ANY OF YOU, DEADMAN.
BUT I NEED YOUR HELP.
I NEED THE JUSTICE LEAGUE DARK.

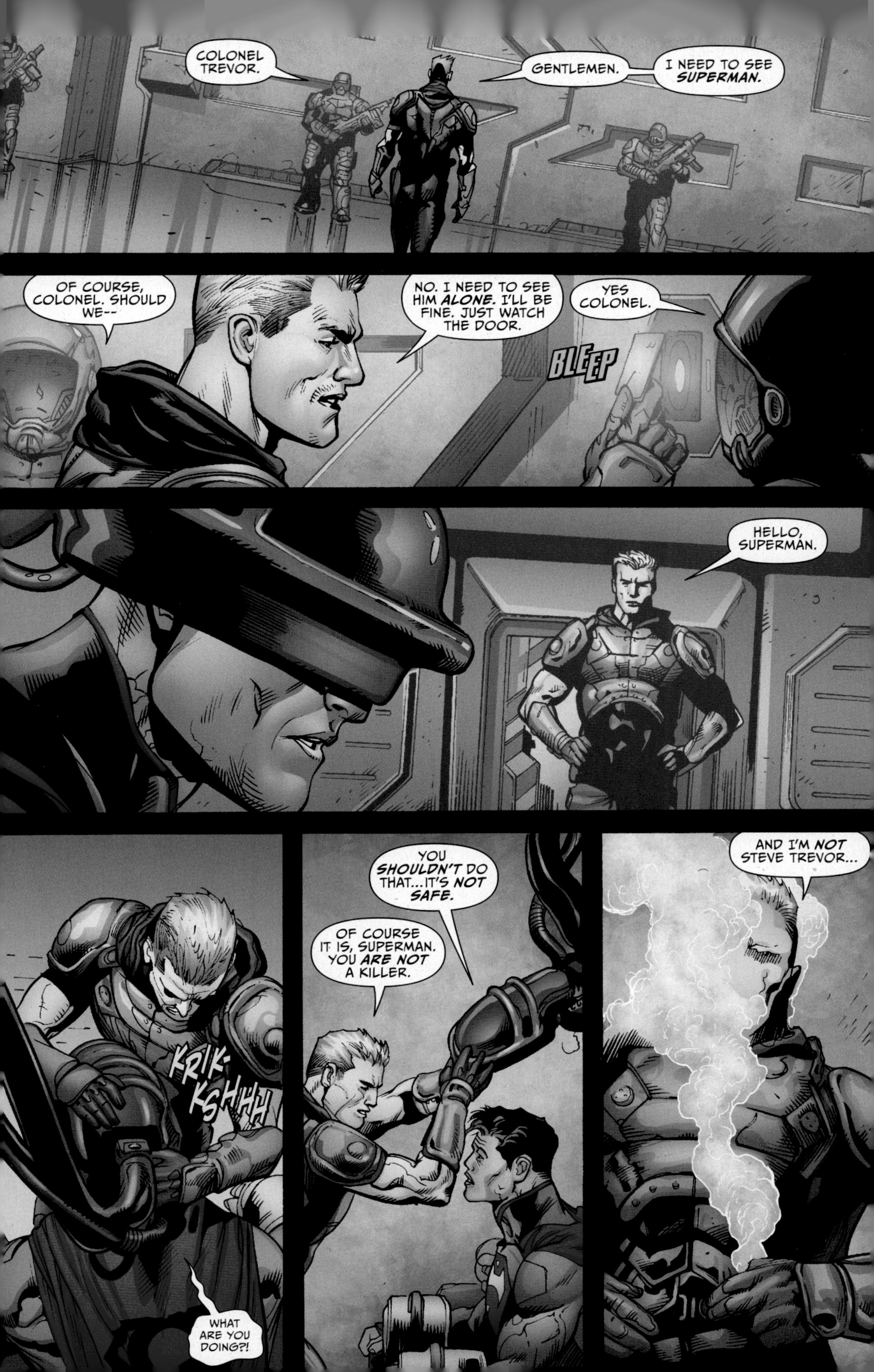
COLONEL TREVOR.
GENTLEMEN.
I NEED TO SEE SUPERMAN.
OF COURSE, COLONEL. SHOULD WE--
NO. I NEED TO SEE HIM ALONE. I'LL BE FINE. JUST WATCH THE DOOR.
YES COLONEL.
BLEEP
HELLO, SUPERMAN.
KRIK-KSHHH
WHAT ARE YOU DOING?!
YOU SHOULDN'T DO THAT...IT'S NOT SAFE.
OF COURSE IT IS, SUPERMAN. YOU ARE NOT A KILLER.
AND I'M NOT STEVE TREVOR...

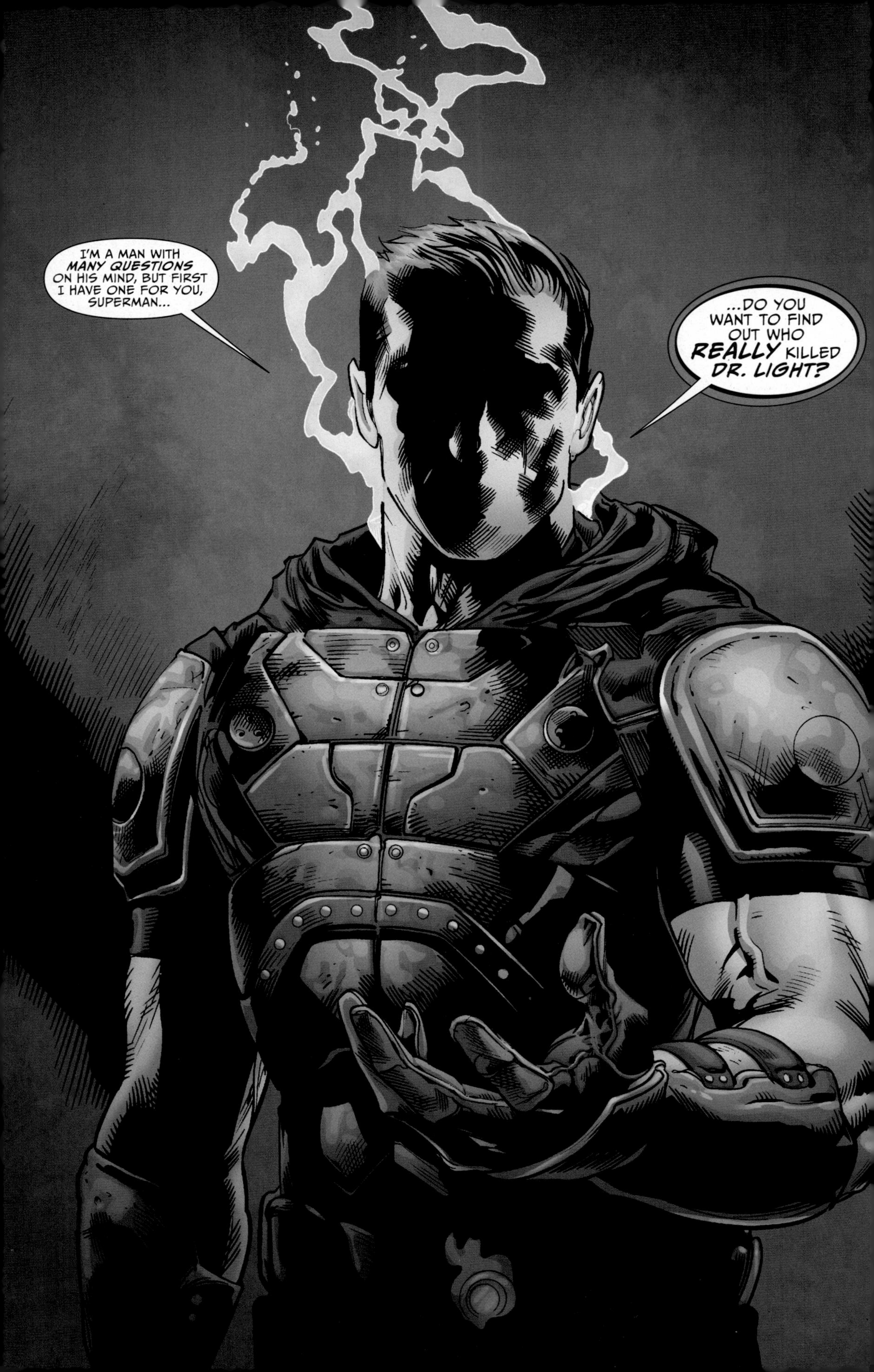
I'M A MAN WITH MANY QUESTIONS ON HIS MIND, BUT FIRST I HAVE ONE FOR YOU, SUPERMAN...
...DO YOU WANT TO FIND OUT WHO REALLY KILLED DR. LIGHT?

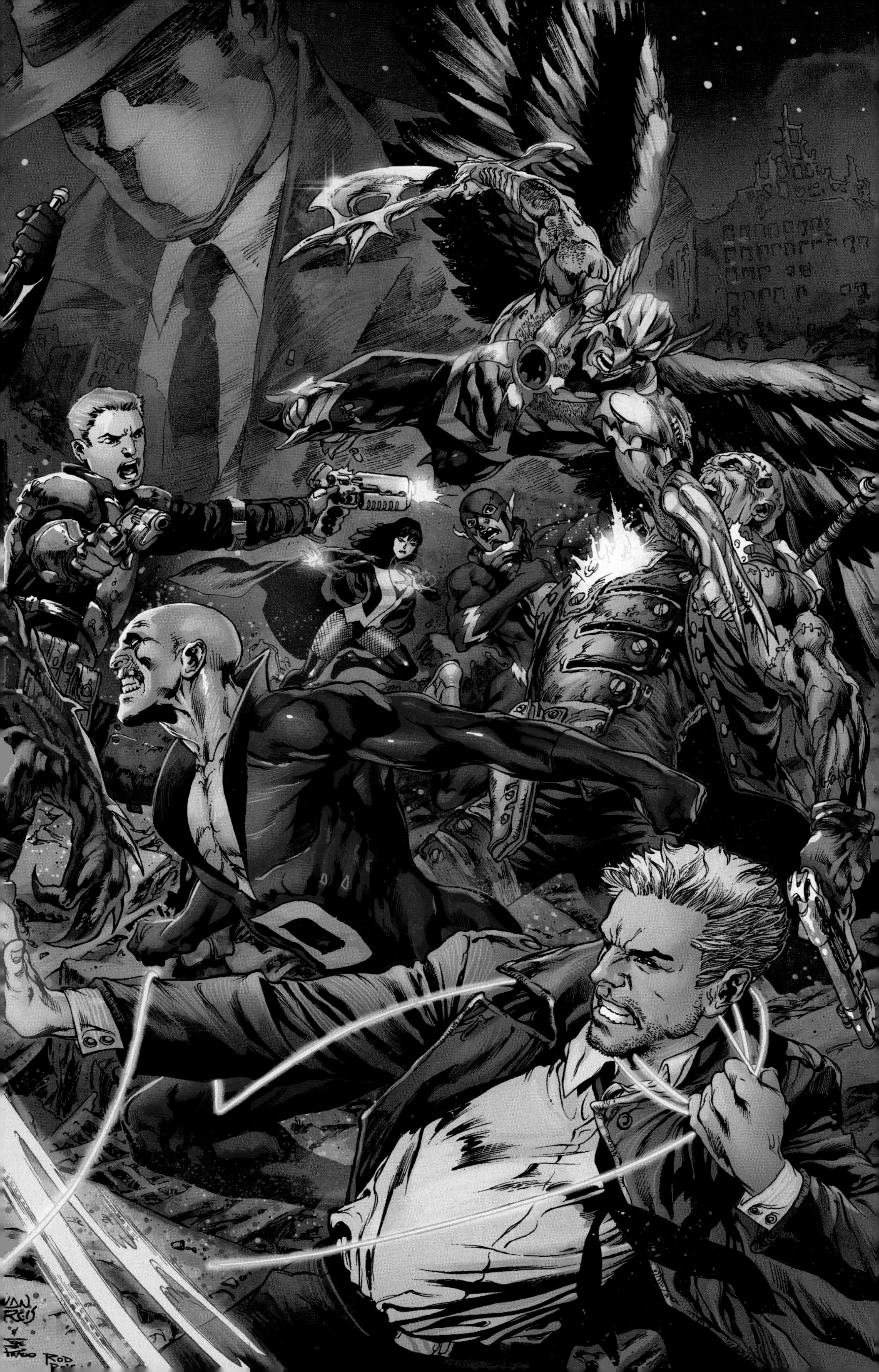

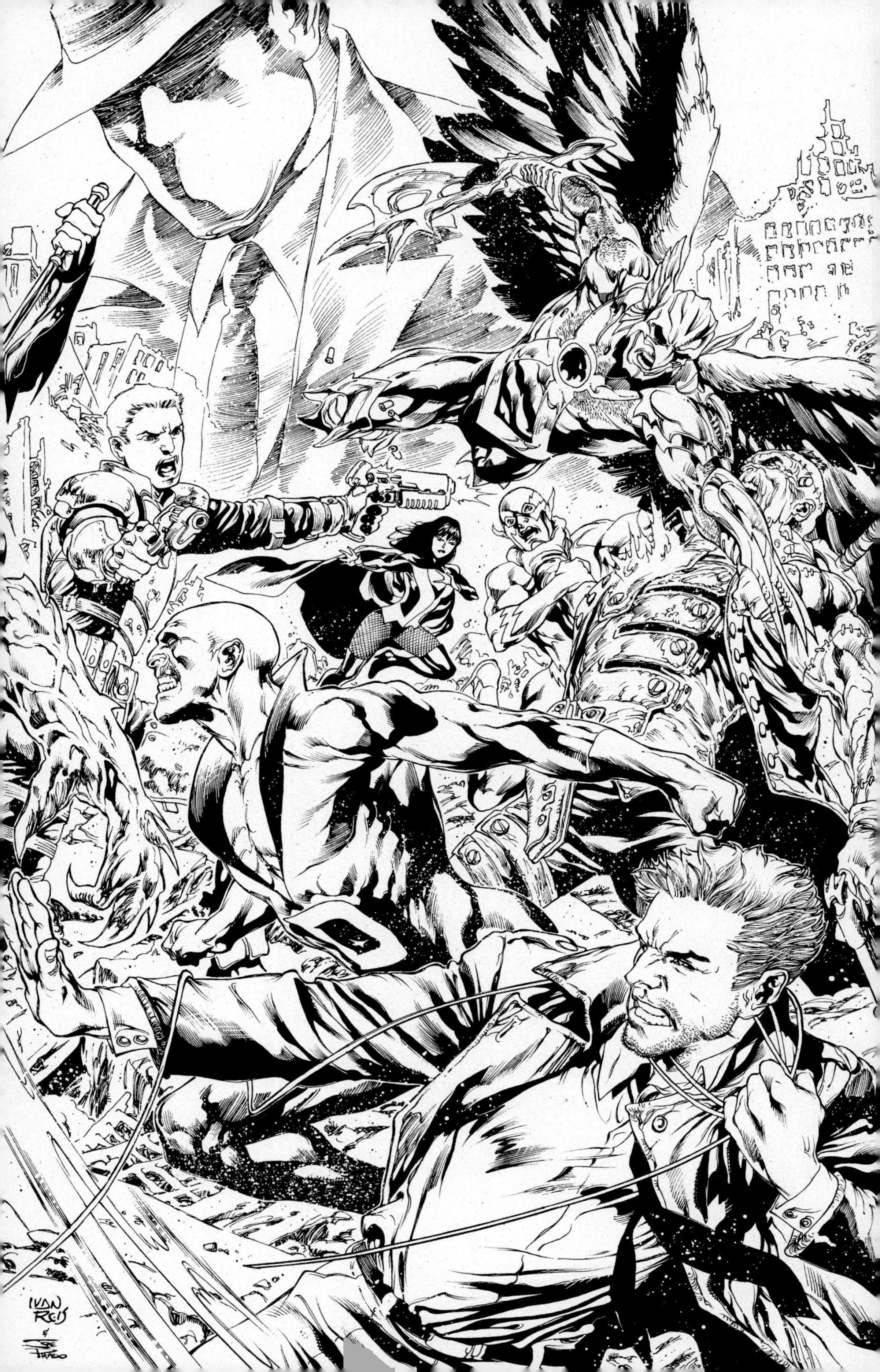
IVAN REIS

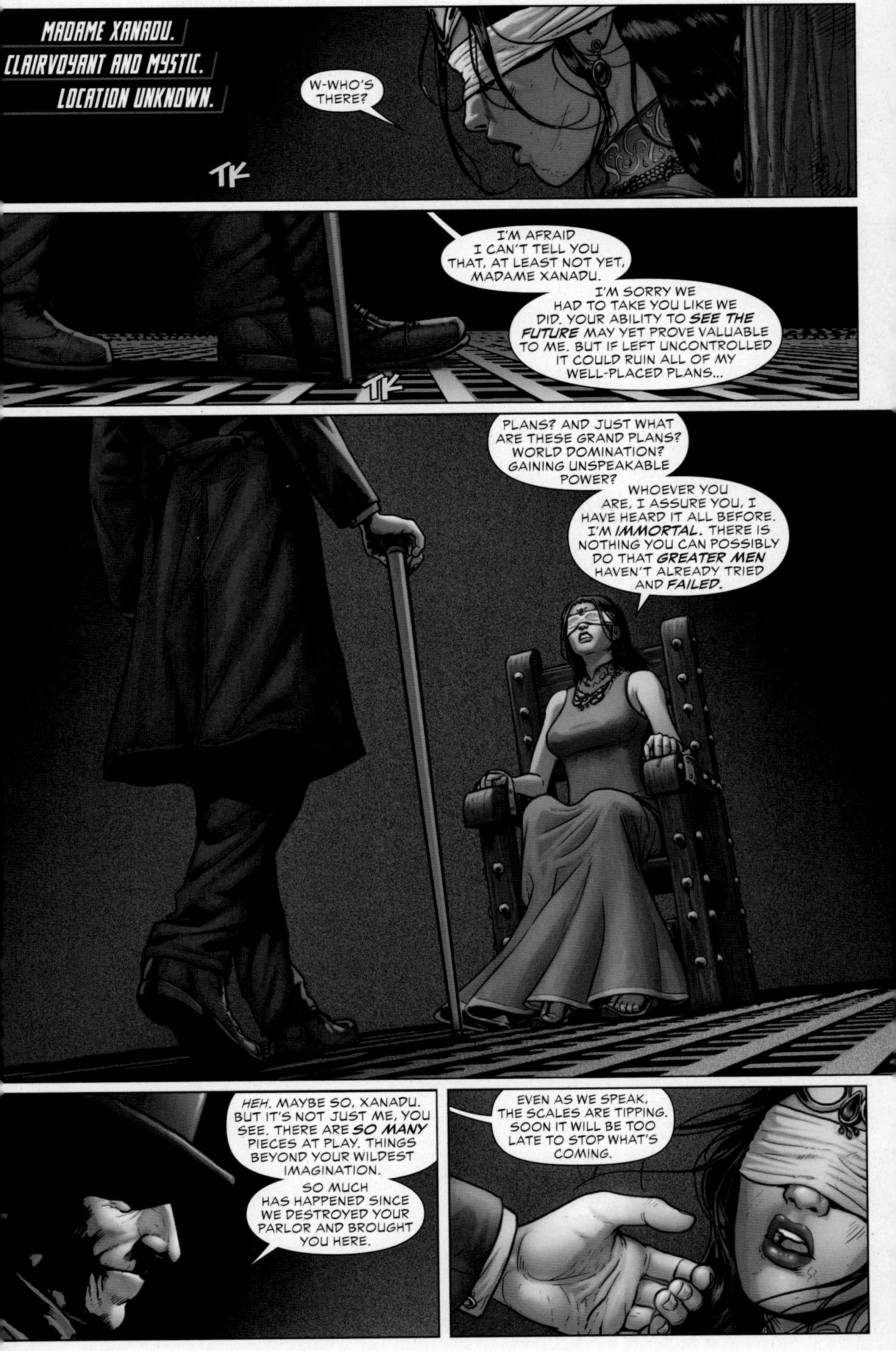
MADAME XANADU.
CLAIRVOYANT AND MYSTIC.
LOCATION UNKNOWN.
W-WHO'S THERE?
TK
I'M AFRAID I CAN'T TELL YOU THAT, AT LEAST NOT YET, MADAME XANADU.
I'M SORRY WE HAD TO TAKE YOU LIKE WE DID. YOUR ABILITY TO SEE THE FUTURE MAY YET PROVE VALUABLE TO ME. BUT IF LEFT UNCONTROLLED IT COULD RUIN ALL OF MY WELL-PLACED PLANS...
TK
PLANS? AND JUST WHAT ARE THESE GRAND PLANS? WORLD DOMINATION? GAINING UNSPEAKABLE POWER?
WHOEVER YOU ARE, I ASSURE YOU, I HAVE HEARD IT ALL BEFORE. I'M IMMORTAL. THERE IS NOTHING YOU CAN POSSIBLY DO THAT GREATER MEN HAVEN'T ALREADY TRIED AND FAILED.
HEH. MAYBE SO, XANADU. BUT IT'S NOT JUST ME, YOU SEE. THERE ARE SO MANY PIECES AT PLAY. THINGS BEYOND YOUR WILDEST IMAGINATION.
SO MUCH HAS HAPPENED SINCE WE DESTROYED YOUR PARLOR AND BROUGHT YOU HERE.
EVEN AS WE SPEAK, THE SCALES ARE TIPPING. SOON IT WILL BE TOO LATE TO STOP WHAT'S COMING.

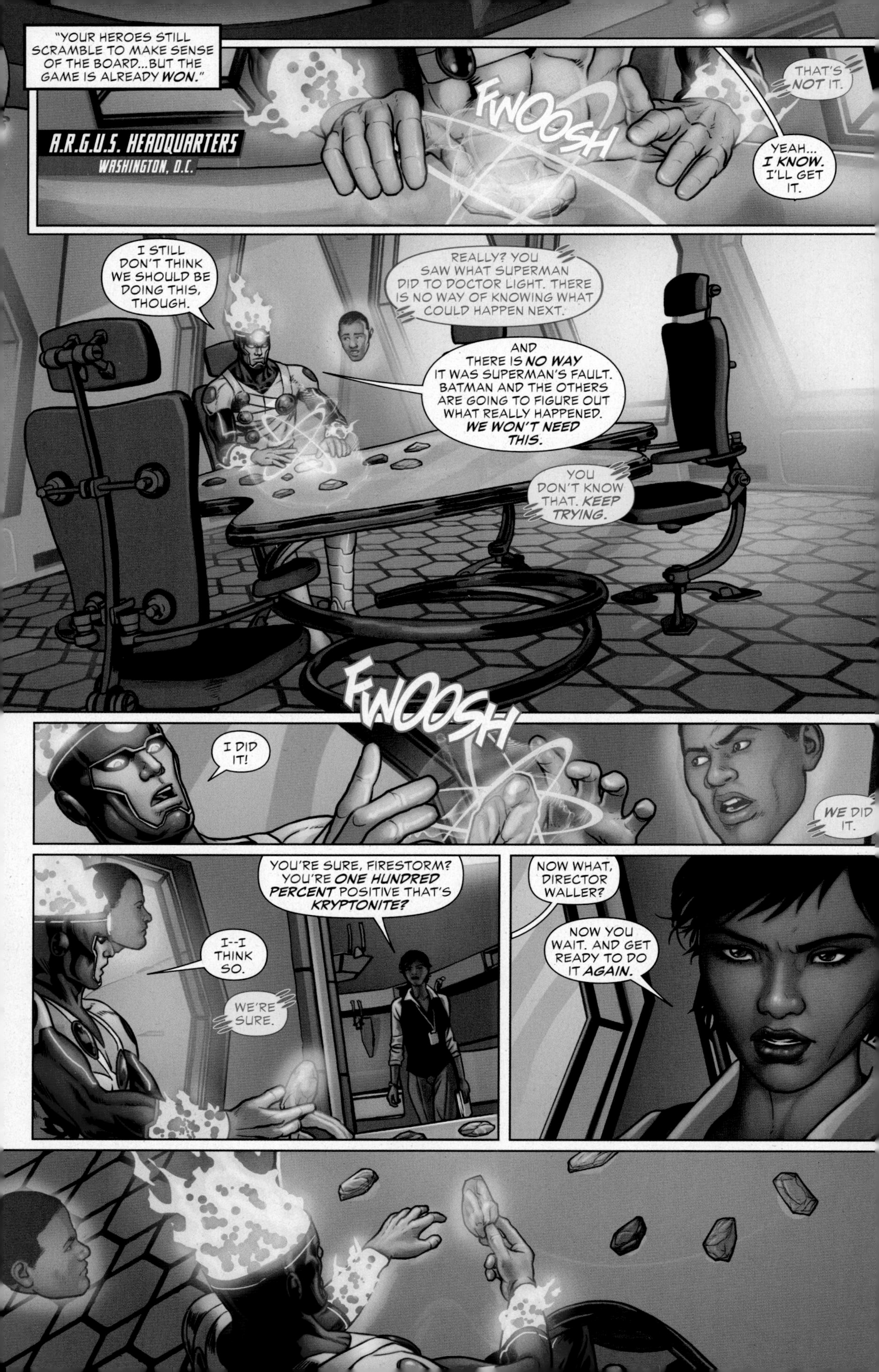
"YOUR HEROES STILL SCRAMBLE TO MAKE SENSE OF THE BOARD...BUT THE GAME IS ALREADY WON."
A.R.G.U.S. HEADQUARTERS
WASHINGTON, D.C.
FWOOSH
THAT'S NOT IT.
YEAH... I KNOW. I'LL GET IT.
I STILL DON'T THINK WE SHOULD BE DOING THIS, THOUGH.
REALLY? YOU SAW WHAT SUPERMAN DID TO DOCTOR LIGHT. THERE IS NO WAY OF KNOWING WHAT COULD HAPPEN NEXT.
AND THERE IS NO WAY IT WAS SUPERMAN'S FAULT. BATMAN AND THE OTHERS ARE GOING TO FIGURE OUT WHAT REALLY HAPPENED. WE WON'T NEED THIS.
YOU DON'T KNOW THAT. KEEP TRYING.
FWOOSH
I DID IT!
WE DID IT.
YOU'RE SURE, FIRESTORM? YOU'RE ONE HUNDRED PERCENT POSITIVE THAT'S KRYPTONITE?
I--I THINK SO.
WE'RE SURE.
NOW WHAT, DIRECTOR WALLER?
NOW YOU WAIT. AND GET READY TO DO IT AGAIN.

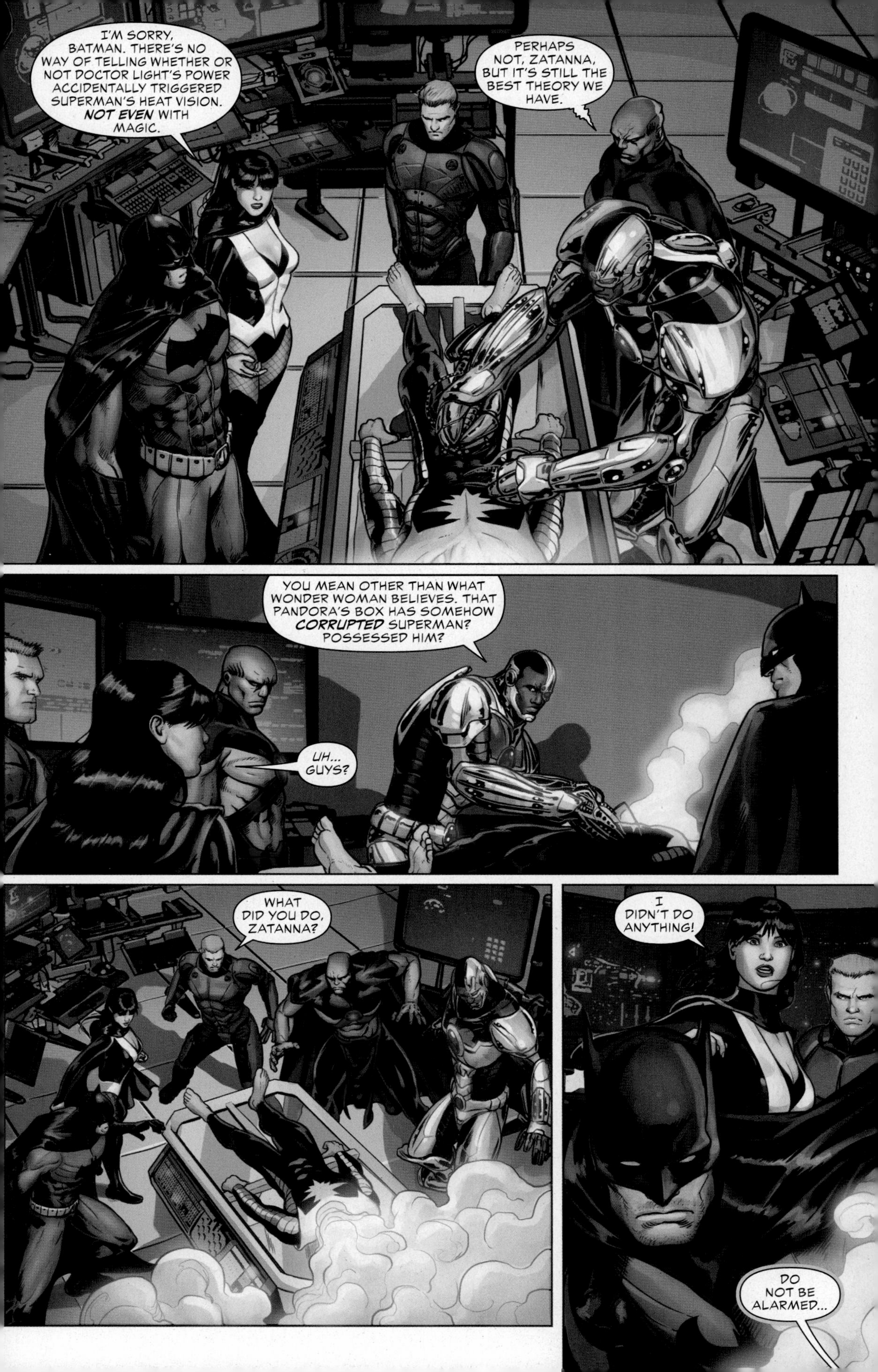
I'M SORRY, BATMAN. THERE'S NO WAY OF TELLING WHETHER OR NOT DOCTOR LIGHT'S POWER ACCIDENTALLY TRIGGERED SUPERMAN'S HEAT VISION. ***NOT EVEN*** WITH MAGIC.
PERHAPS NOT, ZATANNA, BUT IT'S STILL THE BEST THEORY WE HAVE.
YOU MEAN OTHER THAN WHAT WONDER WOMAN BELIEVES. THAT PANDORA'S BOX HAS SOMEHOW ***CORRUPTED*** SUPERMAN? POSSESSED HIM?
UH... GUYS?
WHAT DID YOU DO, ZATANNA?
I DIDN'T DO ANYTHING!
DO NOT BE ALARMED...

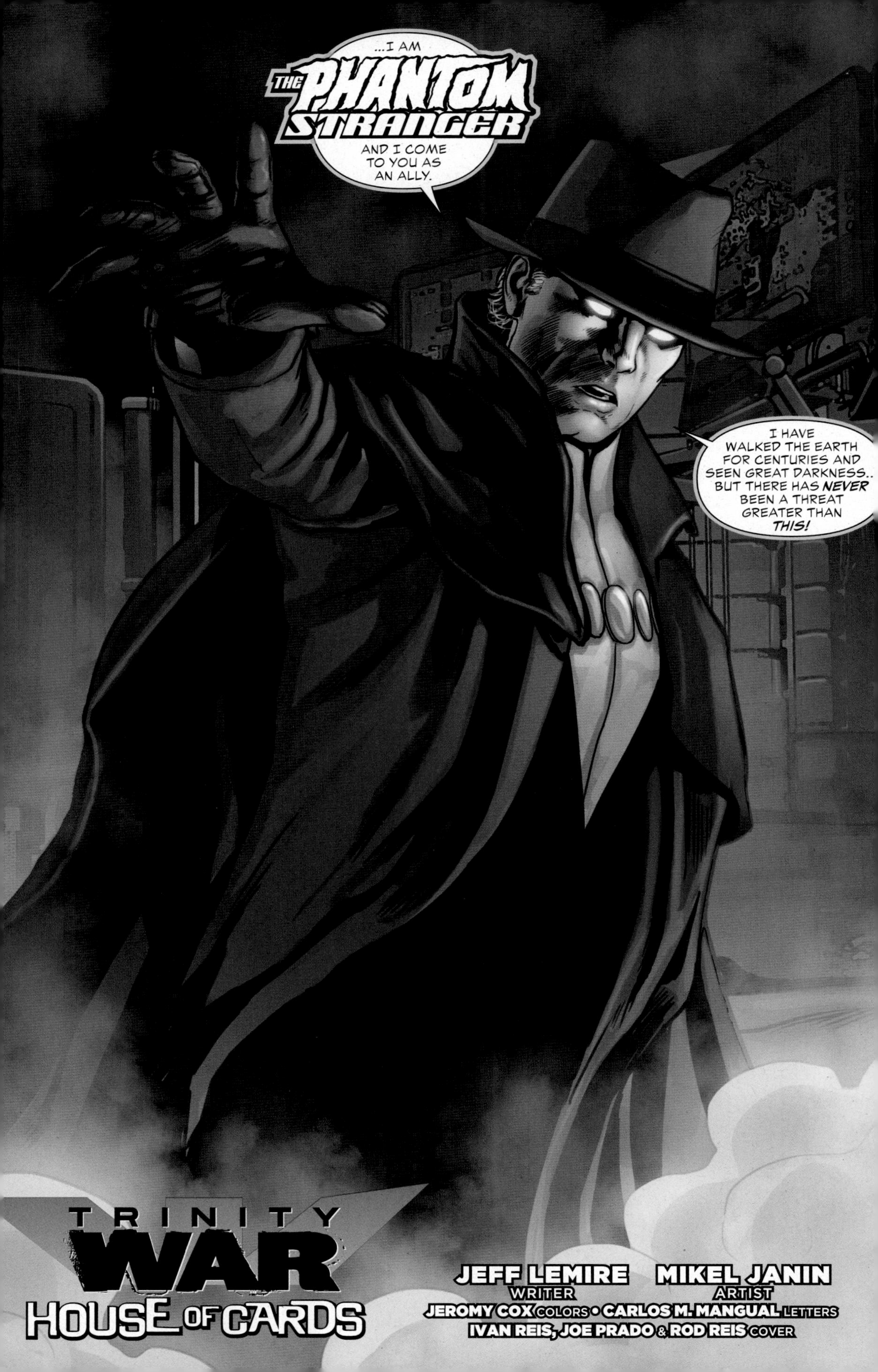
...I AM THE PHANTOM STRANGER AND I COME TO YOU AS AN ALLY.
I HAVE WALKED THE EARTH FOR CENTURIES AND SEEN GREAT DARKNESS.. BUT THERE HAS NEVER BEEN A THREAT GREATER THAN THIS!
TRINITY WAR
HOUSE OF CARDS
JEFF LEMIRE WRITER
MIKEL JANIN ARTIST
JEROMY COX COLORS • CARLOS M. MANGUAL LETTERS
IVAN REIS, JOE PRADO & ROD REIS COVER

AS WE SPEAK, WONDER WOMAN IS IN NEW YORK SEEKING THE ASSISTANCE OF THE MAGICAL ADVENTURERS YOU MAY KNOW AS THE JUSTICE LEAGUE DARK.

SHE HOPES TO RECRUIT THEM TO HELP HER LOCATE A WOMAN NAMED PANDORA. IF THEY SUCCEED IT WILL BE THE DEATH OF ALL.

MY FATHER TRUSTED HIM, BUT...

BUT SHOULD WE?

IT'S NOT A MATTER OF TRUST, BATMAN. WE CAN'T LET DIANA GET ANYWHERE NEAR PANDORA'S BOX.

BUT WHAT IF WONDER WOMAN IS RIGHT, TREVOR? WHAT IF THIS BOX CORRUPTED SUPERMAN?

IT'S TOO DANGEROUS, J'ONN. I'VE SEEN WHAT THAT BOX CAN DO. MY FIRST--AND LAST--MISSION WITH TEAM 7 WAS TO RETRIEVE THE BOX. THE TEAM WAS DECIMATED.

CYBORG, CALL FLASH. WE'RE GOING AFTER WONDER WOMAN. BUT I NEED YOU HERE IN CASE SUPERMAN'S CONDITION GETS ANY WORSE.

AND I'M LEAVING FIRESTORM, ELEMENT WOMAN AND THE ATOM. THEY ARE NOT READY FOR THIS.

GOT IT.

J'ONN! I'M LEAVING YOU AND GREEN ARROW HERE TO HOLD THE FORT.

THE OTHERS ARE WITH ME.

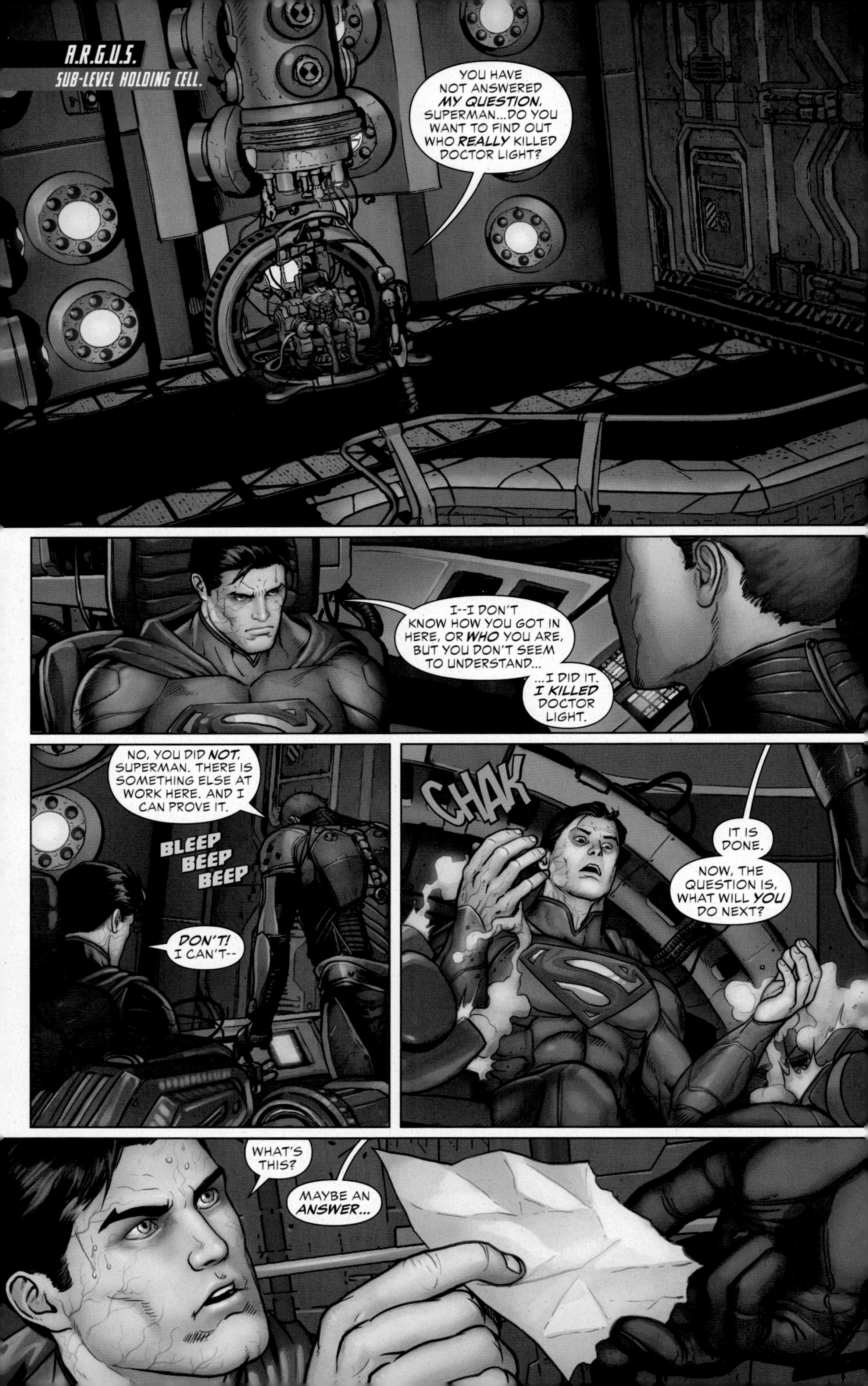
A.R.G.U.S.
SUB-LEVEL HOLDING CELL.
YOU HAVE NOT ANSWERED MY QUESTION, SUPERMAN...DO YOU WANT TO FIND OUT WHO REALLY KILLED DOCTOR LIGHT?
I--I DON'T KNOW HOW YOU GOT IN HERE, OR WHO YOU ARE, BUT YOU DON'T SEEM TO UNDERSTAND...
...I DID IT. I KILLED DOCTOR LIGHT.
NO, YOU DID NOT, SUPERMAN. THERE IS SOMETHING ELSE AT WORK HERE. AND I CAN PROVE IT.
BLEEP BEEP BEEP
DON'T! I CAN'T--
CHAK
IT IS DONE.
NOW, THE QUESTION IS, WHAT WILL YOU DO NEXT?
WHAT'S THIS?
MAYBE AN ANSWER...

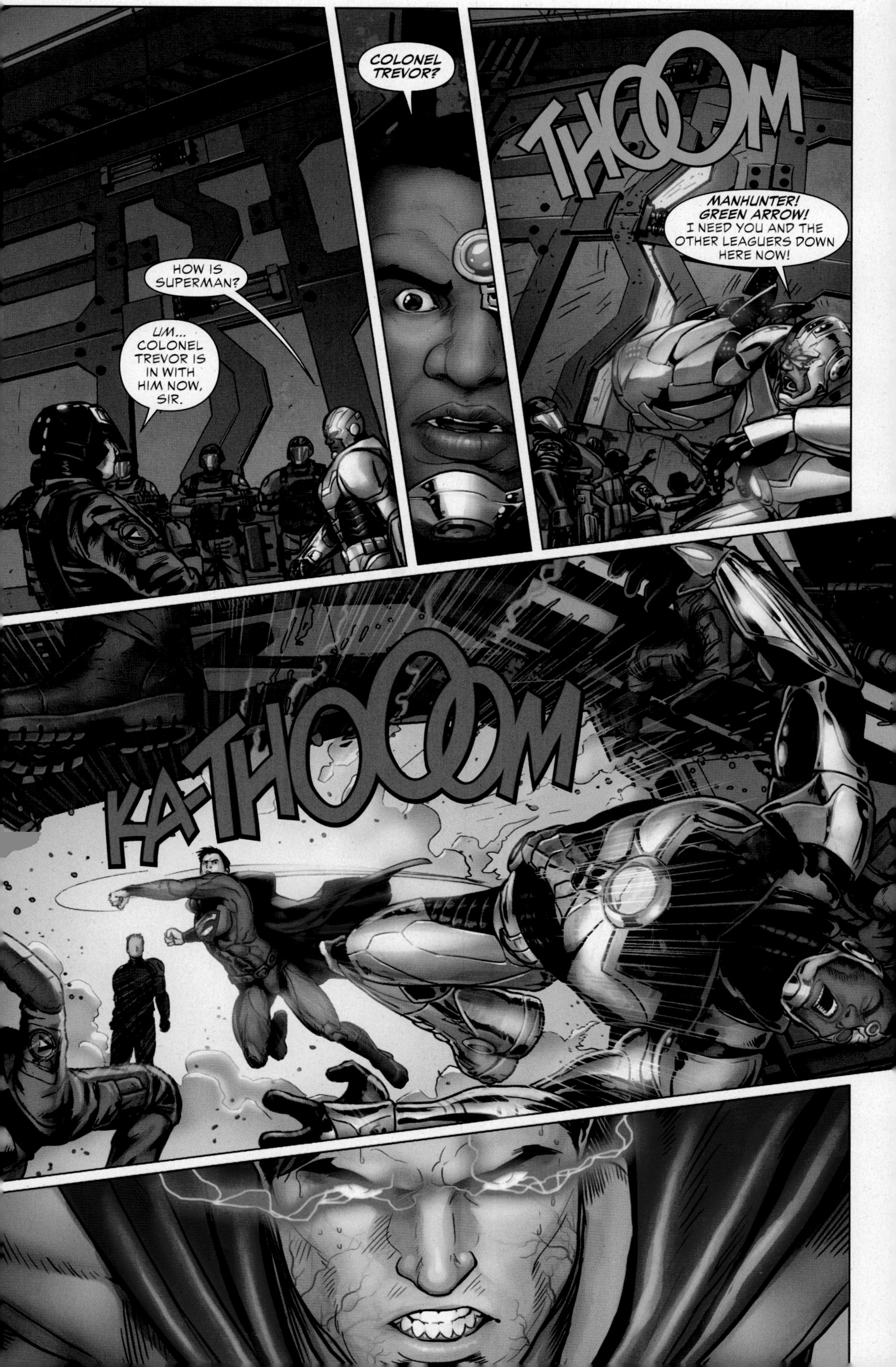
HOW IS SUPERMAN?
UM... COLONEL TREVOR IS IN WITH HIM NOW, SIR.
COLONEL TREVOR?
THOOOM
MANHUNTER! GREEN ARROW! I NEED YOU AND THE OTHER LEAGUERS DOWN HERE NOW!
KA-THOOOM

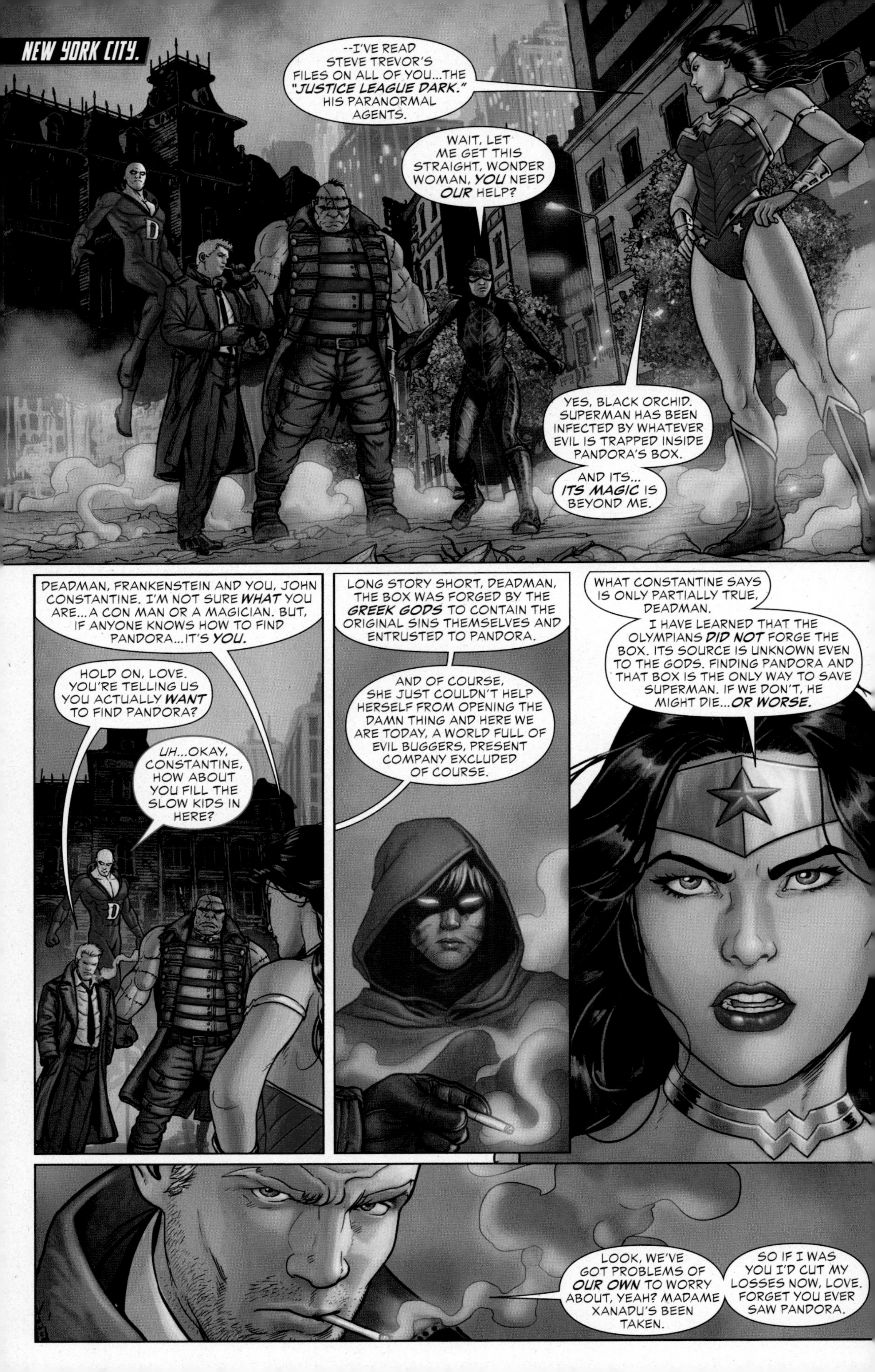
NEW YORK CITY.
--I'VE READ STEVE TREVOR'S FILES ON ALL OF YOU...THE "JUSTICE LEAGUE DARK." HIS PARANORMAL AGENTS.
WAIT, LET ME GET THIS STRAIGHT, WONDER WOMAN, YOU NEED OUR HELP?
YES, BLACK ORCHID. SUPERMAN HAS BEEN INFECTED BY WHATEVER EVIL IS TRAPPED INSIDE PANDORA'S BOX.
AND ITS... ITS MAGIC IS BEYOND ME.
DEADMAN, FRANKENSTEIN AND YOU, JOHN CONSTANTINE. I'M NOT SURE WHAT YOU ARE...A CON MAN OR A MAGICIAN. BUT, IF ANYONE KNOWS HOW TO FIND PANDORA...IT'S YOU.
HOLD ON, LOVE. YOU'RE TELLING US YOU ACTUALLY WANT TO FIND PANDORA?
UH...OKAY, CONSTANTINE, HOW ABOUT YOU FILL THE SLOW KIDS IN HERE?
LONG STORY SHORT, DEADMAN, THE BOX WAS FORGED BY THE GREEK GODS TO CONTAIN THE ORIGINAL SINS THEMSELVES AND ENTRUSTED TO PANDORA.
AND OF COURSE, SHE JUST COULDN'T HELP HERSELF FROM OPENING THE DAMN THING AND HERE WE ARE TODAY, A WORLD FULL OF EVIL BUGGERS, PRESENT COMPANY EXCLUDED OF COURSE.
WHAT CONSTANTINE SAYS IS ONLY PARTIALLY TRUE, DEADMAN.
I HAVE LEARNED THAT THE OLYMPIANS DID NOT FORGE THE BOX. ITS SOURCE IS UNKNOWN EVEN TO THE GODS. FINDING PANDORA AND THAT BOX IS THE ONLY WAY TO SAVE SUPERMAN. IF WE DON'T, HE MIGHT DIE...OR WORSE.
LOOK, WE'VE GOT PROBLEMS OF OUR OWN TO WORRY ABOUT, YEAH? MADAME XANADU'S BEEN TAKEN.
SO IF I WAS YOU I'D CUT MY LOSSES NOW, LOVE. FORGET YOU EVER SAW PANDORA.

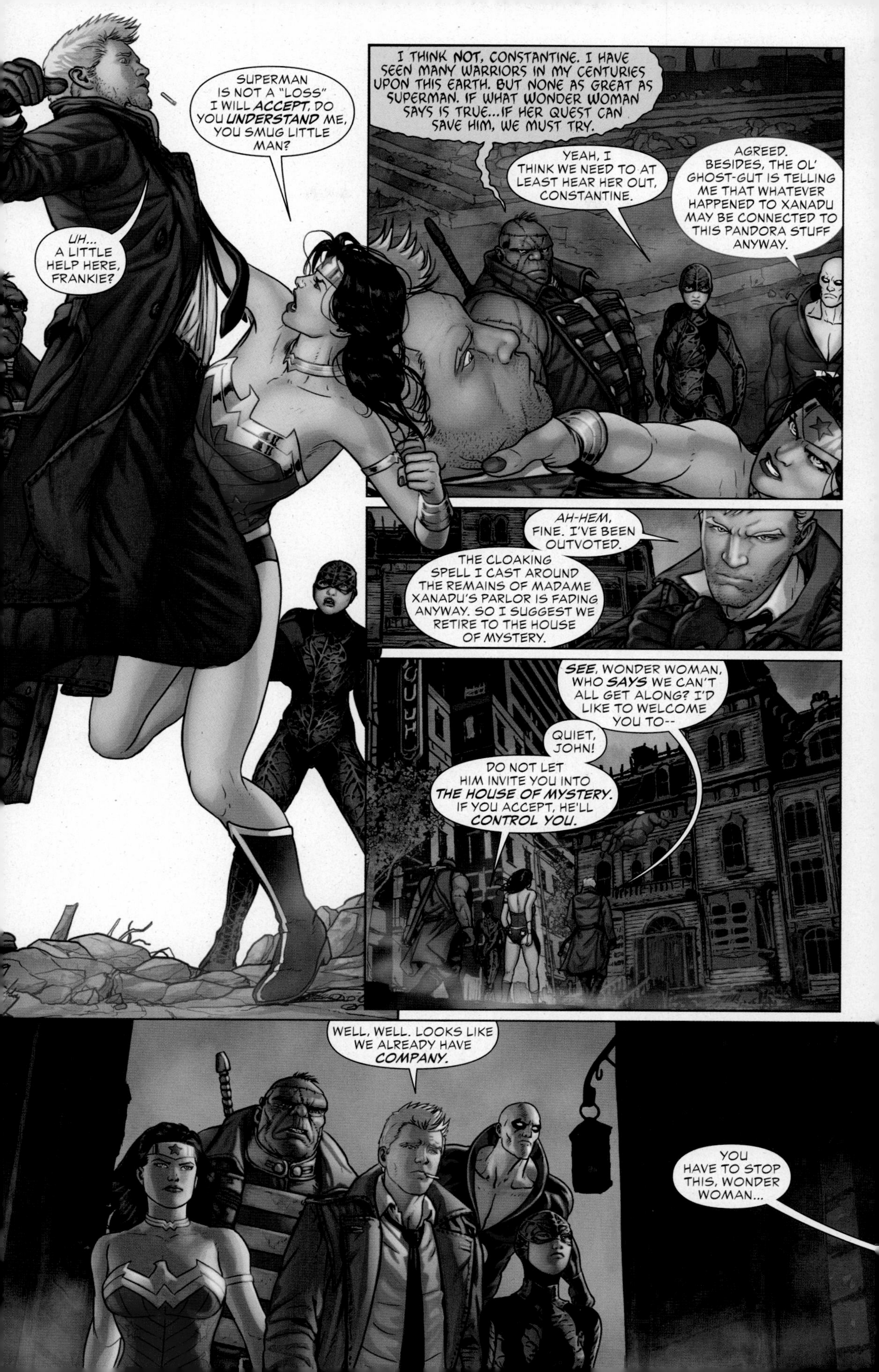
SUPERMAN IS NOT A "LOSS" I WILL ACCEPT, DO YOU UNDERSTAND ME, YOU SMUG LITTLE MAN?
UH... A LITTLE HELP HERE, FRANKIE?
I THINK NOT, CONSTANTINE. I HAVE SEEN MANY WARRIORS IN MY CENTURIES UPON THIS EARTH. BUT NONE AS GREAT AS SUPERMAN. IF WHAT WONDER WOMAN SAYS IS TRUE...IF HER QUEST CAN SAVE HIM, WE MUST TRY.
YEAH, I THINK WE NEED TO AT LEAST HEAR HER OUT, CONSTANTINE.
AGREED. BESIDES, THE OL' GHOST-GUT IS TELLING ME THAT WHATEVER HAPPENED TO XANADU MAY BE CONNECTED TO THIS PANDORA STUFF ANYWAY.
AH-HEM, FINE. I'VE BEEN OUTVOTED.
THE CLOAKING SPELL I CAST AROUND THE REMAINS OF MADAME XANADU'S PARLOR IS FADING ANYWAY. SO I SUGGEST WE RETIRE TO THE HOUSE OF MYSTERY.
SEE, WONDER WOMAN, WHO SAYS WE CAN'T ALL GET ALONG? I'D LIKE TO WELCOME YOU TO--
QUIET, JOHN!
DO NOT LET HIM INVITE YOU INTO THE HOUSE OF MYSTERY. IF YOU ACCEPT, HE'LL CONTROL YOU.
WELL, WELL. LOOKS LIKE WE ALREADY HAVE COMPANY.
YOU HAVE TO STOP THIS, WONDER WOMAN...

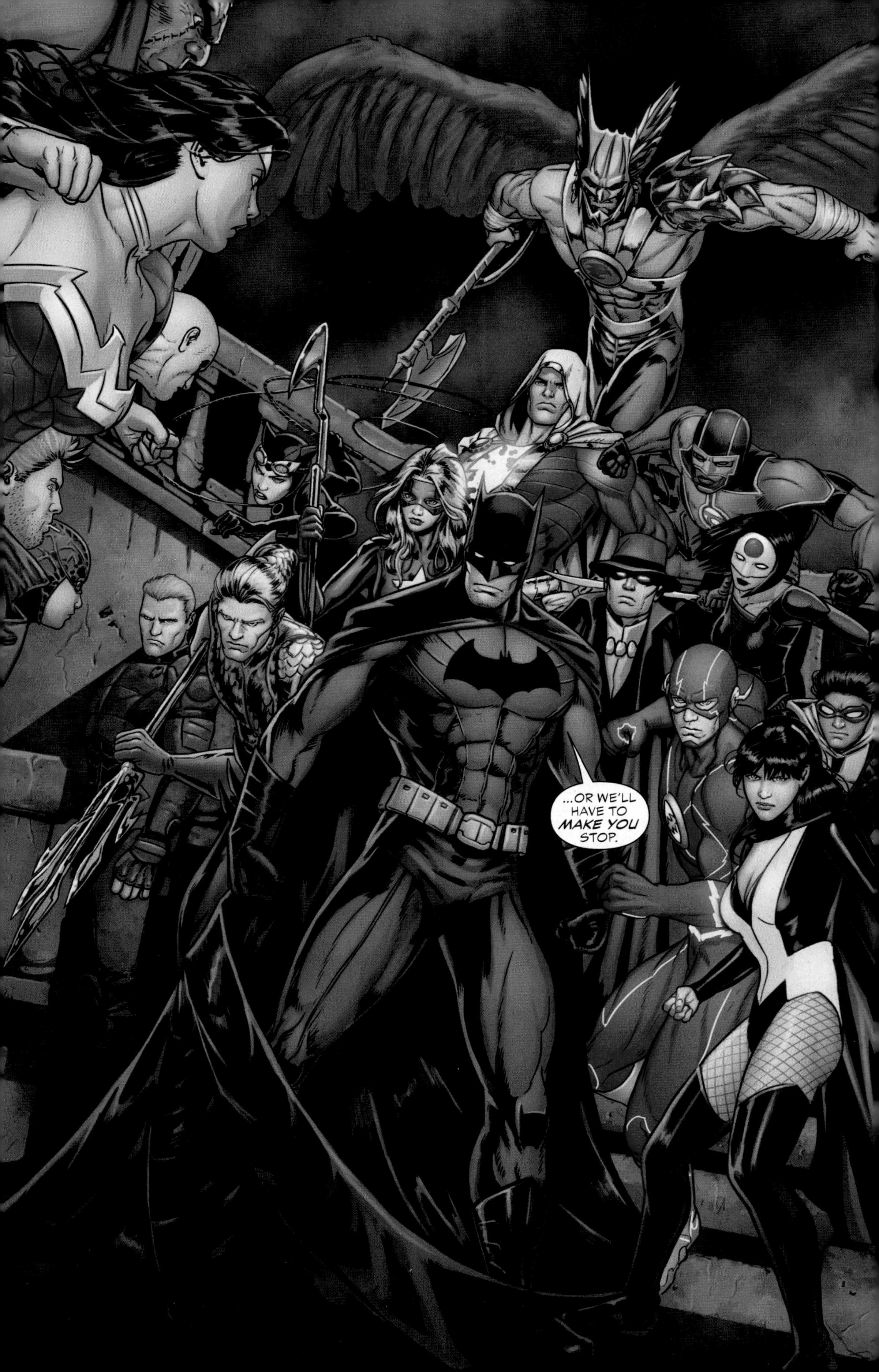
...OR WE'LL HAVE TO MAKE YOU STOP.

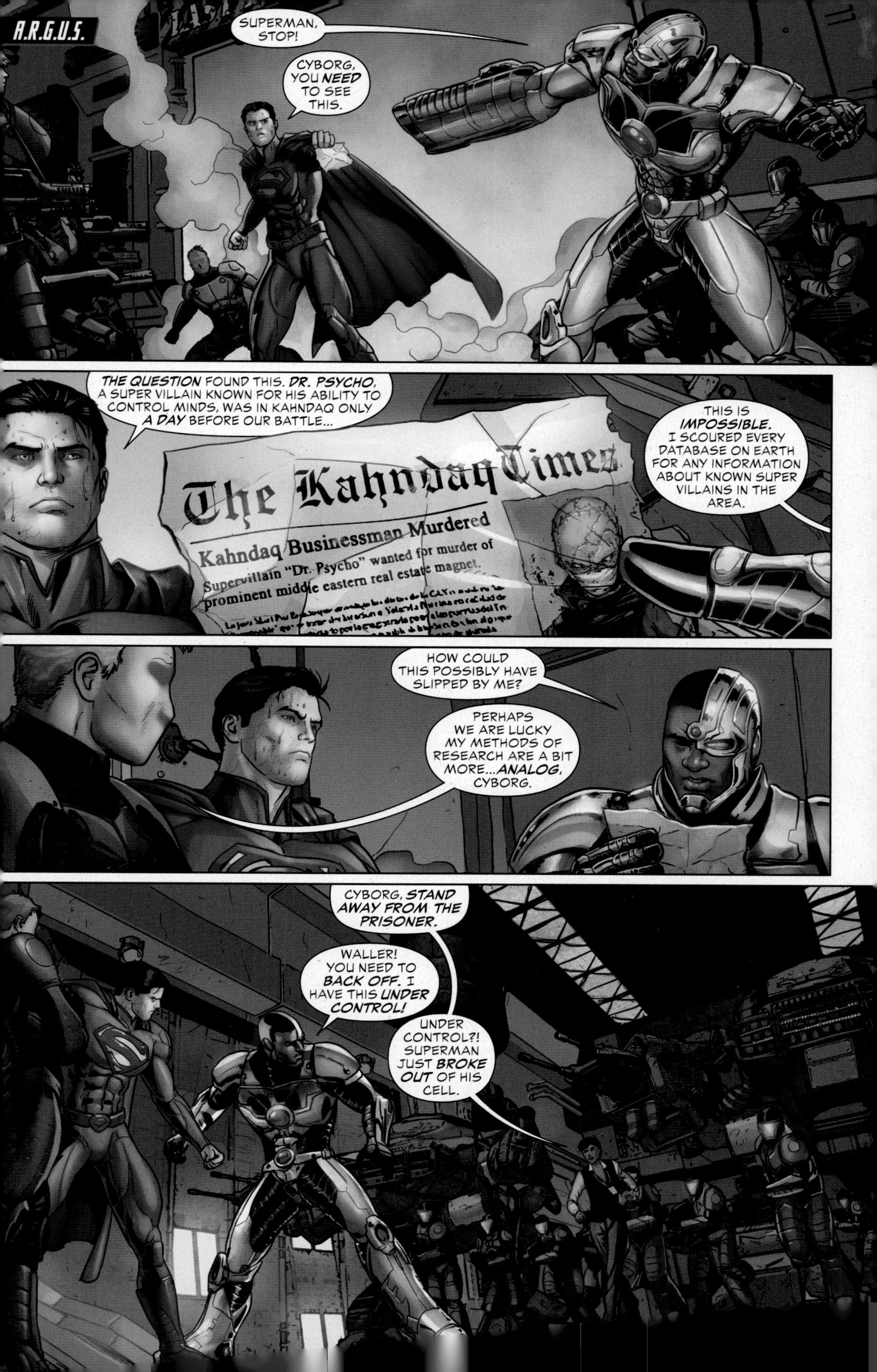
A.R.G.U.S.
SUPERMAN, STOP!
CYBORG, YOU NEED TO SEE THIS.
THE QUESTION FOUND THIS. DR. PSYCHO, A SUPER VILLAIN KNOWN FOR HIS ABILITY TO CONTROL MINDS, WAS IN KAHNDAQ ONLY A DAY BEFORE OUR BATTLE...
The Kahndaq Times
Kahndaq Businessman Murdered
Supervillain "Dr. Psycho" wanted for murder of prominent middle eastern real estate magnet.
THIS IS IMPOSSIBLE. I SCOURED EVERY DATABASE ON EARTH FOR ANY INFORMATION ABOUT KNOWN SUPER VILLAINS IN THE AREA.
HOW COULD THIS POSSIBLY HAVE SLIPPED BY ME?
PERHAPS WE ARE LUCKY MY METHODS OF RESEARCH ARE A BIT MORE...ANALOG, CYBORG.
CYBORG, STAND AWAY FROM THE PRISONER.
WALLER! YOU NEED TO BACK OFF. I HAVE THIS UNDER CONTROL!
UNDER CONTROL?! SUPERMAN JUST BROKE OUT OF HIS CELL.

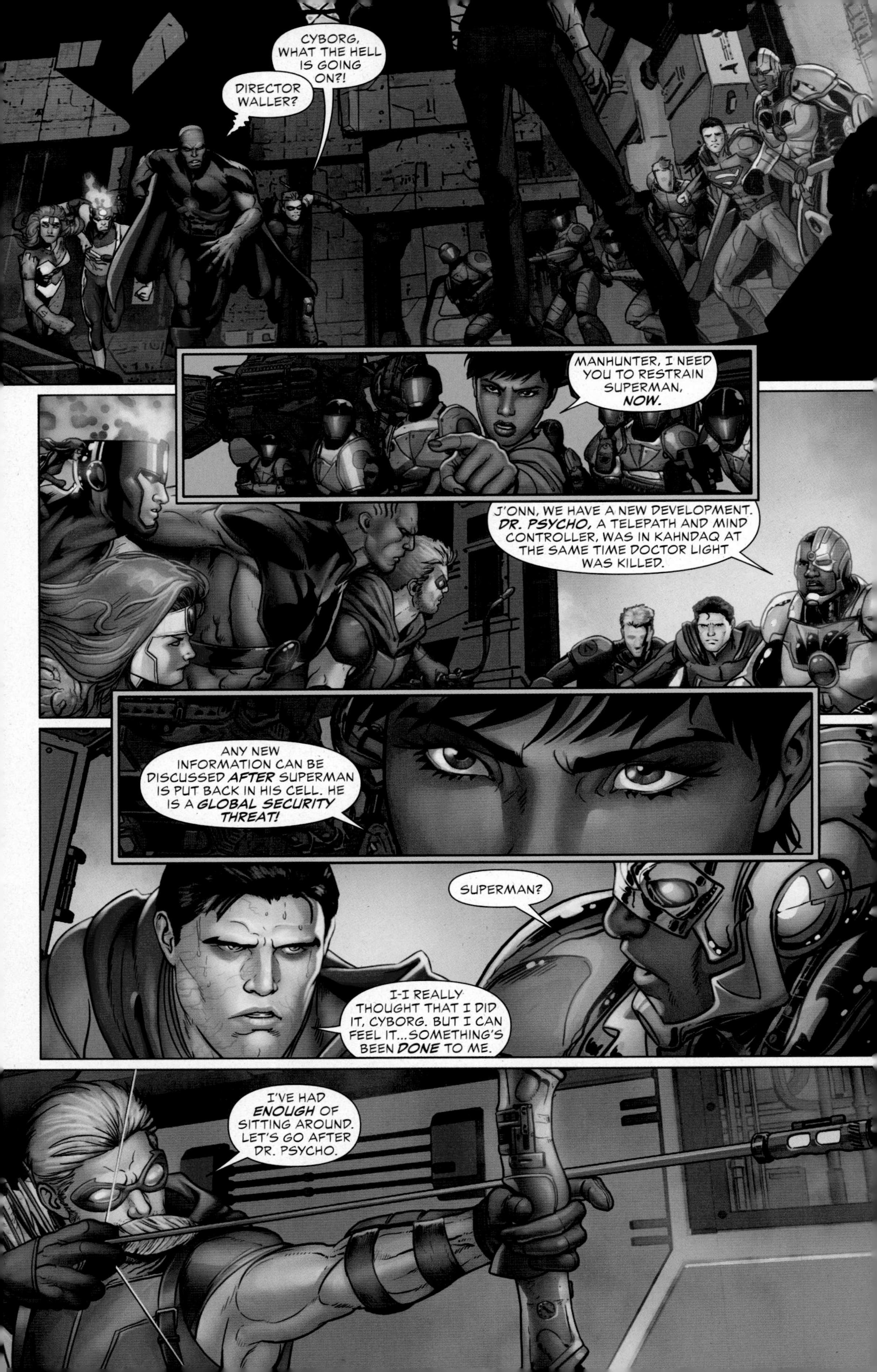
DIRECTOR WALLER?
CYBORG, WHAT THE HELL IS GOING ON?!
MANHUNTER, I NEED YOU TO RESTRAIN SUPERMAN, NOW.
J'ONN, WE HAVE A NEW DEVELOPMENT. DR. PSYCHO, A TELEPATH AND MIND CONTROLLER, WAS IN KAHNDAQ AT THE SAME TIME DOCTOR LIGHT WAS KILLED.
ANY NEW INFORMATION CAN BE DISCUSSED AFTER SUPERMAN IS PUT BACK IN HIS CELL. HE IS A GLOBAL SECURITY THREAT!
SUPERMAN?
I-I REALLY THOUGHT THAT I DID IT, CYBORG. BUT I CAN FEEL IT...SOMETHING'S BEEN DONE TO ME.
I'VE HAD ENOUGH OF SITTING AROUND. LET'S GO AFTER DR. PSYCHO.

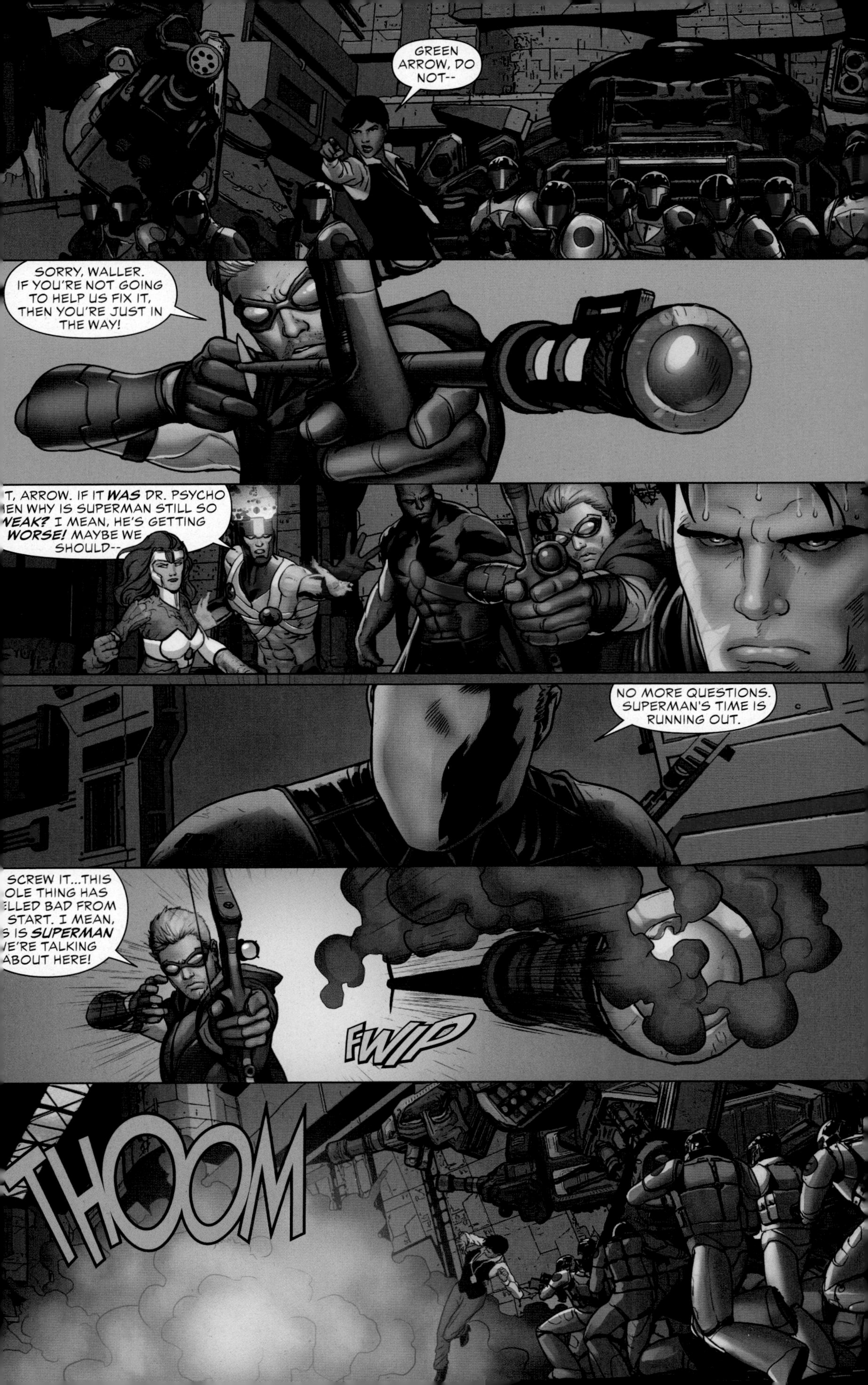
GREEN ARROW, DO NOT--
SORRY, WALLER. IF YOU'RE NOT GOING TO HELP US FIX IT, THEN YOU'RE JUST IN THE WAY!
T, ARROW. IF IT WAS DR. PSYCHO EN WHY IS SUPERMAN STILL SO WEAK? I MEAN, HE'S GETTING WORSE! MAYBE WE SHOULD--
NO MORE QUESTIONS. SUPERMAN'S TIME IS RUNNING OUT.
SCREW IT...THIS OLE THING HAS ELLED BAD FROM START. I MEAN, S IS SUPERMAN E'RE TALKING ABOUT HERE!
FWIP
THOOM

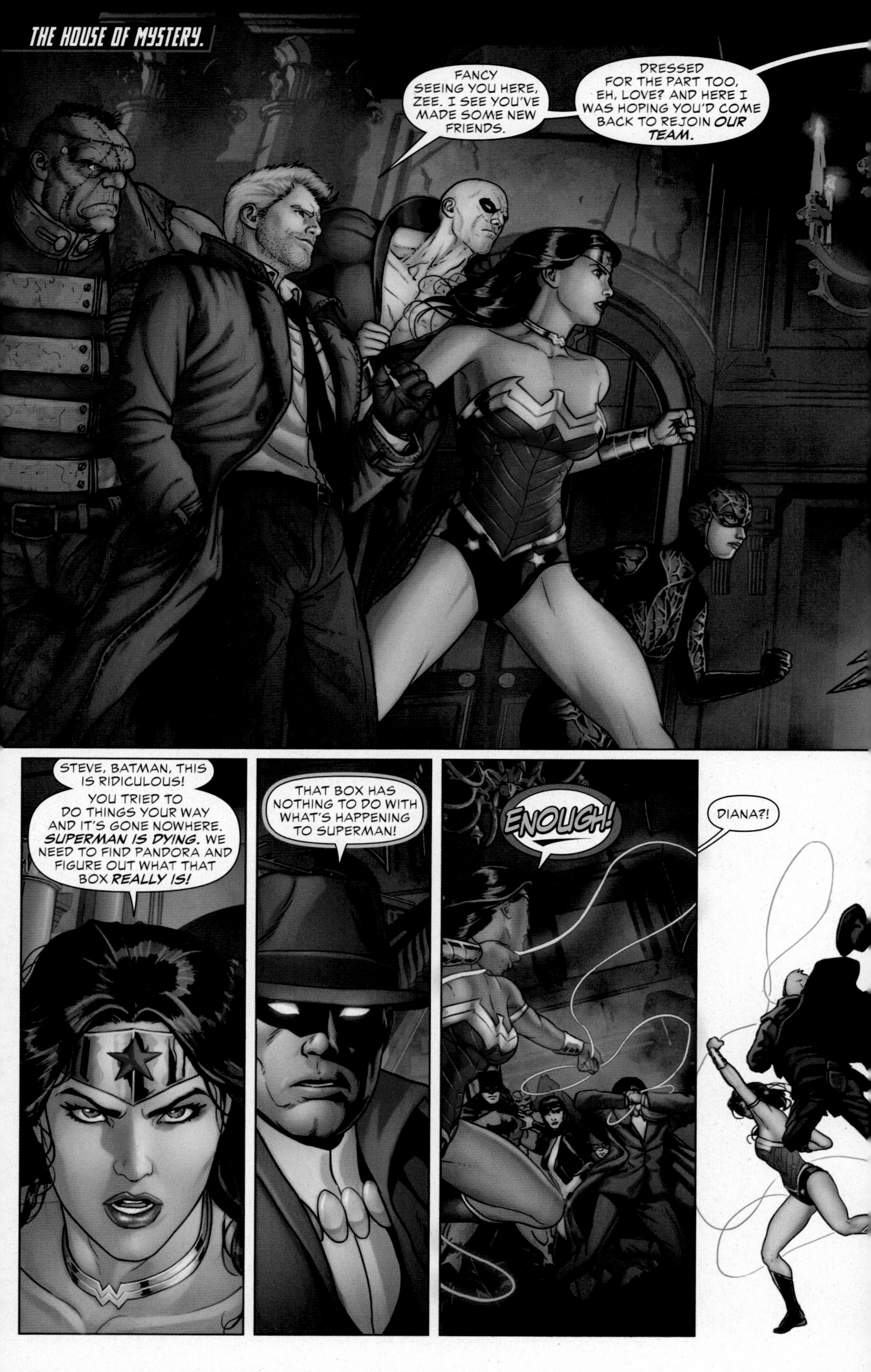
THE HOUSE OF MYSTERY.
FANCY SEEING YOU HERE, ZEE. I SEE YOU'VE MADE SOME NEW FRIENDS.
DRESSED FOR THE PART TOO, EH, LOVE? AND HERE I WAS HOPING YOU'D COME BACK TO REJOIN OUR TEAM.
STEVE, BATMAN, THIS IS RIDICULOUS!
YOU TRIED TO DO THINGS YOUR WAY AND IT'S GONE NOWHERE. SUPERMAN IS DYING. WE NEED TO FIND PANDORA AND FIGURE OUT WHAT THAT BOX REALLY IS!
THAT BOX HAS NOTHING TO DO WITH WHAT'S HAPPENING TO SUPERMAN!
ENOUGH!
DIANA?!

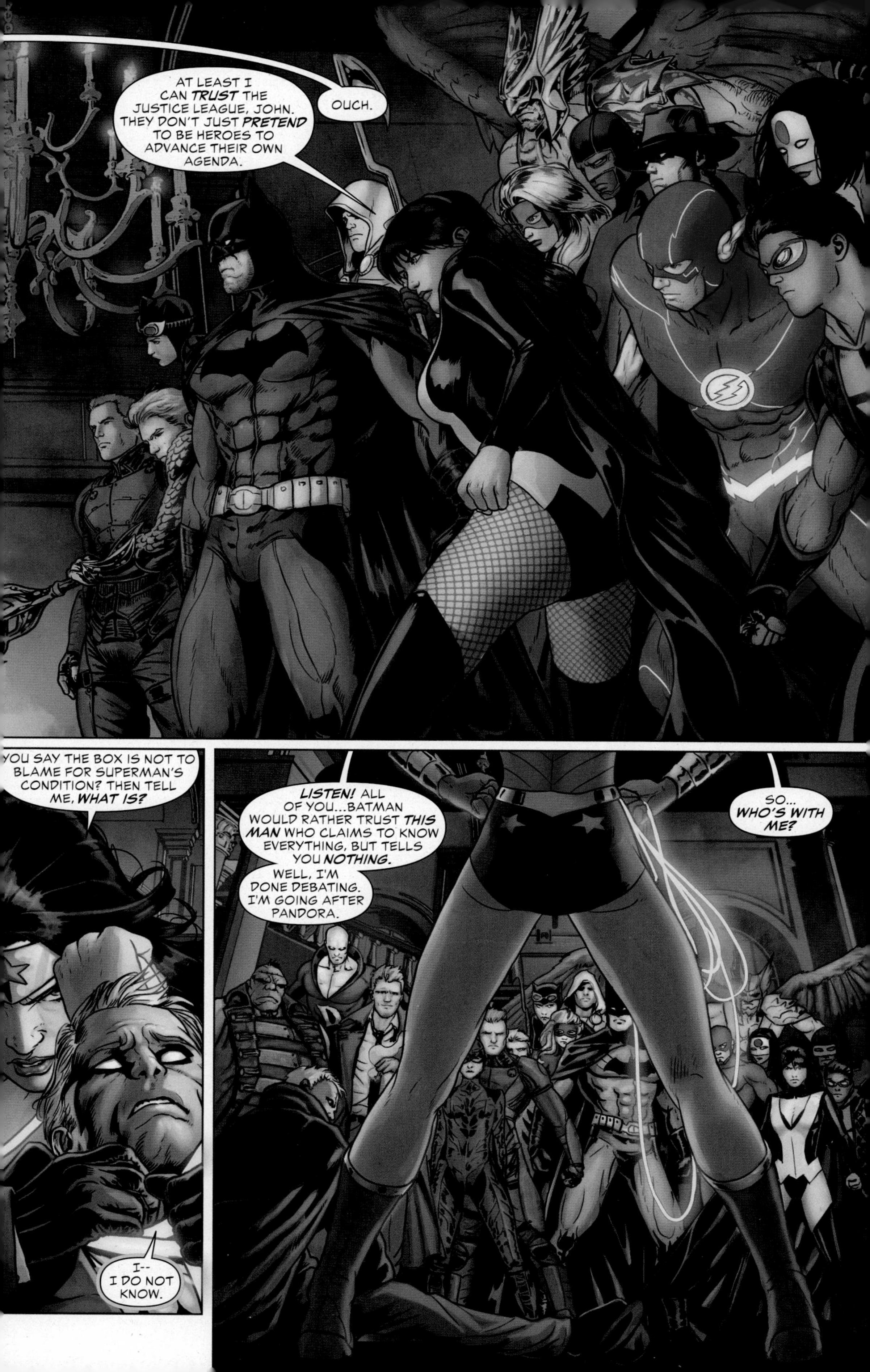
AT LEAST I CAN TRUST THE JUSTICE LEAGUE, JOHN. THEY DON'T JUST PRETEND TO BE HEROES TO ADVANCE THEIR OWN AGENDA.
OUCH.
YOU SAY THE BOX IS NOT TO BLAME FOR SUPERMAN'S CONDITION? THEN TELL ME, WHAT IS?
I-- I DO NOT KNOW.
LISTEN! ALL OF YOU...BATMAN WOULD RATHER TRUST THIS MAN WHO CLAIMS TO KNOW EVERYTHING, BUT TELLS YOU NOTHING.
WELL, I'M DONE DEBATING. I'M GOING AFTER PANDORA.
SO... WHO'S WITH ME?

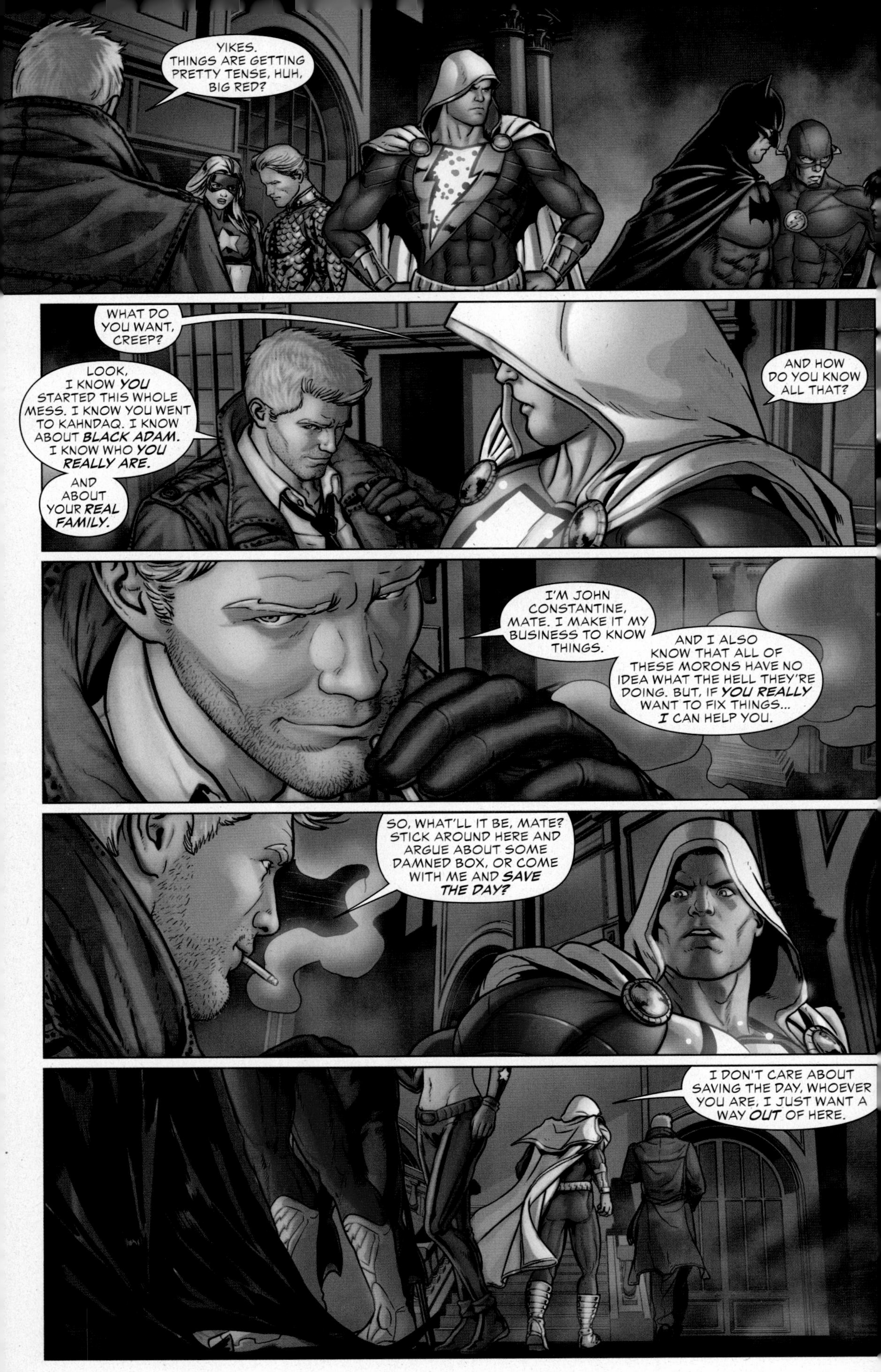
YIKES. THINGS ARE GETTING PRETTY TENSE, HUH, BIG RED?
WHAT DO YOU WANT, CREEP?
LOOK, I KNOW YOU STARTED THIS WHOLE MESS. I KNOW YOU WENT TO KAHNDAQ. I KNOW ABOUT BLACK ADAM. I KNOW WHO YOU REALLY ARE.
AND ABOUT YOUR REAL FAMILY.
AND HOW DO YOU KNOW ALL THAT?
I'M JOHN CONSTANTINE, MATE. I MAKE IT MY BUSINESS TO KNOW THINGS.
AND I ALSO KNOW THAT ALL OF THESE MORONS HAVE NO IDEA WHAT THE HELL THEY'RE DOING. BUT, IF YOU REALLY WANT TO FIX THINGS... I CAN HELP YOU.
SO, WHAT'LL IT BE, MATE? STICK AROUND HERE AND ARGUE ABOUT SOME DAMNED BOX, OR COME WITH ME AND SAVE THE DAY?
I DON'T CARE ABOUT SAVING THE DAY, WHOEVER YOU ARE, I JUST WANT A WAY OUT OF HERE.

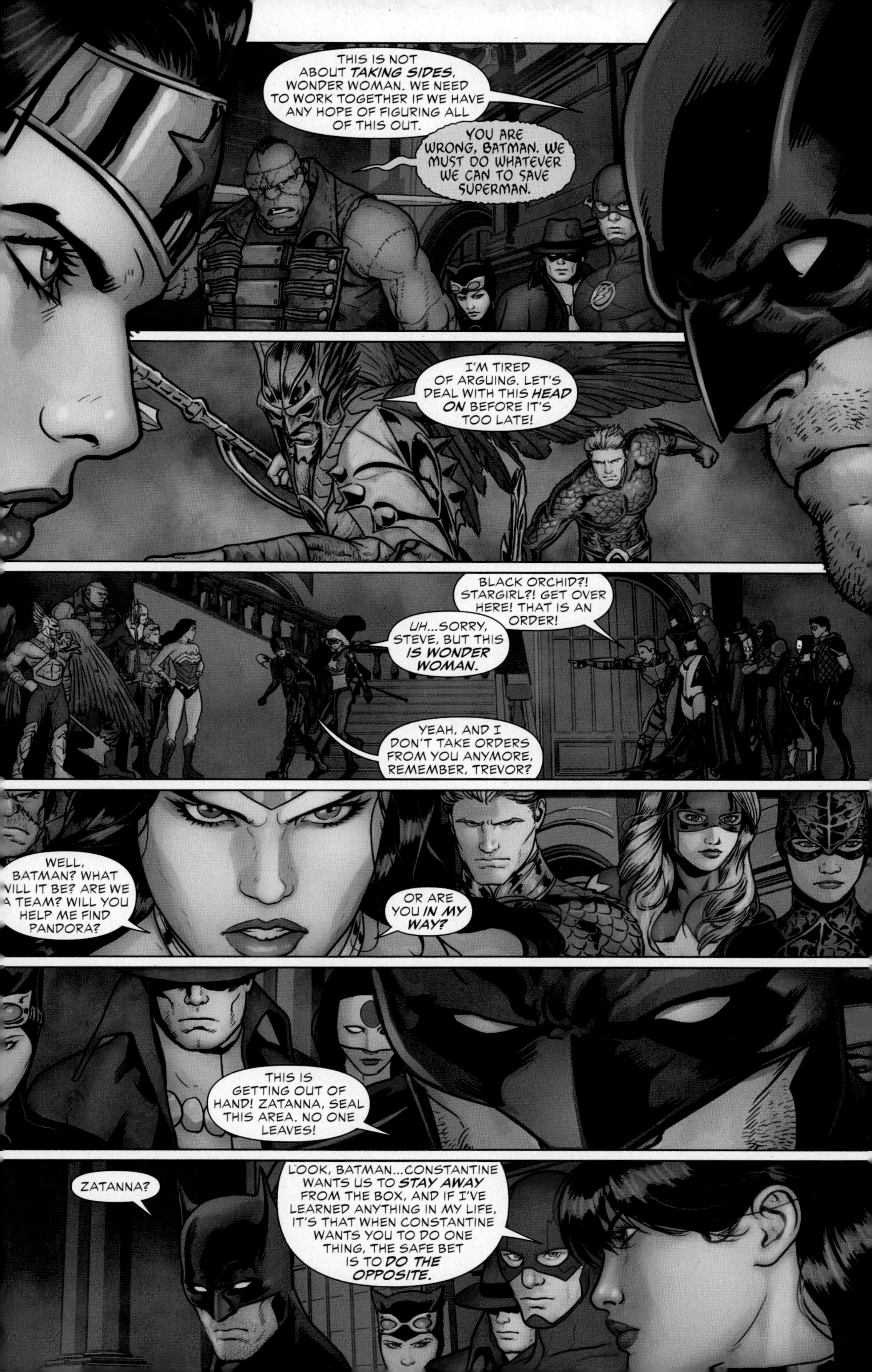
THIS IS NOT ABOUT TAKING SIDES, WONDER WOMAN. WE NEED TO WORK TOGETHER IF WE HAVE ANY HOPE OF FIGURING ALL OF THIS OUT.
YOU ARE WRONG, BATMAN. WE MUST DO WHATEVER WE CAN TO SAVE SUPERMAN.
I'M TIRED OF ARGUING. LET'S DEAL WITH THIS HEAD ON BEFORE IT'S TOO LATE!
BLACK ORCHID?! STARGIRL?! GET OVER HERE! THAT IS AN ORDER!
UH...SORRY, STEVE, BUT THIS IS WONDER WOMAN.
YEAH, AND I DON'T TAKE ORDERS FROM YOU ANYMORE, REMEMBER, TREVOR?
WELL, BATMAN? WHAT WILL IT BE? ARE WE A TEAM? WILL YOU HELP ME FIND PANDORA?
OR ARE YOU IN MY WAY?
THIS IS GETTING OUT OF HAND! ZATANNA, SEAL THIS AREA. NO ONE LEAVES!
ZATANNA?
LOOK, BATMAN...CONSTANTINE WANTS US TO STAY AWAY FROM THE BOX, AND IF I'VE LEARNED ANYTHING IN MY LIFE, IT'S THAT WHEN CONSTANTINE WANTS YOU TO DO ONE THING, THE SAFE BET IS TO DO THE OPPOSITE.

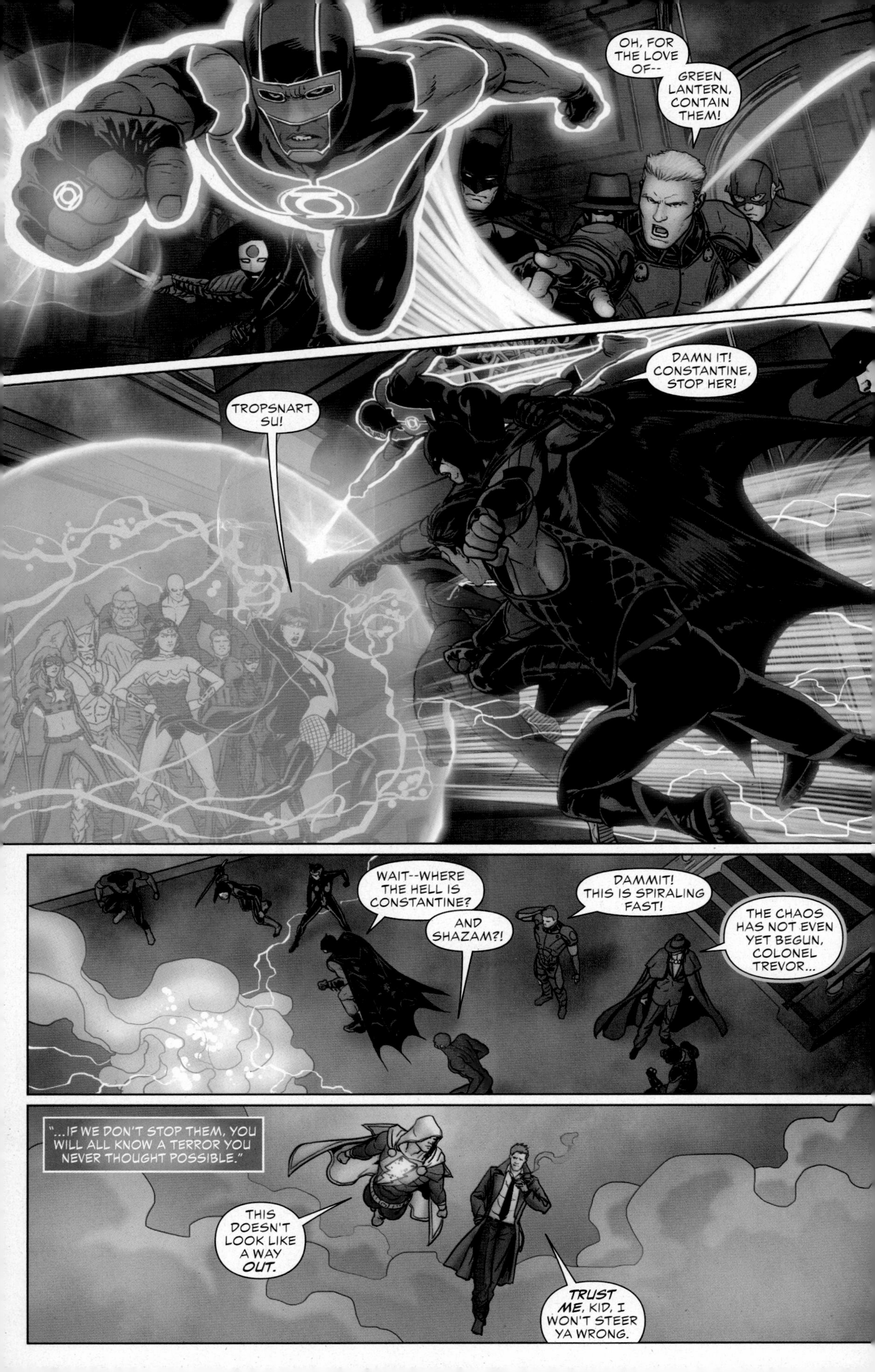
OH, FOR THE LOVE OF--
GREEN LANTERN, CONTAIN THEM!
DAMN IT! CONSTANTINE, STOP HER!
TROPSNART SU!
WAIT--WHERE THE HELL IS CONSTANTINE?
AND SHAZAM?!
DAMMIT! THIS IS SPIRALING FAST!
THE CHAOS HAS NOT EVEN YET BEGUN, COLONEL TREVOR...
"...IF WE DON'T STOP THEM, YOU WILL ALL KNOW A TERROR YOU NEVER THOUGHT POSSIBLE."
THIS DOESN'T LOOK LIKE A WAY OUT.
TRUST ME, KID, I WON'T STEER YA WRONG.

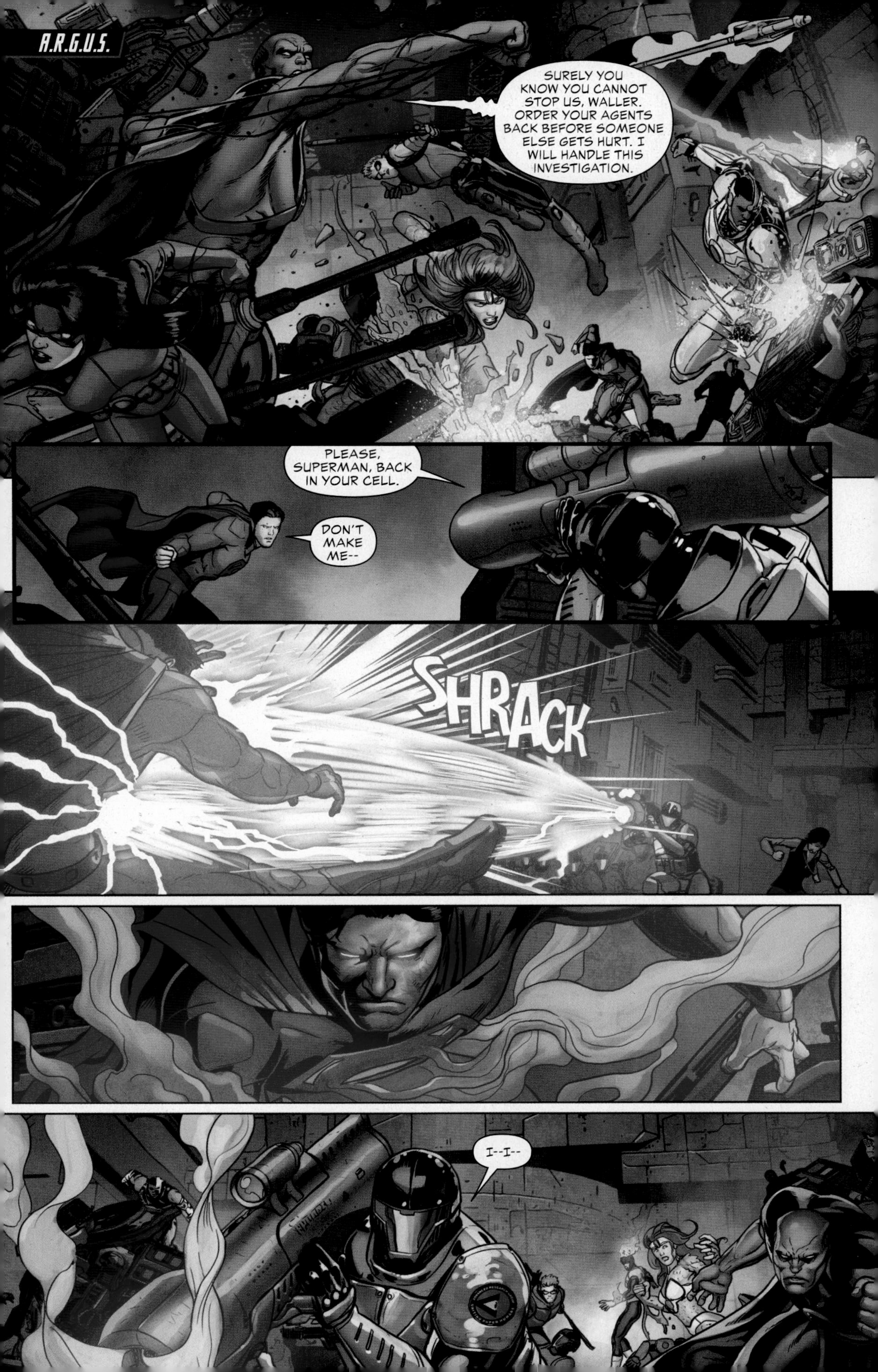
SURELY YOU KNOW YOU CANNOT STOP US, WALLER. ORDER YOUR AGENTS BACK BEFORE SOMEONE ELSE GETS HURT. I WILL HANDLE THIS INVESTIGATION.
PLEASE, SUPERMAN, BACK IN YOUR CELL.
DON'T MAKE ME--
SHRACK
I--I--

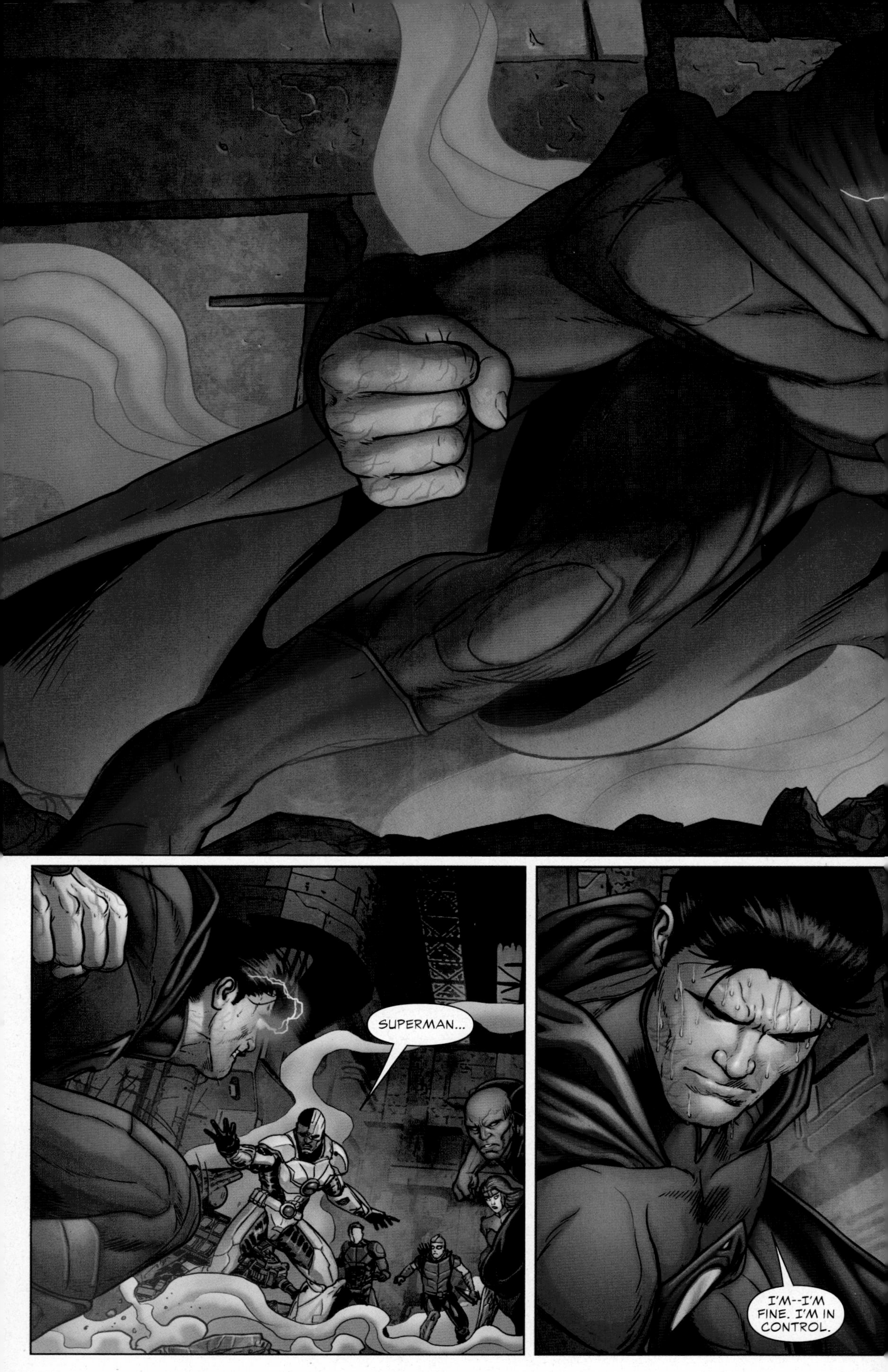
SUPERMAN...
I'M--I'M FINE. I'M IN CONTROL.

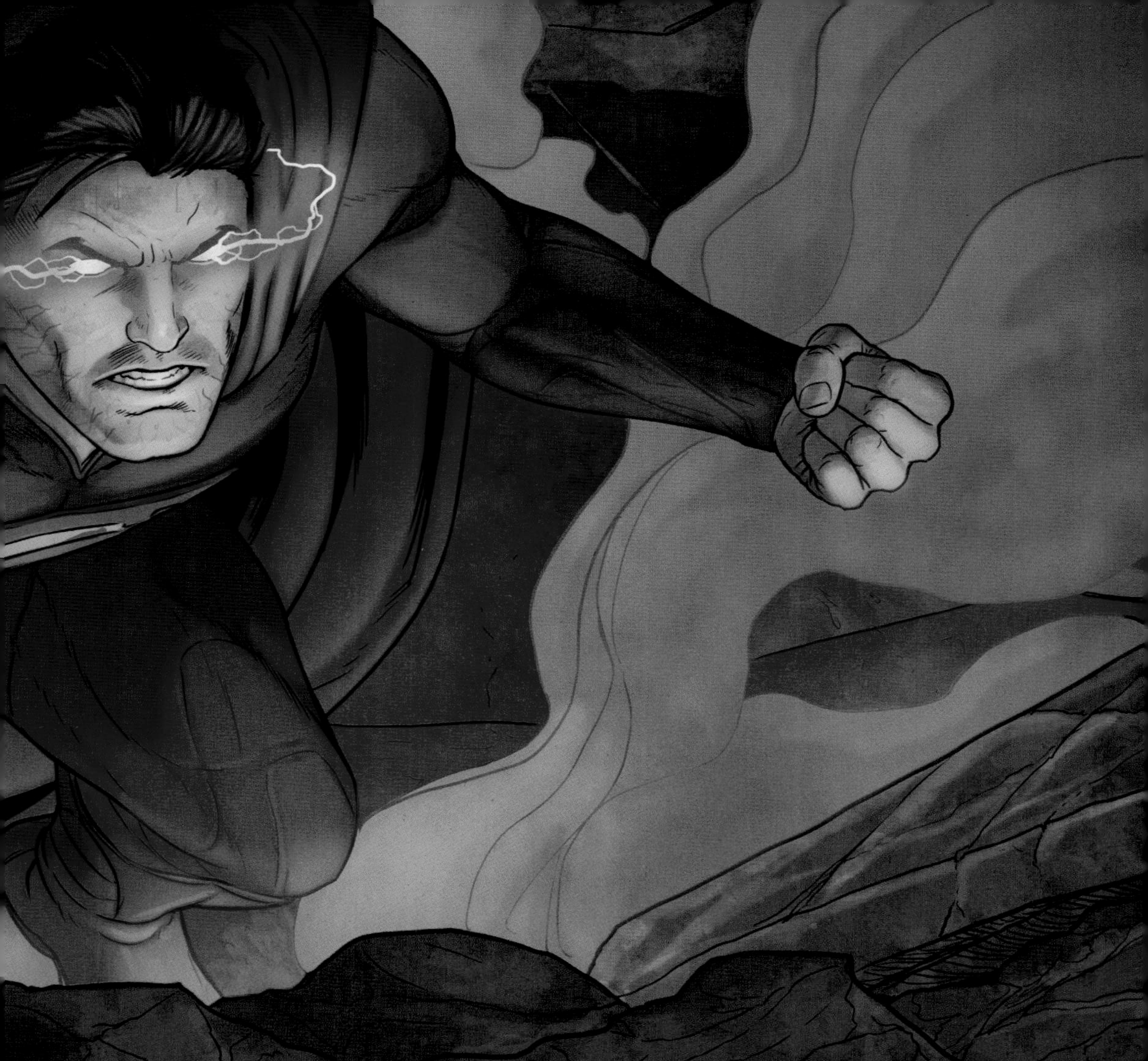

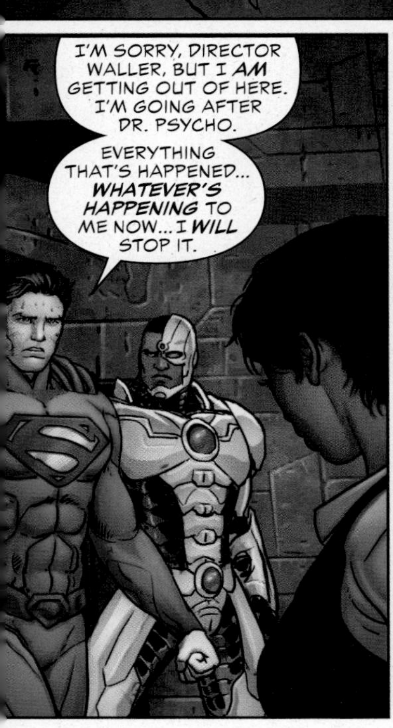
I'M SORRY, DIRECTOR WALLER, BUT I AM GETTING OUT OF HERE. I'M GOING AFTER DR. PSYCHO.
EVERYTHING THAT'S HAPPENED... WHATEVER'S HAPPENING TO ME NOW... I WILL STOP IT.

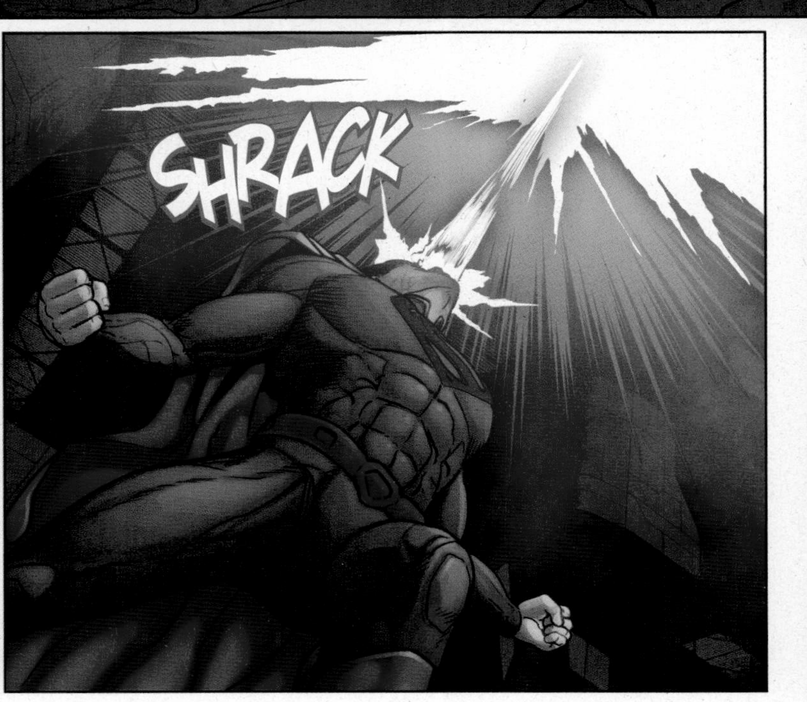
SHRACK

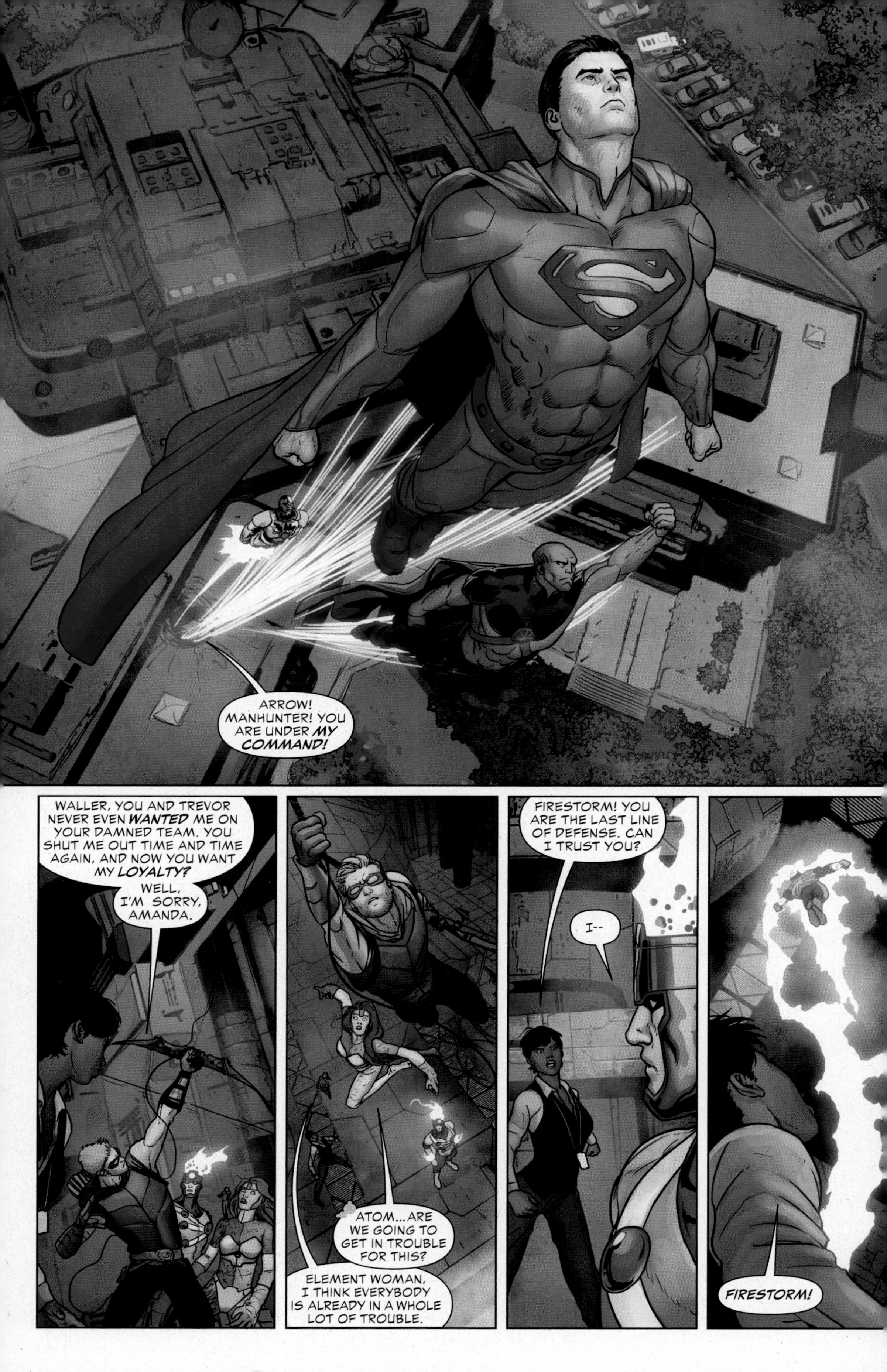

ARROW! MANHUNTER! YOU ARE UNDER MY COMMAND!
WALLER, YOU AND TREVOR NEVER EVEN WANTED ME ON YOUR DAMNED TEAM. YOU SHUT ME OUT TIME AND TIME AGAIN, AND NOW YOU WANT MY LOYALTY?
WELL, I'M SORRY, AMANDA.
ATOM... ARE WE GOING TO GET IN TROUBLE FOR THIS?
ELEMENT WOMAN, I THINK EVERYBODY IS ALREADY IN A WHOLE LOT OF TROUBLE.
FIRESTORM! YOU ARE THE LAST LINE OF DEFENSE. CAN I TRUST YOU?
I--
FIRESTORM!

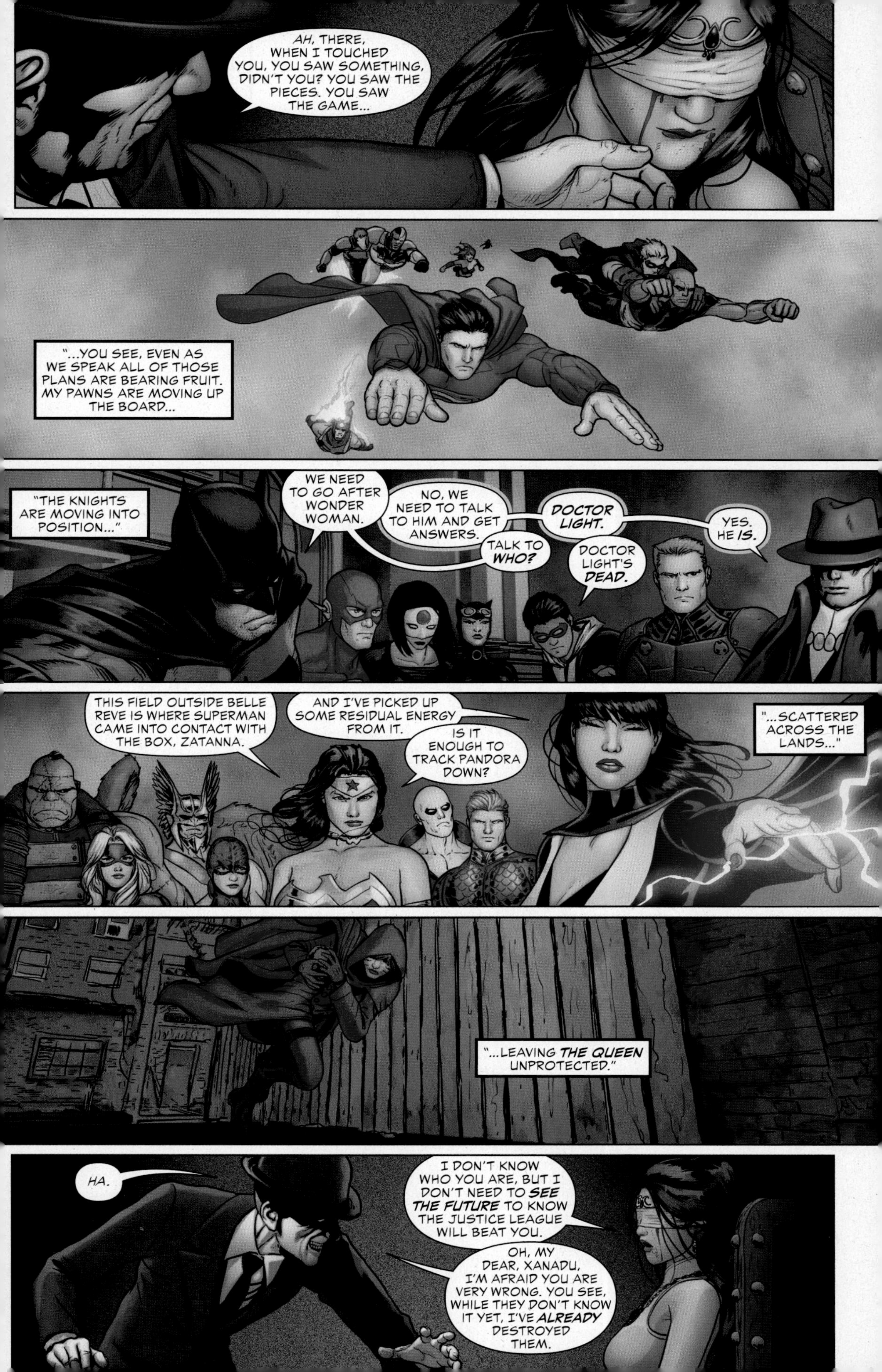
AH, THERE, WHEN I TOUCHED YOU, YOU SAW SOMETHING, DIDN'T YOU? YOU SAW THE PIECES. YOU SAW THE GAME...
"...YOU SEE, EVEN AS WE SPEAK ALL OF THOSE PLANS ARE BEARING FRUIT. MY PAWNS ARE MOVING UP THE BOARD...
"THE KNIGHTS ARE MOVING INTO POSITION..."
WE NEED TO GO AFTER WONDER WOMAN.
NO, WE NEED TO TALK TO HIM AND GET ANSWERS.
TALK TO WHO?
DOCTOR LIGHT.
DOCTOR LIGHT'S DEAD.
YES. HE IS.
THIS FIELD OUTSIDE BELLE REVE IS WHERE SUPERMAN CAME INTO CONTACT WITH THE BOX, ZATANNA.
AND I'VE PICKED UP SOME RESIDUAL ENERGY FROM IT.
IS IT ENOUGH TO TRACK PANDORA DOWN?
"...SCATTERED ACROSS THE LANDS..."
"...LEAVING THE QUEEN UNPROTECTED."
HA.
I DON'T KNOW WHO YOU ARE, BUT I DON'T NEED TO SEE THE FUTURE TO KNOW THE JUSTICE LEAGUE WILL BEAT YOU.
OH, MY DEAR, XANADU, I'M AFRAID YOU ARE VERY WRONG. YOU SEE, WHILE THEY DON'T KNOW IT YET, I'VE ALREADY DESTROYED THEM.

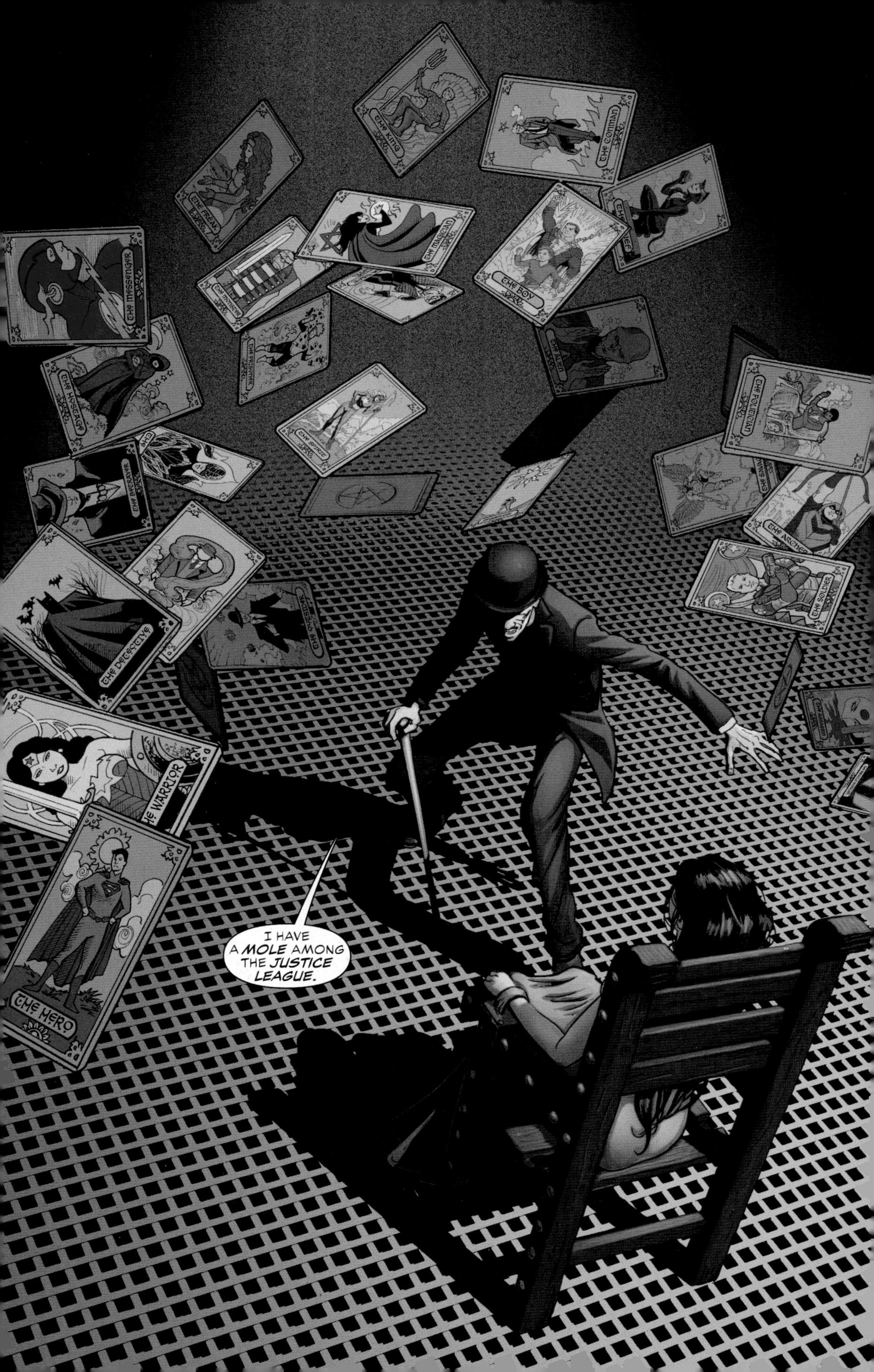
THE KING
THE CONMAN
THE MAGICIAN
THE MESSENGER
THE BOY
THE POLITICIAN
THE SOLDIER
THE DETECTIVE
THE HERO
I HAVE A MOLE AMONG THE JUSTICE LEAGUE.

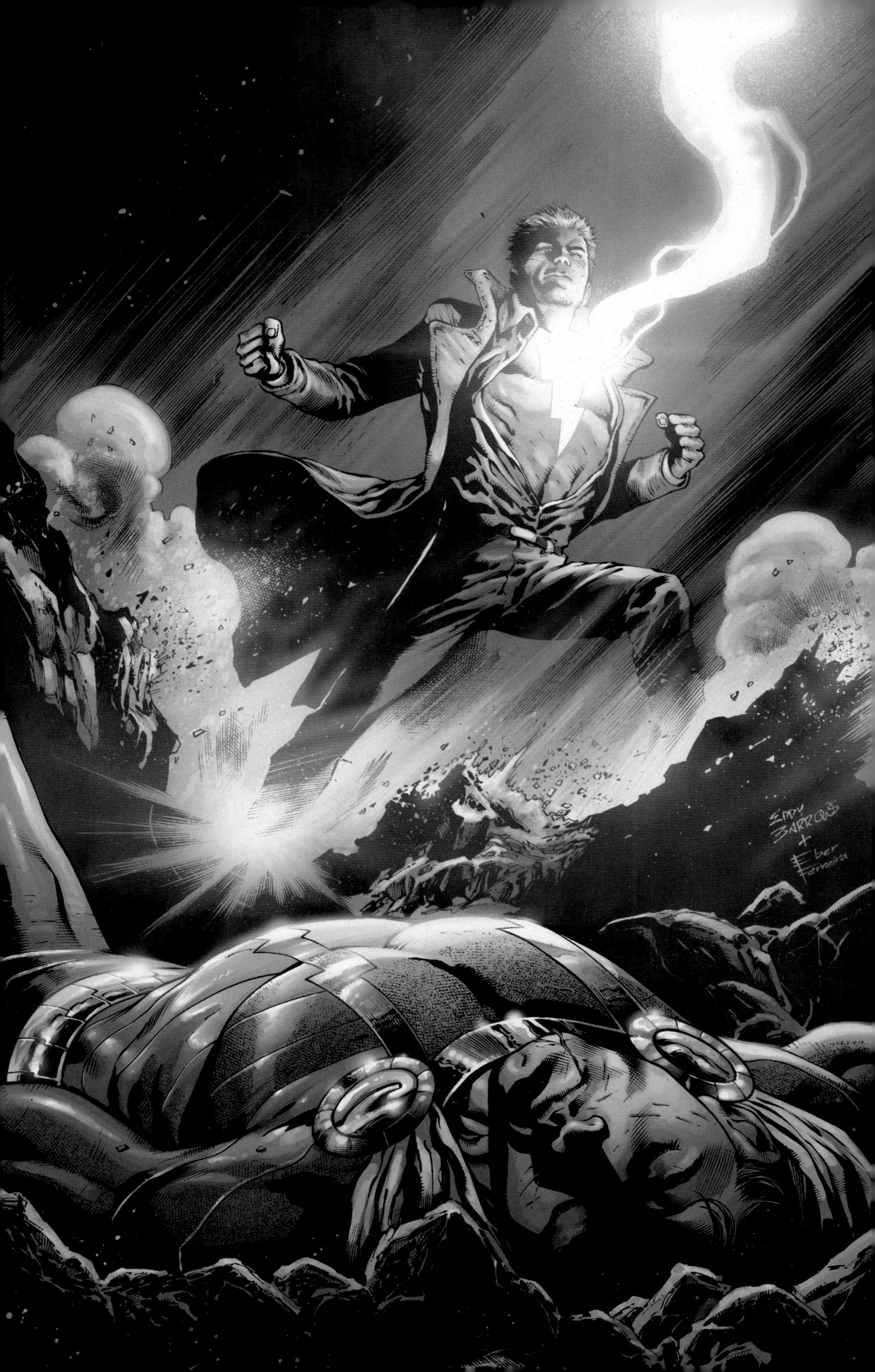
EDDY BARROWS
+
Eber Ferreira

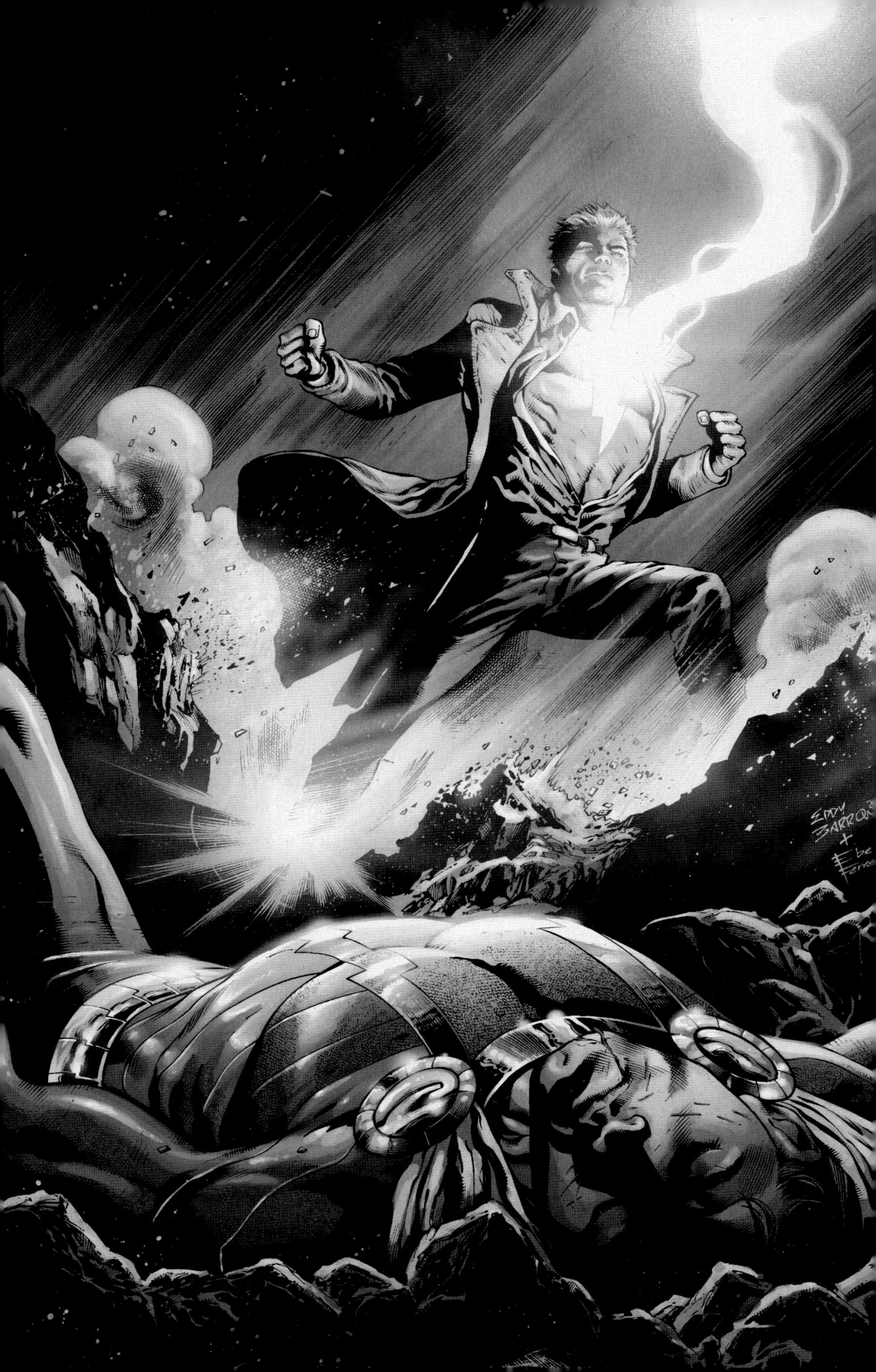

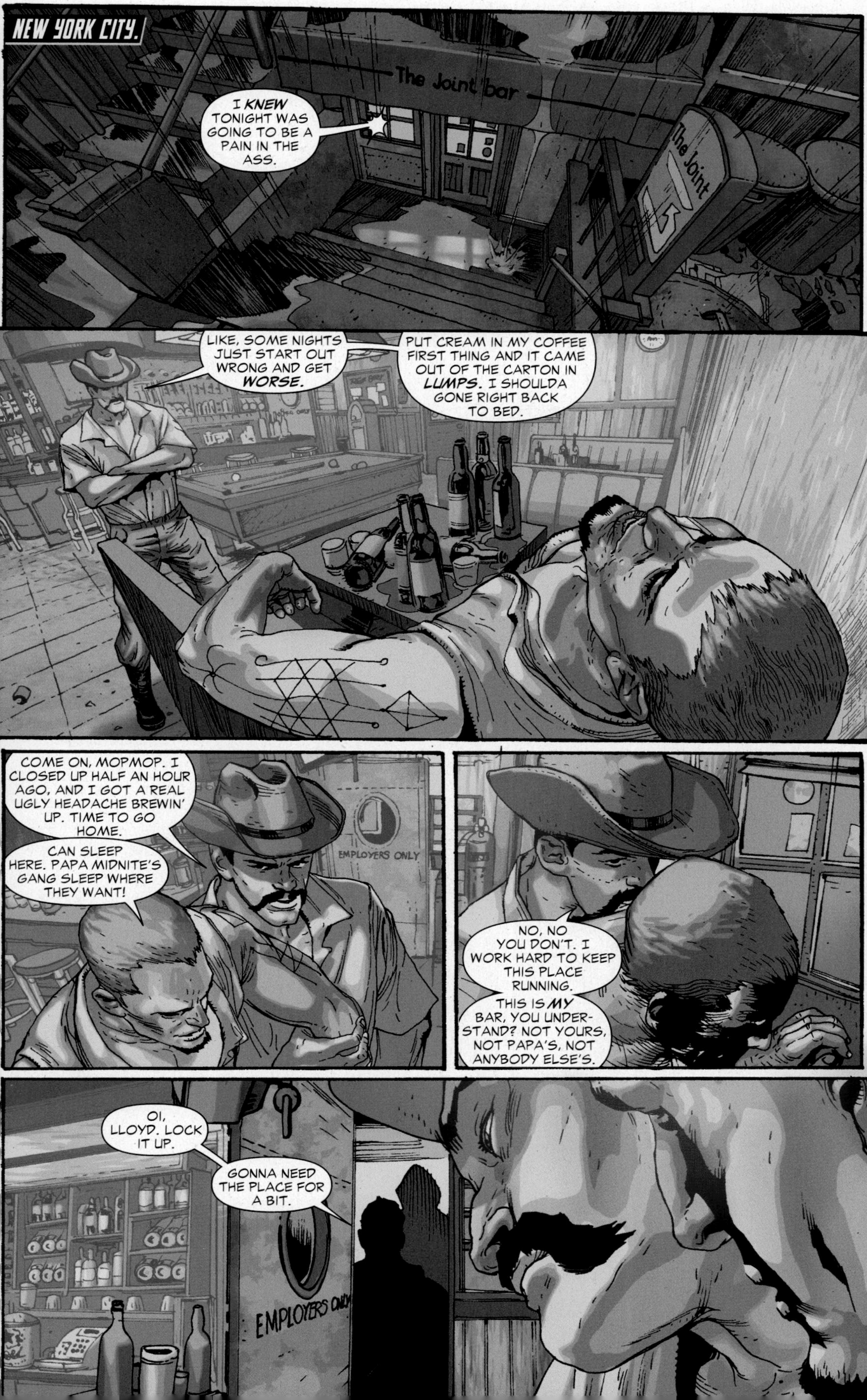
NEW YORK CITY.
The Joint bar
I KNEW TONIGHT WAS GOING TO BE A PAIN IN THE ASS.
The Joint
LIKE, SOME NIGHTS JUST START OUT WRONG AND GET WORSE.
PUT CREAM IN MY COFFEE FIRST THING AND IT CAME OUT OF THE CARTON IN LUMPS. I SHOULDA GONE RIGHT BACK TO BED.
COME ON, MOPMOP. I CLOSED UP HALF AN HOUR AGO, AND I GOT A REAL UGLY HEADACHE BREWIN' UP. TIME TO GO HOME.
CAN SLEEP HERE. PAPA MIDNITE'S GANG SLEEP WHERE THEY WANT!
EMPLOYERS ONLY
NO, NO YOU DON'T. I WORK HARD TO KEEP THIS PLACE RUNNING.
THIS IS MY BAR, YOU UNDERSTAND? NOT YOURS, NOT PAPA'S, NOT ANYBODY ELSE'S.
OI, LLOYD. LOCK IT UP.
GONNA NEED THE PLACE FOR A BIT.
EMPLOYERS ONLY

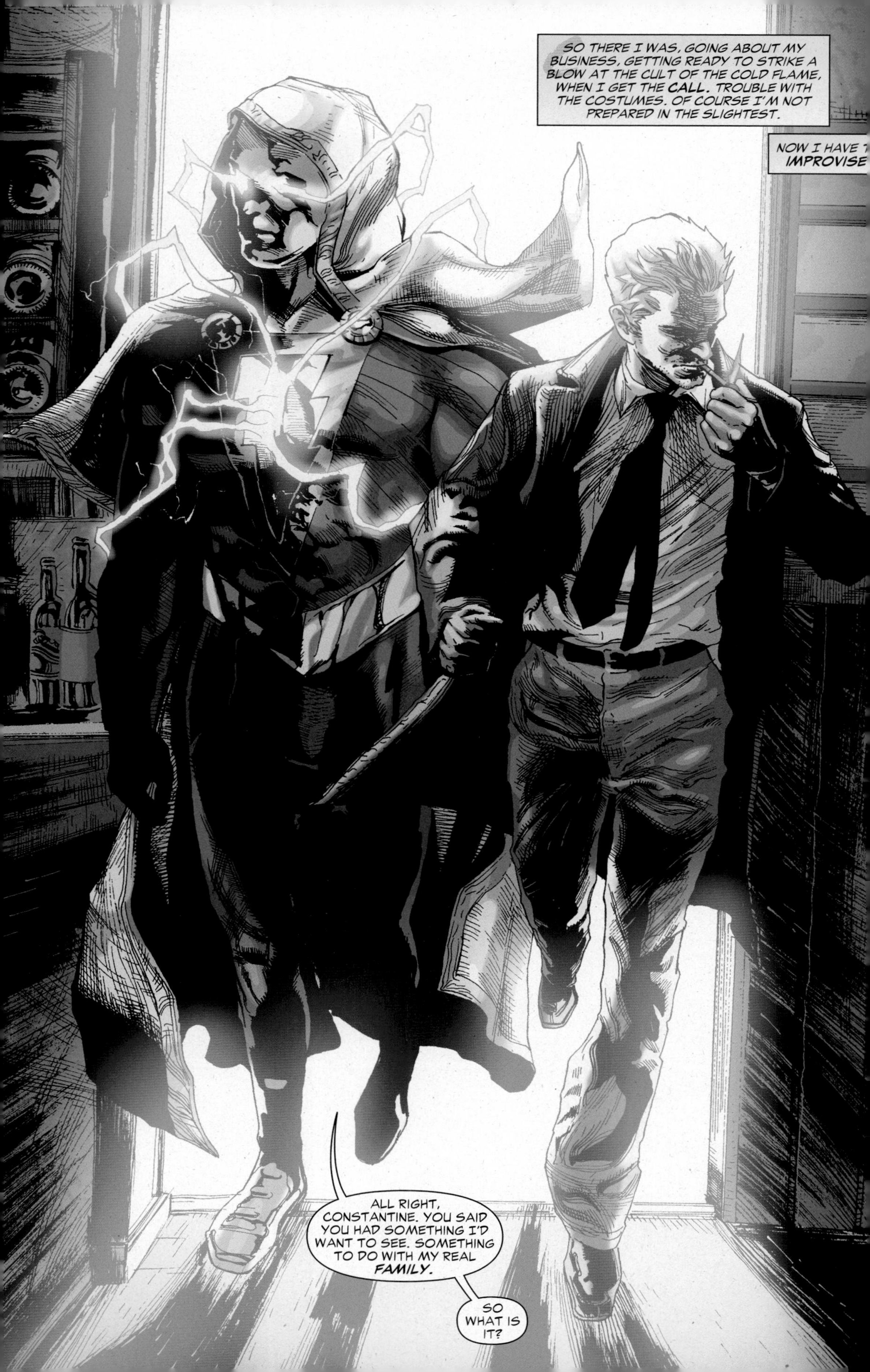
SO THERE I WAS, GOING ABOUT MY BUSINESS, GETTING READY TO STRIKE A BLOW AT THE CULT OF THE COLD FLAME, WHEN I GET THE **CALL.** TROUBLE WITH THE COSTUMES. OF COURSE I'M NOT PREPARED IN THE SLIGHTEST.
NOW I HAVE T **IMPROVISE**
ALL RIGHT, CONSTANTINE. YOU SAID YOU HAD SOMETHING I'D WANT TO SEE. SOMETHING TO DO WITH MY REAL ***FAMILY.***
SO WHAT IS IT?

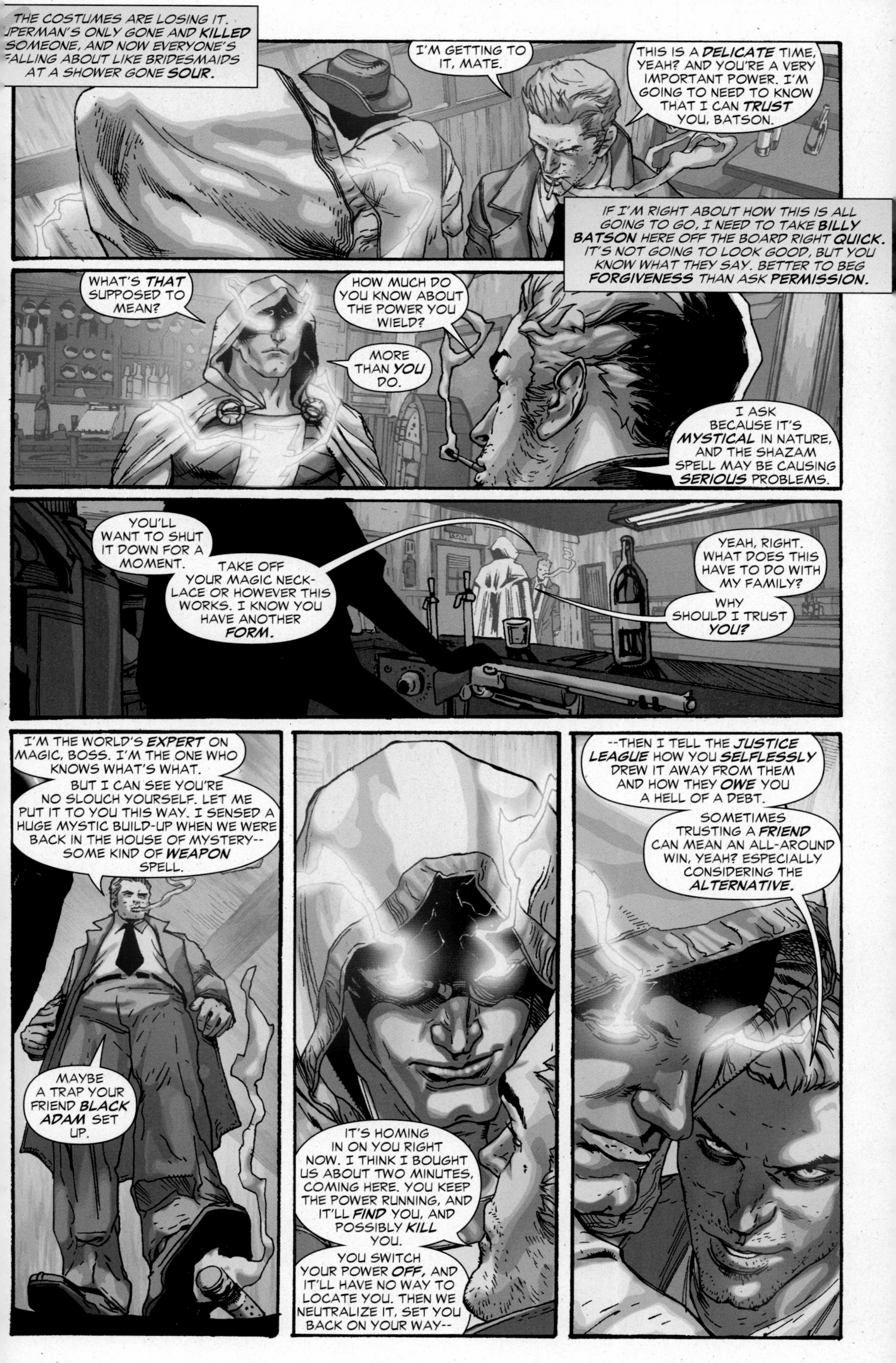
THE COSTUMES ARE LOSING IT. SUPERMAN'S ONLY GONE AND KILLED SOMEONE, AND NOW EVERYONE'S FALLING ABOUT LIKE BRIDESMAIDS AT A SHOWER GONE SOUR.
I'M GETTING TO IT, MATE.
THIS IS A DELICATE TIME, YEAH? AND YOU'RE A VERY IMPORTANT POWER. I'M GOING TO NEED TO KNOW THAT I CAN TRUST YOU, BATSON.
IF I'M RIGHT ABOUT HOW THIS IS ALL GOING TO GO, I NEED TO TAKE BILLY BATSON HERE OFF THE BOARD RIGHT QUICK. IT'S NOT GOING TO LOOK GOOD, BUT YOU KNOW WHAT THEY SAY. BETTER TO BEG FORGIVENESS THAN ASK PERMISSION.
WHAT'S THAT SUPPOSED TO MEAN?
HOW MUCH DO YOU KNOW ABOUT THE POWER YOU WIELD?
MORE THAN YOU DO.
I ASK BECAUSE IT'S MYSTICAL IN NATURE, AND THE SHAZAM SPELL MAY BE CAUSING SERIOUS PROBLEMS.
YOU'LL WANT TO SHUT IT DOWN FOR A MOMENT.
TAKE OFF YOUR MAGIC NECKLACE OR HOWEVER THIS WORKS. I KNOW YOU HAVE ANOTHER FORM.
YEAH, RIGHT. WHAT DOES THIS HAVE TO DO WITH MY FAMILY?
WHY SHOULD I TRUST YOU?
I'M THE WORLD'S EXPERT ON MAGIC, BOSS. I'M THE ONE WHO KNOWS WHAT'S WHAT.
BUT I CAN SEE YOU'RE NO SLOUCH YOURSELF. LET ME PUT IT TO YOU THIS WAY. I SENSED A HUGE MYSTIC BUILD-UP WHEN WE WERE BACK IN THE HOUSE OF MYSTERY-- SOME KIND OF WEAPON SPELL.
MAYBE A TRAP YOUR FRIEND BLACK ADAM SET UP.
IT'S HOMING IN ON YOU RIGHT NOW. I THINK I BOUGHT US ABOUT TWO MINUTES, COMING HERE. YOU KEEP THE POWER RUNNING, AND IT'LL FIND YOU, AND POSSIBLY KILL YOU.
YOU SWITCH YOUR POWER OFF, AND IT'LL HAVE NO WAY TO LOCATE YOU. THEN WE NEUTRALIZE IT, SET YOU BACK ON YOUR WAY--
--THEN I TELL THE JUSTICE LEAGUE HOW YOU SELFLESSLY DREW IT AWAY FROM THEM AND HOW THEY OWE YOU A HELL OF A DEBT.
SOMETIMES TRUSTING A FRIEND CAN MEAN AN ALL-AROUND WIN, YEAH? ESPECIALLY CONSIDERING THE ALTERNATIVE.

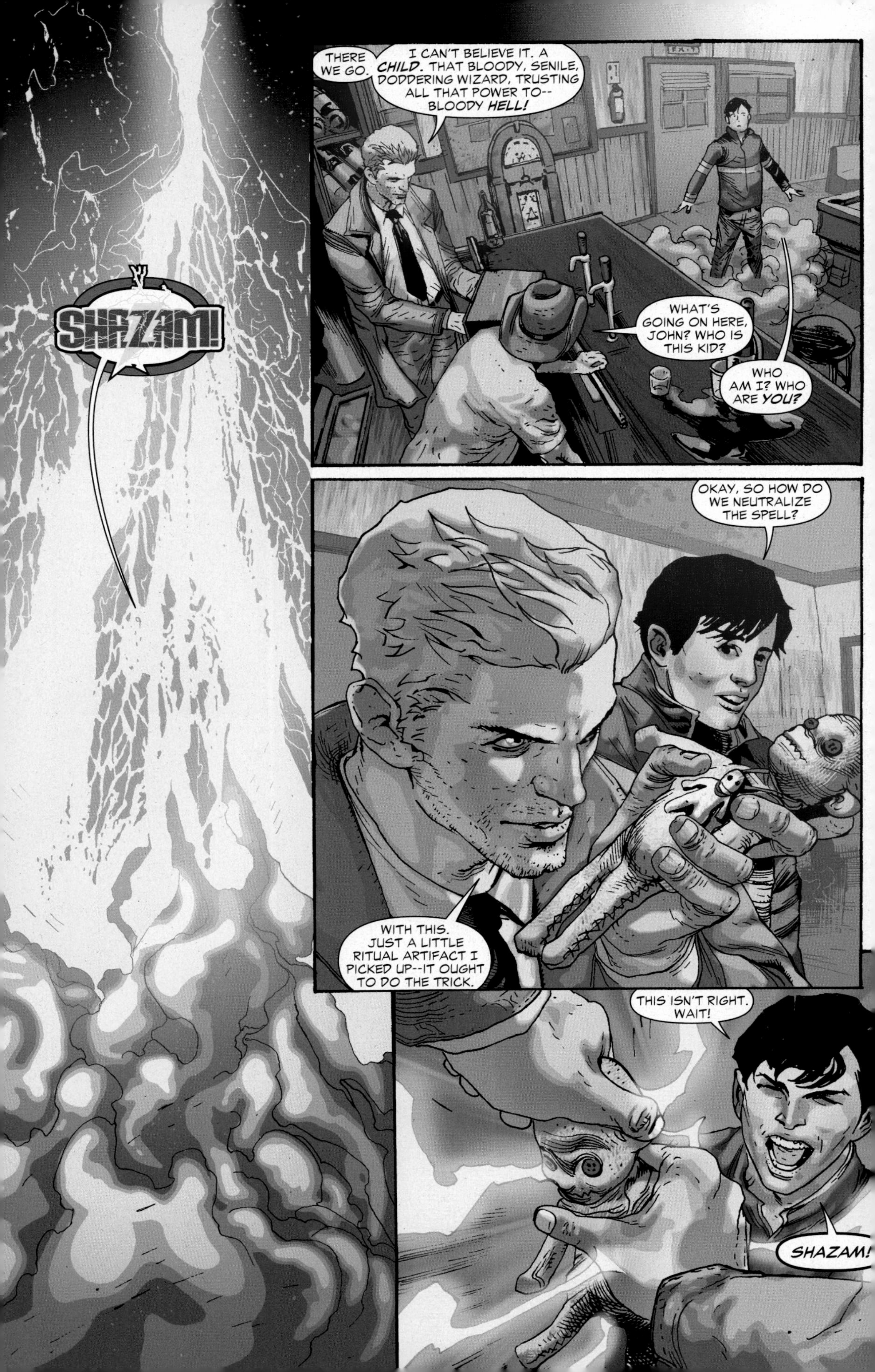
SHAZAM!
THERE WE GO.
I CAN'T BELIEVE IT. A CHILD. THAT BLOODY, SENILE, DODDERING WIZARD, TRUSTING ALL THAT POWER TO-- BLOODY HELL!
WHAT'S GOING ON HERE, JOHN? WHO IS THIS KID?
WHO AM I? WHO ARE YOU?
OKAY, SO HOW DO WE NEUTRALIZE THE SPELL?
WITH THIS. JUST A LITTLE RITUAL ARTIFACT I PICKED UP--IT OUGHT TO DO THE TRICK.
THIS ISN'T RIGHT. WAIT!
SHAZAM!

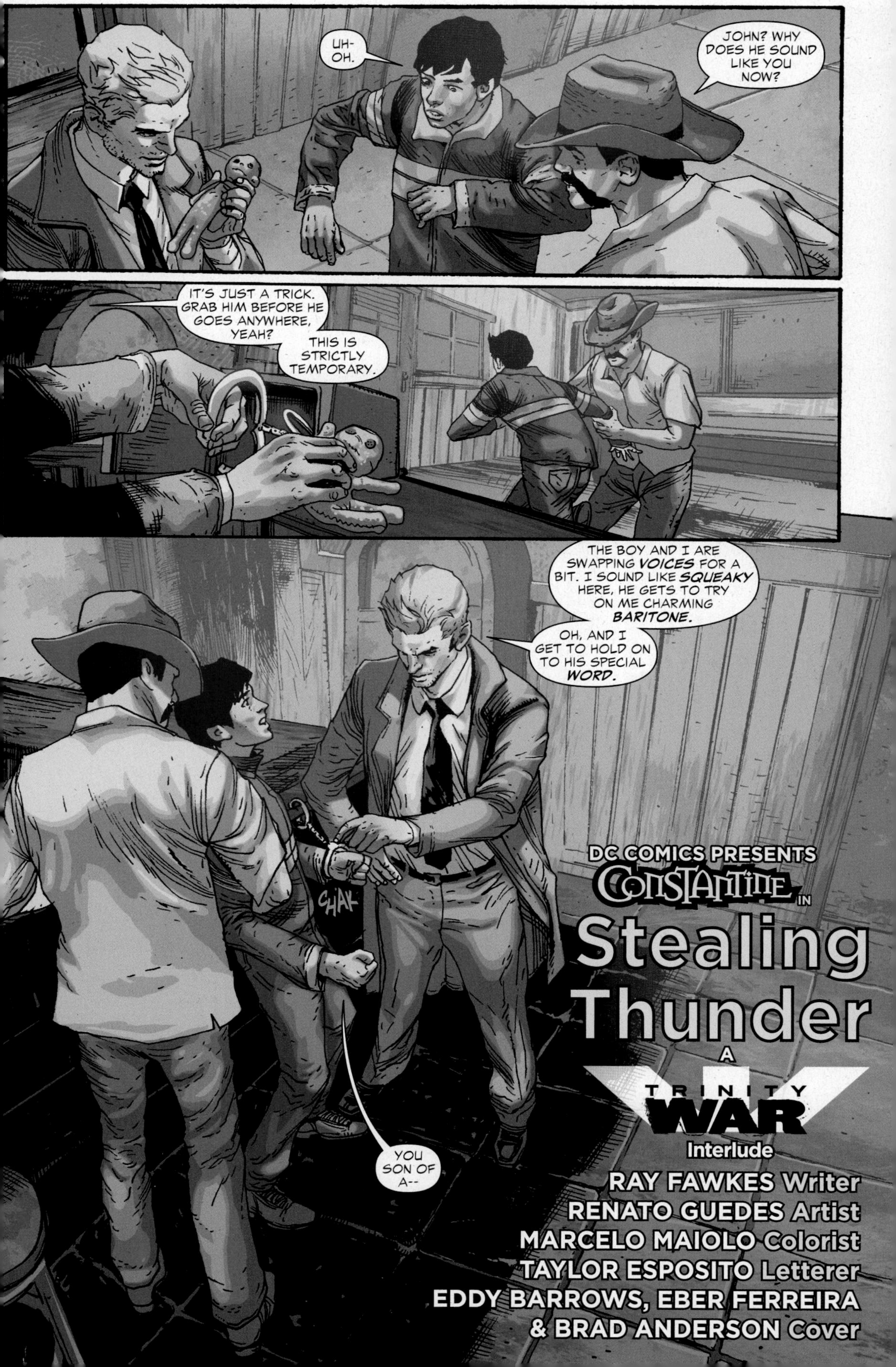
UH-
OH.
JOHN? WHY
DOES HE SOUND
LIKE YOU
NOW?
IT'S JUST A TRICK.
GRAB HIM BEFORE HE
GOES ANYWHERE,
YEAH?
THIS IS
STRICTLY
TEMPORARY.
THE BOY AND I ARE
SWAPPING VOICES FOR A
BIT. I SOUND LIKE SQUEAKY
HERE, HE GETS TO TRY
ON ME CHARMING
BARITONE.
OH, AND I
GET TO HOLD ON
TO HIS SPECIAL
WORD.
CHAK
YOU
SON OF
A--
DC COMICS PRESENTS
CONSTANTINE IN
Stealing
Thunder
A
TRINITY
WAR
Interlude
RAY FAWKES Writer
RENATO GUEDES Artist
MARCELO MAIOLO Colorist
TAYLOR ESPOSITO Letterer
EDDY BARROWS, EBER FERREIRA
& BRAD ANDERSON Cover

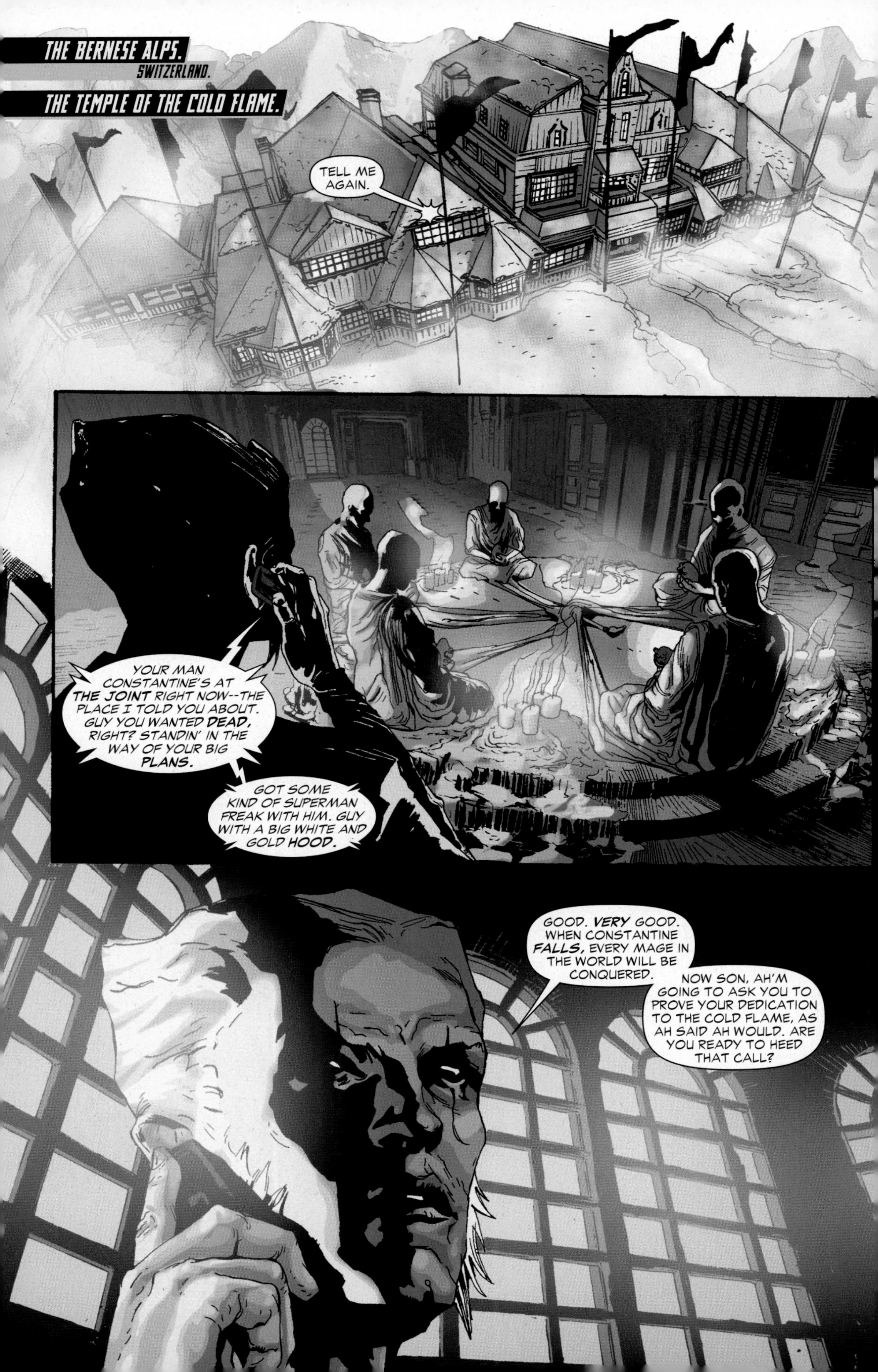
THE BERNESE ALPS.
SWITZERLAND.
THE TEMPLE OF THE COLD FLAME.
TELL ME AGAIN.
YOUR MAN CONSTANTINE'S AT THE JOINT RIGHT NOW--THE PLACE I TOLD YOU ABOUT. GUY YOU WANTED DEAD, RIGHT? STANDIN' IN THE WAY OF YOUR BIG PLANS.
GOT SOME KIND OF SUPERMAN FREAK WITH HIM. GUY WITH A BIG WHITE AND GOLD HOOD.
GOOD. VERY GOOD. WHEN CONSTANTINE FALLS, EVERY MAGE IN THE WORLD WILL BE CONQUERED.
NOW SON, AH'M GOING TO ASK YOU TO PROVE YOUR DEDICATION TO THE COLD FLAME, AS AH SAID AH WOULD. ARE YOU READY TO HEED THAT CALL?

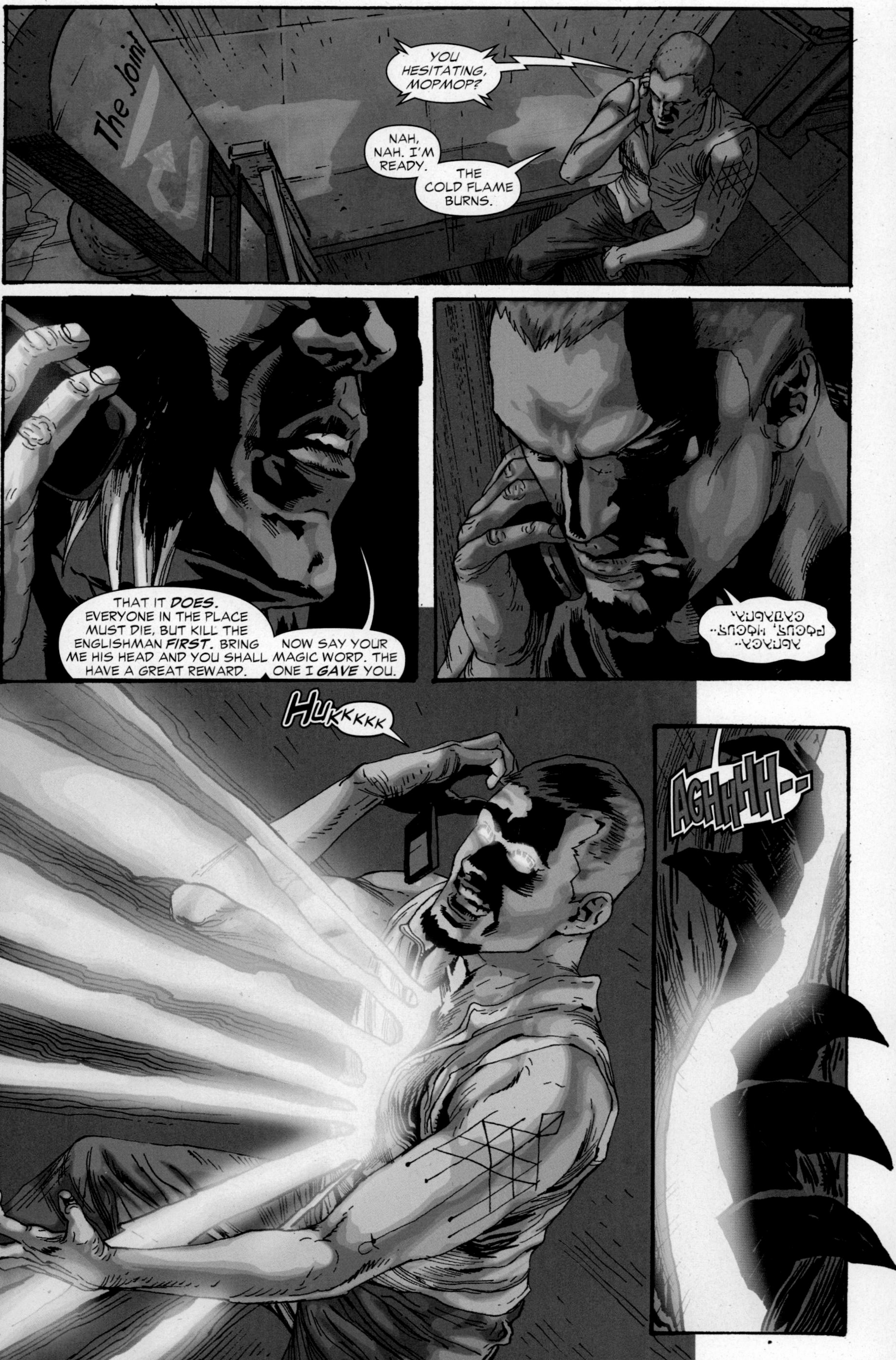
The Joint
YOU HESITATING, MOPMOP?
NAH, NAH. I'M READY.
THE COLD FLAME BURNS.
THAT IT DOES. EVERYONE IN THE PLACE MUST DIE, BUT KILL THE ENGLISHMAN FIRST. BRING ME HIS HEAD AND YOU SHALL HAVE A GREAT REWARD.
NOW SAY YOUR MAGIC WORD. THE ONE I GAVE YOU.
HUKKKKK
AGHHHH--

BDEEP
SHOW ME NEW YORK.

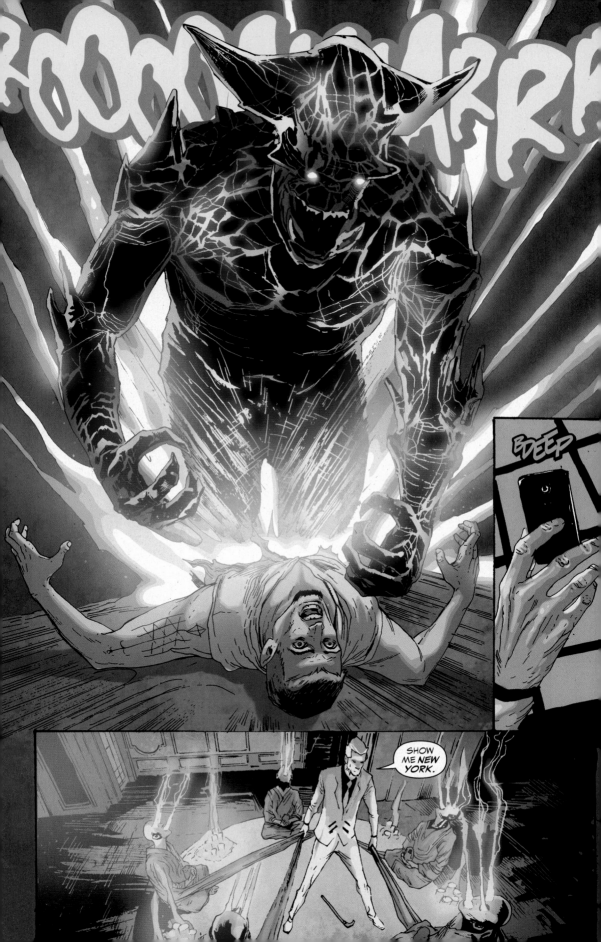

DON'T WORRY, MATE. I'M NOT AFTER YOUR POWER FOR MYSELF. LAST THING I WANT IS TO SLAP ON YOUR ENCHANTED LONGJOHNS. SEEMS MUTUAL, TOO--I CAN FEEL IT TRYING TO GET OUT.
I'LL JUST BOTTLE IT UP HERE, AND THEN YOU AND I ARE GOING TO TALK.
JOHN, CAN YOU DO THIS SOMEWHERE ELSE? YOU KNOW I HATE THIS FREAKY CRAP IN MY BAR.
YOU ALL SOUNDING LIKE A CREEPY LITTLE BOY.
NO CHOICE, LLOYD. THIS KID HAS NO IDEA HOW DISASTROUS IT COULD BE IF HE RUNS LOOSE WITH THIS MAGIC RIGHT NOW.
DOING THE WRONG THING FOR THE RIGHT REASON AND WE'RE ALL IN A WORLD OF PAIN AND DARKNESS.
BUT IT'S MY MAGIC. WHAT GIVES YOU THE RIGHT TO DECIDE IF I CAN USE IT?
BOOOOM
AAAH!
ROOOAA
CRASH
WHAT IS THAT THING?
GIVE ME THE POWER BACK, JERK-WAD! NOW!
HNNH!
YUU DEAD
YUU DEAD RRRINGOOO
MOPMOP?
VHOK
SH--
SHAZAM--

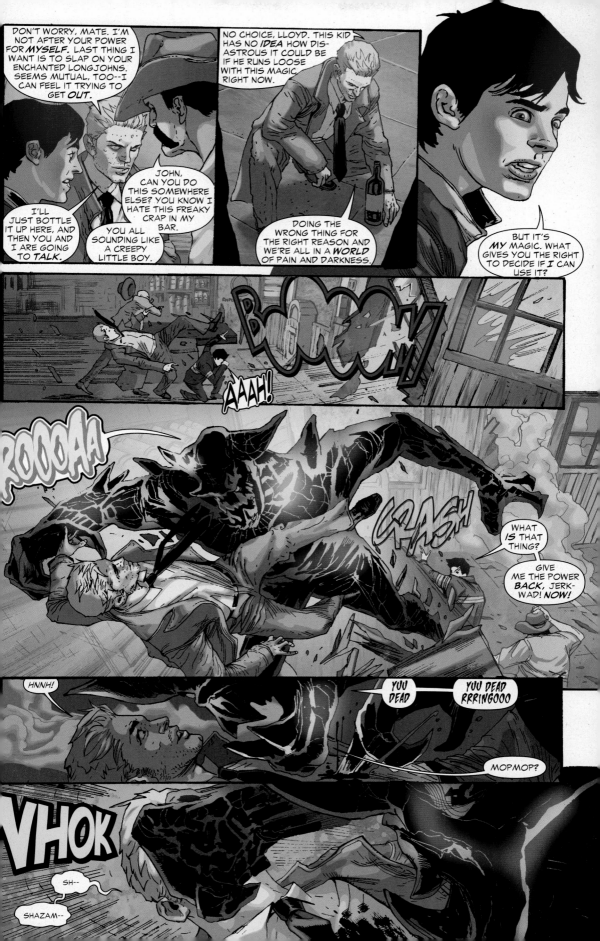

BOOM

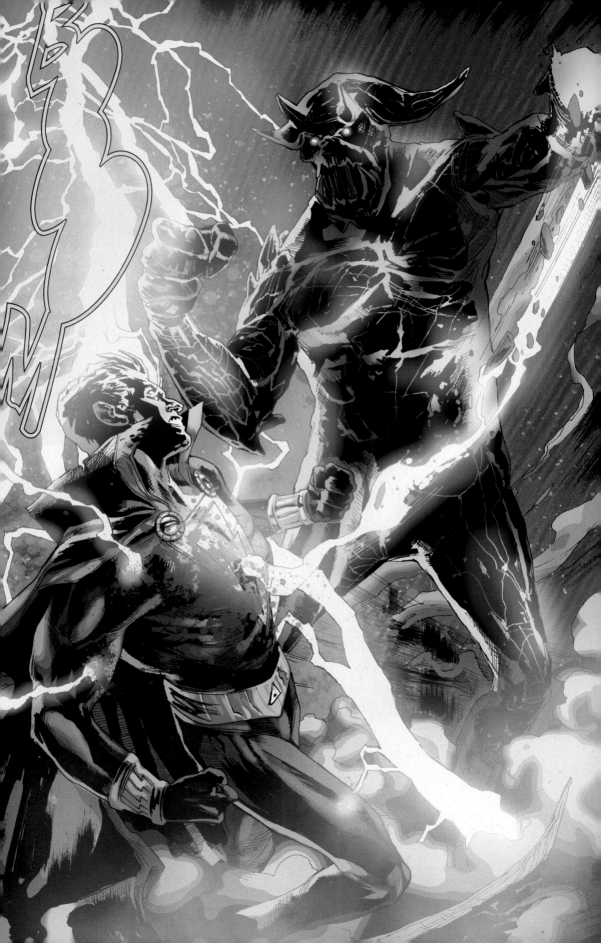

THE POWER... IS AGONY.

SHHZZZTTT

WON'T...BE ABLE TO CONTAIN IT... FOR LONG...

BAM

CRASH

RRAAA

DON'T TOUCH, KID. I DON'T WANT TO HAVE TO HIT YOU. JUST TAKE COVER.

TRUST ME, MOPMOP. I LIKE THIS LESS THAN YOU DO.
WHAM
LOOKS LIKE WE'RE BOTH STEPPING OUT OF TYPE, YEAH?
WHAM
SHRAAAAKKKKKK
DAMN IT! AGH!
KILLL YUUU
WAIT A SEC.
YUUU DIIIE
IT'S AFTER HIM. BUT I'VE GOT HIS VOICE. I SOUND LIKE HIM.
SO?

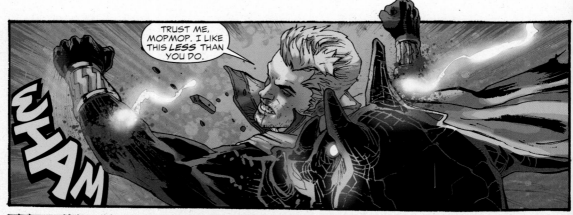

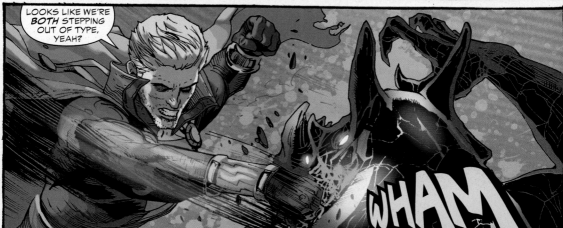

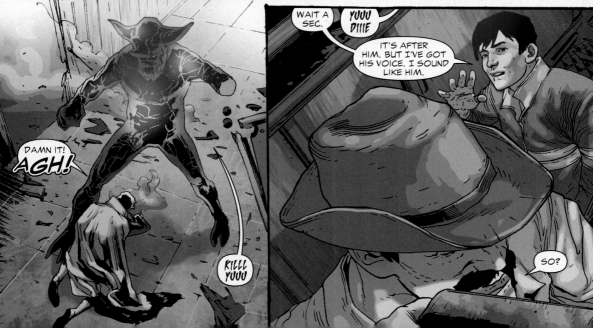

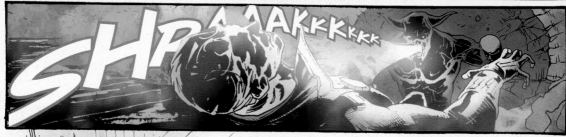

UH, OI!
OI, UGLY! YOU'RE AFTER *ME*, AREN'T YOU?
...UH, *MATEY?*
QUITE A TRICK, EH, YA STUPID *WANKER?* I BLOODY SWITCHED BODIES WITH THE BOY, DIDN'T I?
UH, BOLLOCKS ON YOU! UMM...
THUU ENGLISSHHMANN
BLAM
KKKKKK
UUUAAUUU

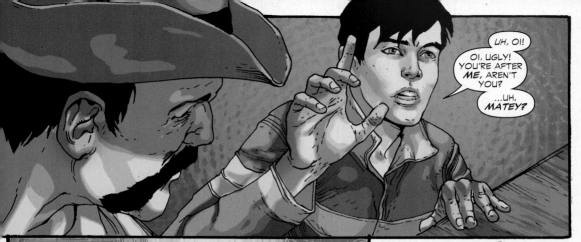

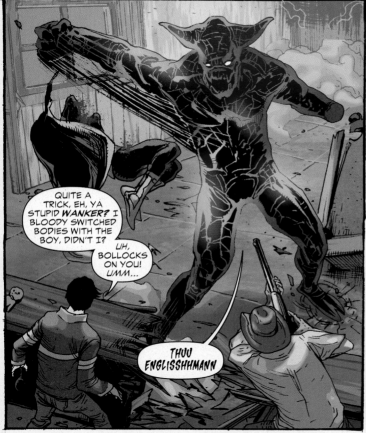

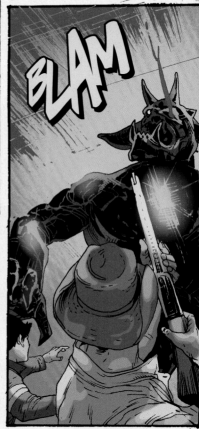

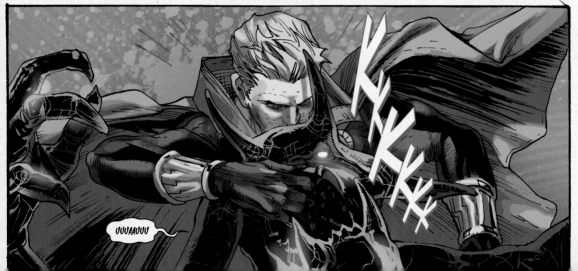

KKKRACKKKK

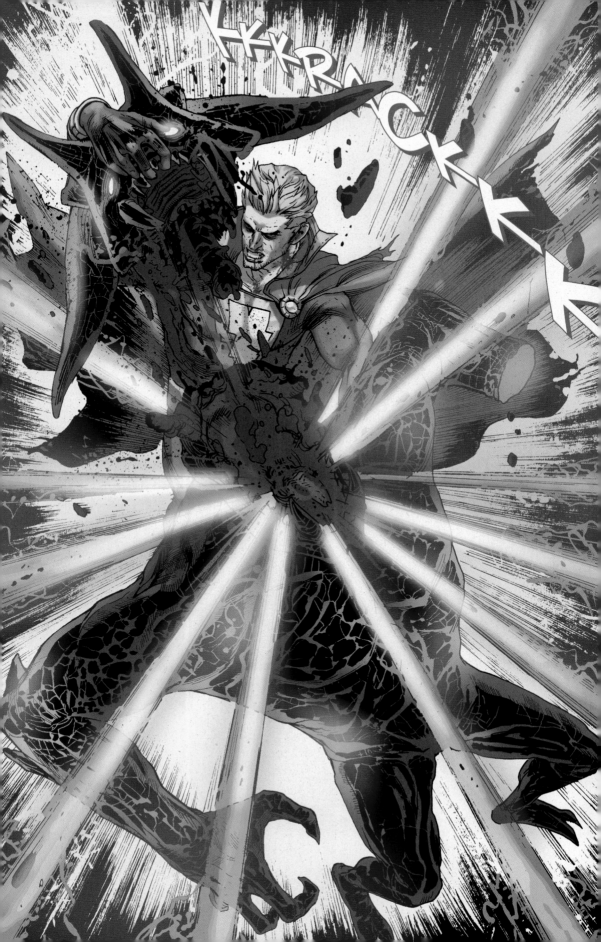

THIS POWER... TEARING ME UP INSIDE...
BLUM
NICE PLAY, KID.
YOU GOT SOME BALLS.
NO, WAIT!
SHAZAM!

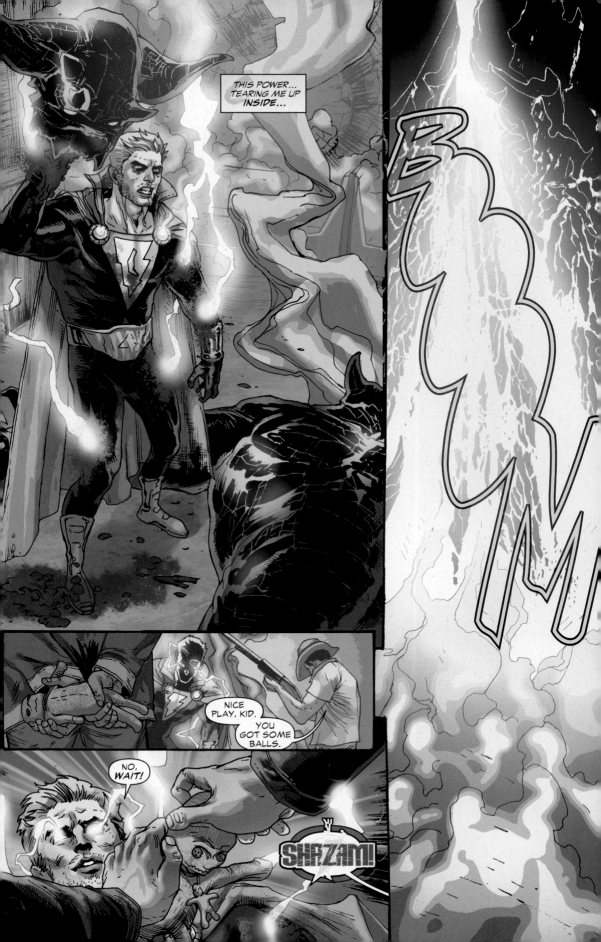

THAT'S BETTER.
THE CHANGE REALLY KNOCKS YOU OUT, HUH? IT MUST TOTALLY SUCK FOR AN OLD GUY.
HNGH!
YOU'RE LUCKY I'M NOT KICKING THE CRAP OUT OF YOU FOR WHAT YOU DID. LYING TO ME ABOUT MY FAMILY.
YEAH--
YEAH, YOU'RE A REAL SWEETHEART, BATSON.
THE OLD WIZARD TRUSTED ME WITH THIS POWER. I'M THE ONE WHO'S SUPPOSED TO DECIDE WHAT TO DO WITH IT.
I'M GONNA ASK YOU AGAIN. WHAT MAKES YOU THINK YOU HAVE THE RIGHT TO TAKE IT AWAY?
LISTEN TO ME.
YOU LISTEN. I OWE YOU ONE.
THE BOX. THE BOX THAT LOOKS LIKE A SKULL WITH THREE EYES.
THE ONE ALL THE COSTUMES ARE FIGHTING OVER. IT'S NOT WHAT IT LOOKS LIKE. IT'S A GLOBAL BOMB. THE COUNCIL--THE WIZARDS WHOSE POWER YOU CARRY. THEY HAD NO IDEA.
LISTEN.

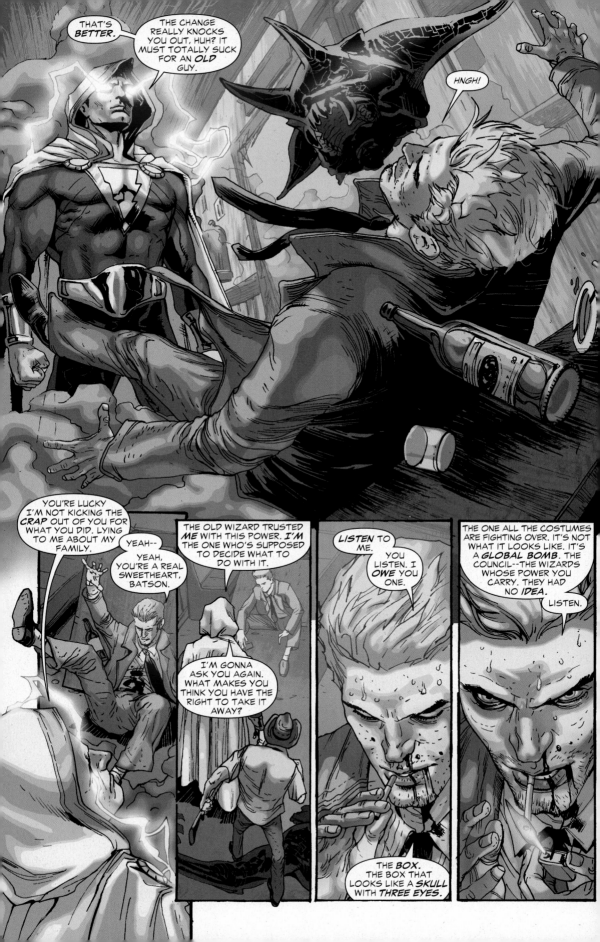

JOHN--

DON'T **TOUCH** IT, KID. YOU'LL THINK YOU'RE DOING THE RIGHT THING, BUT YOU'LL ONLY **LIGHT** THE **FUSE**.

THIS COMING FROM THE GUY WHO **KIDNAPS** ME, **LIES** TO ME, AND **STEALS** MY POWER.

HOW DO I KNOW YOU'RE NOT TELLING ME THE **OPPOSITE** OF WHAT I SHOULD DO?

I WOULDN'T-- NNH--

I WOULDN'T HAVE DONE ANY OF THAT IF I KNEW I COULD **TRUST** YOU. THE POWER YOU HAVE IS **TOO BIG** FOR MAYBES, KID.

RIGHT. YOU'RE A REAL **JERK**, CONSTANTINE. I HOPE I **NEVER** SEE YOU AGAIN.

‡COUGH‡

>COUGH<
>COUGH<
I DON'T GET IT, JOHN. WHAT WAS THE PLAY HERE?
WHAT WAS IN IT FOR YOU?

JOHN, AW NO, MOPMOP GOT YOU!
LET ME GET MY KIT. I'M GONNA GET MY KIT.

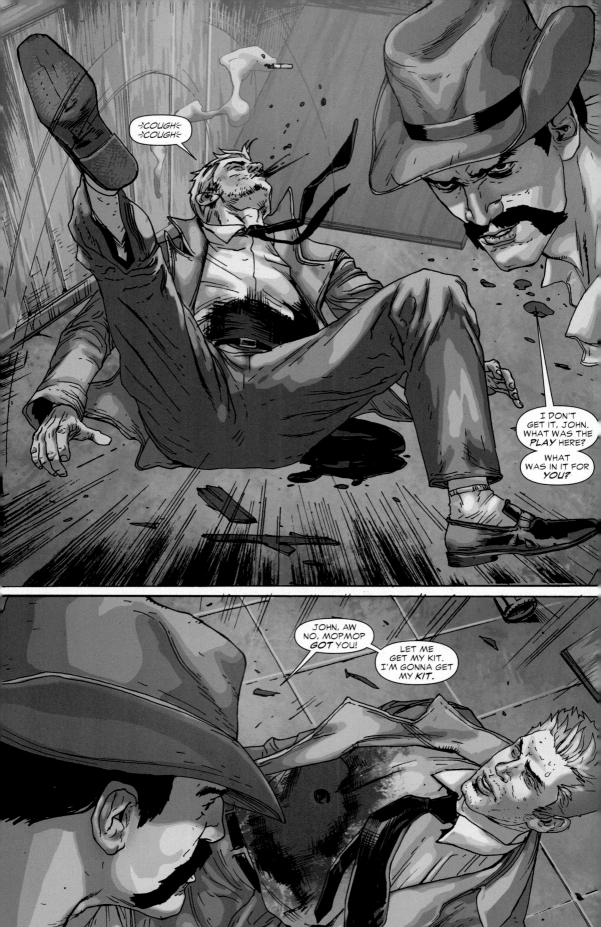

LLOYD.
LLOYD. SORRY ABOUT THE BAR.
DON'T TRY TO TALK. I'M GONNA CALL FOR HELP.
YOU'RE GONNA BE ALL RIGHT.
BLOODY HELL.
WELL, WELL, WELL...

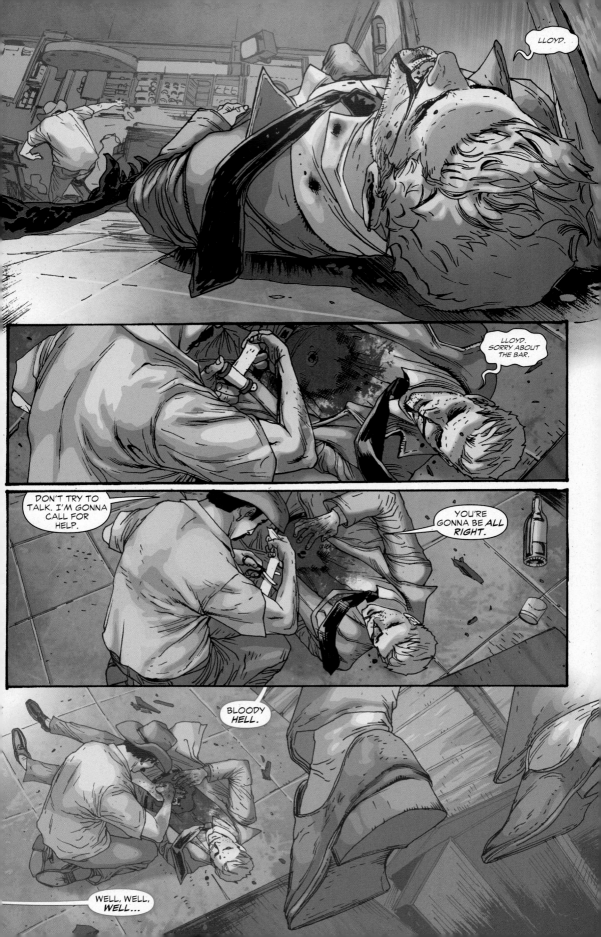

...LOOK WHO IT IS, GETTING ALL OUT-OF-BODY, LIGHT-AT-THE-END-OF-THE-TUNNEL.
HI, JOHN. REMEMBER ME? IT'S CHRIS, THE GUY YOU KILLED A COUPLE WEEKS AGO. GUESS WHAT?
IT'S TIME FOR PAYBACK.
ERS ONLY
EXIT

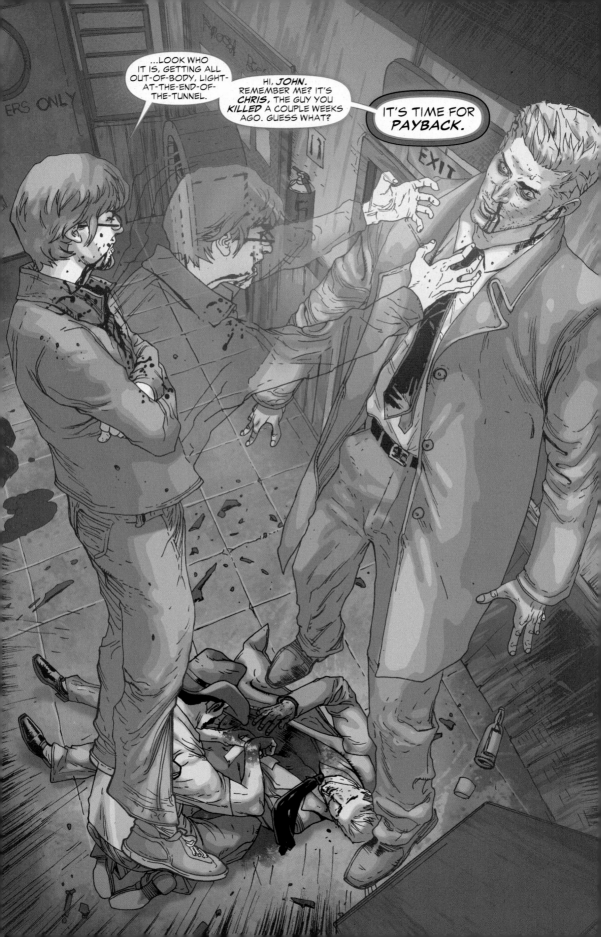

SOOK

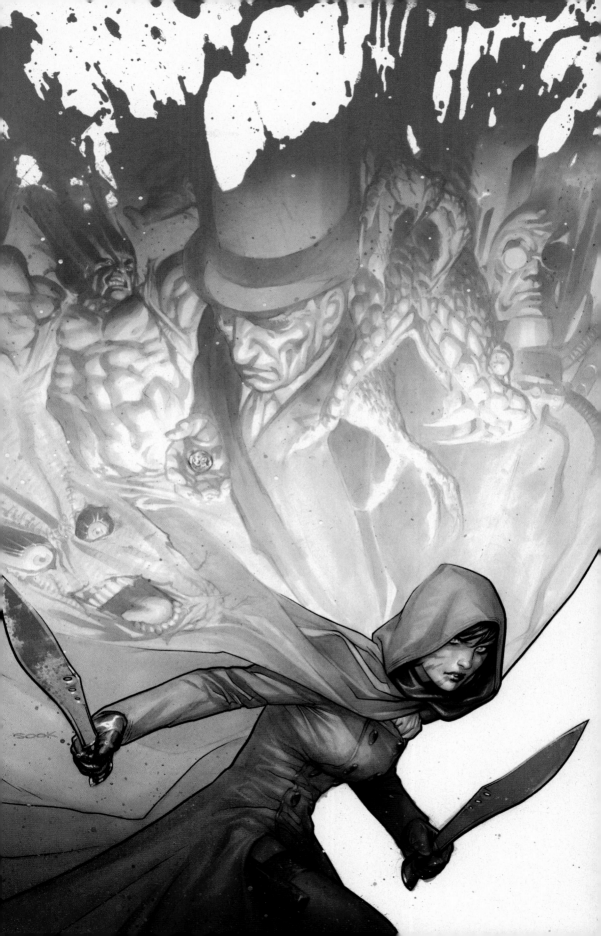

SOOK
SOOK

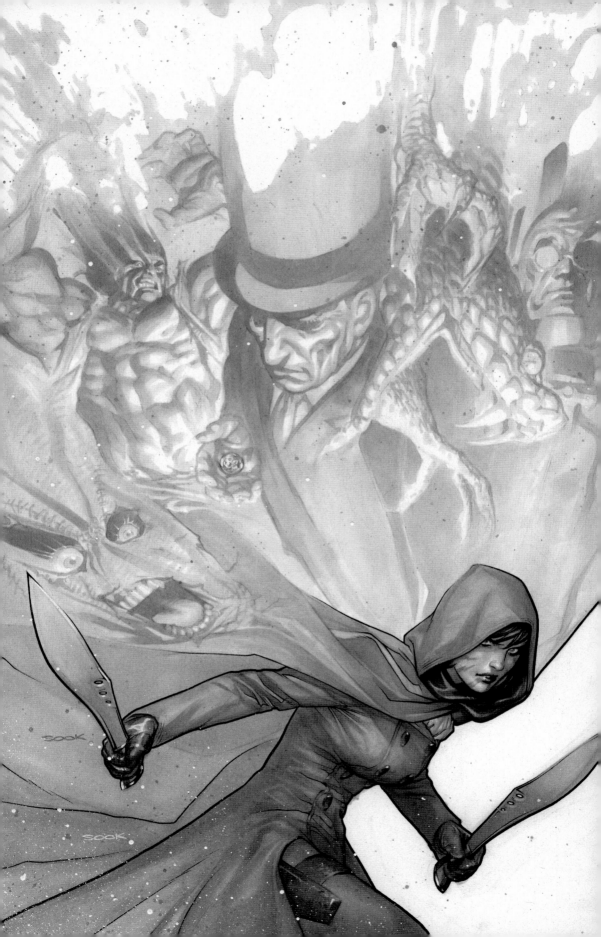

A, EGYPT.
I'M HERE, PRIDE. WHAT'S YOUR NEED?
AH,
SILENCE NOW, BROTHER ENVY, WHILE THE HOT SUN SETS. THIS SHIMMERING SPECTACLE PLEASES ME.
NOW IT'S SET. MAY I SPEAK?
YOU'VE NAUGHT WORTH HEARING. BUT LISTEN CLOSELY.
PANDORA UNDYING SEEKS TO ERASE US. OUR OWN MOTHER.
...THAT'S NOT NEW.
NO? THE WIZARD'S DEAD, BUT GIVEN HER A CLUE. SHE'S GOT THE BOX NOW, SHE'LL PUZZLE IT OUT.
SHE MOVES QUICKLY. GO. BLOCK HER, DELAY HER.
TO WHAT END?
TO THE END THAT I DESIGN. NOW DO IT. THE NIGHT'S JUST FALLEN...

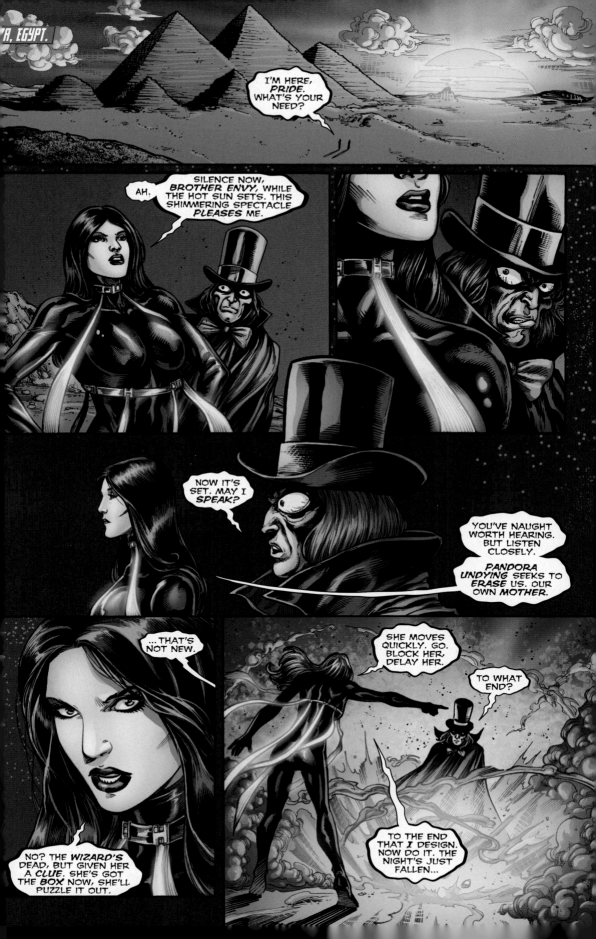

"...AND I'VE OTHER AGENTS WHO NEED TENDING."

TERREBONNE PARISH, LOUISIANA. BELLE REVE PENITENTIARY.

WHAT A WAY TO START THE WEEKEND. WHAT'S THE STORY?

WE'VE GOT ONE *JUSTICE LEAGUE* MEMBER DEAD, AND IT LOOKS LIKE SUPERMAN KILLED HIM, RIGHT? I HAVE A FEELING YOUR WEEKEND BARBECUE PLANS OR WHATEVER HAVE BEEN *DEPRIORITIZED.*

WE'VE GOT SECURITY FOOTAGE OF SUPERMAN AND WONDER WOMAN MEETING UP WITH THIS UNIDENTIFIED WOMAN RIGHT *HERE* YESTERDAY, AND WE'RE READING RESIDUE OF A FRANKLY LUDICROUS ENERGY DISCHARGE AT THIS SPOT.

SENSORS SPINNING ON THEIR DIALS AND BREAKING LIKE SOMETHING OUT OF A SLAPSTICK CARTOON.

SHE'S *NOT* UNIDENTIFIED.

EXCUSE ME?

THIS SAME WOMAN RECENTLY BROKE INTO A SECURE A.R.G.U.S. FACILITY KNOWN AS THE *BLACK ROOM* AND STOLE AN ARTIFACT FROM US. HER CODENAME IS *PANDORA.*

WELL, HOORAY FOR INTERDEPARTMENTAL *COMMUNICATION.* BECAUSE S.H.A.D.E.* HAS BEEN TRYING TO IDENTIFY AND *CLASSIFY* HER HERE.

OKAY, SO YOUR JOB IS DONE. I'M TELLING YOU SHE'S A METAHUMAN THREAT SO SHE'S NOT YOUR PROBLEM.

SPECIAL AGENT *KINCAID,* I'M SPECIAL AGENT *PAUL CHANG,* A.R.G.U.S.* INTELLIGENCE. THIS ONE'S MY JURISDICTION.

HOLD ON. WE HAD ONE OF OUR PSYCHICS HERE AT THE SCENE--HE WENT INTO *CONVULSIONS* THE MOMENT HE STEPPED OUT OF THE CAR.

WOW, A PSYCHIC WITH A *VAGUE* PROCLAMATION AND NO FOLLOW-UP.

I'M *SHOCKED.*

SAID SOMETHING ABOUT "TEN THOUSAND YEARS OF UNDYING PAIN" BEFORE HE SLIPPED INTO A *COMA.* THE SUSPECT MIGHT BE *PARAHUMAN.*

VERY FUNNY. I'LL SAY THIS: I GET THE IMPRESSION JURISDICTION ISN'T QUITE SO CLEAR HERE...

*SUPER-HUMAN ADVANCED DEFENSE EXECUTIVE

*ADVANCED RESEARCH GROUP UNITING SUPER-HUMANS

CHANG, P.
CLEARANCE 3-BT10

..I THINK THIS IS
A PROBLEM FOR
EVERYBODY."
ALTIMORE, MARYLAND
YOU SAY YOU'VE SEEN ME THROUGH TWO HUNDRED REINCARNATIONS. YOU EVER ASK ME TO ARM YOU UP LIKE THIS?
I THOUGHT I COULD END MY CURSE, MARCUS, BUT IT LOOKS LIKE I'VE IGNITED SOME KIND OF WAR INSTEAD.
DC COMICS PROUDLY PRESENTS
TRINITY OF SIN:
PANDORA
DRAWING BLOOD
AY FAKWES-WRITER
ANIEL SAMPERE-PENCILLER
VICENTE CIFUENTES-INKER HI-FI-COLORIST DEZI SIENTY-LETTERER RYAN SOOK-COVER

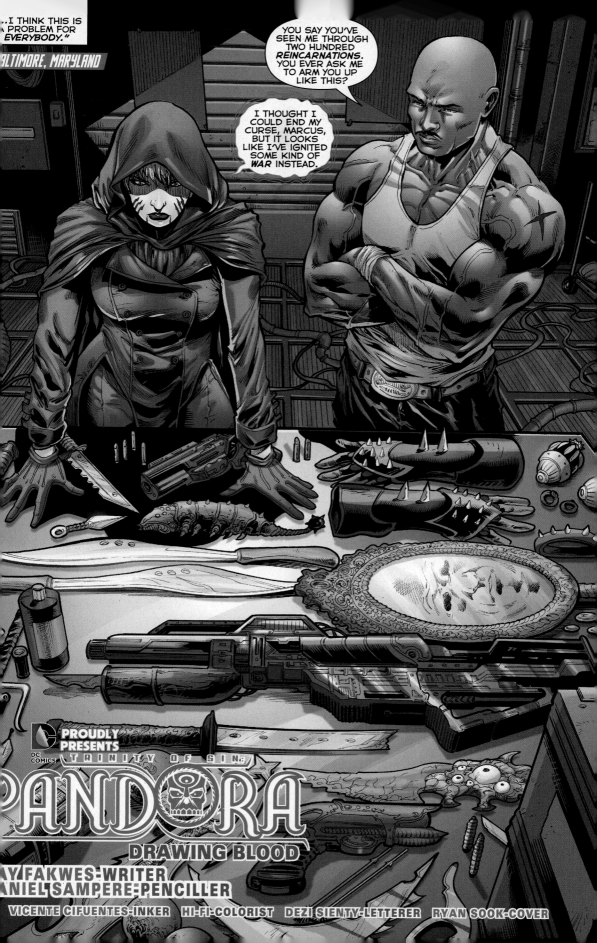

I DIDN'T WANT ANY OF THIS TO HAPPEN.
WHAT ARE WE TALKING ABOUT HERE? SOMEBODY GOING TO TRY TO TAKE YOU DOWN?
THAT'S NOT WHAT I'M WORRIED ABOUT...
"...IT'S THIS FEELING I HAVE-- THAT EVERYTHING'S SPIRALING OUT OF CONTROL."
I LIKE IT.
LOOKS LIKE OUR LADY PANDORA REALLY CUT LOOSE HERE.
IT'S NOT SO BIG.
YOU SHOULD SEE THE SUBATOMIC DISTORTIONS I'M READING. PLUS, OUR SPIES ARE TELLING US THAT A.R.G.U.S. HAS CLASSIFIED THIS A SUPERCRIME.
THIS IS WHERE SHE ATTACKED SUPERMAN AND ESCAPED.
NO KIDDING?
SCOUT'S HONOR, GIGANTA. WE'VE GOT ENERGY OUTPUT ON A COLOSSAL SCALE HERE.
SO YEAH, SHE USED THE BOX.
"SIGNALMAN." CAN YOU FIND HER?
UH, WELL, I'M CERTAINLY GOING TO TRY, SIR.

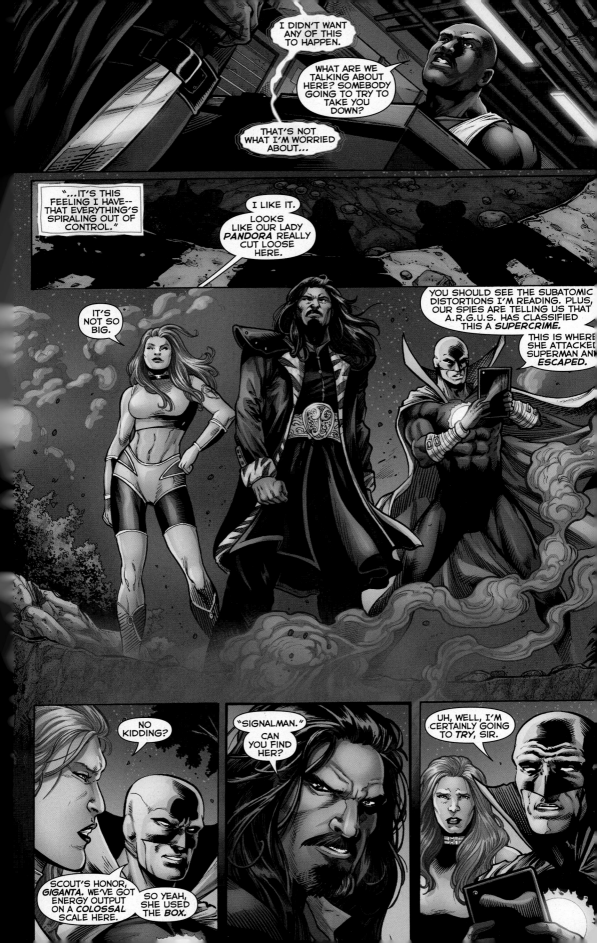

I'M JUST ...NING SIX HACKED ...TARY SATELLITES ...E IN PARALLEL SO ...T I CAN GET MY ...CAN-AND-TRACK CALCULATIONS DONE.
NO BIG DEAL.
SECRET SOCIETY COMMAND SAYS THAT IF WE GET OUR HANDS ON THAT BOX, THE WORLD IS *OURS.*
YEAH, BUT WHAT DOES THAT EVEN *MEAN?*
WHAT *IS* THIS THING?
IT MEANS IF WE *TAKE* IT, WE CAN HAVE WHATEVER WE *WANT*. WHAT MORE DO YOU NEED TO KNOW?
RIGHT, RIGHT.
SO I GET MY MANSION PLAYGROUND WITH UNLIMITED TOYS AND YOU GET TO *SMASH* STUFF, KAIJU-STYLE. BUT WHAT DOES *THAT* SCARY BASTARD WANT?
WELL?
HEY, I'M THE GUY WHO SEES THE *SIGNALS.*
IF SHE SHOWS UP AGAIN, I'LL FIND A WAY TO *SPOT* HER. 'COURSE, I'LL NEED ACCESS TO MORE *RESOURCES.* THE BOSS OUGHT TO AUTHORIZE THAT, DON'T YOU THINK?
I AM *VANDAL SAVAGE*, PEON.
YOU WOULD *TREMBLE* TO KNOW MY THOUGHTS.

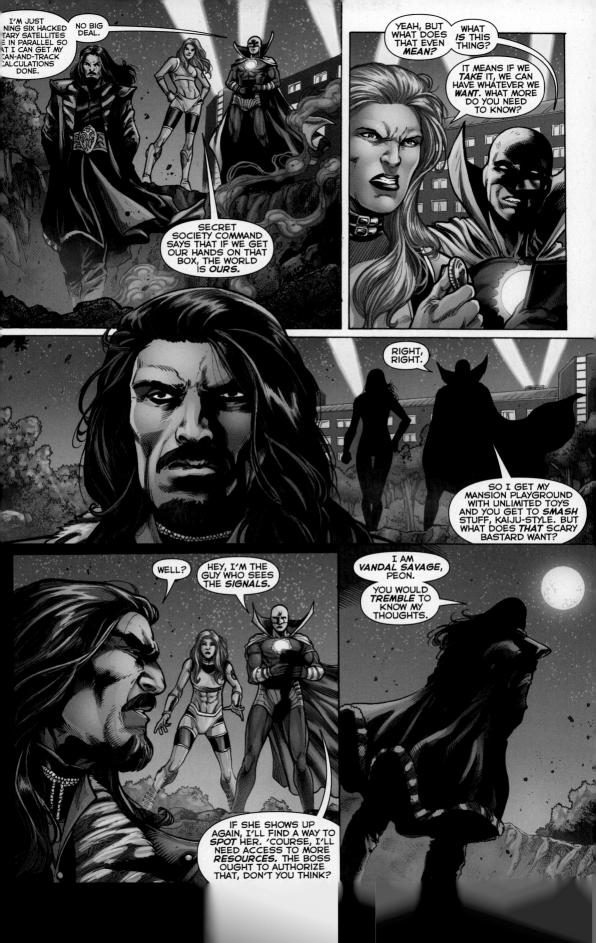

...REPORTS THAT SUPERMAN IS ACCUSED OF KILLING AN AGENT OF THE AMERICAN GOVERNMENT IN KAHNDAQ...
WHOA.
PENNY FOR YOUR THOUGHTS.
LAST TIME I TALKED TO YOU, YOU SAID HE WAS THE ONE YOU NEEDED TO SEE.
DID YOU DO SOMETHING TO SUPERMAN?
I DID.
NONE OF THIS WILL MATTER WHEN I GET THE BOX OPEN MARCUS. THE WORLD WILL BE PURGED OF THE EVIL IT UNLEASHED AND WE WILL BE MADE ANEW.
I HOPE SO. I REALLY DO.
I GET THE STAKES, PANDORA. I'M JUST--I'M GETTING WORRIED IS ALL.
HE WAS MY BEST OPTION, BUT HE WASN'T MY LAST.
"THE PUREST OF HEART OR THE DARKEST" CAN OPEN IT AND REVERSE THE CURSE. THERE ARE NO HEARTS AS PURE AS THE ONES I'VE ALREADY GONE TO.
BUT THE DARKEST EVIL...
UH-OH.
I SENSE IT. I KNEW IT WOULD COME.
A HEART SO OLD THAT EVERYTHING GOOD IN IT HAS TURNED TO DUST. ALL THAT REMAINS IS SIN.
EXIT
AND YOU'RE GONNA, WHAT--GO THERE? SHAKE HANDS?
MAKE AN OFFER?

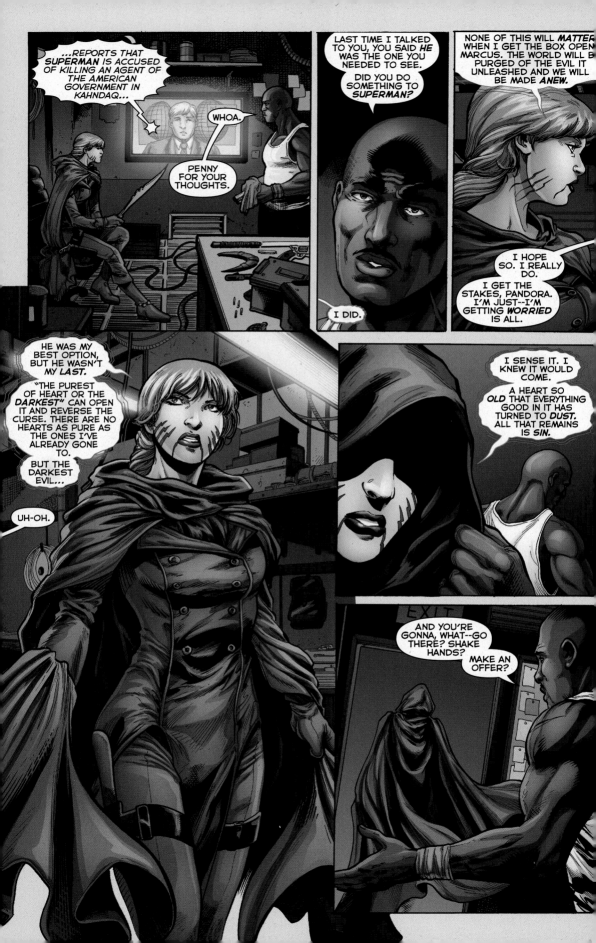

I'M GOING TO DO WHAT HAS TO BE DONE."
OKAY, I'VE GOT SOMETHING. ENERGY SIGNATURE.
I'VE GOT IT!
WHERE?
WHOA. RIGHT HERE.
RIGHT BEHIND US!
LET ME HANDLE THIS.
IF SHE'S HUMAN, THIS OUGHT TO INDUCE BLINDNESS AND SEIZURE.
THEN YOU CAN MOP HER UP.
PAF
UH... SAVAGE? SAVAGE?
YES. I WANT TO TALK TO VANDAL SAVAGE.

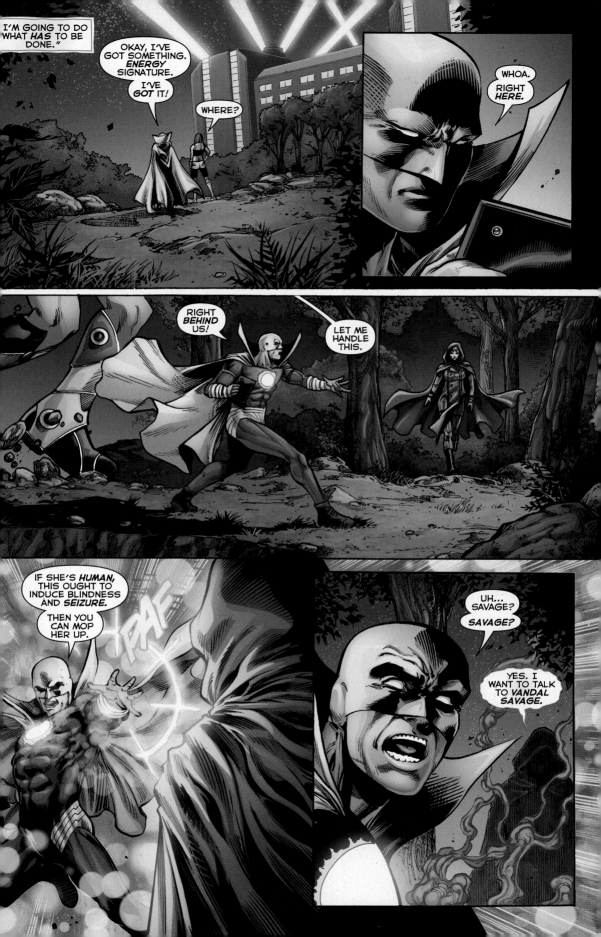

TALK TO THIS.

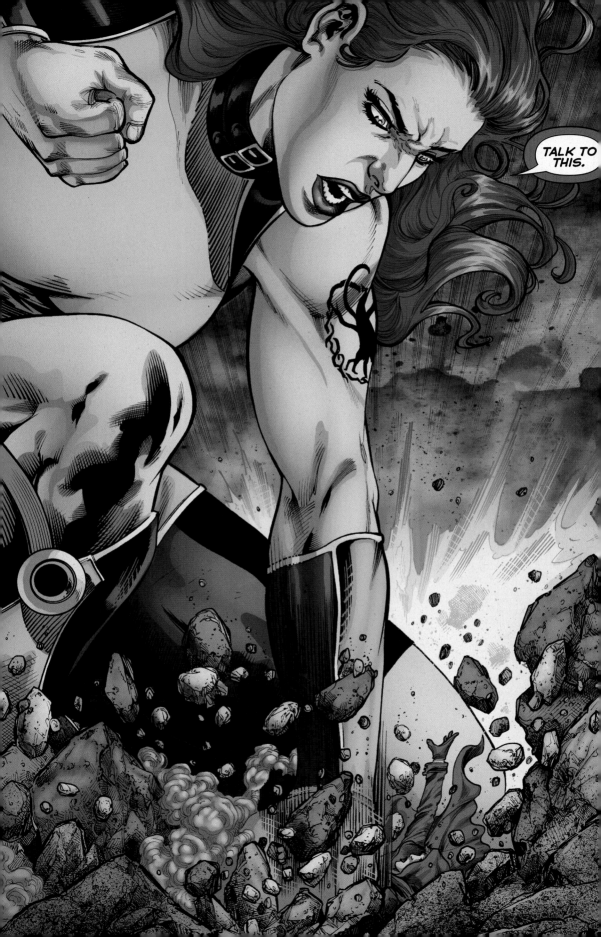

SHE'S NOT DOWN!
HIT HER AGAIN!
RELAX.
I SAID I'LL HANDLE THIS.
KRAKKK
I--

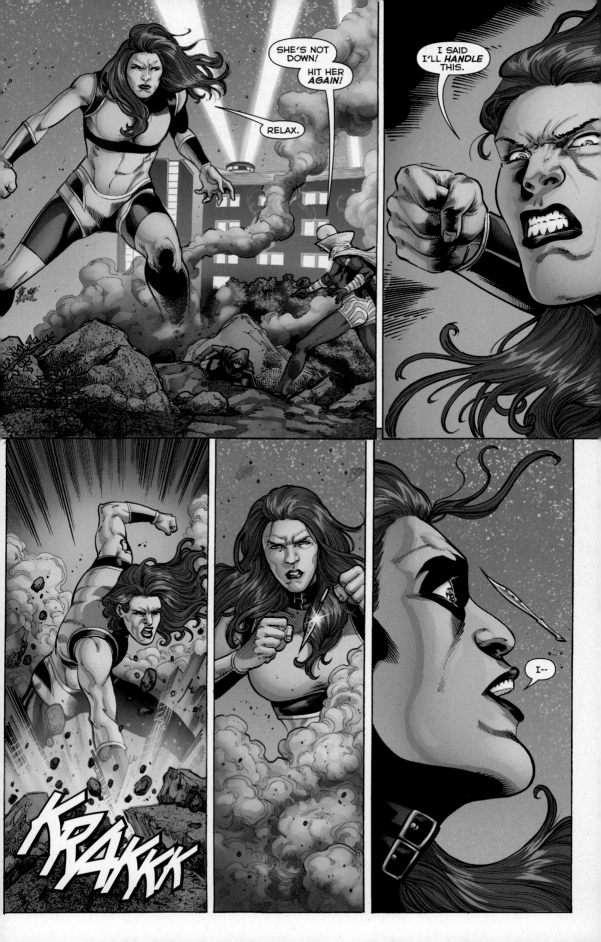

AAIIIII!
BOOOOM
OH, MAN.
EEEIGGGH!

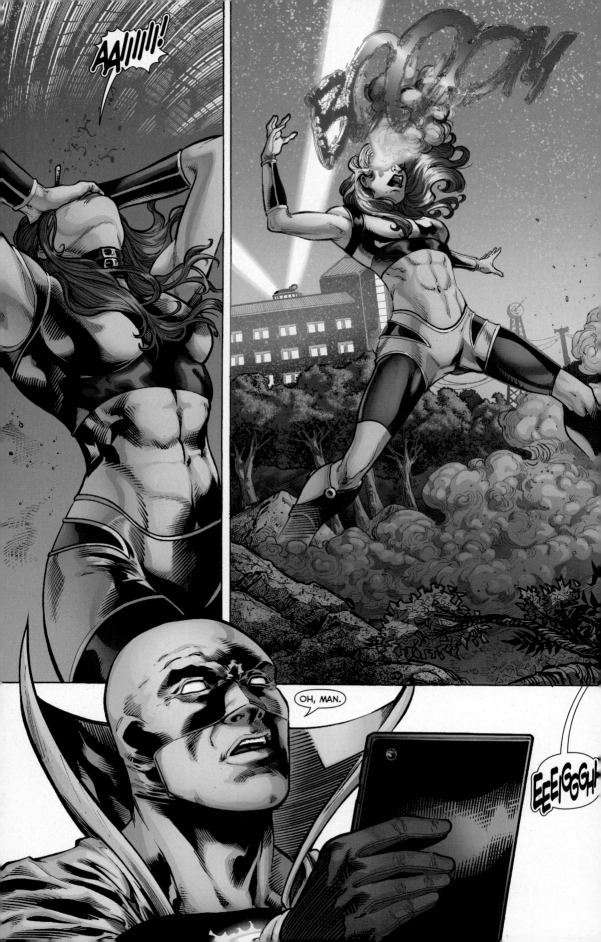

CRASSHH
OUUGGODD MY EYEEEE...
SIGNALMAN TO COMMAND: 'E'RE ENGAGING THE TARGET.
GIGANTA IS DOWN! I'M SENDING WHATEVER DATA I CAN GATHER ON PANDORA.
I'M READING A COMPOUND FRACTURE ON ONE FEMUR THERE--IT'S ALREADY KNITTING ITSELF BACK TOGETHER.
SKULL FRACTURE TOO, AND A COUPLE OF VERTEBRAE. DIDN'T SLOW HER DOWN A BIT, SO WE'RE LOOKING AT PARAHUMAN ENDURANCE AND MOBILITY.
NEUROSCAN SHOWS THAT SHE'S IN ALL KINDS OF PAIN, BUT SHE'S JUST-- GOD, SHE'S JUST CARRYING IT.
VAPOR ANALYSIS OF THE SMOKE SEEMS TO INDICATE THAT SHE'S NOT BREATHING.
SOME KIND OF MYSTIC ENERGY IGNATURE ON HER EAPONS, BUT ONLY WHEN SHE'S HOLDING THEM.
EXPLOSIVE N THE HILT ON HE BLADES, AND DICATION THAT E DOESN'T NEED) ACTUALLY SEE TO HIT HER TARGET.
SAVAGE IS MOVING IN TO ENGAGE.
RRRAH!
UNGH!

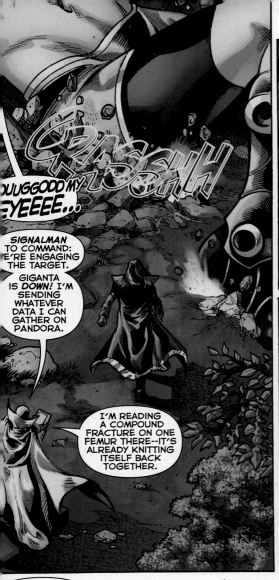

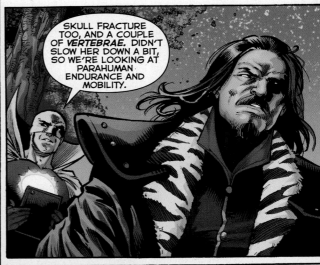

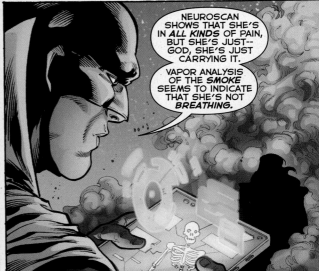

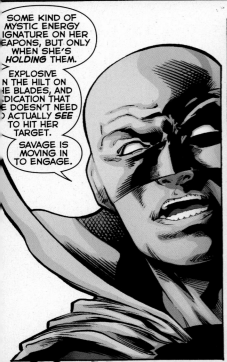

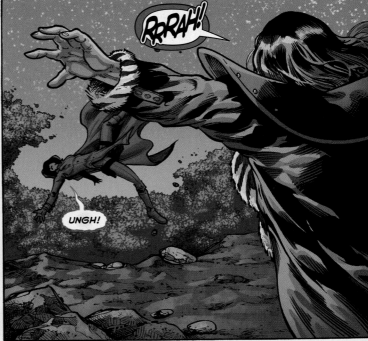

WAIT!
SKSSSSS
HAH!
CHK
BLAMM

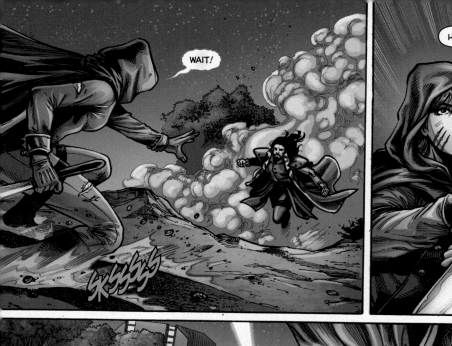

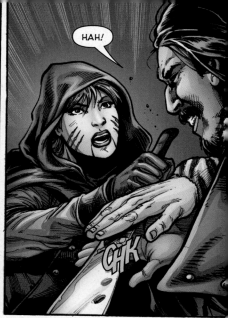

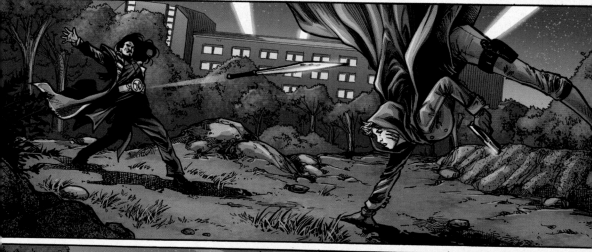

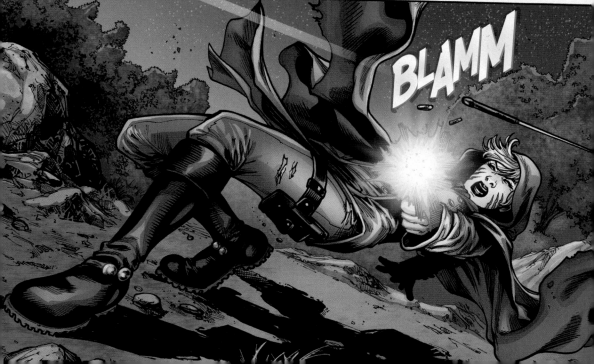

BLAMM
BLAMM
BLAMM
BLAMM
THEP
UNH?!

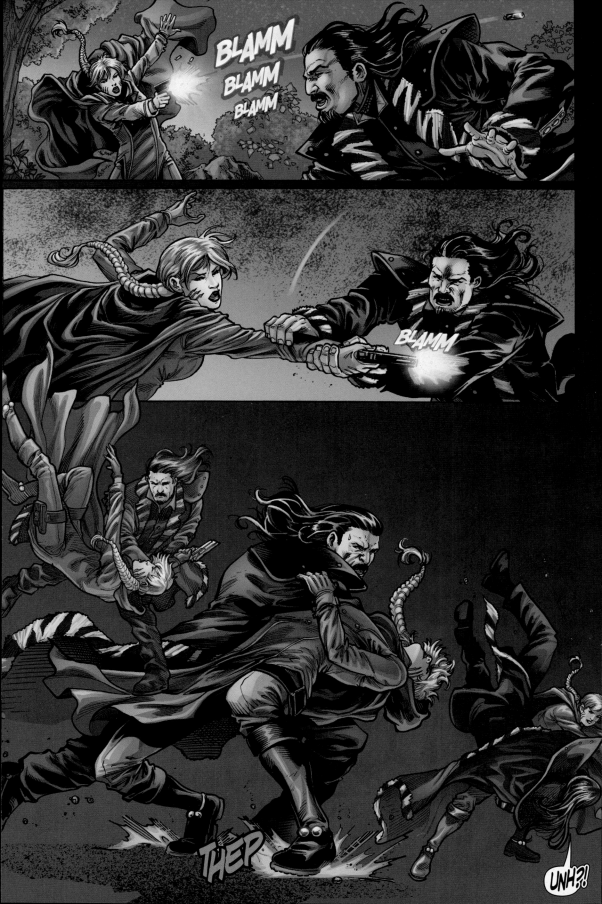

HEH. YOU THINK YOU CAN STOP ME?

YOU KNOW I'M NOT LIKE ANYONE ELSE. *NOTHING* CAN STOP ME.

REALLY?

BLAMM

YOU... YOU... YOU *KILLED* HIM.

HE WOULDN'T STOP. HE WOULDN'T *LISTEN.*

IT'S BEEN A THOUSAND YEARS, PANDORA, SINCE WE LAST SPOKE.
I OFFERED YOU MY SYMPATHY.
YOU CAN CONSIDER THAT OFFER RESCINDED.
CRACK
TARGET'S NECK IS SNAPPED AT THE SIXTH AND SEVENTH CERVICAL VERTEBRAE...

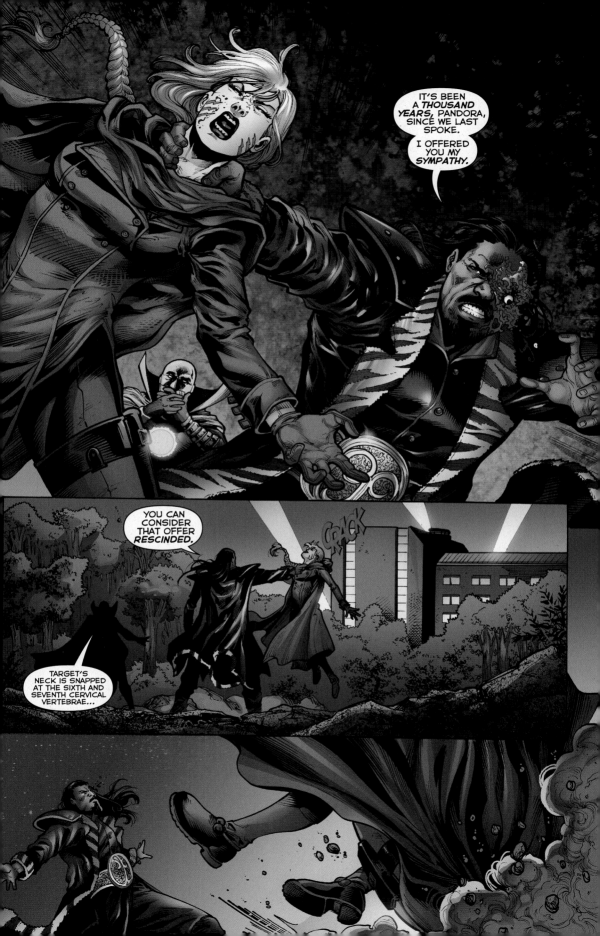

I TOLD YOU.
I CAN'T BE KILLED. I AM THE UNSTOPPABLE FORCE.
BLAMM
BLAMM
BLAMM
GIVE ME THE BOX OR THIS GOES ON UNTIL I FIND OUT HOW TO DESTROY YOU.
GRK
BUT THAT'S WHAT I WANT.
DON'T YOU UNDERSTAND?

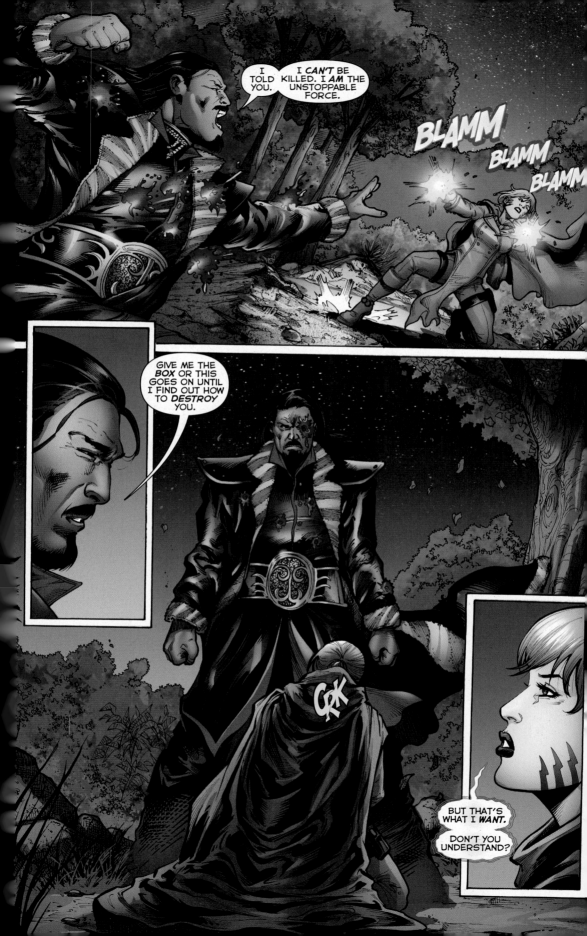

EXCUSE ME?

I *WANT* YOU TO *TAKE* IT.

I CAN SEE THE EVIL IN YOU.

IT RUNS SO *DEEP.*

IT'S A *UNIQUE* VINTAGE. BY THE GODS, I'LL MAKE YOU *SUFFER* IF THIS IS SOME SORT OF--

THE PUREST OF HEART OR THE *DARKEST.*

TAKE IT.

OPEN IT, IF YOU CAN. THEN THERE WILL *FINALLY* BE PEACE.

NO, I--

THE *POWER* I SENSE. WHAT *IS* THIS?

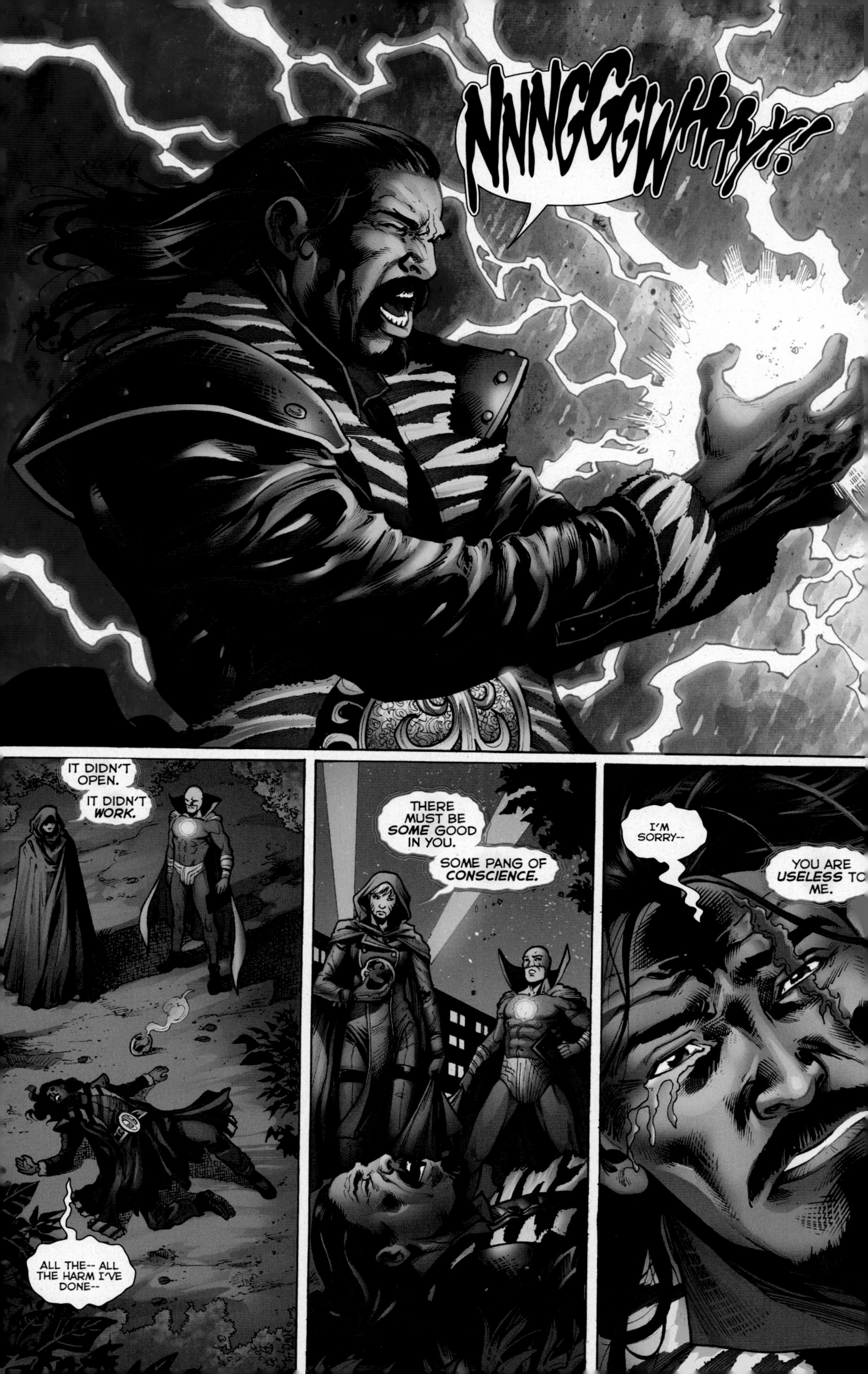

NNNGGGWHHY!?
IT DIDN'T OPEN.
IT DIDN'T WORK.
ALL THE-- ALL THE HARM I'VE DONE--
THERE MUST BE SOME GOOD IN YOU.
SOME PANG OF CONSCIENCE.
I'M SORRY--
YOU ARE USELESS TO ME.

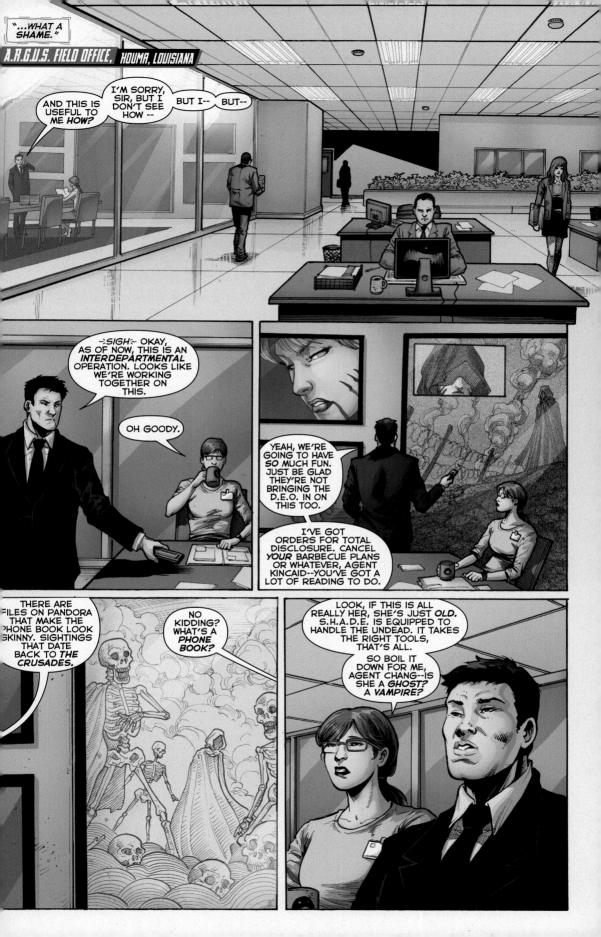

"...WHAT A SHAME."
A.R.G.U.S. FIELD OFFICE, HOUMA, LOUISIANA
AND THIS IS USEFUL TO ME HOW?
I'M SORRY, SIR, BUT I DON'T SEE HOW --
BUT I--
BUT--
-SIGH- OKAY, AS OF NOW, THIS IS AN INTERDEPARTMENTAL OPERATION. LOOKS LIKE WE'RE WORKING TOGETHER ON THIS.
OH GOODY.
YEAH, WE'RE GOING TO HAVE SO MUCH FUN. JUST BE GLAD THEY'RE NOT BRINGING THE D.E.O. IN ON THIS TOO.
I'VE GOT ORDERS FOR TOTAL DISCLOSURE. CANCEL YOUR BARBECUE PLANS OR WHATEVER, AGENT KINCAID--YOU'VE GOT A LOT OF READING TO DO.
THERE ARE FILES ON PANDORA THAT MAKE THE PHONE BOOK LOOK SKINNY. SIGHTINGS THAT DATE BACK TO THE CRUSADES.
NO KIDDING? WHAT'S A PHONE BOOK?
LOOK, IF THIS IS ALL REALLY HER, SHE'S JUST OLD. S.H.A.D.E. IS EQUIPPED TO HANDLE THE UNDEAD. IT TAKES THE RIGHT TOOLS, THAT'S ALL.
SO BOIL IT DOWN FOR ME, AGENT CHANG--IS SHE A GHOST? A VAMPIRE?

SHE MAY OR MAY NOT BE THE PANDORA OF ANCIENT MYTH. YOU KNOW, THE ONE WHO OPENED THE URN OF THE GODS AND SET LOOSE ALL THE EVILS OF THE WORLD?

UH-*HUH.*

AND SHE MA OR MAY NOT *SANTA CLAUS* A MAGIC SOC PUPPET.

I'M ASKING YO IF YOU KNO WHAT SHE *IS.*

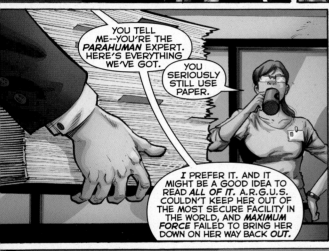

YOU TELL ME--YOU'RE THE *PARAHUMAN* EXPERT. HERE'S EVERYTHING WE'VE GOT.

YOU SERIOUSLY STILL USE PAPER.

I PREFER IT. AND IT MIGHT BE A GOOD IDEA TO READ *ALL OF IT.* A.R.G.U.S. COULDN'T KEEP HER OUT OF THE MOST SECURE FACILITY IN THE WORLD, AND *MAXIMUM FORCE* FAILED TO BRING HER DOWN ON HER WAY BACK *OUT.*

AND AN EXECUTIVE ORDER JUST CAME IN, STRAIGHT FROM THE *TOP.*

AS OF RIGHT NOW, PANDORA IS PRIORITY TARGET *ONE* FOR BOTH OUR AGENCIES.

ALL AVAILABLE RESOURCES ARE DIVERTED TO THIS MISSION. NO DELAYS, NO EXCUSES. THE TARGET IS TO BE *LIQUIDATED* WITH ABSOLUTE PREJUDICE.

TRINITY OF SIN: THE PHANTOM STRANGER
C OMICS ROUDLY RESENTS
SO TELL ME AGAIN WHERE WE ARE...?
IT DOESN'T HAVE A NAME, BATMAN, BUT YOU CAN CALL IT...HEAVEN'S BASEMENT--
--A REGION OF THE AFTERLIFE CLOSEST TO THE EARTH-PLANE--WHERE SOULS OF THE DEAD THAT ARE UNABLE TO DETACH THEMSELVES FROM PHYSICAL EXISTENCE GATHER--
--SENDING TENDRILS OF THEMSELVES DOWN THROUGH THE ETHERS--
--TO FEED ON THE EMOTIONS AND EXPERIENCES OF THE LIVING.
I'LL TELL YA, STRANGER-- THIS PLACE GIVES ME THE CREEPS...AND I'M A FREAKIN' GHOST!

THEY SEEM MORE INTERESTED IN WHAT LIES BELOW, *DEADMAN*--THAN IN US.

TAKE ANOTHER LOOK, *KATANA.*

WE'VE GOT TO *LEAVE.* NOW.

ENTITIES LIKE THIS HAVE BEEN INVADING MY LIFE FOR *YEARS* NOW. THE BEST WAY TO DEAL WITH THEM IS TO *STAY*--

--AND SHOW THEM WHAT THE *LIVING* ARE CAPABLE OF!

THESE AREN'T THE DEAD YOU'RE *ACCUSTOMED* TO, KATANA.

GIVEN THE CHANCE, THEY'LL DRINK DEEPLY AT THE *WELL OF OUR SOULS*--

--SUCKING OUT EVERY LAST *DREAM* AND *DESIRE*...EVERY *THOUGHT* AND *FEELING*-- UNTIL WE'RE *HOLLOWED OUT*--

--AND LEFT *LESS* THAN DEAD.

IF WE *LET* THEM!

NO! DON'T ENGAGE THEM!

WHAT? *WHY?*

THIS IS A *BREAKING AND ENTERING JOB,* KATANA--AND THE *LAST* THING WE WANT TO DO--

--IS DRAW THE *ATTENTION* OF THE LOCAL *AUTHORITIES.*

THE QUICKER WE CAN MOVE *THROUGH* HERE AND ON TO THE *NEXT LEVEL* OF THE AFTERLIFE--

--THE LESS OF A CHANCE THAT WE'LL BE *NOTICED.*

CONSIDERING THIS PLACE IS RUN BY A GUY WHO'S *OMNIPOTENT* AND *OMNIPRESENT*--

--I DON'T REALLY SEE IT *HAPPENING!* THAT *SAID*--

--I'VE GOT AN IDEA!

COME ON, YOU HUNGRY BASTARDS--YOU WANNA FEED ON SOMEONE--

--FEED ON ME!

BRAND-- *NO!* DIDN'T YOU HEAR WHAT THE STRANGER *SAID?* THEY GET THOSE TENTACLES *INTO* YOU AND--

AND...?

WHAT *HAPPENED?*

THESE SOULS GAIN STRENGTH...PURPOSE...FROM FEEDING ON THE *LIVING.* FEEDING ON A *GHOST* HAS THE...*OPPOSITE* EFFECT.

WHICH IS WHY I *PUT* THE IDEA IN BRAND'S MIND IN THE *FIRST* PLACE.

GOOD THING IT *WORKED...* OR I'D BE *SERIOUSLY* PISSED.

I ASSUME THEY'LL REVIVE *QUICKLY...?*

CORRECT.

THEN YOU'D BETTER FIND THE DOOR OUT OF HERE--

NOT A *DOOR* EXACTLY... MORE A SHIFT IN *PERCEPTION*. HELL, HEAVEN... AND *ALL* THE REALMS BETWEEN--

--ARE MORE *STATES OF CONSCIOUSNESS* THAN *ACTUAL PLACES.* THEY--

SPARE ME THE METAPHYSICS, STRANGER.

A MAN'S *LIFE* IS ON THE LINE.

I DON'T WANT *EXPLANATIONS*--

--I WANT *RESULTS.*

"WE ARE," SOMEONE ONCE WROTE, "WHAT WE *PRETEND* TO BE."

IF THAT'S THE CASE, PRETENDING TO BE THE BATMAN IS A *VERY* DANGEROUS GAME.

HOW LONG BEFORE THE *ROLE* CONSUMES THE *MAN?* BEFORE THE *MASK* BECOMES THE *REALITY?*

SOON, PERHAPS--BUT NOT *YET.*

BENEATH THE *COLD AUTHORITY* IN HIS VOICE...BENEATH THE *ARROGANCE* AND *SUSPICION...*

...THERE'S A *HUMANITY* HE TRIES DESPERATELY TO HIDE.

...WE JUST CAN'T STAND AROUND HERE WAITING. I'M GOING *IN* THERE.

BATMAN AND THE PHANTOM STRANGER--INSIDE *THAT* PLACE?

TAKE IT FROM *ME,* TREVOR: ANY *ONE* OF THOSE IS REASON ENOUGH TO STAY *OUTSIDE.*

BRAND, WHY ARE YOU EVEN HERE? I THOUGHT YOU WERE WITH WONDER WOMAN'S GROUP AT BELLE REVE.

IT WAS A BUST PANDORA'S BOX WASN'T THERE.

THEY'RE GONNA KEEP LOOKING, BUT THOUGHT I'D BE OF BETTER US WITH THIS GROUP.

LUCKY ME.

I SWEAR-- EVERY TIME I LOOK IN THROUGH THE *WINDOW*...I SEE A *DIFFERENT* ROOM.

A DEEP *COMPASSION*

AND A DEEPER *FEAR*.

...I CAN'T BELIEVE *YOU*, OF ALL PEOPLE, ARE *SUGGESTING* THIS.

BUT ISN'T THIS KIND OF THING YOUR *STOCK IN TRADE*?

A *FEAR* I UNDERSTOOD ALL TOO *WELL*.

THE *AFTERLIFE* IS FOR THE *DEAD*, BATMAN--NOT THE *LIVING*. AND...AS I'VE *RECENTLY* LEARNED--

--IT'S *BEST* TO LEAVE THE DEAD *ALONE*.

AN *HOUR* AGO--OR PERHAPS IT WAS AN *INSTANT* (IMPOSSIBLE TO TELL WHEN YOU'RE AT THE *CROSSROADS* OF TIME AND SPACE)...

...WE STOOD WITHIN *THE HOUSE OF MYSTERY*...

DOCTOR LIGHT IS DEAD, STRANGER. *KILLED*--OR SO MOST PEOPLE BELIEVE--BY *SUPERMAN*.

THAT SINGLE EVENT TRIGGERED A *CHAIN REACTION* THAT'S RIPPLED ACROSS THE *WORLD*. BROUGHT THREE *JUSTICE LEAGUES* TO *WAR*--AND THEN UNEASY *PEACE*.

...PONDERING THE *IMPOSSIBLE*.

I KNOW THAT SUPERMAN'S NOT RESPONSIBLE--

--AND I'M WILLING TO BET THAT *LIGHT* DOES, TOO.

IF WE CAN *INTERROGATE* HIM...GET SOME EVIDENCE THAT WILL LEAD US TO THE ONES *BEHIND* THIS, THEN--

I'M *SORRY*, BATMAN--BUT THE ANSWER IS *NO*.

DON'T TURN YOUR *BACK* ON ME--

AND DON'T *YOU* MEDDLE IN THINGS THAT ARE BEYOND YOUR *PATHETICALLY LIMITED* COMPREHENSION!

I'M... *SORRY*.

THERE'S SOMETHING YOU'RE NOT *TELLING* ME--

THERE WERE *MANY* THINGS I WASN'T TELLING HIM.

HOW I'D JOURNEYED FROM THE BOWELS OF *HELL* TO THE HEIGHTS OF *HEAVEN* IN SEARCH OF MY MURDERED *WIFE* AND *CHILDREN.*

HOW I'D *LOST* THEM...

...AND BEEN WARNED BY THE ANGEL *ZAURIEL* NEVER TO *RETURN* TO THE AFTERLIFE.

"IF YOU SO MUCH AS *ATTEMPT* IT," HE SAID...

..."YOU WILL BE *ERASED* FROM TIME AND HISTORY."

WE *ALL* HAVE OUR SECRETS.

I ASK THAT YOU RESPECT *MINE.*

FAIR ENOUGH. BUT I ASK *YOU* TO THINK ABOUT A MAN WHO *EMBODIES HOPE.*

WHO'S *SACRIFICED* HIMSELF AGAIN AND AGAIN FOR THE *GREATER GOOD.*

YOU SPEAK OF *SUPERMAN* AS IF HE'S SOME KIND OF... *MESSIAH.*

NO. FOR ALL HIS *POWER*...HE'S JUST A *MAN.* BUT A *GOOD* MAN--

--WHO NEEDS YOUR *HELP.*

STRANGE AS IT SOUNDS, I COULD FEEL THE HOUSE *COME AWAKE* AROUND US...

...EAGER AND INTERESTED...LIKE A VITAL *LIVING* THING.

WAS IT, I WONDERED, MERELY *REFLECTING* OUR THOUGHTS AND FEELINGS...

TELL ME ABOUT THE *VICTIM.* WHO IS THIS...*DOCTOR LIGHT?*

...OR SUBTLY *INFLUENCING* THEM?

FROM ALL I'VE LEARNED, *HE* WAS A GOOD MAN, *TOO.* PULLED INTO *AMANDA WALLER'S J.L.A.* AGAINST HIS WILL--

ARTHUR LIGHT WAS A SCIENTIST...A FAMILY MAN WITH A WIFE...THREE DAUGHTERS.
SOMEONE MANIPULATED SUPERMAN... USED HIM AS A WEAPON--
--AND ROBBED THOSE GIRLS OF THEIR FATHER. ROBBED THAT WOMAN OF HER--
--AND SLAUGHTERED FOR NO GOOD REASON.
I'VE HEARD ENOUGH.
LET'S DO IT.
EXCUSE ME?
IT WON'T BE EASY. WE CAN'T JUST WALK UP TO THE GATES OF HEAVEN AND ANNOUNCE OURSELVES.
WE NEED TO FIND ANOTHER WAY IN.
AND YOU KNOW ONE?
I THINK I DO.
BUT WE'LL NEED HELP.
DEADMAN... KATANA-- YOU'RE FAMILIAR WITH THE REALMS OF THE DEAD--
--SO YOU'RE WITH US.
WE ARE?
WAIT ONE DAMN MINUTE! WHAT THE HELL DO YOU THINK YOU'RE--
I HATE IT WHEN THEY DO THAT.
WELL, DON'T JUST STAND THERE! GO AFTER THEM!
HAPPY TO, COLONEL. ALL YOU HAVE TO DO--

"--IS TELL US WHERE THEY WENT."
WE CLIMBED UP FROM HEAVEN'S BASEMENT...
...MOVING THROUGH CAVERNS OF LONGING, TUNNELS OF GRIEF...
...THEN FINALLY STEPPED OUT INTO THE LIGHT...
WAIT A MINUTE!
THIS--
--IS HEAVEN...?
GIVEN THE CIRCUITOUS ROUTE WE TOOK, WE BYPASSED THE MORE SCENIC REGIONS AND--
WELL, LET'S JUST SAY THIS ISN'T ONE OF THE...BETTER NEIGHBORHOODS.
THERE ARE NEIGHBORHOODS-- IN HEAVEN?
NEIGHBORHOODS, NATIONS. WORLDS AND UNIVERSES.
THERE ARE, IN FACT, AS MANY HEAVENS AS THERE ARE SOULS. EACH ONE TAILORED TO THE BELIEFS THE SOUL HELD ON EARTH.

BUT WHY **THIS** PLACE...?

PERHAPS THESE SOULS THINK THEY DON'T **DESERVE** ANYTHING BETTER. OR PERHAPS **HALLS OF GOLD** AND **HEAVENLY CHOIRS** AREN'T FOR EVERYONE.

HEAVEN IS A **RELATIVE** CONCEPT, AFTER ALL.

EXACTLY.

IN THE END, THIS IS JUST A **TRANSITIONAL REALM.** THE ANGELS WILL EVENTUALLY MOVE ALL OF THESE SPIRITS INTO THE **DEEPER** AFTERWORLDS.

WHAT ABOUT **LIGHT?** IS **HE** HERE?

NO. I'D **KNOW** IT IF HE WAS.

WHICH MEANS WE HAVE TO LOCATE THE **SPECIFIC HEAVEN--**

--THAT HE'S **CREATED** FOR HIMSELF...

WHAT DID YOU SAY, BATMAN?

BATMAN?

GONE. DEADMAN AND KATANA GONE **WITH** HIM. AND IN THAT MOMENT I REALIZED THE TERRIBLE **MISTAKE** I'D MADE.

IN A PLACE WHERE **MIND** CREATES MATTER, WHERE THE INDIVIDUAL **HEART** INSTANTLY MOLDS ITS OWN **PARADISE...**

...I SHOULD HAVE FORESEEN THAT **EACH OF THEM...**

MASEO?

...WOULD BE SWEPT OFF INTO A HEAVEN OF THEIR **OWN** MAKING.

SURPRISED TO SEE YOUR DEAD HUSBAND, **TATSU?**

EVEN A GHOST WHO ROAMS THE EARTH NEEDS A PLACE TO **REST.** SO, FROM TIME TO TIME, I **RETREAT** TO WHAT YOUR FRIEND CALLED...HEAVEN'S BASEMENT.

I CAN'T SAY I CARE FOR THE **NATIVES**...BUT, FOR THE MOST PART, THEY LEAVE ME **ALONE.**

WHEN I SAW *YOU* THERE AMONG THEM, I TOOK A RISK...*FOLLOWED* YOU--

--KNOWING THAT...*TOGETHER*... OUR LOVE WOULD CREATE A *HAVEN* FOR US TO SHARE.

AND HERE WE *ARE.*

FOR *HOW LONG?*

TIME HAS *NO MEANING* HERE.

BUT--

WHY *QUESTION,* TATSU. WHY *OBJECT?*

YOUR LIFE ON EARTH IS A *LIVING HELL* OF PAIN AND SORROW. ENDLESS VIOLENCE.

PUT IT ALL *ASIDE,* MY LOVE--

--AND EMBRACE *HEAVEN.*

NO. YOU RESIST ME. DOES YOUR GUILT...INHIBIT YOU?

YOU *KNOW.*

OF YOUR... *DALLIANCE* WITH MY BROTHER? THE VERY MAN WHO *MURDERED* ME?

IT'S NOT THAT *SIMPLE.*

BUT IN THIS GARDEN--*IT IS.* TAKEO IS WORLDS AWAY.

HERE YOU ARE FREE TO *LOVE ME,* TATSU.

I...DO, MASEO. I--

RUMMMMMM

BACK TO THE *LOWER REGIONS* WHERE YOU BELONG!

MASEO!

BACK, WRAITH!

WHAT HAVE YOU DONE TO MY *HUSBAND?*

WHAT HAVE YOU *DONE?!*

HOW CAN YOU BE SURE THAT *WAS* YOUR HUSBAND?

I KNOW MASEO BETTER THAN I KNOW *MYSELF!*

PERHAPS IT WAS. OR PERHAPS HE WAS A *PROJECTION* OF YOUR OWN DESIRE.

OR...WORSE...ONE OF THOSE *BASEMENT-DWELLERS... MANIPULATING* YOU--IN ORDER TO *FEED* ON YOUR LIFE-FORCE.

IN *ANY* CASE--

--HE WAS A *DISTRACTION* FROM THE MISSION AT HAND.

YOU HAD NO *RIGHT* TO TAKE HIM FROM ME! YOU HAD NO--

SHHHKK

--RIGHT!

CHOK!

FORGIVE ME.

I'M THE ONE WHO NEEDS FORGIVENESS. I SHOULD HAVE *KNOWN* THIS WOULD HAPPEN.

WHERE ARE THE *OTHERS?*

I'M NOT SURE ABOUT *BRAND*...BUT IT WON'T BE DIFFICULT--

"--TO FIND *BATMAN.*"

"...MARLEY WAS DEAD: TO BEGIN WITH. THERE IS NO DOUBT WHATEVER ABOUT THAT. THE REGISTER OF HIS BURIAL WAS SIGNED BY THE CLERGYMAN, THE CLERK, THE UNDERTAKER, AND THE CHIEF MOURNER.

"SCROOGE SIGNED IT: AND SCROOGE'S NAME WAS GOOD UPON 'CHANGE, FOR ANYTHING HE CHOSE TO PUT HIS HAND TO. OLD MARLEY--

"--WAS AS DEAD AS A DOORNAIL.

"*MIND!* I DON'T MEAN TO SAY THAT I KNOW, OF MY OWN KNOWLEDGE, WHAT THERE IS PARTICULARLY DEAD ABOUT A DOORNAIL. I MIGHT HAVE BEEN INCLINED, MYSELF, TO REGARD A COFFIN-NAIL AS THE DEADEST PIECE OF IRONMONGERY IN THE TRADE.

"BUT THE WISDOM OF OUR ANCESTORS IS IN THE SIMILE; AND MY UNHALLOWED HANDS SHALL NOT DISTURB IT, OR THE COUNTRY'S DONE FOR. YOU WILL THEREFORE PERMIT ME TO REPEAT, EMPHATICALLY, THAT MARLEY WAS AS DEAD AS A DOORNAIL."

IT'S GETTING LATE, *THOMAS.* I THINK WE SHOULD GET *BRUCE* TO BED.

BUT HE JUST *STARTED* THE STORY!

YES. FOR THE *SECOND* TIME.

PLEASE, MOTHER...?

:SIGH: *FIVE MORE* MINUTES--

"SCROOGE KNEW HE WAS DEAD? OF COURSE HE DID. HOW COULD IT BE OTHERWISE? SCROOGE AND HE WERE PARTNERS FOR I DON'T KNOW HOW MANY YEARS..."

WHERE *ARE* WE?

A PLACE THAT *NEVER* WAS. A *CHRISTMAS* THAT NEVER HAPPENED.

THAT LITTLE BOY ONCE SPENT THIS HOLIDAY *GRIEF-STRICKEN* AND *ALONE.* BUT HERE HE CAN *REWRITE HISTORY.* HERE--

"--CHRISTMAS CAN LAST *FOREVER.*"

"SCROOGE WAS HIS SOLE EXECUTOR, HIS SOLE ADMINISTRATOR, HIS SOLE ASSIGN, HIS SOLE RESIDUARY LEGATEE--"

"--HIS SOLE FRIEND AND SOLE MOURNER."

ARE YOU SAYING THAT THE BOY ON THE *COUCH*--

--IS *BATMAN?*

IS IT SURPRISING THAT A MAN WHO LIVES WITH DARKNESS AND BRUTALITY *DAY AFTER DAY*--

--WOULD SEEK REFUGE...FIND *HEAVEN*--

--IN A BOY'S LOST *DREAMS?*

NOT SURPRISING AT *ALL.*

AND MAYBE *ONE* DAY...WHEN I'M GIVEN THE CHANCE TO *REST*...I'LL COME *BACK* HERE.

BATMAN? THEN THAT'S *NOT*...?

HE'S A PART OF ME, KATANA--*THEY'RE* A PART OF ME--THAT I WANTED TO GLIMPSE...FOR JUST A *MOMENT.*

"AND EVEN SCROOGE WAS NOT SO DREADFULLY CUT UP BY THE SAD EVENT, BUT THAT HE WAS AN EXCELLENT MAN OF BUSINESS ON THE VERY DAY OF THE FUNERAL--

"--AND SOLEMNIZED IT WITH AN UNDOUBTED BARGAIN."

BUT THAT MOMENT HAS PASSED.

MY APOLOGIES, KATANA-- BUT, IN ORDER TO PROTECT BATMAN'S IDENTITY, I MUST...DIM THE MEMORY OF THIS ENCOUNTER.

WHAT ENCOUNTER?

HAVE YOU LOCATED DOCTOR LIGHT?

NOT YET, BUT--

BUT I HAVE!

BRAND?

WHILE YOU WERE ALL PLAYING "BUILD-A-HEAVEN," I WAS OUT SCOURING EVERY CORNER OF THIS PLACE.

BUT HOW WERE YOU ABLE TO RESIST THE PULL OF--

EASY. I DID SOME PRETTY ROTTEN THINGS WHEN I WAS ALIVE--AND THE POWERS-THAT-BE GAVE ME A SECOND CHANCE.

THAT CHANCE IS BACK IN THE LAND OF THE LIVING-- NOT HERE.

GUESS YOU COULD SAY I'M MORE INTERESTED IN AVOIDING HELL THAN GAINING HEAVEN.

WHAT ABOUT YOU, STRANGER?

I FOUND MY PARADISE ON EARTH, DEADMAN. FOUND IT, LIVED IT, AND--

--LOST IT...?

WHERE... WHERE ARE WE?

PRETTY SPECTACULAR--

--ISN'T IT...?
THERE IS A TRANQUILITY HERE...AN ABSOLUTE SERENITY...THAT I HAVE NEVER FELT BEFORE.
MAKES A STRANGE KIND OF SENSE THAT A MAN WITH THE POWER TO BEND LIGHT AND MANIPULATE ENERGY--
--WOULD CREATE A PERSONAL UNIVERSE COMPOSED OF LIGHT.
IF HE DID...HE DID IT UNCONSCIOUSLY.
LOOK AT HIM--HE'S NOT AWAKE. NOT AWARE.
WHY NOT?
THINK ABOUT IT. THE MAN WAS MURDERED--SUDDENLY AND UNEXPECTEDLY. TORN FROM HIS LIFE WITHOUT WARNING.
THIS PLACE...IS A KIND OF WOMB--
--WHERE HIS CONSCIOUSNESS CAN TRANSITION GENTLY BETWEEN THE WORLDS--AND MAKE PEACE WITH WHAT'S HAPPENED.
GONNA MAKE HIM KINDA HARD TO INTERROGATE.
THEN WE WAKE HIM UP.
WE DON'T KNOW WHAT COULD HAPPEN IF WE TEAR HIM OUT OF THERE.
WE KNOW WHAT WILL HAPPEN IF WE DON'T! WHILE LIGHT FLOATS ALONG IN HIS PERSONAL HEAVEN--
--MY FRIEND IS BURNING IN AN UNDESERVED HELL!
WE CAME HERE TO HELP SUPERMAN--

--AND THAT'S WHAT WE'RE GOING TO *DO*.

KATANA--YOUR *SOULTAKER!*

WAIT! WEREN'T *YOU* THE ONE WHO SAID WE SHOULDN'T DRAW ATTENTION TO--

OOOOOMMM!!

SHRAKK!

--OURSELVES...?

THAT'S NOT AN EXPERIENCE I'D CARE T'REPEAT.

WHAT ABOUT *LIGHT?*

I'LL TAKE CARE OF--

PLEASE, BATMAN...LET *ME* DO THIS. AS YOU'VE JUST *DEMONSTRATED*, YOUR METHODS SOMETIMES LACK A CERTAIN--

--SUBTLETY.

WH... WHAT...?

ARTHUR... CAN YOU *HEAR* ME?

NO! NO! OH, GOD--IT HURTS!
IT HURTS!!!
NO ONE WILL HURT YOU ANY MORE, ARTHUR. I PROMISE.
I PROMISE.
I'M--
I'M DEAD.
YES. BUT DEAD OR NOT--WE NEED YOUR HELP.
WHAT DO YOU REMEMBER, ARTHUR... ABOUT WHEN YOU DIED?
WE KNOW SUPERMAN WASN'T RESPONSIBLE... SO WHO WAS? IF YOU HAVE ANY IDEA...ANY CLUE--
HOW...HOW COULD I?
IT ALL HAPPENED SO FAST. SUDDENLY... I WAS BURNING... AND THEN--
YOU MUST REMEMBER SOMETHING!
I...I WISH I DID, BUT--
DON'T LIE TO ME, LIGHT! DON'T--
BATMAN... HE DOESN'T KNOW.
THEN I'VE FAILED SUPERMAN. AND ALL THIS--
--WAS FOR NOTHING.
NO. THERE'S STILL A WAY.
IF WE TAKE LIGHT BACK WITH US...RETURN HIM TO LIFE--
--THEN THERE NEVER WAS A MURDER. SUPERMAN... IS FREE.
AND YOU, ARTHUR--

--YOU'LL HAVE YOUR *FAMILY* BACK.

NOTHING--IN LIFE OR DEATH--IS MORE IMPORTANT THAN *THAT*.

IS...IS IT *POSSIBLE?*

NO--

--BUT WE'LL DO IT *ANYWAY*.

BRING THE DEAD-- *BACK TO LIFE?*

THAT'S *INSANE*.

I *LIKE* IT.

STRANGER...IF THIS *DOESN'T WORK*...IF YOU CAN'T GET ME *HOME*--

I CAN. I *WILL*.

I DON'T DOUBT YOUR *INTENTIONS*. BUT INTENTIONS AREN'T ALWAYS *ENOUGH*.

SO *TAKE* THIS... PLEASE--

--AND *PROMISE ME* THAT...IF WE *FAIL*... YOU'LL BRING IT TO MY WIFE AND CHILDREN--

--AS A *FINAL GIFT*...

YOU HAVE MY *WORD*.

BUT *LISTEN* TO ME, ARTHUR: WE'RE NOT *GOING* TO FAIL.

LISTEN TO *ME*, STRANGER.

YOU ALREADY HAVE.
ZAURIEL!

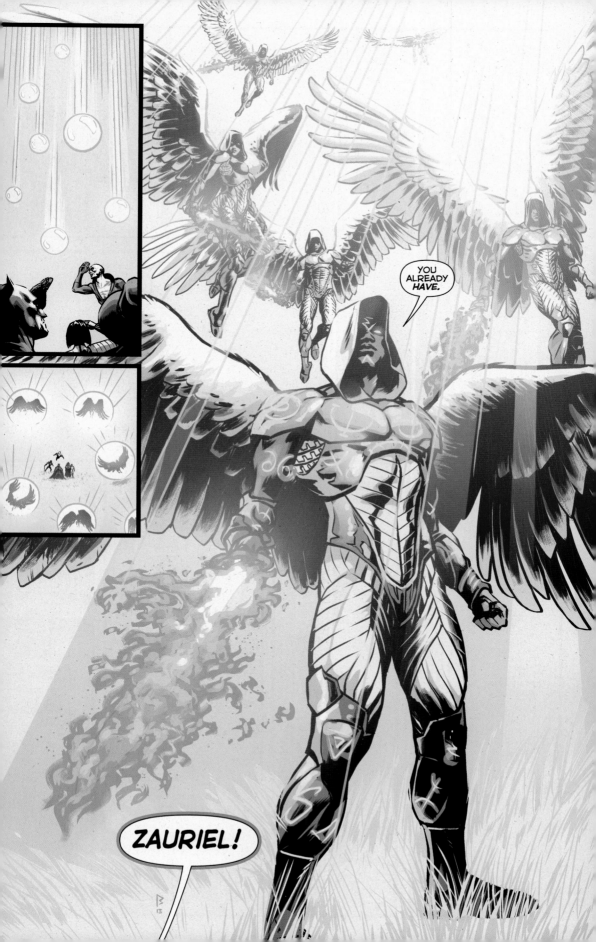

YOU WERE *WARNED,* STRANGER, *NEVER* TO RETURN HERE.

YOU *KNEW* THAT ANOTHER ATTEMPT TO RETRIEVE A SOUL FROM THE AFTERWORLDS WOULD RESULT IN YOUR *EXTINCTION.*

HIS *EXTINCTION...?*

HEY! HEY...*WAIT* A MINUTE! YOU CAN'T *DO* THAT!

STRANGER-- WHY DIDN'T YOU *TELL* US? WE--

YOU THREE HAVE DONE *ENOUGH* DAMAGE.

BEGONE.

PLEASE-- HE WAS ONLY TRYING TO *HELP.*

YOU CAME HERE TO *REST,* ARTHUR LIGHT. TO *HEAL.* SO LET HEAVEN *NURTURE* YOU--

--AND LET *ME* SEE TO THE PHANTOM STRANGER.

WHY *DIDN'T* YOU TELL THEM? AND WHY DID YOU *DO* IT? RISK ALL *YOU ARE* FOR PEOPLE YOU HARDLY KNEW.

I HAD NO *ANSWER.* IT WAS--AS THE ANGEL SAID--A *FOOLISH* ACT.

BUT, ONCE, TWO THOUSAND YEARS AGO, I *SERVED* A MAN THAT SOME CALLED A FOOL.

I KNEW THE *RISKS*, ZAURIEL. IF THE PRICE I PAY FOR WHAT I DID HERE TODAY IS --THEN *SO BE IT.* TO HAVE MY EXISTENCE *ERASED* FROM TIME AND MEMORY--

AND I THINK, PERHAPS, THAT HE MIGHT BE *PLEASED...*

...BY WHAT I DID HERE TOD--

FOOLISH MAN

J.M. DEMATTEIS writer
FERNANDO BLANCO artist
BRAD ANDERSON colorist
TRAVIS LANHAM letterer
GUILLEM MARCH cover

THEY SAY I'M A BAD MAN.
AS IF PEOPLE WERE AS EASILY DEFINED AS NIGHT AND DAY.
CHARGES OF FRAUD AND CONSPIRACY WILL ALSO BE DROPPED, MR. LUTHOR.
WE COULD HAVE YOU OUT OF HERE AS EARLY AS TONIGHT.
I SUPPOSE THAT'S WHAT SIMPLER MINDS NEED TO DO TO CONVINCE THEMSELVES THEY UNDERSTAND HOW THE WORLD WORKS.
MR. LUTHOR?
THEY PUT THINGS IN COLUMNS OF GOOD OR EVIL.
LIKE CHILD
I'VE NEVER LIKED CHILDREN.
MR. LUTHOR, WE'RE TALKING ABOUT FINALLY GETTING YOU OUT OF HERE A FREE MAN.
YOU'LL REGAIN FULL CONTROL OF LEXCORP.
YOU WILL HAVE YOUR LIFE BACK, SIR.
WHAT'S IN THE NEWSPAPER THAT'S MORE IMPORTANT THAN THAT?
DAILY PLA
SUPERMAN ACCUSED OF MANSLAUGHTER
Newest Member of the JLA Dead

ONE'S SET THE ALIEN OR A FALL. AND FOR ANGE IT WASN'T ME.
I'M A BIT JEALOUS, I'LL ADMIT.
BUT I'M MOR CURIOUS.
MR. LUTHOR? WE NEED YOUR UNDIVIDED ATTENTION FOR A MOMENT SO WE CAN--
YOU'RE ALL FIRED.
WHAT?
BUT, MR. LUTHOR--?
GO.
NOW.
WHO DID THIS TO THE SELF-RIGHTEOUS BOY SCOUT?
HOW?
WHY?
LEX LUTHOR.
I TOLD YOU TO LEAVE.

I AM PANDORA
WHOEVER YOU ARE, IF YOU'RE COUNTING ON ME TO REACT WITH SHOCK AND AWE THAT YOU'VE APPEARED OUT OF THIN AIR, PREPARE TO BE DISAPPOINTED.
DAILY PLANET
SUPERMAN ACCUSED OF MANSLAUGHTER
Newest Member of the JLA Dead
I'VE SEEN A MAN FLY.
I AM ON A MISSION TO SAVE THE WORLD FROM THE EVIL I ONCE UNLEASHED UPON IT.
AN EVIL THAT HAS TAKEN ROOT AND FESTERED IN HEARTS LIKE YOURS.
DARK HEARTS.
DO ANY OF YOU PEOPLE EVER ACTUALLY LISTEN TO YOURSELVES?
TAKE THIS.
IT WAS ONCE A PRISON TO THE ESSENCE OF EVIL. IT CAN BE AGAIN.
IT ONLY HAS TO BE OPENED.

ARE YOU INSIDE?
KLAK
WASHINGTON, D.C.
A.R.G.U.S.
THE MORGUE.
YES.
OUR FRIEND HAS SHUT DOWN SURVEILLANCE THROUGHOUT THE LOWER LEVELS...
"...BUT THEY'LL BLAME IT ON SUPERMAN'S ESCAPE."
THE LEAGUE WENT WITH SUPERMAN, MR. PRESIDENT.
BECAUSE THEY THINK SOMEONE ELSE IS RESPONSIBLE FOR KILLING DOCTOR LIGHT.
IT'S TIME DOCTOR LIGHT'S METAMORPHOSIS BEGAN.
HAVE YOU PREPARED THE BODY?
YES. DOCTOR LIGHT IS SET.
BEEP
PLASTIQUE OUT.

IF EVERYONE SAW THE WORLD THE WAY I DO, THEY'D KNOW WHY I HATE IT SO MUCH.

I HAVE DISSECTED THE MINDS OF *PRIESTS*, *SOCIAL ACTIVISTS* AND *PHILANTHROPISTS*.

I HAVE SEARCHED FOR YEARS FOR SOMEONE THAT IS FREE OF *SELFISHNESS, HATE* AND *PERVERSION*.

BUT *NO ONE* IS *UNSULLIED*. NO ONE IS WITHOUT *EVIL* THOUGHTS.

AND YOUR THOUGHTS ARE AS CLEAR TO ME AS THEY ARE TO GOD.

IF SUCH A *FAIRY TALE* EXISTED.

KRRRNNGG

P-PLEASE, LET US GO. PLEASE, DON'T KILL US!

I'M NOT GOING TO KILL YOU, MY DEAR.

YOU'RE GOING TO KILL *EACH OTHER.*

IT ONLY TAKES THE *SLIGHTEST* TELEPATHIC PUSH FOR MOST PEOPLE.

YOU *UGLY* PEOPLE WHO THINK *UGLY* THOUGHTS.

NOW YOU'LL DO *UGLY* THINGS.

DOCTOR PSYCHO!

NNGG!

NO. THE MARTIAN.

HE'S *FOUND* ME.

KKKKHHHHHH

SO.
WE GOING TO DO THIS *EASY* OR *HARD*, PSYCHO?
I'D PREFER HARD MYSELF, CYBORG. MY BOW FINGER'S ITCHING.
WE NEED TO GET THOSE PEOPLE OUT OF HARM'S WAY *FIRST*, ARROW.
ROGER *THAT*, TINKERBELL.

GEOFF JOHNS AND JEFF LEMIRE WRITERS
DOUG MAHNKE PENCILLER
CHRISTIAN ALAMY, KEITH CHAMPAGNE, MARC DEERING, DOUG MAHNKE & WALDEN WONG INKERS
NATHAN EYRING, PETE PANTAZIS & GABE ELTAEB COLORISTS · ROB LEIGH LETTERER
DOUG MAHNKE AND ALEX SINCLAIR COVER

TRINITY
WAR
TINKERBELL? HER NAME'S THE ATOM.

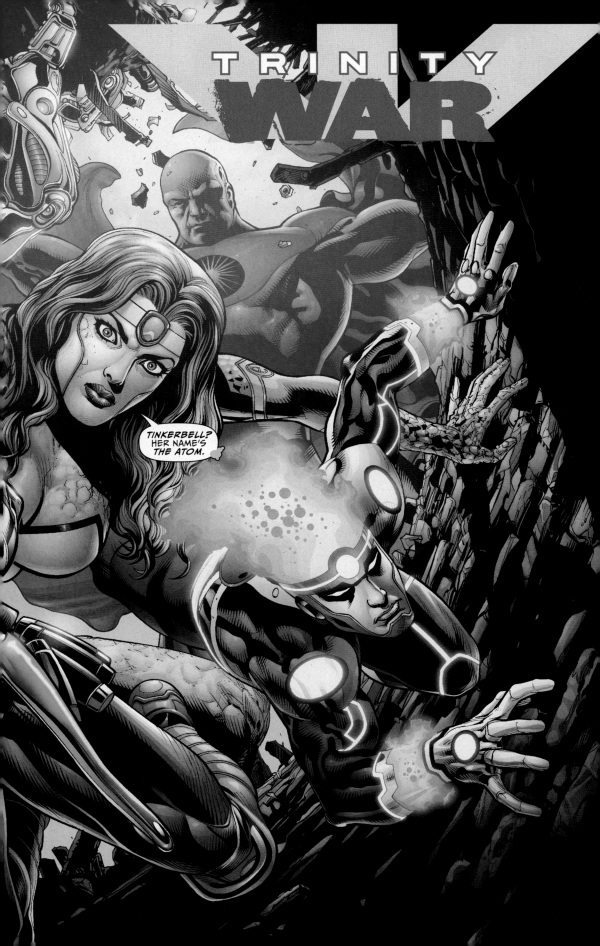

NO!
NO, THIS ISN'T FAIR!
DON'T WORRY!
EVERYTHING'S GOING TO BE OKAY, OKAY?
ELEMENT WOMAN! WAIT!
THE COUCHES ARE RIGGED WITH EXPLOSIVES.
THAT'S C-4, RONNIE. CYCLOTRIMETHYLENE-TRINITRAMINE.
C-4 TOLD ME EVERYTHING I NEEDED TO KNOW, JACE. SO I'LL TRANSMUTE THE...
JUST UNRAVEL THE NITRATE.
FZZAMMM
THIS IS DOCTOR PSYCHO! I NEED EXTRACTION!
I NEED HELP!
THERE'S THE LITTLE SPUD. SMALL TARGET. MAKES IT MORE FUN.
WHAT KIND OF ARROW IS THAT?
A REGULAR OLD GREEN ARROW, QUESTION.
ARROW, WAIT! THAT'S NOT--
TWANG

BOOOMMM
AAAHHH!
I SWEAR IT WAS A RAZOR-TIP ARROW...AND THAT I WAS AIMING AT PSYCHO.
WHEN YOU WERE ACTUALLY AIMING AT CYBORG.
HE WAS IN YOUR MIND.
"WELL, WHERE THE HELL IS HE NOW?"
I DID WHAT YOU ASKED! NOW YOU HELP ME!
THE JUSTICE LEAGUE IS HERE!
KRRKKKK

KKRAKOOM
SUPERMAN IS HERE!

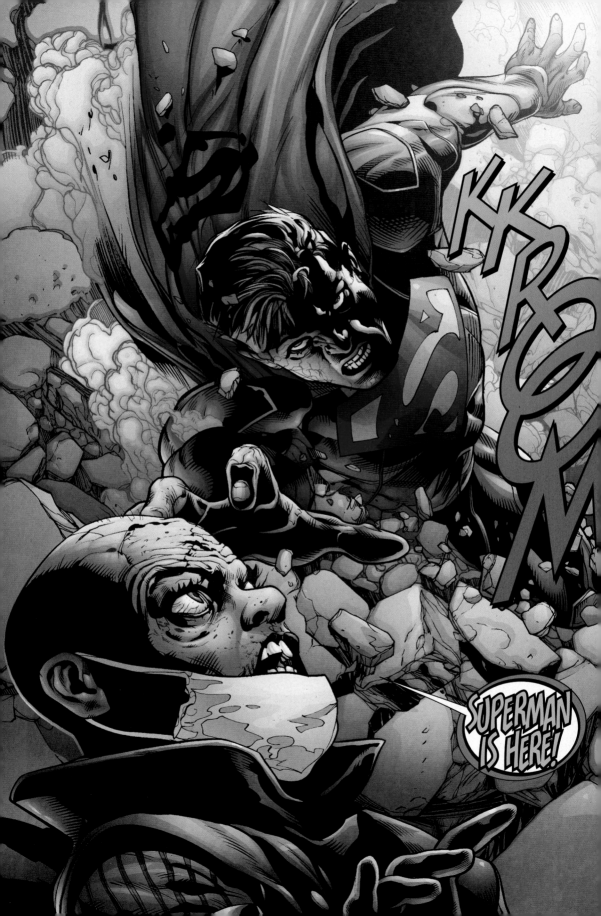

DOCTOR PSYCHO...WHAT DID YOU...DO TO ME?
I... I DIDN'T DO ANYTHING...
FWUMP
...BUT IT LOOKS LIKE I CAN NOW.
WHAT'S IN THAT MIND?! HA HA!
AARR!
YES! I SEE...THE FARM...THE GLASSES... MY GOD, YOU GREW UP ON THIS PLANET?
YOUR NAME IS CLARK KE--
--AAARRHHH!!
THAT WILL BE FORGOTTEN.
WHAT ARE YOU DOING TO HIM?
WHATEVER I HAVE TO DO TO GET ANSWERS.
EVEN IF IT MEANS TEARING HIS TWISTED LITTLE MIND APART.
ARRRGGHHH!!!

THE HOUSE OF MYSTER
HEADQUARTERS OF JUSTICE LEAGUE DA
C'MON, RING!
DO NOT EMBARRASS ME IN FRONT OF EVERYONE AGAIN.
KRRKSSHH
COME ON, LANTERN. THE HOUSE OF MYSTERY IS OUR ONLY LEAD ON FINDING OUT WHERE PHANTOM STRANGER TOOK BATMAN, KATANA AND DEADMAN.
SO KEEP TRYING TO GET US BACK IN.
IT'S NOT WORKING.
HAL COULD DO IT.
THE STRANGER SAID THEY WERE GOING TO TALK TO DOCTOR LIGHT (WHO'S DEAD) AND HE DISAPPEARED WITH HALF OUR CREW.
WHAT?
SORR IT JUS CAME O

LOOK, I KNOW DON'T HAVE A LOT OF PERIENCE WITH THE RING, UT WHATEVER KIND OF FUNHOUSE THIS IS, MY CONSTRUCTS AREN'T AFFECTING IT.
AND NEITHER ARE MY VIBRATIONAL BLASTS. I CAN'T EVEN GET THE WIND CHIMES TO...CHIME.
WHY WOULD THE STRANGER TAKE THOSE THREE AND LEAVE US HERE?
CONSTANTINE SAID THE HOUSE OF MYSTERY WAS "ALIVE," STEVIE. MAYBE HE CAN TELL US WHERE THEY WENT.
THE HOUSE OF MYSTERY IS A "HE," CATWOMAN?
YES, IT IS.
KREEEEK
HOW DID YOU GET THAT DOOR OPEN?
WHILE YOU BOYS WERE TRYING TO BREAK IT DOWN, I ASKED THE HOUSE TO UNLOCK IT.
YOU SAID THAT WOULDN'T WORK.
JUST GET INSIDE.
SO. THIS LOOKS TOTALLY DIFFERENT THAN WHEN WE WERE IN HERE TWENTY MINUTES AGO.
YEAH. THERE'S FOOD!
DON'T EAT ANYTHING, VIBE. NOT IN A PLACE LIKE THIS.
THE HOUSE IS ONLY BEING CONSIDERATE. IT WANTS US TO FEEL COMFORTABLE.
SO WHERE ARE PHANTOM STRANGER AND THE OTHERS?
LET'S ASK HIM.
MIRROR, MIRROR, ON THE WALL... WHERE'S THE STRANGEST OF THEM ALL?

THE PHANTOM STRANGER! AND HE'S SOMEWHERE... CLOUDY.
SO WHERE'S EVERYONE ELSE, FLASH?
THEY ARE CAUGHT BETWEEN LIFE AND DEATH.
WE ATTEMPTED TO INTERROGATE DOCTOR LIGHT'S SOUL.
BUT HE KNEW NOTHING. I'VE MADE A TERRIBLE MISTAKE...AND I'LL PAY THE ULTIMATE PRICE.
KZZZAAAT
I HAVE THE STRENGTH ENOUGH...TO SAVE YOUR FRIENDS.
IF NOT MYSELF!
KRRAKKSSH
"BE CAREFUL!"

HIS MIND IS POWERFUL, J'ONN...
I HAVE SIFTED THROUGH THOUSANDS OF MINDS, SUPERMAN. DOCTOR PSYCHO MAY BE A TELEPATH, BUT HE IS NO THREAT TO ME.
YOU SHOULD'VE WAITED OUTSIDE. YOU'RE TOO WEAK--
I HAVE TO KNOW.
DID DOCTOR PSYCHO MAKE ME INTO A MURDERER?
THAT'S WHAT I'M ABOUT TO FIND OUT.
WERE YOU IN KAHNDAQ WHEN DR. LIGHT WAS KILLED?
Y-YES...
...THE SECRET SOCIETY SENT ME THERE.

WHAT DID YOU DO TO SUPERMAN WHEN YOU WERE IN KAHNDAQ?
NOTHING!
THEY TOLD ME TO GO THERE...THEY SENT ME TO A HOTEL AND...AND I WAS TO WAIT FOR ORDERS...BUT THEY NEVER CAME.
THEY KNEW YOU'D FIND OUT I WAS THERE AND THAT YOU'D BLAME ME FOR THIS.
THEY USED ME!
DID YOU CONTROL SUPERMAN'S MIND? DID YOU MAKE HIM KILL DR. LIGHT?
I--I--
--I D-DIDN'T EVEN KNOW YOU WERE THERE. I SWEAR!
I AM AN UGLY LITTLE MAN!
HE'S TELLING THE TRUTH.
SO HE KNOWS SQUAT?! WHAT'S THE DEAL, QUESTION? YOU SAID IT WAS PSYCHO.
THE QUESTIONS THAT APPEAR IN MY HEAD AREN'T AS STRAIGHTFORWARD AS THEY FIRST APPEAR, ARROW.
DOCTOR PSYCHO MAY NOT BE DIRECTLY RESPONSIBLE, BUT HE'S POINTED US IN THE RIGHT DIRECTION.
HE SAID A SECRET SOCIETY SENT HIM IN THERE.
THEN IS IT THE BOX? IS WONDER WOMAN RIGHT?
AND WHAT'S THE...SECRET SOCIETY?
YOU SHOULD ALREADY KNOW THAT, SUPERMAN. OH, GOD. MAYBE WE COULD'VE PREVENTED ALL OF THIS FROM HAPPENING...
...MAYBE WE COULD'VE SAVED DOCTOR LIGHT AND PROTECTED SUPERMAN IF...IF I HADN'T LIED TO YOU.

LIED? ABOUT WHAT?
ATOM, NOT NOW.
WHAT'S THE ATOM TALKING ABOUT, J'ONN?
I'M SORRY, MANHUNTER, BUT THEY HAVE TO KNOW WHY THE JUSTICE LEAGUE OF AMERICA WAS REALLY PUT TOGETHER.
AMANDA WALLER CREATED THE JLA AS A FAIL-SAFE AGAINST THE JUSTICE LEAGUE.
EACH ONE OF US...EACH ONE OF US WAS RECRUITED SPECIFICALLY TO ATTACK ONE OF YOU.
AND I AGREED TO IT. I'VE BEEN SPYING ON THE JUSTICE LEAGUE. THAT'S WHY THEY KNEW WE WERE IN KAHNDAQ.
THAT CAN'T BE TRUE.
WE'RE TEAMMATES, ATOM. WE'RE FRIENDS.
I'M SORRY, EMILY.
BUT I SWEAR I NEVER WOULD'VE HURT ANY OF YOU.
IT WAS ALL A LIE?

YOU WERE ASSEMBLED TO FIGHT US?
I DIDN'T KNOW ABOUT IT, CYBORG!
NONE OF US DID!
SOME OF YOU DID.
I HAD REASONS FOR IT. JUST LIKE I HAD REASONS FOR QUITTING THE LEAGUE.
EVERYTHING I DO, I DO IN THE INTEREST OF THIS PLANET AND ITS PEOPLE.
WALLER WANTED THIS TO HAPPEN, SUPERMAN.
SHE WANTED TO REPLACE THE JUSTICE LEAGUE.
BUT SHE COULDN'T BE BEHIND THIS... COULD SHE?
VIC, TAKE US BACK TO WALLER.

"RIGHT NOW."
YOU CAN SAVE US, LEX LUTHOR.
ALL RIGHT.
FWP
OH, THIS SHOULD BE INTERESTING.
WHAT ARE YOU DOING?

DROP THE BOX, PANDORA.
IT'S COMING WITH US.

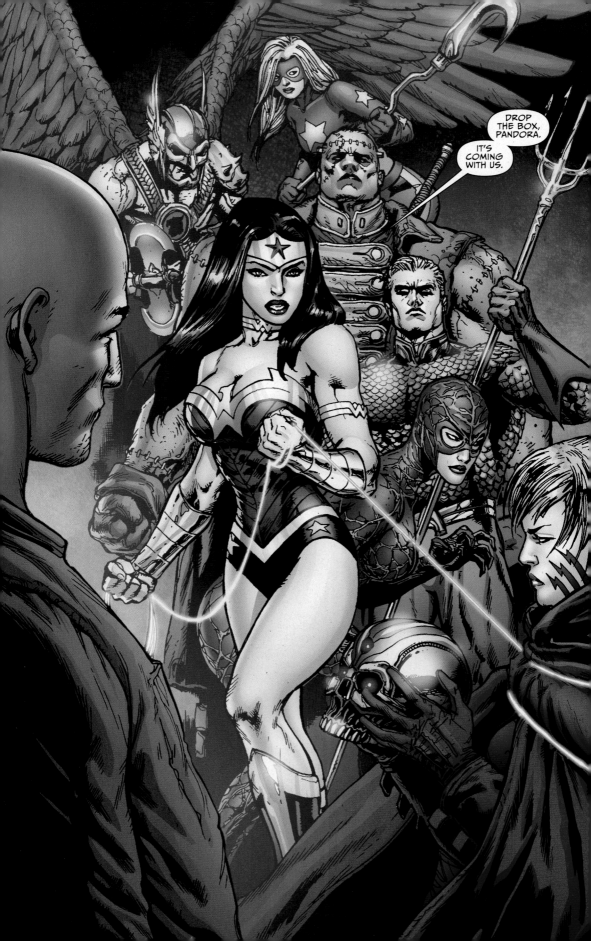

IF YOU WANT THAT BOX, WONDER WOMAN--
--SO DO I!
NO!
BATMAN!
YOU NEED TO FIND MADAME XANADU. SHE'S STILL ALIVE.
SHE KNOWS THE TRUTH BEHIND THE BOX! SHE KNOWS WHAT IT REALLY CAN DO AND WHO IS AFTER IT!
WE'VE ALL BEEN TRICKED THE BOX IS REALLY
AAARRRRR!!!
SUPERMAN? YOU'VE COME BACK.
WE NEED TO TALK, WALLER...WE KNOW ABOUT THE JLA...WE...
SUPERMAN AND THE OTHERS HAVE RETURNED TO A.R.G.U.S.
HA.
DETONATE DOCTOR LIGHT, MY FRIEND.
BEEP
BEEP
HAVE A NICE DAY
"HAVE A NICE DAY"?
WHAT THE HELL IS GOING--

BOOOMM
STRANGER?

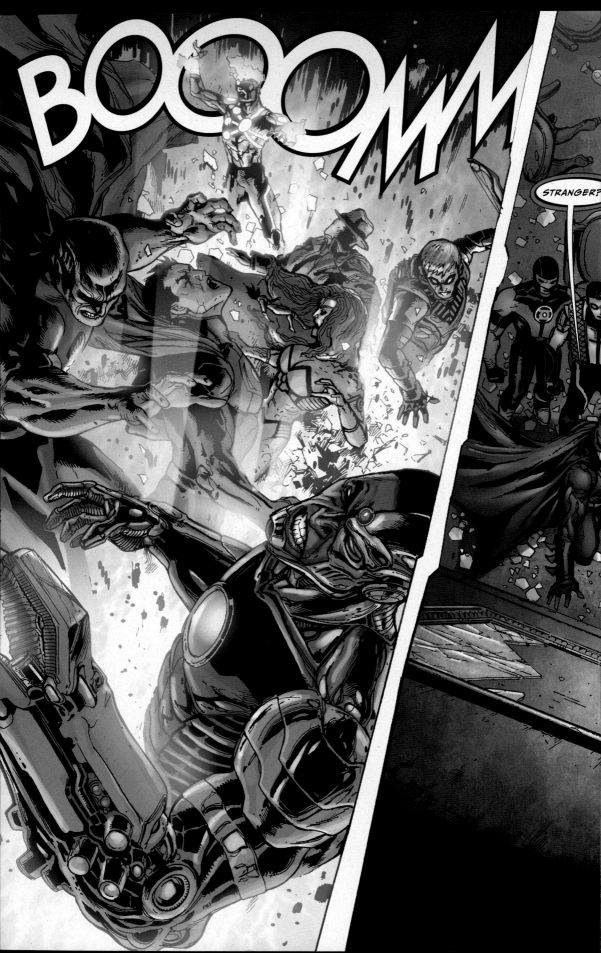

HE'S GONE.
NO. HE'S DEAD.
HE'S FINALLY DEAD.
I HAVE THE BOX!

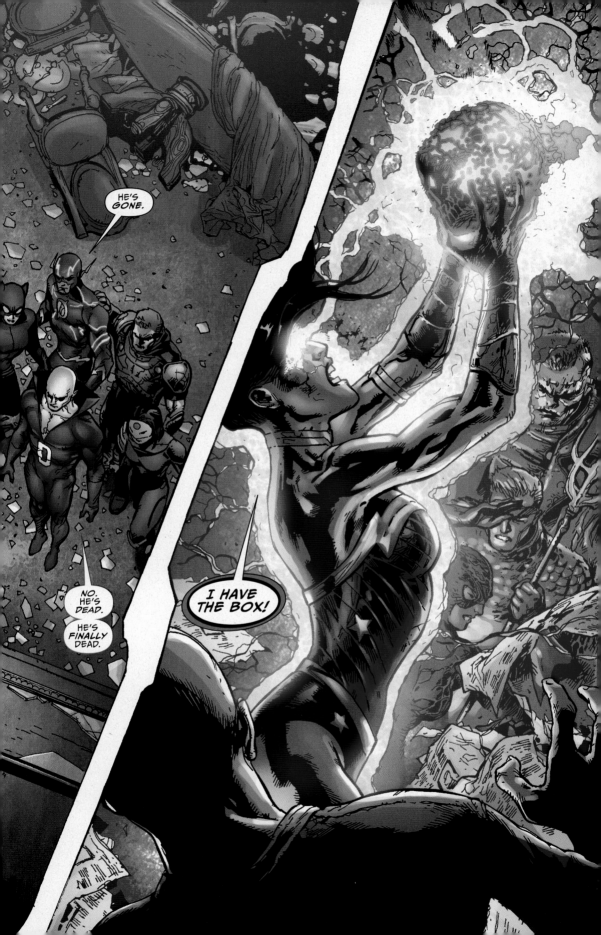

AND THE BOX...
...HAS
ME!

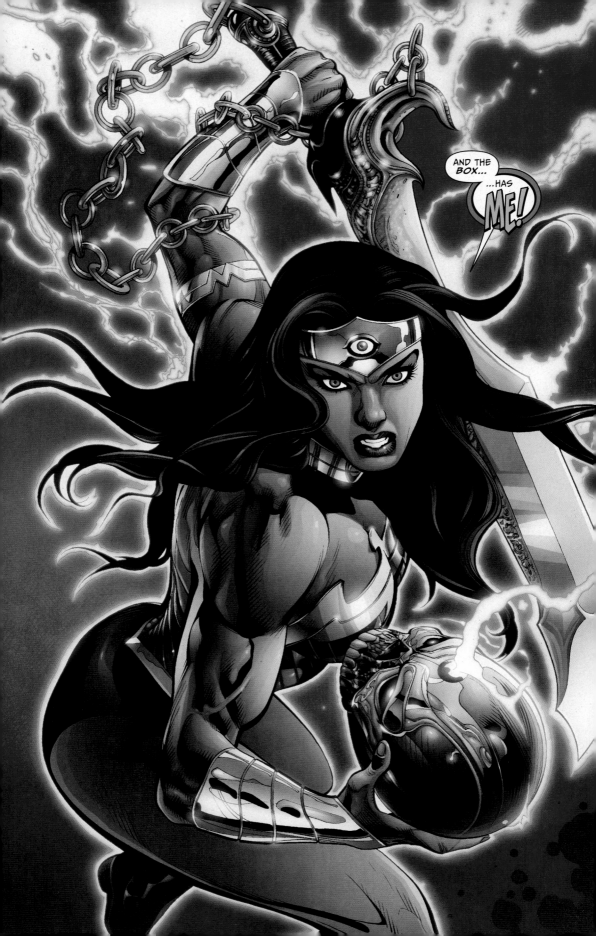

OUNT SONG, 1330 C.E.
WHAT IS EVIL?

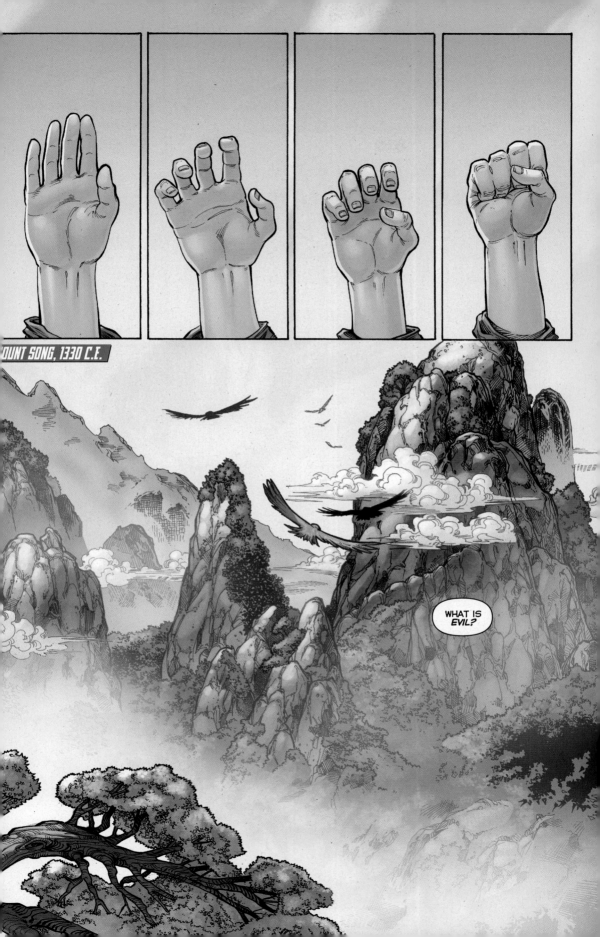

CAN YOU TOUCH IT? CAN YOU DRAW IT FORTH, LIKE A VENOM?
NO, PANDORA.
EVIL IS NOT A SUBSTANCE. EVIL IS A RESULT.
WHEN ONE DENIES THE COURSE OF NATURE, ONE GENERATES EVIL.
RAISE UP THAT WHICH IS MEANT TO BURROW, IT WILL COLLAPSE TOWARDS THE EARTH.
CONTAIN THAT WHICH IS MEANT TO FLOW, IT WILL BURST FORTH IN A TORRENT.
WOULD YOU STRIKE THE FALL? CAN YOU KICK THE FLOOD?
YOU'RE WRONG.
I'VE SEEN EVIL. IT WALKS THE EARTH.
IT WEARS SEVEN MONSTROUS FORMS. THEY SPEAK TO ME... THEY...
AH.
SO YOU HAVE SAID.
AND YOU WISH TO KILL THIS EVIL.

YES.

MORE THAN ANYTHING. I WAS HOPING--

I WAS HOPING YOU WOULD *TEACH* ME HOW.

I HAVE *ALREADY* BEEN TEACHING YOU. IF YOU WISH IT, I WILL TEACH YOU FOR MANY YEARS MORE. YOU *ARE* IMMORTAL.

WITH WHAT YOU ALREADY KNOW, AND WHAT YOU MAY YET LEARN, YOU WILL HAVE DIFFICULTY FINDING A FOE YOU COULD *NOT* KILL.

BUT A TIME WILL COME.

YOU WILL DRAW YOUR WEAPONS AT THE *FALL*. YOU WILL FACE THE *FLOOD*...

THE U.S. MILITARY-RUN PRISON DESIGNED TO HOLD LEX LUTHOR.
NOW.
"...AND I PRAY YOU WILL REMEMBER MY WORDS."
THE HEROES OF THE WORLD ARE AT WAR. THEY BATTLE FOR THE PRIZE-- THE BOX THAT ONCE HELD ALL THE SINS OF THE WORLD, AND NOW HOLDS THE KEY TO MY CURSE.

AND THE SEVEN DEADLY SINS FLOAT UNSEEN ABOVE THEM, REVELING IN THE CHAOS. THERE MUST BE A WAY TO STOP THIS...BUT HOW? WHAT CAN I DO?
DC COMICS PROUDLY PRESENTS
TRINITY OF SIN:
PANDORA
KICK THE FLOOD
RAY FAWKES WRITER DANIEL SAMPERE PENCILLER
VICENTE CIFUENTES INKER HI-FI COLORIST
DEZI SIENTY LETTERER RYAN SOOK COVER

LISTEN TO ME! WE'VE BEEN TRICKED!
WE'VE ALL BEEN TRICKED!
GET AWAY FROM THE BOX!
SOMETHING'S HAPPENED TO IT! IT'S CHANGING US!
O MOTHER, I WEEP.
YOU ARE ALL INVISIBLE TO THEM...THEY JUST KEEP FIGHTING EACH OTHER...

TO SEE YOU RUGGLE WHEN U SHOULD BE PROUD.
HAT KINDNESS AS THIS WORLD ER SHOWN YOU? ESE SO-CALLED "HEROES" ARE NOTHING TO YOU.
THEY OVERFLOW WITH SIN. SEE THEM FEED US?
THEIR ENVY, THEIR PRIDE. ARE THESE SQUABBLERS GOOD?
YOU BROUGHT US FORTH INTO THIS MORTAL REALM. THE TERRIBLE TRUTH IS YOURS TO SEE NOW.
THIS IS OUR CRUEL WORLD...

GLUTTONY
LUST
ENVY
...WE HAVE CONQUERED IT.
AND WE'LL PUNISH IT IN YOUR BLESSED NAME.
WRAT
GREED
PRIDE
WILL YOU NOT LOVE US FOR IT, O MOTHER?
SLOTH
WITH EVERY SHOUTED CURSE, EVERY DROP OF SPILLED BLOOD, THE SINS GROW STRONGER. THEY'RE FEEDING OFF THESE HEROES, BLOATING WITH POWER EVEN AS THEIR TWISTED INFLUENCE WHIPS THE WARRIORS TO FURTHER SAVAGERY.
THEY GIGGLE AND TWITCH. THEY CAN BARELY CONTAIN THEMSELVES. I THINK O THE COUNTLESS BILLIONS WHO HAVE SUFFERED FOR THEIR PERVERSION AND CRUELTY, AND I SEE THEM POISONING TH VERY BEST THIS WORLD HAS TO OFFER. M BODY ACHES. MY MIND REELS.
HOW CAN THIS BE TOLERATED?

NANTES, 1594 C.E.
THAT'S A DAMNED GOOD QUESTION.
"WHY WOULD GOD PERMIT EVIL TO EXIST?"
YES, THAT'S INTERESTING. THOMAS AQUINAS SAID THAT EVIL MUST SOMEHOW BE REQUIRED BY THE PERFECTION OF THE UNIVERSE.
I COULD NEVER ACCEPT THAT, ADALGER.
WELL, IT DOES SOUND FACILE WHEN I SAY IT.
WHEN I FIRE, REMEMBER WHAT I TAUGHT YOU: YOU ARE THERE AND NOT THERE. THE ARROW IS THERE AND NOT THERE. READY?
AQUINAS WAS JUST INTERPRETING AUGUSTINE, WHO SAID THAT EVIL IN ITSELF IS NOTHING. THAT IT'S ONLY A LACK OF GOOD, AS DARKNESS IS A LACK OF LIGHT.
WITHOUT DEGREES OF LIGHT AND DARK, WE WOULD BE BLIND TO BOTH. IT FOLLOWS THAT THEY ARE BOTH REQUIRED.
HMM.
I'M--
--READY.

NO.
HOW THE GILDED CREATURES' TEMPERS RUN HOT!
HOW EASILY THEY BEND THEIR THOUGHTS TO RAGE!
A FINE MEAL THEY MAKE.
WITH THIS POWER, I'LL TURN THE WHOLE WORLD RED!
WHAT, DRAW WEAPONS? YOU KNOW THE MIGHTY WRATH WILL NOT BLEED.
I DON'T KNOW WHAT TO DO.
I DON'T KNOW.
THEN SHALL I TELL YOU?...

SIMPLE! JUST GIVE UP.

SHE WON'T, *BROTHER SLOTH.* SHE WANTS TO *HURT* US. I *TASTE* HER DESIRE.

STOP IT!

BLAMM

HA!

ALL YOUR *TRAINING'S* FOR NAUGHT. YOU CAN'T *TOUCH* US.

AND YOU *NEVER* WILL.

I CARRY THE BLAME FOR THE SINS. I'LL CARRY THIS TOO.

THIS IS A *NIGHTMARE.*

FLENSBURG, 1703 C.E.
IT SEEMS HOPELESS, DOESN'T IT?
EVIL IS DRAWN INTO THE ROOT WITHOUT WARNING. WE DON'T KNOW WHY.
GOODNESS SOURS AND MONSTERS ARISE, EH?
WHICH DO WE CUT AWAY? THE ROOT? THE BLIGHTED GOOD? THE MONSTERS?
AND THEN WHAT? I DON'T KNOW. I DON'T KNOW.
YOU ARE VERY OLD-- YOU TELL ME.
BUT THEY SAID YOU COULD HELP ME, LEHRER. THAT I COULD COME TO YOU FOR HIDDEN WISDOM.
HEE HEE HEE!
YOU DIDN'T COME TO ME FOR WISDOM.
YOU CAME TO ME TO LEARN HOW TO DESTROY BODILESS SPIRITS.

LOOK INTO THIS HERE.
THERE IS NO LIQUID IN THE BOWL. YOU ARE LOOKING AT A SLUMBERING SPIRIT.
VERY COMFORTABLE IN ITS LITTLE WOODEN BED! HAHA! I SANG IT A LULLABY.
YOU CANNOT TOUCH IT. YOU CANNOT POUR IT OR CUT IT OR BURN IT. BUT YOU CAN SEE YOURSELF IN IT, EH?
YOU CAN SEE YOURSELF IN IT.
WISDOM.
-HMPH-
SHALL WE BEGIN YOUR LESSONS?

BALTIMORE, MARYLAND.
I MUST BE CRAZY.
GO AND GET WRAPPED UP WITH--
MARCUS SEVERIN?
WHO THE HELL ARE YOU?
I'M SPECIAL AGENT PAUL CHANG, AND THIS IS AGENT KINCAID.
WE'D JUST LIKE TO ASK YOU A FEW QUESTIONS, IF YOU DON'T MIND.
IF I DON'T--
SPECIAL AGENT OF WHAT? YOU COPS?
EASY, MARCUS.
EXIT
YOU'LL WANT TO PUT THAT BLADE DOWN, OKAY? WE JUST WANT TO TALK.

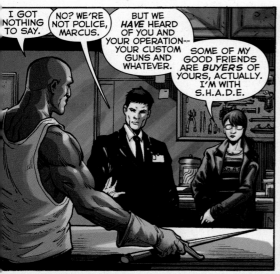

I GOT NOTHING TO SAY.

NO? WE'RE NOT POLICE, MARCUS.

BUT WE *HAVE* HEARD OF YOU AND YOUR OPERATION-- YOUR CUSTOM GUNS AND WHATEVER.

SOME OF MY GOOD FRIENDS ARE *BUYERS* OF YOURS, ACTUALLY. I'M WITH S.H.A.D.E.

AW HELL. YOU KNOW I AIN'T *SUPERNATURAL.*

ROOM *FULL* OF ILLEGAL WEAPONS AND YOU DON'T EVEN KEEP YOUR DOOR LOCKED? YOU MUST HAVE A *HELL* OF A REPUTATION.

OR POWERFUL FRIENDS.

LIKE THIS WOMAN.

DO YOU RECOGNIZE HER?

I TOLD YOU, I GOT NOTHING TO SAY. YOU WANT INFO ON ME, WANT TO KNOW WHO MY FRIENDS ARE? S.H.A.D.E.'S GOT IT ALL.

AND I STILL HAVEN'T SEEN ANY I.D.

HOW'S THIS?

A.R.G.U.S... WHAT'S THAT?

RIGHT. I'M GOING TO GUESS YOU'VE BEEN HERE WORKING ALL DAY AND YOU HAVEN'T SEEN...

...THIS.

JESUS.

A.R.G.U.S. DEALS WITH *METAHUMANS,* MARCUS.

IT DIDN'T TAKE LONG FOR US TO FIGURE OUT THAT THE GUNS *PANDORA* CARRIES ARE YOUR CREATIONS.

THE GUNS AND ALL THE *OTHER* STUFF.

LOOKS LIKE WE'VE GOT A *PROBLEM,* HUH? I MEAN, POWERFUL FRIENDS ARE ONE THING--BUT THIS WOMAN'S A LISTED *SUPERVILLAIN.*

AND WE'RE GOING TO HAVE TO BRING YOU IN.

UNLESS YOU WANT TO TELL US RIGHT NOW...

"...WHERE IS PANDORA?"
I DON'T UNDERSTAND.
NOTHING I DO, NOTHING I SAY CAN *HURT* THESE SINS. THEY ONLY GET MORE AND MORE POWERFUL...
RRROOOAAARRRR
WHILE I...
I...

OH. LEHRER, I UNDERSTAND NOW...

...WHAT YOU WERE TRYING TO *TELL* ME.

I *SEE* MYSELF IN *THEM*.

DO YOU HEAR ME? MAYBE SOMETHING'S HAPPENED TO THE *BOX*. MAYBE SOMETHING'S HAPPENED TO *ME*.

I *SEE* MYSELF!

WHAT'S THIS? SOMETHING'S *CHANGED*...

ALL THESE MANY YEARS...ALL THE PEOPLE I GREW TO *KNOW*...

AND THEY WOULD *LIVE*, AND *LOVE*, AND GROW OLD. THEY, WHO COULD *LAUGH*, WHO COULD FIND *PEACE*...

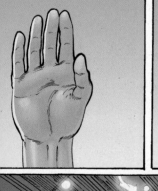

WHO COULD BEAR *CHILDREN*...

AND *DIE*...

SOMETHING'S *DIFFERENT* NOW... HOW *CURIOUS*...

ALL THE THINGS I COULD NEVER DO!
I ENVY THEM--
--SO MUCH!
BLAMM
BLAMM
UKK--

HOW CAN SHE TOUCH HIM?
WHAT? IMPOSSIBLE!
BOOM
IS ENVY DEAD? HOW? HOW?
FSSSSSSSS

OH YES. HE'S GONE.
HOW? I CAN EXPLAIN.
BUT FIRST...

...WHO'S NEXT?

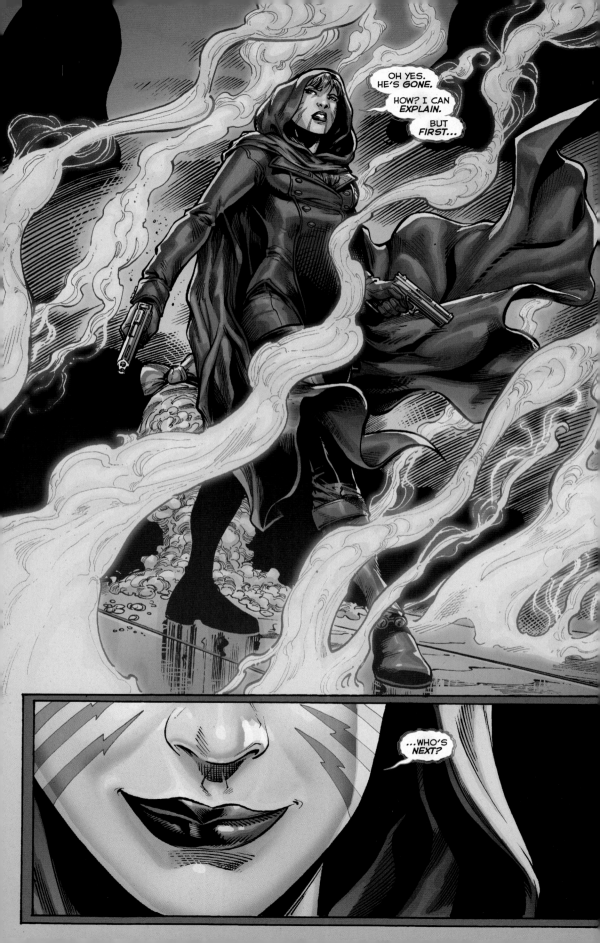

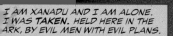

I AM XANADU AND I AM ALONE. I WAS TAKEN. HELD HERE IN THE ARK, BY EVIL MEN WITH EVIL PLANS.

AT FIRST I COULDN'T UNDERSTAND WHY THEY WANTED ME. OF ALL THE SUPER HUMANS CAUGHT UP IN THEIR MACHINATIONS, WHY DID I, A SIMPLE CLAIRVOYANT, POSE SUCH A THREAT TO THESE MEN?

BUT NOW I KNOW. THEY DON'T WANT ME OUT OF THEIR GAME BECAUSE I CAN MOVE MOUNTAINS OR SHAKE THE EARTH...THEY NEED ME HERE BECAUSE I CAN SEE.

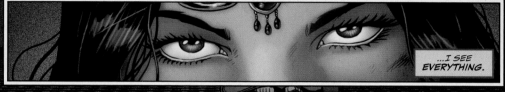

...I SEE EVERYTHING.

JEFF LEMIRE Writer
MIKEL JANIN Artist

I SEE THE MIGHTY FALL.

A.R.G.U.S., THE HUB OF THE JUSTICE LEAGUES, HAS BEEN DESTROYED... SUPERMAN AND HIS COMPANIONS CAUGHT IN THE CENTER OF THE APOCALYPTIC BLAST.

JEROMY COX Colorist • ROB LEIGH Letterer

I SEE THE GUILTY PUNISHED.

BATMAN AND HIS TEAM WENT ALL THE WAY TO HELL AND BACK TO LOOK FOR THE SECRETS THAT COME SO EASILY TO ME...AND INSTEAD FOUND THE PHANTOM STRANGER DESTROYED.

DOUG MAHNKE and ALEX SINCLAIR Cover

I SEE THE CON MAN, CAUGHT AT LAST.

JOHN CONSTANTINE, THE TRICKSTER, TRIED TO TAKE THE POWERFUL SHAZAM OUT OF THE GAME TO USE HIM FOR HIS OWN GAIN, AS CONSTANTINE IS ALWAYS WONT TO DO.

BUT IN THE YOUNG-HEARTED SHAZAM, CONSTANTINE MAY HAVE MET HIS MATCH AT LAST.

BUT ALL OF THIS IS JUST NOISE...

AND WHEN I LOOK PAST IT ALL, WHEN I BLOCK EVERYTHING ELSE OUT, I SEE THE REAL BATTLE AT THE HEART OF ALL THIS CHAOS.

...I SEE THE FINAL BATTLE JUST BEGINNING.
TAKE HER DOWN! GET THAT BOX AWAY FROM HER!
WONDER WOMAN AND HER ALLIES SOUGHT TO DESTROY PANDORA'S BOX...BUT ALL IT HAS DONE IS CORRUPT HER TOO.
HRRN... IT SEEMS THE TASK IS OURS, ATLANTEAN! BUT BE CAREFUL, SHE IS VERY--
AARRGH!!!
BUT NOW I SEE WHAT THAT BOX IS. IT'S SOMETHING BEYOND THEIR WILDEST IMAGINATIONS...
STAY BACK!
THWAK

SOMETHING EVIL.
HAWKMAN'S DOWN...STAY BACK, I GOT HER!
DON'T YOU SEE? NO ONE ELSE COULD BE WORTHY OF THIS POWER...THIS IS WHAT I WAS MEANT TO BE...
AND THE MORE THEY STRUGGLE TO POSSESS IT, THE CLOSER IT GETS TO UNLEASHING THAT EVIL.
...A GODDESS!!
LIKE A POT ABOUT TO BOIL OVER...ALL IT NEEDS IS A LITTLE MORE HEAT...
WHAT THE HELL HAS THAT THING DONE TO HER?!
KRA-KOOOM

WONDER WOMAN?
THAT CREEP CONSTANTINE TRIED TO TRICK ME...STEAL MY POWERS. I SHOULDN'T HAVE LEFT. I KNOW THAT NOW. YOU GUYS NEEDED ME.
I KNOW WHY YOU REALLY CAME BACK, SHAZAM...TO STEAL THE POWER. TO TAKE IT FOR YOURSELF!
BE CAREFUL, SHAZAM, THAT THING HAS DONE SOMETHING TO HER.
ZATANNA?
S-SOMETHING--
pfft--I'M NOT SCARED OF HER...
SHAZAM?! WHERE WERE YOU?! NOT EXACTLY A GOOD TIME TO TAKE OFF, YOU KNOW?
--SOMETHING'S NOT RIGHT.

SUPERMAN SHOULD HAVE KILLED YOU IN KANDHAQ!
WHAP
THIS STUPID BOX HAS CAUSED ENOUGH PROBLEMS--
IT'S-- IT'S--
...IT'S MINE.
OH GOD... NO!

SHAZAM!

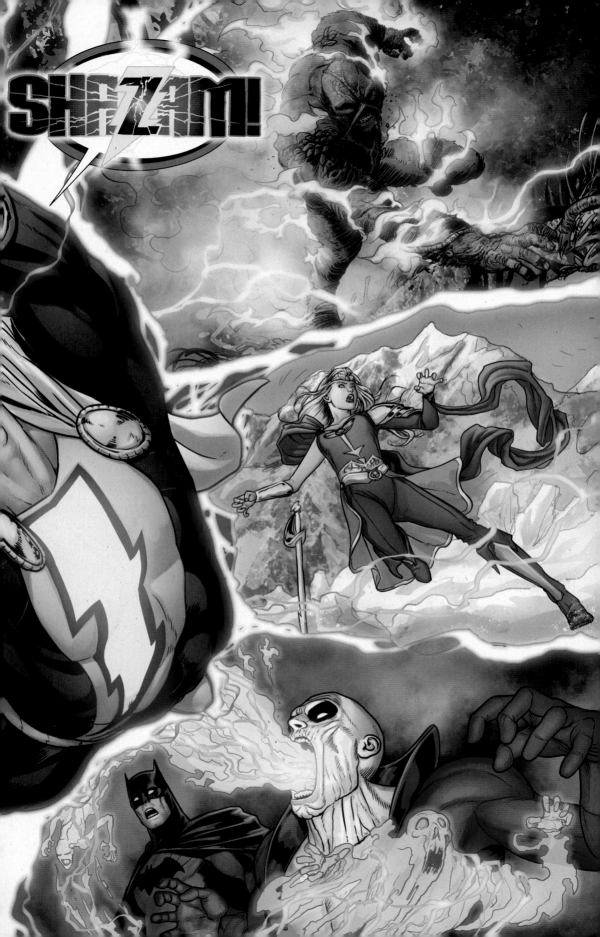

DEADMAN, ARE YOU OKAY?!

I--I THINK SO, FLASH. FELT LIKE MY HEAD WAS GONNA EXPLODE THERE FOR A MINUTE... 'COURSE, I'M ALREADY DEAD, SO I GUESS TECHNICALLY THAT'S IMPOSSIBLE.

WHAT THE HELL WAS THAT, BRAND?

SOME KIND OF MAJOR DISTURBANCE IN THE MAGICAL PLAINS. AND I DO MEAN MAJOR.

RIPPED RIGHT THROUGH EVERYTHING. FOR A SECOND IT WAS LIKE EVERYTHING MAGICAL WAS INSIDE ME SCREAMING TO GET OUT...

I MEAN I COULD FEEL EVERYONE...ZATANNA, CONSTANTINE, EVEN SOME GUY WITH A GOLD HELMET I'D NEVER SEEN BEFORE.

...AND THAT NEW GUY, SHAZAM, HIM MOST OF ALL. I SENSED HIM AT THE HEART OF IT ALL.

SHAZAM?

WAIT A MINUTE, DEADMAN. YOU SAID YOU SENSED EVERYONE?

YES, I--

MADAME XANADU!

THINK I CAN FIND HER!"

WASHINGTON, D.C.
FORMERLY THE SITE OF A.R.G.U.S. HEADQUARTERS.
THOOM
WHAT THE HELL JUST HAPPENED?!
THE ENERGY READINGS FROM DR. LIGHT'S BODY WENT OFF THE CHARTS. I THINK--I THINK HE EXPLODED!

I--I DIDN'T EVEN THINK. I JUST SURROUNDED US ALL IN THE HARDEST METALS I COULD.
WELL, YOU DID GOOD, EM...YOU SAVED OUR BUTTS BIG TIME!
LOOK AROUND US! THERE MUST HAVE BEEN HUNDREDS OF PEOPLE INSIDE A.R.G.U.S.! YOU'RE GOING TO ANSWER FOR THIS, WALLER!
ME? WHAT ARE YOU TALKING ABOUT?
THE ATOM TOLD US EVERYTHING. HOW YOU PUT THE JLA TOGETHER TO TAKE DOWN THE LEAGUE.
YOU SET THIS WHOLE THING UP, DIDN'T YOU?! DR. LIGHT'S MURDER?! FRAMING SUPERMAN?!
YOU'RE OUT OF YOUR DAMNED MINDS!
I DON'T KNOW WHAT THE ATOM TOLD YOU, BUT I PROMISE YOU, I'M TRYING TO FIGURE THIS ALL OUT JUST LIKE YOU! NOW GET THAT ARROW OUT OF MY FACE BEFORE I SHOVE IT UP YOUR DAMNED QUIVER!
UH, GUYS...
RONNIE, DON'T!
QUIET! WE HAVE TO TELL THEM!

WHAT IS IT, FIRESTORM?! IF YOU KNOW SOMETHING--
WALLER HAD ME LEARN HOW TO MAK KRYPTONITE. SHE TOLD ME IT WAS JUS A FAILSAFE, BUT--
ARE YOU KIDDING ME?! THESE WERE MY PEOPLE... MY FAMILY! YES, I HAD HIM MAKE KRYPTONITE, BECAUSE LIKE ALL OF YOU, I HAVE NO IDEA WHAT THE HELL HAPPENED TO SUPERMAN!
NOW, YOU CAN ALL STAND AROUND BLAMING ME LATER IF YOU WANT, BUT RIGHT NOW I'M GOING TO START LOOKING FOR SURVIVORS!
SHE'S RIGHT. THERE MAY STILL BE PEOPLE ALIVE HERE. WE NEED TO STOP FIGHTING AND HELP THEM!
YOU HEARD THE MAN...SEARCH AND RESCUE. MOVE!
MANHUNTER, STAY WITH SUPERMAN. ARROW, YOU KEEP THAT BOW ON WALLER.
I STILL DON'T BELIEVE A DAMNED WORD SHE'S SAYING.

WELL, 'REN'T YOU IDIOTS GOING TO DO SOMETHING?
QUIET, LUTHOR!
LISTEN, BOY... THAT THING IS VILE, AND I FEAR ITS EVIL SPREADS TO ALL WHO POSSESS IT. MY UNDEAD SOUL MAY BE THE ONLY THING IMMUNE...
BE CAREFUL, FRANK.
SHANK
THE TIME FOR CARE IS LONG PAST, ZATANNA! SUPERMAN IS DYING...AND THAT CURSED THING IS THE KEY TO HELPING HIM!
I'M TIRED OF EVERYONE TELLING ME WHAT TO DO!
ENOUGH, CHILD!

FORGET IT, FREAK! I AM A KING. I SHOULD HAVE IT!
I AM THE ONLY ONE WHO'S HEART IS PURE ENOUGH TO WITHSTAND--
--WITHSTAND--
WHAT'S HAPPENING... DON'T FEEL--
IT'S NOT YOU, STARGIRL...THE BOX IS SIMPLY DOING WHAT IT ALWAYS DOES... CORRUPTING EVERYTHING AROUND IT NOW!
PANDORA'S RIGHT. SHAZAM'S MAGIC IS HAVING SOME SORT OF REACTION TO THE BOX'S... THEY'RE FEEDING OFF EACH OTHER, SPREADING LIKE A VIRUS.
I THINK I CAN CAST A PROTECTIVE SPELL AROUND US WITH MY BACKWARDS MAGIC, BUT I DON'T KNOW HOW LONG IT WILL HOLD OUT...

SINNERS... ABOMINATIONS. ALL OF YOU!
Uh-oh...
TCETORP EW EERHT MORF EHT XOB!
I--I FEEL BETTER. BUT WHAT ABOUT THEM, THEY'LL TEAR EACH OTHER APART IF WE DON'T GET THAT BOX AWAY!
DON'T WORRY, STARGIRL, I'VE GOT THIS...

ENOYREVE TEG YAWA MORF EHT XOB!

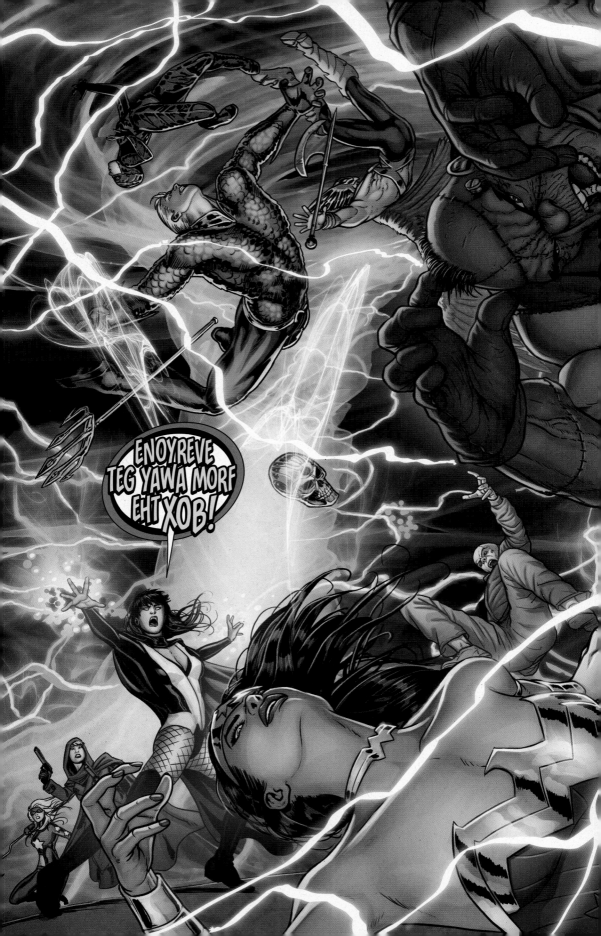

COVER ME, I'M GOING TO GET THAT THING THE HELL OUT OF HERE!
SORRY, BIG GREEN GUY!
HRRN!
SHRACK
GIVE IT BACK TO ME!
BLAMM
SNIAHC!
BLAMM
SHRAKK
OUTTA MY WAY!
--UNGH!

GET YOUR HANDS OFF OF HER!
BLAMM BLAMM
AGGH! STOP THAT!
STARGIRL, ARE YOU OKAY?
OKAY? NO, I'M NOT OKAY...
NOT UNTIL I GET THAT BOX!
SHRAKK
STARGIRL?! --UNGH!
DAMN IT, MY SPELL IS WEARING OUT!
THEN JUST GIVE ME THE BOX, I WON'T HURT YOU.
SGNIW FO DAEL!
YOU TRIED TO TRICK ME SO YOU COULD HAVE IT, ZATANNA!
STARGIRL, STOP!

NOITCELFED!
ARRGH!
SHRAKK
ZATANNA!
WHA-?
WHAM
NO!
YOU?!

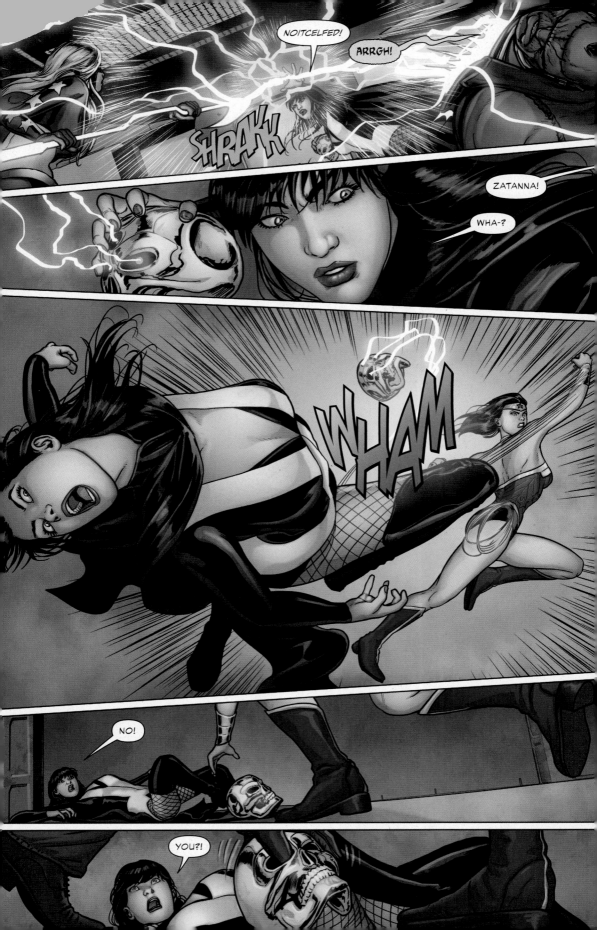

MISS ME?
JOHN. DON'T TOUCH IT! IT WILL--
CORRUPT ME? CAN'T SOIL A POT THAT'S ALREADY FILTHY, LOVE.
WHAT SAY WE GET OUT OF HERE, ZEE?
FWOOSH
HELL, YES.

WHERE ARE WE?

GREEK RUINS... *TEMPLE OF HEPHAESTUS?* I WAS TRYING TO BRING US TO LONDON. I THINK THIS BLOODY THING HAS A MIND OF ITS OWN.

FWOOSH

JOHN--SOMEONE'S *HERE*...FAMILIAR MAGIC. CAN'T QUITE PLACE IT--

I FEEL IT TOO, BUT THERE'S NO ONE ELSE HERE, ZEE...

NOT HERE-- BENEATH US!

NEPO EHT DNUORG.

SOME KIND OF BUNKER...

MADAME XANADU?!

XANADU? TALK TO US, LOVE...WHO THE HELL DID THIS TO YOU?

--NOT A PRISON...

WHAT?

ZEE? JOHN? WHAT THE HELL?!

HAND OVER THAT BOX, CONSTANTINE.

BEST LET ME HANG ONTO IT, BATS. MAGIC HANDS, YOU KNOW.

QUIET! I THINK XANADU HAS BEEN DRUGGED. SHE'S TRYING TO TELL US SOMETHING...

HOLD IT RIGHT THERE!

I SEE IT!

EASY--

NO! TH--THEY TRIED TO KEEP ME BLIND...BUT I SAW IT! I SAW WHAT IT *REALLY* IS!

PANDORA WAS WRONG--YOU WERE ALL WRONG! IT'S NOT A PRISON...IT'S A *DOORWAY!*

SHE'S RIGHT. IT *IS* A DOORWAY...

...AND NOW IT'S TIME TO OPEN IT.

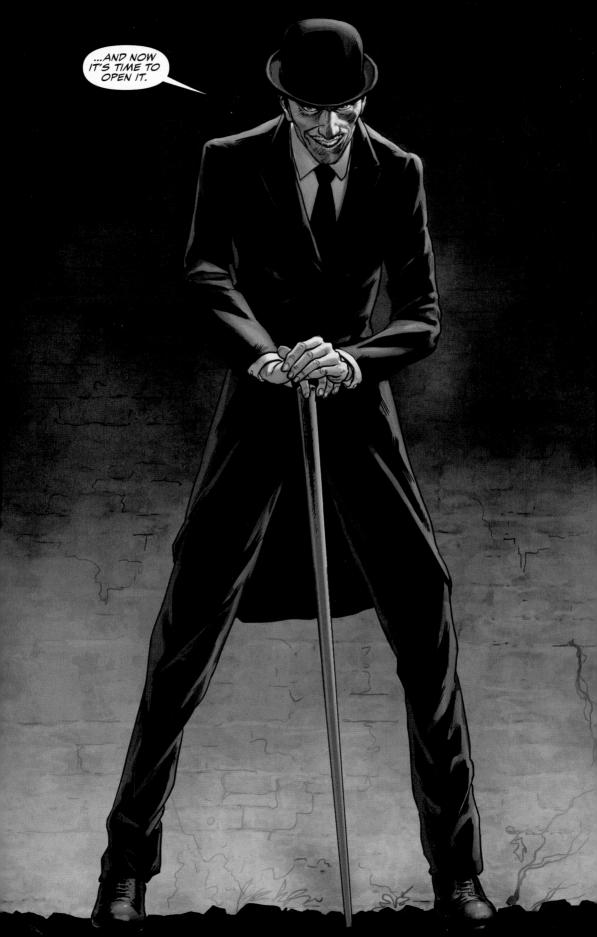

ALL STARTED
VE YEARS AGO.
THE PLANET WAS ATTACKED BY ONE OF THE MOST POWERFUL BEINGS IN EXISTENCE -- A WORLD CONQUEROR CALLED
DARKSEID.
THE JUSTICE LEAGUE CAME TOGETHER TO STOP HIM FROM ENSLAVING EARTH.

ON THAT *SAME DAY*, WHILE THE BARRIERS BETWEEN UNIVERSES WERE WEAKENED, I FINALLY *ESCAPED* FROM WHAT WAS *LEFT* OF *MY* WORLD.

BUT MY MASTER DID NOT.

THEY DIDN'T MAKE IT.

THE JUSTICE LEAGUE CONTINUED TO BATTLE *OVERT THREATS* TO THE WORLD WHILE WE STAYED *HIDDEN*.

NO, MY DEAR, BUT WE DID.

HA.

AND SO MY MISSION TO SAVE HIM BEGAN.

WHEN I DISCOVERED THE *EXISTENCE* OF PANDORA'S *BOX* I FELT *HOPE*.

I *RECOGNIZED* IT.

I KNEW WHERE IT CAME FROM AND WHAT IT COULD DO.

I RECRUITED THE LEAGUE'S MANY ENEMIES, STARTING WITH *PROFESSOR IVO*.

FOR THE FIRST YEAR, I STRUGGLED TO COMPREHEND THE CULTURE AND RULES OF THIS BIZARRE PLACE.

EVEN THE VERY BASIC OF IDEAS APPEARED TWISTED AND TURNED INSIDE OUT.

EAST IS WEST AND WEST IS EAST.

WHILE THE LEAGUE CONTINUED ON, I SEARCHED FOR A WAY TO HELP THE MAN WHO RESCUED ME FROM MY DESTITUTE LIFE.

I HAD MANY MOMENTS OF DOUBT AND DESPERATION DURING THIS TIME.

I FELT ALONE.

BUT I REFUSED TO FAIL MY MASTER.

I BEGAN BUILDING THE *SECRET SOCIETY* TO BE AT THE READY FOR MY MASTER'S ARRIVAL.

THEN I PLANTED AN AGENT WITHIN THE JUSTICE LEAGUE'S RANKS.

AND WITH THE HIGH LEVEL OF *DISTRUST* BETWEEN THE LEAGUES, I KNEW IT WAS ONLY A MATTER OF TIME BEFORE OPPORTUNITY WOULD PRESENT ITSELF.

WHEN THE LEAGUES CAME INTO CONFLICT, I MADE THE WORLD BELIEVE SUPERMAN HAD KILLED ONE OF HIS WOULD-BE TEAMMATES. THEY THOUGHT IT TO BE BECAUSE OF HIS ENCOUNTER WITH *PANDORA'S BOX.*

SO THE LEAGUES SET OFF TO *FIND* IT. THEY'VE DONE MY JOB FOR ME.

HA.

I AM AN *OUTSIDER* TO THIS WORLD.

I AM *THE* OUTSIDER.

AND I SERVE MY MASTER WELL.

I'VE TRACKED BATMAN'S SIGNAL HERE.
WHERE IS HERE, CYBORG?
THE TEMPLE OF HEPHAESTUS IN ATHENS.
THERE ARE OTHERS ALREADY INSIDE, BUT MY TELEPATHY IS AGAIN BEING BLOCKED.
THE SOCIETY MUST BE HERE TOO.
OR AT LEAST, ITS LEADER.
ALTHOUGH MY WORLD IS FOREVER LOST...THIS ONE CAN BE OURS.
THE BOX ISN'T A PRISON, BATMAN, IT'S A DOORWAY.
A DOORWAY TO WHERE, MADAME XANADU?
YOU NEED TO GO AWAY, BATS. GET EVERYONE OUTTA HERE RIGHT NOW.
SO WE CAN LEAVE THE BOX IN YOUR HANDS, CONSTANTINE?

THIS ONE WILL BE OURS.
THEY BROUGHT THE BOX HERE, WONDER WOMAN. BACK TO WHERE I FIRST FOUND IT.
YOU NEED TO LET ME HELP--
YOU'VE HELPED ENOUGH, PANDORA.
WHAT'S WRONG, VIBE?
I'VE GOT ONE OF MY, UH, "VIBE" HEADACHES, FLASH...
...THERE'S SOMETHING THAT'S NOT FROM OUR UNIVERSE NEARBY. OR SOMEONE. MAYBE BOTH.
THE BLOODY THING CORRUPTS WHOEVER TOUCHES IT. 'CEPT FOR ME, RIGHT? I'M ALREADY GOOD AN' GONE.
BUT YOU CAPES DON'T KNOW HOW TA EAL WITH THAT DARK CE CREEPING IN YOUR EADS. IT'S ALREADY GOT SHAZAM!
TELL 'EM, LUV. ZATANNA?
ZEE?
IF MY FATHER WERE ALIVE, HE'D HAVE KILLED YOU FOR THE WAY YOU TREATED ME.
BLIMEY.
NOT YOU TOO.

NOT EVERYONE.

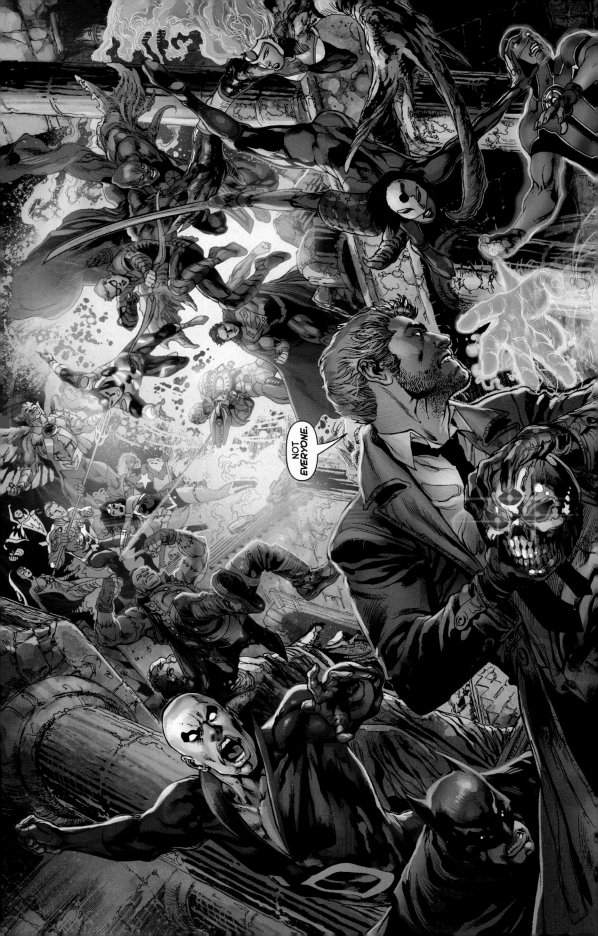

EVIG EM EHT XOB!
TRINITY WAR CONCLUSION
GEOFF JOHNS WRITER
IVAN REIS PENCILLER
JOE PRADO, OCLAIR ALBERT & EBER FERREIRA INKERS
ROD REIS COLORS • NICK J. NAPOLITANO LETTERS
DOUG MAHNKE & ALEX SINCLAIR COVER

I CAN'T BE THE ONLY ONE WITH MY HEAD SCREWED ON STRAIGHT. DON'T YOU BLOODY SEE?
WHATEVER EVIL IS INSIDE TH BOX IS LEAKIN' OUT. IT'S ALREAD INFECTING Y--
SHUT UP, OLD MAN.
--AAAARGHHH!!
HA. IT'S TIME.

BATMAN'S GOT THE BOX! WE CAN HELP SUPERMAN--
YOU THINK I CARE ABOUT WHAT HAPPENS TO SUPERMAN, LANTERN?
HE TOOK DIANA FROM ME, SIMON. LET HIM ROT.
YOU'RE JUST A MAN.
I'M NOT AFRAID OF YOU, BATMAN. I'M THE GREEN LANTERN.
BUT YOU'RE NO HAL JORDAN.
HEY, NEW GUY.

YOU SHOULD WORRY ABOUT ME.

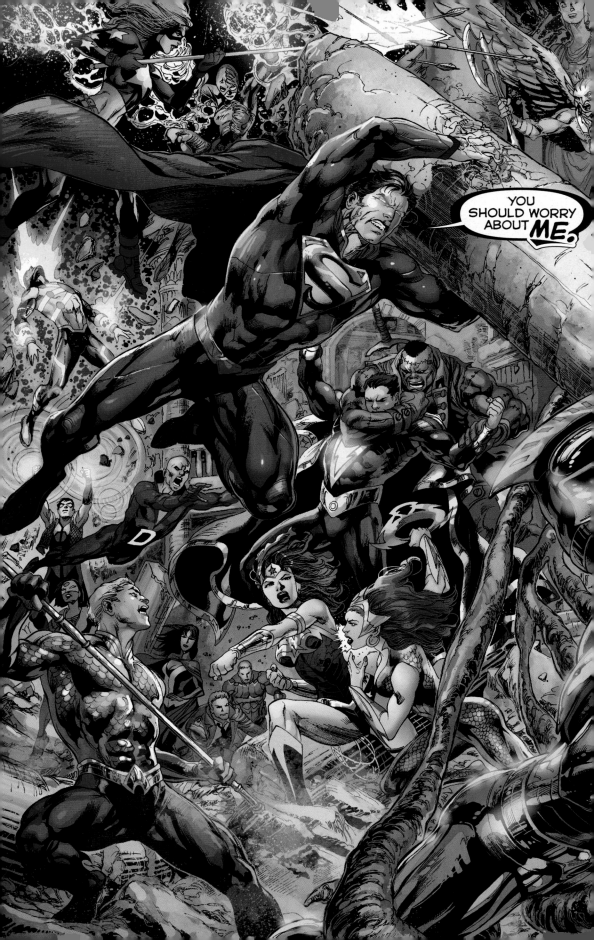

I'VE GOT MUSCLES, FRANKIE.

N-NO, YOU D-DON'T.

SHAZAM!

KRAKK KOOOMMM

MERA? WHAT ARE YOU DOING HERE?

SHE'S NOT.

BLAMM

WHAT HAPPENS IF I OPEN THE BOX? WOULD I EARN FORGIVENESS IN THE EYES OF THE GODS? WOULD I FINALLY GET THE ANSWER TO: WHO AM I?

I CANNOT ALLOW THAT TO HAPPEN, QUESTION!

YOU'LL BECOME MORE DANGEROUS THAN THE BOX ITSELF!

GIVE IT TO ME, BATMAN. I CAN DESTROY IT.
WHICH WOULD OPEN IT, DIANA. AND THAT'S THE LAST THING I THINK WE SHOULD BE DOING.
WE NEED TO SAVE SUPERMAN.
I'M HERE, DIANA.
BUT YOU'RE SICK. AND I'M WORRIED YOU'LL DIE IF BATMAN DOESN'T HAND IT OVER.
WHAT?
AND AFTER I DIE WHAT WILL YOU DO? WILL YOU GO BACK TO STEVE?
OR WILL YOU GO TO BATMAN?
THIS IS ALL GOING BAD, TREVOR. WE'VE GOT WAVES OF EVIL THOUGHTS HITTING EVERYONE.
I HOPE SUPERMAN DIES.
THE BOX IS AFFECTING US. WE NEED TO--
DON'T TELL ME WHAT I NEED TO DO, BATMAN. I WANT TO LIVE A FULL LIFE AND THAT INCLUDES SHARING IT.
AND I WON'T LET YOU TAKE HER AWAY FROM ME.
SUPERMAN, STOP!

I WON'T STOP UNTIL BATMAN IS DEAD!

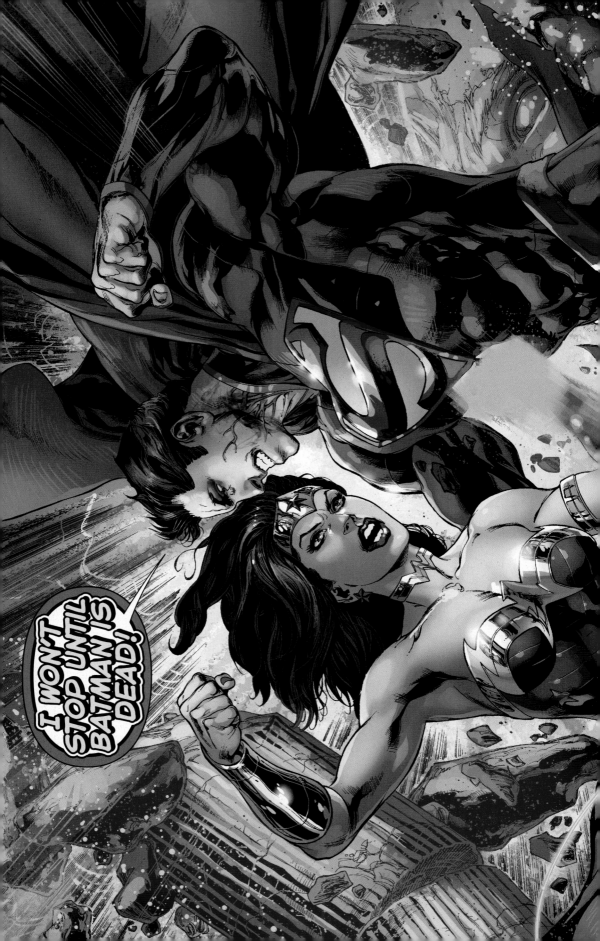

BOOOOOOMMMM
KZZZT
THOOOMM
SUPERMAN?!
NOBODY TOUCH THE BOX!
IT'S GONE DORMANT FOR THE MOMENT.
EVERYBODY STAY BACK.
WHY IS THE BOX HURTING SUPERMAN PHYSICALLY, BUT NOT US?
WONDER WOMAN?

THE BOX MIGHT BE MAKING ALL OF US A LITTLE *CRAZY* IN THE HEAD, BUT I DON'T THINK IT'S WHAT'S MAKING SUPERMAN *SICK.*

I DIDN'T SEE IT BEFORE BECAUSE IT'S SO *FAINT,* BUT...IT'S GETTING *STRONGER.*

I SEE IT TOO, RONNIE.

WHAT IS IT, FIRE-STORM?

SUPERMAN'S EMITTING SOME KIND OF *RADIOACTIVE AURA*... IT'S...

WE WOULDN'T HAVE RECOGNIZED IT WITHOUT WALLER'S HELP.

IT'S *KRYPTONITE.*

HE'S BEING *POISONED* BY *KRYPTONITE?* WHERE IS IT?

I THINK IT'S COMING FROM *INSIDE* SUPERMAN.

I CAN FIND IT.

I CAN TURN INTO *OXYGEN* AND ENTER HIS *BLOODSTREAM.* THEN TRACE THE *DYING CELLS* BACK TO THE SOURCE.

IT... IT'S IN HIS *BRAIN.*

HIS *BRAIN?*

THERE'S A *MICROSCOPIC SLIVER* OF *KRYPTONITE* IN THERE.

HOW'D A MICROSCOPIC SLIVER OF KRYPTONITE GET *IN* HIS BRAIN?

OH, THAT'S AN *EASY QUESTION* TO ANSWER, CYBORG.

I PUT IT IN THERE.

YOU?

"WHEN WE WERE GOING UP AGAINST THE *JLA*--

"--I WENT INTO SUPERMAN'S BRAIN WITH THE *SLIVER* OF *KRYPTONITE* I TOOK FROM BATMAN'S RING.

"I *HIT* A *NERVE...*

"...AND *TRIGGERED* HIS *HEAT* VISION."

I KNOW YOU THOUGHT I WAS PART OF THE *JUSTICE LEAGUE*--AND THE *JLA* THINKS I WORK FOR *THEM,* BUT THE TRUTH IS I DON'T WORK FOR *ANY* OF YOU.

SO YOU'RE A TRAITOR?
OH, VIC.
HONEY.
SO ARE YOU.
VEET
YES.
I HAVE NO NEED FOR THIS FLESH ANYMORE.
N-NO...
AND IT IS A WEAKNESS I PREFER TO BE WITHOUT.
SO I WILL SEPARATE FROM IT.
CHANK
CHANK
CHANK

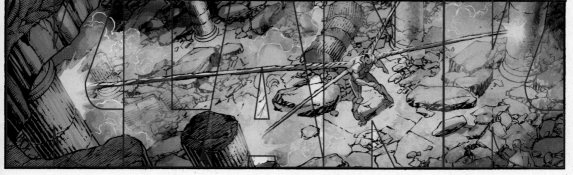

AARRGHHHHH!

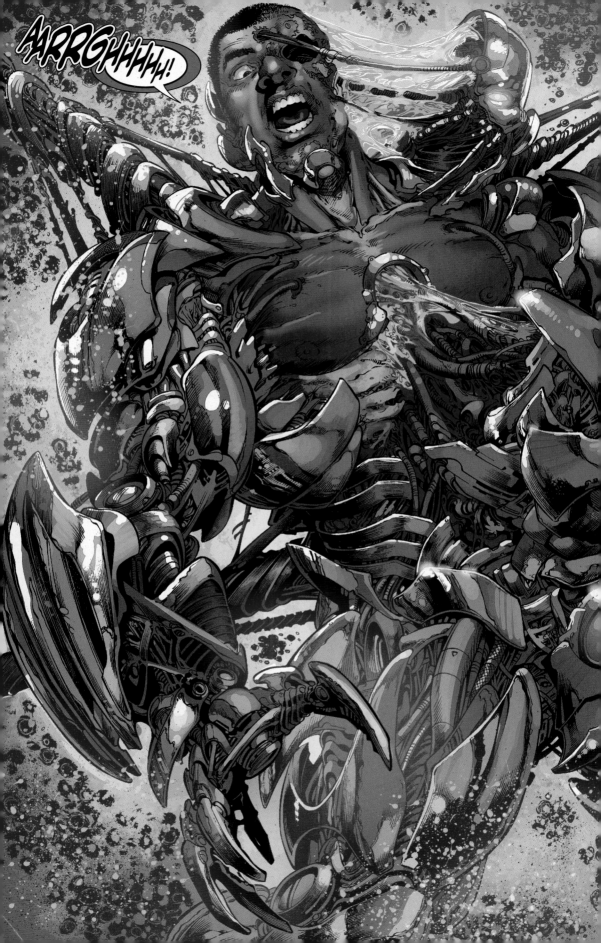

VICTOR!
KRRZZZAAATTT
KRRAAZZZZAARTTTT
RRRAAAARR!
VIC?!
KW-KW-KW
KZZKZZAAATTT
KLINK

GRID
ON-LINE.

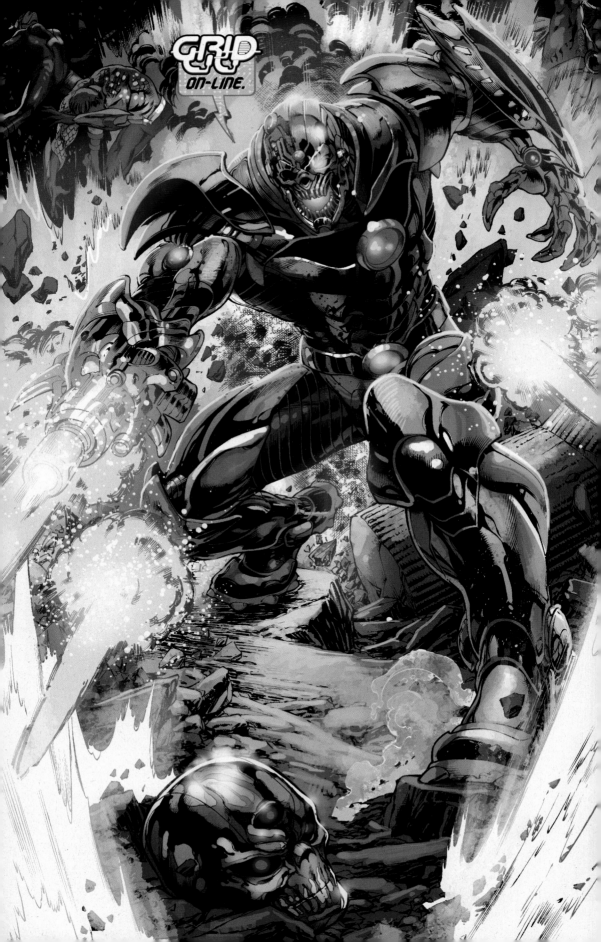

IT'S OURS.

KKRRAKKKZZITTT

WHOEVER YOU ARE, YOU CAN'T YAAAHH!

IT'S TOO LATE, FLASH.

I DON'T UNDERSTAND.

YOU NEVER DID, PANDORA.

SINCE THE GODS WHO DAMNED YOU FIRST FOUND THIS BOX, THEY BELIEVED IT TO BE MAGIC.

BUT THEY WERE WRONG.

IT'S SCIENCE.

ALL THIS TIME YOU SEARCHED THIS WORLD FOR SOMEONE WHO COULD *OPEN* THE BOX. BUT ONLY SOMEONE FROM *OUR* WORLD CAN DO THAT, PANDORA.

HA.

LIKE THE *MOTHER BOX*, THIS IS ONLY *ONE* OF *MANY*. AND LIKE THE *MOTHER BOX*, "*PANDORA'S BOX*" CAN *OPEN* A *GATEWAY* TO *ANOTHER* UNIVERE.

OUR UNIVERSE.

THE *BIRTHPLACE* OF *EVIL*.

KHOOOMMMMM
IT WAS CREATED ON MY WORLD LONG AGO. AND LEFT HERE.
ALL THIS TIME YOU WERE LOOKING FOR WHO WAS BEHIND THIS...AS YOU SAY ON YOUR WORLD...
...THE BUTLER DID IT.
KRRAKKOOOM
WHAT'S HAPPENING, DEADMAN?
HE JUST OPENED SOME KIND OF PORTAL.
SOMEONE'S COMING THROUGH.

BATMAN?
STAY WITH ME, VIC.
WHO IS THAT? WHAT THE HELL IS GOING ON?

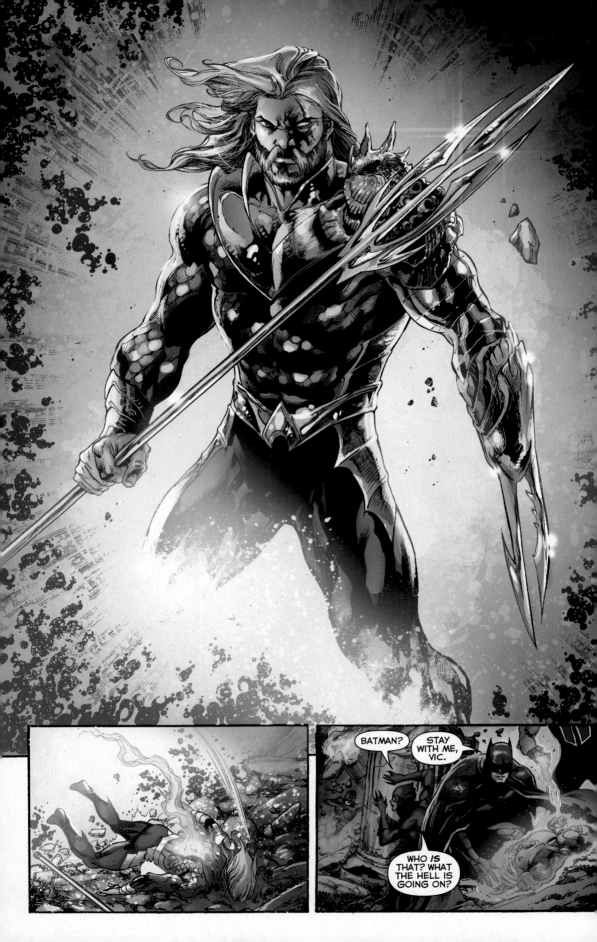

THE BOX HAS BEEN **DESTROYED.**

BUT **EVIL** HASN'T BEEN **IMPRISONED,** PANDORA. ONLY **UNLEASHED!** THE **TRINITY**... IT WASN'T ABOUT YOU...

...IT WAS THE **NUMBER**... THE **TRUE NUMBER** OF EVIL.

THREE. **EARTH- THREE.**

FINALLY!

THOUGH THE **SEA KING** DIDN'T MAKE IT...

...WE HAVE SURVIVED.

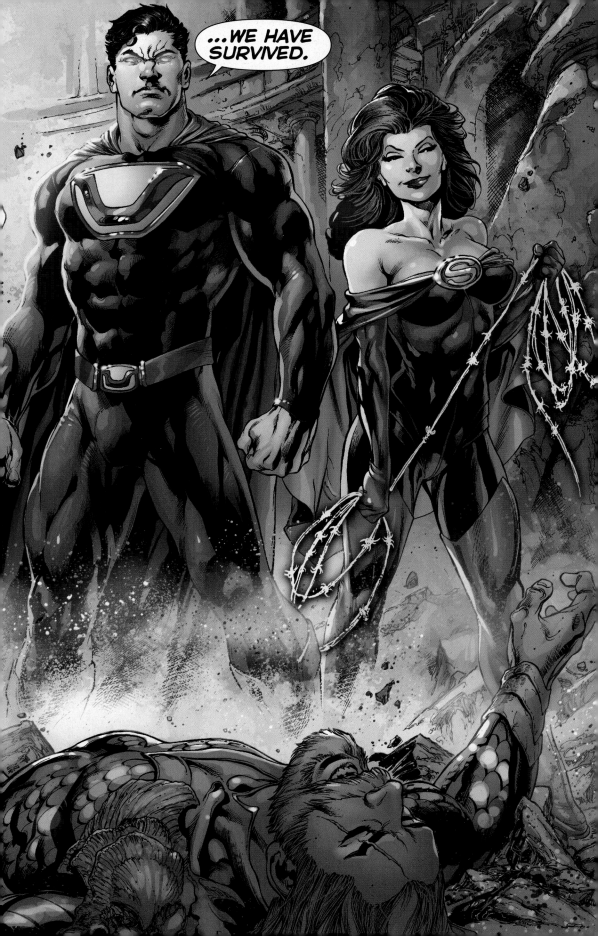

WHO ARE THEY?
I DON'T KNOW, CATWOMAN. EVERYONE REGROUP.
NOW!
JOHNNY?!
ATOMICA!
ATOMICA?
SHE'S ONE OF THEM.
OH, JOHNNY, DID I MISS YOU.
THIS WORLD IS SUCH A DRAG.
WE'LL MAKE IT FUN, BABY. PROMISE.
WELCOME TO YOUR NEW HOME, MASTER THOMAS.
HA.
IT TOOK YOU LONG ENOUGH, ALFRED.
B-BUT IS IT S-SAFE OWLMAN?
IT DOESN'T LOOK S-SAFE!

IT LOOKS DANGEROUS!
CALM YOURSELF, WER RING. THIS IS A SCINATING WORLD, OT A DANGEROUS ONE. NOT TO US.
B-BUT DEATHSTORM--
KEEP PANICKING AND YOU WILL ONLY MAKE YOUR CONDITION WORSE.
B-BUT WHAT IS THAT?!
THIS IS GRID.
I MET HIM WHEN I WAS HACKING INTO CYBORG.
NICE FIND, BABY.
GRID IS A SENTIENT COMPUTER VIRUS FROM THIS WORLD WITH ASPIRATIONS BEYOND CORRUPTING FILES.
HAVE A NICE DAY.
IF WE HAVE ANYTHING TO WORRY ABOUT, POWER RING, IT'S OUR PRISONER.
WE SHOULD'VE LEFT THE BASTARD ON OUR WORLD.
WE NEED TO REMOVE THE KRYPTONITE FROM SUPERMAN!
WE NEED TO GET VIC STABILIZED.
THE REST OF YOU, THOSE THAT CAN STAND--
IT'S SO DISCONCERTING, ISN'T IT?
YES.
THEY LOOK LIKE US, SUPER-WOMAN.
AND LIKE OUR LOST ALLIES.
THEY'RE TRYING TO GET UP! WHAT DO WE DO, ULTRAMAN?!
WE STRETCH OUR LEGS AND HAVE SOME LAUGHS!
WE BEGIN OUR MISSION, JOHNNY.

THIS WORLD NOW BELONGS TO THE CRIME SYNDICATE!

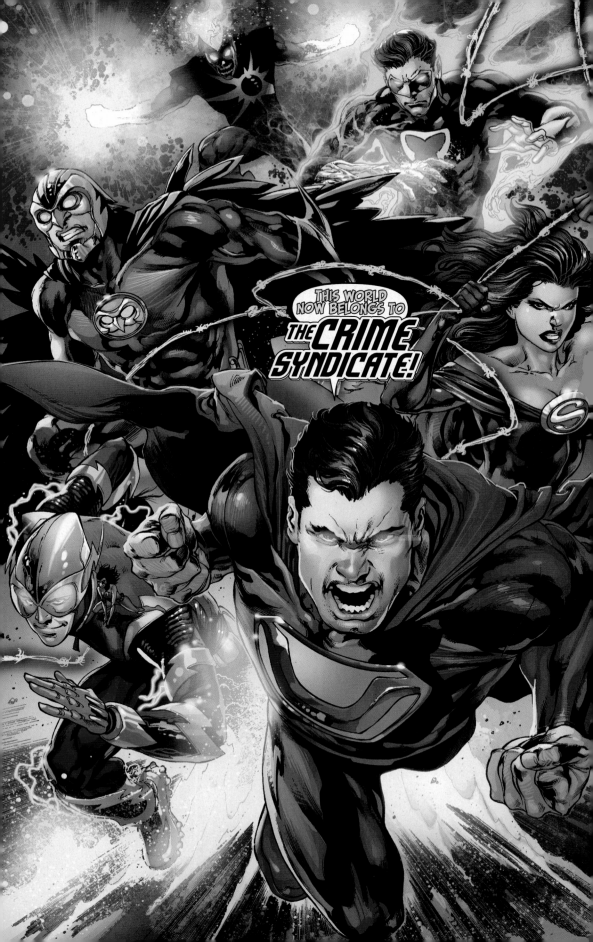

VARIANT COVER GALLERY

TRINITY OF SIN: PANDORA 1
Variant cover by Pasqual Ferry & Brad Anderson

JUSTICE LEAGUE 22
Variant cover by Brett Booth, Norm Rapmund & Andrew Dalhouse

JUSTICE LEAGUE DARK 22
Variant cover by Brett Booth, Norm Rapmund & Andrew Dalhouse

JUSTICE LEAGUE OF AMERICA 6
Variant cover by Brett Booth, Norm Rapmund & Andrew Dalhouse

JUSTICE LEAGUE OF AMERICA 7
Variant cover by Mikel Janin, Vicente Cifuentes & Tomeu Morey

JUSTICE LEAGUE DARK 23
Variant cover by Mikel Janin, Vicente Cifuentes & Tomeu Morey

JUSTICE LEAGUE 23
Variant cover by Mikel Janin, Vicente Cifuentes & Tomeu Morey

Booth '2013'
RAPMUND.
House

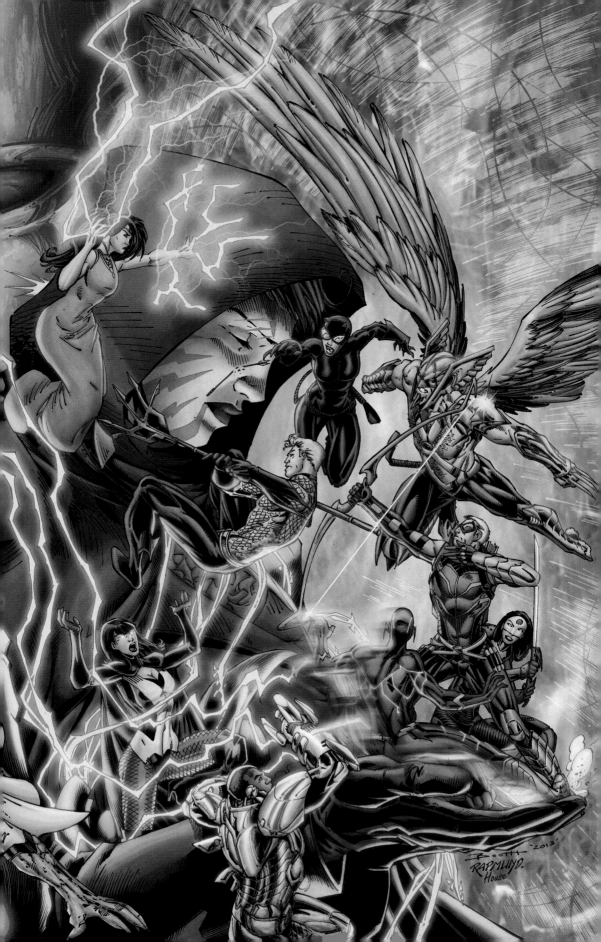

JANÍN
2013

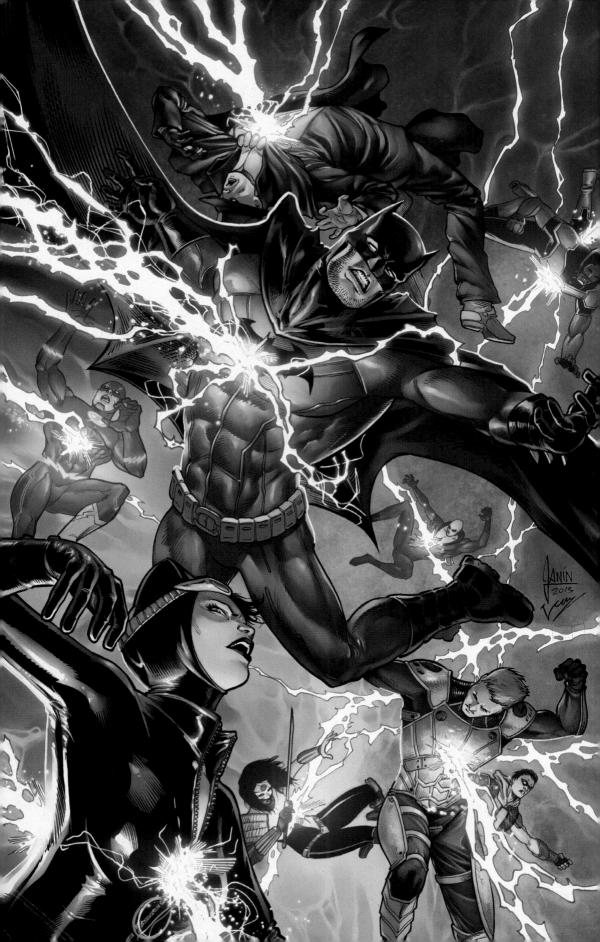

START AT THE BEGINNING!

JUSTICE LEAGUE VOLUME 1:ORIGIN

AQUAMAN VOLUME 1: THE TRENCH

THE SAVAGE HAWKMAN VOLUME 1: DARKNESS RISING

GREEN ARROW VOLUME 1: THE MIDAS TOUCH

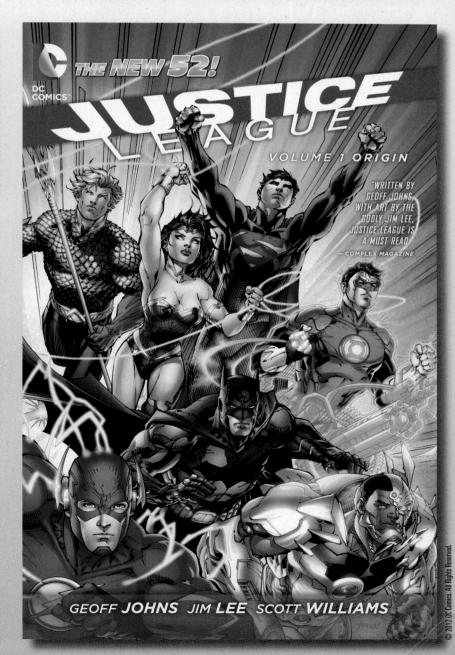

GEOFF **JOHNS** JIM **LEE** SCOTT **WILLIAMS**

DC COMICS™

"If you don't love it from the very first page, you're not human."
—MTV GEEK

"ANIMAL MAN has the sensational Jeff Lemire at the helm."
—ENTERTAINMENT WEEKLY

START AT THE BEGINNING!

ANIMAL MAN VOLUME 1: THE HUNT

DC COMICS™
THE NEW 52!
Animal Man™
VOLUME 1
THE HUNT
"TRAVEL FOREMAN'S ART IS INNOVATIVE AND EXCELLENTLY CREEPY... AS LEMIRE'S EVERYMAN HERO MAKES HIS MARK IN THE NEW DC UNIVERSE."
— USA TODAY
JEFF LEMIRE TRAVEL FOREMAN

JUSTICE LEAGUE DARK
VOLUME 1:
IN THE DARK

THE NEW 52!
JUSTICE LEAGUE DARK
PETER MILLIGAN MIKEL JANIN

RESURRECTION MAN
VOLUME 1:
DEAD AGAIN

THE NEW 52!
RESURRECTION MAN
VOLUME 1 DEAD AGAIN
DAN ABNETT ANDY LANNING FERNANDO DAGNINO

FRANKENSTEIN
AGENT OF S.H.A.D.E.
VOLUME 1: WAR OF
THE MONSTERS

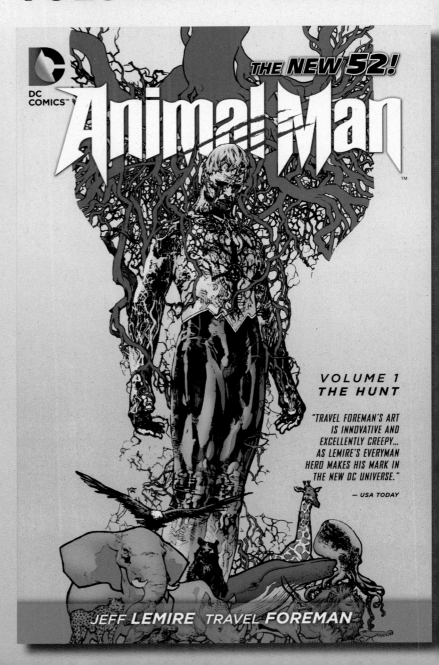

THE NEW 52!
FRANKENSTEIN AGENT OF S.H.A.D.E.
JEFF LEMIRE ALBERTO PONTICELLI